ANDREA DWORKIN

ALSO BY MARTIN DUBERMAN

ANDREA DWORKIN

The Feminist as Revolutionary

Martin Duberman

NEW YORK
LONDON

Requests for permission to reproduce selections from this book
should be made through our website: https://thenewpress.com/contact.

Published in the United States by The New Press, New York, 2020
Distributed by Two Rivers Distribution

ISBN 978-1-62097-585-5 (hc)
ISBN 978-1-62097-586-2 (ebook)
CIP data is available

The New Press publishes books that promote and enrich public discussion and understanding of
the issues vital to our democracy and to a more equitable world. These books are made possible
by the enthusiasm of our readers; the support of a committed group of donors, large and small;
the collaboration of our many partners in the independent media and the not-for-profit sector;
booksellers, who often hand-sell New Press books; librarians; and above all by our authors.

www.thenewpress.com

Book design and composition by Bookbright Media
This book was set in Janson Text

Printed in the United States of America

2   4   6   8   10   9   7   5   3   1

*To Andrea's dream
of a gender-just world*

Imagine: We are linked, not ranked.

—Gloria Steinem (2013)

Contents

1

Beginnings

Andrea's ordeal began on a bitterly cold day in February 1965, when by pre-arrangement she joined a sit-in at the U.S. Mission to the United Nations to protest the escalating U.S. involvement in Vietnam. At the time Andrea was eighteen, a freshman at Bennington College on a nine-week "work break"; already a committed leftist serving as a volunteer at the Student Peace Union, she'd helped the War Resisters League organize the anti-war protest. Expecting to be arrested, Andrea brought along to the sit-in some toilet articles and an extra pair of underwear. As she later remembered it, "this funny, nice little woman" kept going up and down the line of protesters, checking to see that they were all right and asking if she could do anything for them. It was Grace Paley, the well-known writer. As it grew late and an arrest seemed unlikely, Andrea asked Grace to hold on to the extra things she'd brought along, saying she would pick them up in a few hours.[1]

Minutes later, the police suddenly descended, and Andrea was among those carted off to night court. Her legal-aid attorney tried to persuade the presiding judge to free her on her own recognizance, arguing that she posed no danger to society during the period that would precede sentencing. The judge rejected the plea, fixed bail at $500 and, when Andrea said she couldn't pay, remanded her to the notorious bastille in the heart of Greenwich Village known as the Women's House of Detention.

After being showered and searched, she was subjected to a "vaginal exam" by a prison nurse, then taken up to her cell and locked in. The following afternoon she was brought back to the examination room for another "inspection"; when an alarmed Andrea asked a policewoman why, the reply was another question: "Are you a virgin?" Andrea refused to answer. At that point two male doctors entered the room, one explaining loudly to the other that he suspected venereal disease. Andrea was ordered onto the table and told to put her legs in the stirrups. While the one doctor stood by, the other applied pressure initially to Andrea's stomach and then to her breast. "You're hurting me," Andrea protested. Ignoring her, he put on a rubber glove and inserted his hand first into her rectum, then into her vagina. Removing his hand, he explained to the other doctor that he would now probe further with a speculum. Andrea had never heard the word before.[2]

As the exam proceeded and her pain mounted, the second doctor plied her with questions: How many girls at Bennington are virgins? I don't know, Andrea said. How many freshmen at Bennington are virgins? I don't know, Andrea said, as the pain from the forceps grew worse. "*That's* what you should know about," he barked, "not Vietnam." When Andrea started to bleed—it would continue for the next two weeks—the doctor withdrew the forceps and ordered her back to the cell block. On the way, Andrea asked the accompanying policewoman if she could make a phone call. "It's Friday," the officer said. "No calls are allowed on weekends. Monday is George Washington's birthday. You can call on Tuesday."

Released within a few days, Andrea decided to write to every newspaper listed in the Yellow Pages describing conditions at the House of Detention (built to house 400, it currently held 657 inmates) and her own mistreatment there. Somewhat hesitantly she called her parents, fairly certain they'd be appalled at her defiance. She guessed right; her mother Sylvia, in particular, was horrified at the pending "disgrace." Rather than remain at home, subject to her mother's admonitions, and remembering Grace Paley's name,

Andrea looked her up in the phone book and called to ask if she could retrieve her underwear. Grace told her to come right over. She did—and told Grace the whole horrible story. Grace offered her shelter and helped her compose the letter to the newspapers; within a day or two the media started calling. Concerned about Andrea's continual uteral bleeding and pain, Grace persuaded her to see a doctor; he told her she'd been "bruised and injured internally."[3]

The widely read *New York Post* columnist James Wechsler was among the first to respond to Andrea's letter. He found the young woman's story so arresting that he decided to take down her words in the form of a sworn affidavit. Wechsler—long a prominent voice in liberal political circles—listened with mounting anger to the eighteen-year-old as she related, with passionate intensity, her horrendous tale of mistreatment. After receiving her sworn affidavit, Wechsler published the first of his two columns, calling for "a full-scale inquiry, preferably by a commission of independent citizens designated by the Mayor or the Governor." "The original sin," he added, "rests with the self-righteous judge who sent these girls into that horror house for what was essentially a crime of conscience. . . . The truth is that the Women's House is an unfit habitation for any human soul. A sweeping exploration of this case might finally hasten its end."[4]

The mayor of New York City at the time was Robert Wagner, a man (as Wechsler described him) of "studied inactions," though "essentially honest [and] humane." Running true to form, Wagner—a full four days after Andrea's release—had still not made a single comment to the press nor signaled any intention of ordering an official inquiry. When pressed, the Mayor's Office let it be known that he "is patiently waiting for a report from Corrections Commissioner Anna Kross" (who had in fact long since condemned conditions at the Women's House of Detention). Governor Nelson Rockefeller's office, in turn, reminded reporters that a new building for female prisoners was already on the drawing board, the implication being that it would be redundant to bother correcting the state of affairs at the old one.

To appease a mounting public outcry—a Committee of Outraged

Parents had even formed to press for action—the New York State Legislature finally launched two separate inquiries: the Committee on Penal Institutions, headed by Assemblyman Joseph Kottler, and the Committee in Charge of Investigations, headed by Commissioner Herman Stichman. Information gathered from both investigations gradually leaked into the newspapers, and over the next two months the *New York Times* led the pack with no fewer than eight substantial articles on the prison. Commissioner Stichman told the *Times* that he had himself interviewed thirty-seven inmates and that they'd complained bitterly to him about "rats, mice, roaches and flying bugs" (one inmate displayed her badly bitten legs by way of corroboration). Others expressed anger about inadequate medical attention, unpalatable food, and "widespread homosexual practices." The second legislative committee conducted its own inquiry, and its chair, Assemblyman Kottler, confirmed Stichman's findings: the House of Detention, Kottler reported, was a "hellhole" that made him "physically sick."[5]

Though only eighteen, Andrea was already savvy enough to know that fine words are no guarantee of fine deeds, and she continued to press her own case; she gave testimony before the grand jury, and she wrote directly to Corrections Commissioner Anna Kross reiterating the injurious treatment she'd suffered. Kross was sympathetic. She told one reporter that she'd "never held a brief for 'that place,'" and pressured the (female) superintendent of the House of Detention for a full accounting. The superintendent reported back that "complete physical exams were conducted routinely" and always "with the greatest dignity and decorum."

The stalemate led not to a resolution but to yet more commissions and investigations. Deputy Mayor Edward Cavanagh and representatives of volunteer groups (the Salvation Army, Friendly Visitors, etc.) that worked at the House of Detention were among those who managed to get in on the act—the president of the Friendly Visitors announcing to the press that "the prison staff was absolutely dedicated," and characterizing Andrea as "a hysterical young girl." Deputy Mayor Cavanagh, in turn, reported that charges of "snakepit" conditions "were without substance." He cited in support of that conclusion his own interviews with prisoners, who "did not indicate complaint or poor morale," as well as the assertion by the four prison chaplains serving at the women's prison that they were "shocked at the distortions that have been made about conditions." Assemblyman Kottler begged to differ; he insisted that what was underway was nothing less than a deceitful "whitewash"—a charge underscored and confirmed when the doctor who'd brutalized Andrea was promptly reinstated after a brief suspension.

At some point during the period of Andrea's notoriety as *that* girl in the newspapers, she appeared on a television show along with Barbara Deming, a woman she didn't know, who'd long been active in radical causes and had written a book called *Prison Notes* based on her own experiences in jail for civil disobedience—a woman who ten years later would have a significant impact on Andrea's life. During the course of the television discussion, Andrea spoke words that she ever after "deeply regretted": she talked about the terror she'd felt at the widespread lesbianism in the Women's House of Detention, which she described as "rampant, brutal, aggressive . . . the threat of sexual assault was always present. The dykes were like men—macho, brutish, threatening." She'd come out of jail "never wanting to be touched" again by a woman. (By age eighteen, Andrea had in fact already "made love" with a number of women—but she'd never thought of them or herself as "a lesbian"—which in her youthful mind connoted a tough, dangerous, butch woman.)[6]

Traumatized by her House of Detention experience, Andrea turned to her parents in New Jersey for comfort. They had little to offer, though her father Harry, as had been true in the past, offered far more support than did her mother Sylvia. The child of Jewish emigrants from Hungary, Sylvia had for most of Andrea's childhood been in wretched health—deriving from scarlet fever as a child and marked by a series of strokes and heart attacks; when well enough, she worked as a secretary in a high school to help piece out the family income. Andrea was essentially raised by her father, a gentle, nurturing man who became a schoolteacher—at the time a feminized profession—as well as a dedicated socialist.[7]

Harry's parents had fled Russia in their teens to escape persecution and, for his father, pending military service. During Andrea's childhood, Harry Dworkin treated her in much the same way he did her younger brother, Mark: he encouraged her ambition, worked nights in the post office loading trucks to save enough money for both their college educations (and to pay Sylvia's medical bills), and imbued in Andrea his own unshakeable commitment to social justice and racial equality. They were a family, Andrea would later write, "with strong political principles and deep human rights convictions." The Holocaust was ever-present in the family's consciousness; except for the grandparents who'd emigrated, the rest of the family had remained in Europe and almost all had died at Auschwitz.

Like her parents, Andrea as a youngster had been brought up in a secular Jewish community—yet with a difference. Though her parents shared the assimilationist views of the conservative Jewish enclave in which they lived, their social conscience was more pronounced than that of their neighbors—and especially in regard to issues relating to race. They believed that discrimination against black people was fundamentally immoral. Sylvia had insisted on driving Andrea through Harlem to see the direct evidence of black poverty; her father, Harry, for his part, had shamefacedly confessed to her that he harbored some racist feelings against blacks, and that those feelings were wrong and had to be actively combated both within oneself and in the public sphere. Sylvia too had a decidedly maverick side: an upholder of "respectable" views on gender roles, marriage, and family, she supported legal birth control and legal abortion.

"Jewishness," on the other hand, was minimized; what was important above all was to be seen as "normal," to be accepted as part of the local community, to be "just folks." It was important to disassociate oneself from Orthodox Jews, with their peculiar rituals and their chosen isolation from mainstream America. And any dwelling on one's own history back in the "old country" was likewise to be avoided. Harry Dworkin's parents had been Russian immigrants; Sylvia's came from Hungary. All genealogy ended there. Andrea knew only that her father had had seven brothers and sisters. All but one were dead, none had names that could be remembered, nor how they'd died; it was important to face forward, not back; it was the people in *this* room who constituted "family."

Though a number of survivors lived in the vicinity of Camden, the experience of the camps had been too traumatic to become a subject of common conversation. There were few grieving references to the mass slaughter of Europe's Jews. No one gave her *The Diary of Anne Frank* to read, nor did anyone speak of it. Yet she was made aware of the murderous impact of the Nazi reign of terror on her own family. Sent to Hebrew school and made conscious of her Jewishness from an early age, she'd made a point in public school of refusing to sing "Silent Night" along with the rest of her class. As she would later write, "I knew I wasn't a Christian and I didn't worship Jesus. I even knew that Christians had made something of a habit of killing Jews, which sealed the deal for me." She wouldn't be "pushed around" on the subject, and didn't budge about singing "Silent Night." For refusing to give way, she was for a time shunned, and one of her drawings was hung in the hall with the word "KIKE" written across it.

Yet when still in her teens, Andrea strenuously denounced all organized religion as "crap," and the disagreement with her parents over "Jewishness" would continue after Andrea went off to the unconventional all-women's college at Bennington. Sylvia persisted in signing her up to receive "The Scroll," the bulletin of the conservative synagogue Beth Jacob to which she and Harry belonged. As Sylvia must have known, that was the equivalent of trying to convert Senator McCarthy to socialism. Predictably, Andrea's response was indignant: the family needed to understand "once and for all," she wrote home, that she had no interest in Beth Jacob and its "meaningless rituals." If the rest of the family continued to find "satisfaction, beauty, or comfort in them," she would respect that, but as for herself, she found religion's "concomitant moralities . . . repulsive"; "I will not be bound," she added, "by dogmas which limit consciousness or modes of activity," nor participate in "reciting like machines preconceived words."

She exonerated her father ("Dad know[s] what I mean") but let her mother have it between the eyes, capitalizing her words for

added emphasis: "YOU MUST COME TO KNOW ME AND
TO RESPECT ME AS I AM, NOT AS YOU ARE, NOR AS
YOU WANT ME. OTHERWISE, WE CAN NEVER TALK
HONESTLY. AND I LOVE AND RESPECT YOU ENOUGH
(AND THIS IS TRUE AND IMPORTANT) THAT I WANT
YOU TO TALK TO ME NOT TO SOMEONE WHOM YOU
ARE CONSTRUCTING IN YOUR IMAGINATION." This
was *not* a "stage," Andrea emphasized—she was not a "rebellious
adolescent," would not "grow out of it," would never "assimilate."
She mailed back Beth Jacob's loathsome bulletin to her parents,
adding in a final shot—Andrea demonstrated early a penchant for
overemphasis—that she had "never seen such a collection of trivia,
vile writing, and false morality."[8]

Though Andrea, born in 1946, grew up in Camden during the
hyper-conservative fifties, when men and women were viewed as
separate creations with pre-ordained social roles—the male born to
rule, the female to support his needs and raise their children—Harry
Dworkin was a considerable oddity, a man who (as Andrea would
later put it) "valued learning and intellectual dialogue" and vowed
that his children—his daughter as well as his son—"would become
whatever they wanted." From an early age, he gave Andrea books
to read and talked with her about his hopes and dreams for a more
just society. She also credited her father with serving as a model for
being a good listener—a quality for which Andrea herself would,
as an adult, be much admired. "My father," Andrea later wrote in
Heartbreak, "could listen to anyone: sit quietly, follow what they had
to say even if he abhorred it . . . strong enough to hear without being
overcome with anger or desperation or fear. . . . I saw someone with
principles who had no need to call attention to himself."[9]

 "My mother," Andrea wrote years later, "was out of the running as
an influence. My father . . . set the tone and taught both my brother
and me that our proper engagement was with the world." She adored
her father but as a young woman "had no sympathy for my mother,"
other than reluctantly acknowledging her bravery in the face of
considerable physical suffering. Andrea thought her mother's mind
"uninteresting"; she seemed "small and provincial"; "an ignorant

irritant" concerned only that her daughter be "presentable," that she clean up her room, wear "proper" clothes, marry a "nice" man, and have obedient children. Yet as Andrea grew older, she gradually became more sympathetic, better understood that her mother had grown up in poverty, had never been encouraged to read books, never been asked for her opinion about anything important, never been encouraged to think well of herself or her prospects. As soon as she graduated from high school, Sylvia had become a secretary and, when well enough, a part-time salesgirl as well in order to add to the family's income. Harry remained deeply in love with his wife and extraordinarily loyal to her; he tended quietly, usually silently, to side with her when she exploded at Andrea.

During Sylvia's frequent bouts of illness, she was only intermittently able to take care of the children, and since Harry held down two—and occasionally three—jobs, Andrea and her brother Mark, who was younger by three years, lived with relatives for varying periods of time. Andrea felt that as a result of this enforced separation she "grew up very fast and very early in all ways . . . learned resilience, and how to handle 'aloneness'"; she felt she'd "really been adult since about twelve . . . I learned to have a private life when I was very young. I wasn't the usual naive middle class wide eyed child at all, and still, in the muck and with lots of trouble all around, I thought humans were worth loving and life was splendid."

When Sylvia was relatively healthy, she became—to Andrea's angry astonishment—a person who gave orders and stood her ground, and she and her daughter often had (as Andrea put it) "a very hard time with each other." Over the years, never less than annoyed at Sylvia's "bossy" demands, Andrea's compassion for her mother's unlucky life grew. She did come to appreciate, at least intermittently, Sylvia's strength of character, her "mordant sense of humor," her remarkable physical courage, *and* her sharp intelligence. It was Sylvia, Andrea would learn, who—despite her mostly conventional views—supported birth control and abortion "long before" (as Andrea would put it) "these were respectable beliefs"; Sylvia was in fact one of the earliest members of Planned Parenthood. And it was Sylvia who gave Andrea permission to take out Vladimir Nabokov's *Lolita* and Grace Metalious' *Peyton Place* from the public library.

Yet this same unorthodox Sylvia would continue to "blow up" over Andrea's "reckless" penchant for "total honesty," her willful, argumentative, precocious defiance of traditional habits of mind and behavior. Their fights, Andrea later wrote, "were awful and I don't doubt that, then as now, I fought to win." In particular, tempers would flare over Andrea's rebellious dismissal of gender conventions—at what Sylvia called her "wildness." She simultaneously insisted that Andrea never lie and that she "had to lose at games to the boys if I wanted them to like me." "I was the wrong child for my mother to have had," Andrea later concluded. "My emotions were too extravagant for her own more literal sensibility. . . . She valued conformity and never even recognized the brazen emotional ploys of a child to hold on to her. . . . I loved her madly when I was a child, which she never believed. . . . When I would be stretching my brain in curiosity—and dancing my brain in front of her to dazzle her—she thought it was defiance . . . to the extent that she knew me, there was no doubt that she did not like me, and also that I could not be the child that she would find likable. . . . I did stop loving her when I was older and exhausted by her repudiations of me." Later summing up the melancholy contradictions of their relationship, Andrea would sadly conclude that we have all "been robbed of our mothers. I knew only the narrowness of her life, nothing of its depths. She was kept from me, cloistered, covered from my gaze by impenetrable layers of cultural lies."

After Andrea's release from the Women's House of Detention, apparently neither Harry nor Sylvia offered her as much comfort or support as she felt appropriate to the ordeal she'd been through. Perhaps Harry felt embarrassment over references in the press to her vaginal bleeding; perhaps Sylvia drew back from what she viewed as her daughter's penchant for dramatic overstatement, leading her to minimize the extensive abuse Andrea had suffered. The best guess may be that Harry, sympathetic to his daughter's act of conscience, deferred to Sylvia's anger over the family's "good name" being publicly associated with public protest and prison. Possibly, too, Andrea had exaggerated expectations of her parents' ability (or willingness) to match her own indignation. Harry had long since

told Andrea that though he loved her deeply—and she never doubted it (she called it "the one great gift of my life")—he was appalled at
the ongoing conflict between her and her mother, and that Sylvia's
well-being would always come first with him.[10]

Andrea was no better pleased with her reception when she returned
to Bennington. At the time, she'd been living off-campus with two
male roommates, and when she reappeared, her wounds not yet fully healed, they treated her (as she later described it) with "a typical
male reaction to Blood Down There, a kind of *his*terical stiffen-
ing of every muscle, a stony indifference, a strained withdrawing of
mind and body." Her current boyfriend, a black man named Arthur,
offered no more sympathy when Andrea told him the details of her
mistreatment in prison: "White girl," he responded, "that's what
they do!" That was more, Andrea later wrote, "than I could stand to
know about his real life, and so I never saw him again."

Wherever she turned, it seemed, she met with "contempt, or
silence, or indifference," and it left her feeling "choked and enraged,
filled with fury and confusion." Then it dawned on her: she'd been
turning primarily to men. When she finally told her story to two
Bennington undergraduates who she barely knew, the response was
quite different: "They knew viscerally, absolutely, what had happened to me." Over time, Andrea also saw with heightened clarity
that the brutality she'd experienced in the House of Detention had
an added dimension, a deeper personal meaning that related to a
Jewish upbringing she otherwise rejected. It had "conjured up the
Nazi doctors who had tortured flesh of my flesh and blood of my
blood, and an aunt who had survived to tell me, retching in terror
and memory." On one level her treatment at the House of Detention "was what it was, the violation of one woman by two particular
men," but on another level it had also resurrected "that near history
of my living flesh and so it had a resonance beyond itself—a sound,
an echo, through 6,000,000 bodies."[11]

Distraught by the experience and the mostly unsympathetic
response it had evoked, Andrea started to question what she was
doing with her life, why she had ever enrolled at Bennington. From
early adolescence she'd felt that she would become either a writer or

a lawyer, but what did either vocation, she now asked herself, have
to do with matriculating at Bennington College? It was, she now
decided, exclusive, expensive, "isolated from the Vermont community in which it was situated" and with "an *apocryphal* self-image of
being a haven for intellectual and sexual experimentation." Even
before the House of Detention incident, she'd had some doubts
about the school's "ingrown" way of life and its "limited scope of
taste"; a mere two months after arriving she'd felt there was "something deadening (speaking in terms of creativity) about being up
here" and predicted "that there will be a time when I will have out-
grown this place." *Any* place, she sensibly added, "can take one just
so far, can give only so much, and then it becomes a killing thing to
stay for a 'degree', etc." She'd already developed, she wrote home, "a
keen perception of what eternal academic life is, and I don't like it."

Yet she acknowledged that Bennington offered "more actual freedom for women" than almost any other school at the time and even
encouraged them "to take themselves seriously." She'd found considerable encouragement of her talent and sympathy for her edgy
views. "People here," she'd written her parents early in her freshman year, "are terribly concerned about how I am, all highly sympathetic." Initially, she had especially enjoyed her classes in music
and French, but it was a course on ethics and social change that
proved centrally important to her. The reading started with Plato's
Republic, moved on to utilitarianism, and ultimately included Marx,
Gandhi, Martin Luther King, and Aristotle.

One premise of the course resonated for Andrea with special
force. It was the distinction between "conventional morality (that
which is insisted upon by tradition) and 'reflective' morality (that
which is arrived at through individual reasoning and experiencing
processes)." As she herself described it, "the former is the common
condition, is wrong, is immoral . . . the latter is the responsibility
of every thinking individual." She credited Bennington with being
mostly "removed from the academic realm," with being "pertinent
to now, to what would be important to anyone who gives a damn
about what's happening in the world." In a letter home she undiplomatically dotted the "i": "to take it out of the abstract realm,"
she wrote, "it means that if my religious conviction is not Judaic,

it would be wrong of me to go through the motions in order to appease those who value conventional morality."

A number of well-established literary figures were frequently in and out of the Bennington campus, including Stanley Kunitz, Bernard Malamud, Howard Nemerov, Stanley Edgar Hyman, and Richard Wilbur, but Andrea makes reference in her letters only to having met Malamud and Kunitz ("a goddam bore, a real bore. And so was his poetry."). She herself issued an invitation—having become interested in non-authoritarian education—to Peter Anderheggen, who was associated with A.S. Neill's famously unstructured school, Summerhill, in England, to give a talk at Bennington—which she pronounced "wonderful."

But it was several full-time, less prominent figures on the faculty who lavished attention on Andrea, praised her writing, and proved of "outstanding" help—along with being "nice, warm, non-pretentious people." With their encouragement, she slowly began to submit poems and other pieces to avant-garde publications, and even got one reply, from Ralph Ginzburg, editor of the political journal *FACT* and the former editor of *Eros*, a magazine of glossy erotica launched in 1962; it appeared only four times before Ginzburg was indicted on charges of violating federal obscenity laws and sentenced to five years in prison (he served about eight months). Andrea got hold of a copy of *Eros* and described it to her parents as "very well done . . . and not obscene." Ginzburg offered her a job with *FACT* "any time," adding that they could not pay much but sending "all his best wishes and personal respect." Andrea was "very pleased."

Her literary education, she later wrote, focused on "an almost exclusively male tradition of literature." While in high school, she'd begun to read Lawrence Ferlinghetti, James Baldwin, William S. Burroughs (*Naked Lunch* is "an extraordinary satirical work"), and Allen Ginsberg (who within a few years she'd come to know personally), and had launched a protest, to her parents' embarrassment, when the school library removed *The Catcher in the Rye* from its shelves. The nineteen-year-old Andrea was an unmitigated champion of writers like Norman Mailer ("America's most talented novelist"), Henry Miller (his *Black Spring* was "tremendous . . .

exquisite . . . essential for understanding America"), D.H. Lawrence, and Jean Genet—writers she would later brand "the most misogynist and brutal male writers in existence." Yet even then she'd continue to credit them with having given her "a tremendous sense of freedom and audacity," as well as a willingness "to use the language to confront the society around you."[12]

She "wouldn't read anyone who didn't have an apocalyptic message"; her favorites included Burroughs, Orwell's *Down and Out in Paris and London*, anything by Rimbaud (in his case, she remained "hooked for life"), and, above all, Kafka and his "monuments of ravaged and ravaging male consciousness"—this "tubercular, frightened, insignificant German Jew [who can] . . . force the world into a new shape." Despite the deficiencies of focusing on the male tradition, it did not (as she later wrote) "teach coyness or fear: the writers I admired were blunt and not particularly polite. I did not understand that—even as a writer—I was supposed to be delicate, fragile, intuitive, personal, introspective. I wanted to claim the public world of action, not the private world of feelings."[13]

As a youngster, the only woman writer Andrea read was George Eliot's assigned *Silas Marner*, which, like most schoolchildren, she'd "hated" (over time, she'd decide that *Middlemarch* was the greatest of all novels). It would only be in 1970, after reading Kate Millett's *Sexual Politics*, that Andrea's visceral feminism took charge and her reading habits "totally turned" around. (In 1965, of course, the feminist movement had barely surfaced, though Simone de Beauvoir had already published *The Second Sex* and, taking their inspiration from her, Mary King and Casey Hayden, stalwarts of the Student Nonviolent Coordinating Committee [SNCC], had issued a bold position paper decrying "the assumption of male superiority" in the white civil rights movement.)

Andrea had an active social life at Bennington. Decidedly counter-cultural, she was a firm believer in sexual liberation, in "the unqualified goodness of sex, its sensuousness, its intensity, its generosity." She later made oblique references to having slept with the wife of one of the deans and at one point dated two young men simultaneously (one was from Kenya and studying international relations). Two of her closest undergraduate friends were also black:

Lynn Jones, a young transfer student from Chicago, and Emmy Annan, an African nationalist from Nairobi who'd traveled widely and who in her three or four years of schooling in the United States had experienced (as Andrea wrote home) "more cruelty, hatred, and agony than you or I could imagine, let alone contend with."[14]

Her enthusiasm for Bennington would wax and wane. After the first few months of acclimation had passed, Andrea enthusiastically wrote her parents—and she rarely gilded the lily—that she was "really happy here now, discovering a great many things about myself, about my own worth, about what's right and wrong, many of which you probably wouldn't be happy with, but which are giving me a real sense of self-respect." Yet even early on, she described the "Bennington experience" in one jaundiced letter as "a very distressing kind of playpen where wealthy young women were educated to various accomplishments which would insure good marriages for the respectable and good affairs for the bohemians."[15]

Following her return to campus after the House of Detention episode and her mixed, mostly negative, reception, her attitude toward Bennington settled into disdain. In those years, most colleges across the country continued to view themselves as serving *in loco parentis*—as custodians of the morality of the young placed in their charge. Students lived in gender-segregated dorms and had to abide by strict parietal rules; at Bennington, between the hours of 2 a.m. and 6 a.m. no males were tolerated on the premises. "One could have sex with another girl," Andrea would later mockingly write, "and many of us did, myself certainly included"—but male lovers had to disappear into the night.[16]

On returning to Bennington, Andrea discovered that the college had a new president, one more conventional than his predecessors. Andrea lived in Franklin House—"a hotbed of treason," as she saw it, that voted down parietal rules and "seceded" from the school. Suddenly, "stringy, hairy boys" were appearing in the bathrooms at 4 a.m.; "a pleasant anarchy reigned." That is, until the faculty—a number of them notorious for sleeping with students—decided to at least appear to side with the president. When Andrea was elected to the Judicial Committee, which had the right to expel students, she helped push through a "test case" whereby a significant number of students signed a piece of paper acknowledging that they'd broken the parietal rules, for which crime the committee "expelled" all of them. The president promptly reacted by refusing to re-admit any student who failed to sign a loyalty oath pledging to obey the school's rules. Andrea was among the few who refused. She had decided it was time to leave Bennington—indeed to leave the country, to leave her family. She felt it was essential to break free from the strictures of home and college alike—to go far away, to go out of reach. She wasn't, she sometimes thought, "afraid of anything"—or as she put it in another formulation, "I was equally afraid of everything, so that nothing held a special terror and no action that interested me was too dangerous."

She now knew, irrevocably, that she wanted to become not a lawyer but a writer: "I wanted to write books that, once experienced, could not be forgotten." What she didn't yet know, as she would later acknowledge, was what it meant, deeply meant, to be a woman, an American woman. She felt she *did* know about "white Amerikan (the then-fashionable counter-cultural spelling to which Andrea adhered throughout her life) ignorance"—not only middle-class ignorance, but one that was "democratically distributed." She did *not* yet know that she was a feminist—that cultural eye-opener was only beginning to blink—but she did know that Amerikan ignorance remained largely untouched, even as Vietnamese villages were being widely burned, and both Vietnamese and Americans pointlessly killed.

Besides becoming a writer, Andrea had one other foregrounded hope. At eighteen she could only describe it in somewhat grandiloquent terms: to help create "a new social order in which people could live in a new way . . . lives would not be without pain, but they would be without certain kinds of pain. They would be lives untouched by prisons and killings and hunger and bombs . . . a world without institutionalized murder and systematic cruelty. I imagined that I could write a book that would make such a world possible . . . I had a hunger to know and to tell and to do everything that could be done. I had an absolute faith in my own will to survive."[17]

She initially considered spending the summer of 1965 teaching in

Mississippi, joining the multitude of other Northern students participating in the black struggle for civil rights. But the deep South, finally, didn't seem far enough away. It was Amerika she wanted to leave behind, not least her own family's version of it. For their sake, she pretended otherwise: "Please know that my leaving school is not a rejection of you in any way, shape or form. Ok? . . . I hope that when I come home there won't be any rending of chests"; she didn't want to defend her decision, she wrote, "although I'd love to share it." She told her parents that she'd managed to locate a ship that catered primarily to students and charged only $129 for a one-way ticket to Europe—it "recognizes students' poverty. America recognizes very little." Over the anguished protest of her parents, Andrea embarked for Europe on September 15, 1965, just days before her nineteenth birthday. As it would turn out, she'd need every ounce of that faith in her will to survive.

Toward the end of the cross-Atlantic trip, a gale in the English Channel made Andrea seasick, but that aside, the voyage proved "terribly exciting—students, artists, professors mostly"—and for icing on the cake the presence of Mario Savio, leader of the Free Speech Movement in Berkeley that had recently turned the campus upside down, whom she'd admired from a distance, as well as the Living Theater experimental company led by Judith Malina and Julian Beck, with both of whom she would later become fast friends.

Arriving in England, Andrea briefly visited two distant cousins and then, traveling alone, took a "terribly uncomfortable" (as she wrote home) train ride through "some of the world's most beautiful land"—Switzerland and Yugoslavia—and moved straight on to Athens. Her reaction to the city and its inhabitants was positive from the start: the ancient ruins "indescribably beautiful" and the city itself the only one she knew of where "one can go out at night and feel perfectly safe." She attributed the lack of street violence to the fact that "so much social life is in the streets," outdoor cafes ("tavernas") were everywhere, multiple musicians moved among the crowd, and on nearly every corner men sold souvlaki (a doughy pancake filled with lamb meat, tomatoes, onions, and half a dozen condiments). For Andrea's tight budget, the inexpensive and plentiful food—at least outside the tourist areas—was a godsend; if she ordered beef, she got a full plate of it, a "salad" would turn into a large platter of huge, tasty tomatoes. Dinner cost 15 or 20 drachmas (at most $0.60 in American money).

She took special pleasure in the bouzouki music omnipresent in the tavernas, as was the sight of Greek men spontaneously dancing together "with great precision and grace, the rougher, more virile the man, the more desired he is as a dancer," a throwback, she chose to believe, "of the ancient Greek homosexual societies." The scene in the tavernas inspired her to compose a paean to maleness (she who would later be summarily denounced as a "man-hater"): "I have known men who have allowed me my youth, my anger, my stupidity . . . I have known men who have known what it is to be afraid . . . I have known men who have had the courage to be free, to be good, to suck the earth dry . . . I have known men who have refused to die in vain, and I have even known men who have refused to live in vain . . . I have known the beautiful men of here and now. I have slept with them, and sheltered them, and loved them, breathed into their manly pores, housed their gentle fluid erections, fed them milk from out my breasts . . ."[18]

Moving on to Crete's capital, Heraklion (also known as Iraklion, which is how Andrea spelled it), she quickly found an enchanting apartment on the outskirts of the city overlooking the Mediterranean. Perhaps more important, as the days turned into weeks she began to find "something called 'peace'"—explaining it as the absence of wealth that in America bred "false values." She adored Iraklion; it dated back thousands of years to the Minoan civilization and contained, among much else of beauty, the ruins of the palace of Knossos; plus the light was "exquisite, and the combination of mountain and sea powerful." She loved, too, the absence of the huge, polluting cars omnipresent in the States; on Crete the chief mode of transportation was the human-sized motorcycle and (for the less prosperous) the donkey cart or bicycle.

Though food and rent were cheap in Iraklion, some everyday items like postage stamps or a dictionary were unexpectedly high, and Andrea's need to rent a typewriter pretty much busted her budget. Within a month (as she reported to her parents) she became seriously involved with a "really wonderful" twenty-one-year-old French-Greek man, who she described as fluent in four languages (though not in English; they spoke French together) and "compassionate in the sense of empathetic and gentle." The affair reached the point where he asked Andrea to marry him—"don't panic," she wrote her parents, "I'm not planning to, yet." Alas, after nearly pledging eternal troth, he had to return to his studies in France, promising to return within a few months—though he never did.[19]

Andrea would later describe herself during her late teens as "sexually carnivorous" rather than self-identifying as gay, straight, or bisexual. As early as age fourteen, she and her closest friend (known only as "M") had been deeply in love, and, as she would later write, that love had "exploded into touching and kissing and passion . . . eroticism suffused our bodies and brought us to each other, and all night long, neither of us knowing anything conceptual or verbal about what was happening between us, we made love . . . consuming, passionate, tender, lusty love, over and over. . . . Everything just happened, there were no names, no shame or guilt, almost no memory."

Starting in junior high school, Andrea also had, along with two of her classmates, what she later called a "sexualized relationship" with one of her favorite male teachers ("who liked little girls, especially little Jewish girls. I don't mean five year olds, although maybe he liked them too."). He was by far the hippest teacher in the school, the one who affirmed her right to be "disobedient." He liked jazz (which Andrea adored), smoked marijuana, introduced her to Sartre and Camus ("though not de Beauvoir, certainly not"). He drew pictures for her "of all the sex acts, including oral and anal sex," instructed her "in how to pursue men, not boys," and suggested that she "become a prostitute"—as he put it, "it was more interesting than becoming a hairdresser." In her 2002 memoir *Heartbreak*, Andrea would explicitly state that the teacher "fucked" one of the two classmates who was competing with her for his attention, "and kept up an emotionally abusive relationship with her for years." More ambiguous about the extent of her own involvement with the teacher, Andrea nevertheless insisted that she became so smitten with him that "I almost committed suicide at sixteen because

I didn't think he loved me" (he reassured her "in a hot and heavy phone call" that he did). As Andrea later wrote, "it took me longer—far too long—to become anti-pedophilic."

She would later also acknowledge that as early as high school, when she "needed money or dinner," she'd prostitute herself, and would continue to do so "in New York, in Vermont, in Crete." While in Europe—both on Crete and then later in Amsterdam—she also freely indulged, as she put it, in a life full of dope, fucking, and "the romance of radical ideas." She described herself in Crete as "a person who always had her legs open, whose breast was always warm and accommodating, who derived great pleasure from passion with tenderness, without tenderness, with brutality, with violence, with anything any man had to offer." "I was a person who did not know that there was real malice in the world . . . I had no notion at all of the damage that people sustain and how that damage drives them to do harm to others."

Andrea devoted two hours a day to learning at least rudimentary Greek, and enjoyed the process. There were Americans on the island, and she occasionally had a coffee with one, but it was a fourteen-year-old "academically talented" Greek boy who became her best friend and who she helped with his English. Writing to her brother, Mark, who Andrea missed more than she did her parents, she emphasized how comfortable she felt with Greek people and their culture, how little she missed life in the States where "all the forces of television, government, newspapers, etc." emphasize that "good guys" wear $300 suits and "bad guys" wear beards, where "the rich get richer, the poor get poorer, and who gives a bloody damn?" In Greece, in contrast, almost everyone was poor, but there was "no Harlem . . . nothing that ugly, that sick, that fetid."

With the perspective of distance, she contrasted the Greeks—cognizant of the past and surrounded by history—to the standard American, with "no knowledge of their own country, none of others . . . the most ignorant group of people around." Americans seemed, as Andrea wrote her brother, "inbred . . . [convinced] of their own innate, god-given superiority . . . a country of slogans, the product of endless committees of empty minds, and the empty mind is the dangerous mind." One reason she'd come to Greece, she added, "was that my mind was filled with garbage, now it is emptying and will rest. . . . I have just recently learned how to take an idea and chew it, to live with it for days, months, in the skull, and to chew it slowly, over and over."[20]

Yet she wasn't oblivious to some of the less admirable aspects of Greek culture. She arrived in the country at a time of political turmoil, even if she herself managed to find a measure of personal peace. The year 1965 saw King Constantine's ousting of George Papandreou's government, in which Papandreou's son Andreas—who'd studied and taught in the States and married an American woman—had served as his father's chief economic advisor. Over the next two years, Greece would experience a period of political instability and agitation, ending with a military junta seizing power in a 1967 coup. Sent into exile, Andreas would form a progressive (and somewhat anti-American) coalition that, in 1981, would ultimately return him to power as prime minister.[21]

The apartment Andrea rented in the Iraklion suburb of Poros was part of the Katsirdakis family compound, and she was warmly received by its members. The father was a "quiet, gentle man who likes reading the newspaper and was a Papandreou partisan." His wife, his daughter, and her fiancé all spoke English, and the family "every day/night . . . sits around, drinks coffee, talks," while the mother sewed clothes to sell to the poor in distant villages. "They are treating me," Andrea wrote her parents, "as a daughter." Mrs. Katsirdakis helped her every night with learning Greek, and the entire family assured her that if civil war broke out, Crete was a safe place to be, "as it's the only part of all Greece which is almost unanimous for Papandreou." For a mere twenty drachmas a day, the family fed her a hearty diet of vegetables, meat, and eggs, provided her with a warm community, and yet gave her the considerable privacy she needed to write (she had slowly begun to accumulate pages—and rejection slips).[22]

For two months she worked feverishly on a manuscript that used up "every bit of energy I had," her eyes feeling "like they've been knocked out in jungle warfare"—and then decided to burn it, showing a capacity for self-criticism that in the future few would credit. She then began a "long prose poem," which she'd started while at

Bennington, and this time around she decided, on completion, that it was good enough to send out for possible publication. She chose the three leading avant garde publishers in the United States—Grove, City Lights, and New Directions—but all three rejected it. Andrea tried to be philosophical: "It is inevitable, it always happens that organs that begin to showcase . . . a group of writers fail to grow to encompass other writers." New Directions now contented itself, in her opinion, "with reprinting William Carlos Williams (who had to publish his own first 3 books)"; Grove "prints and reprints Henry Miller and Samuel Beckett," both, she thought, "great writers," though getting on in years.

Like so many radical women, Andrea's political energy before leaving for Greece had gone into ending segregation and protesting the war in Vietnam. A committed leftist, she'd had decidedly anarchist (anti-authoritarian) leanings. When her father—though himself on the left—tried to persuade her in regard to Vietnam that given human nature, warfare of some sort would always be with them, Andrea replied with a question: Does war "feel inevitable in your *gut*" or merely "in your brain"? She rejected his view that violence was intrinsic to the human condition rather than a function of misguided government policies, and dismissed as well the wartime rationale of "freedom" that both sides in a given conflict employed (she reminded him that Hitler had spoken of freeing the German people from the Jews). In Andrea's view, "freedom begins where political institutions end, and political institutions can only end when the sheep are no longer in the majority." She suggested that her father read, or reread, Thoreau's "Essay on Civil Disobedience."

With America's involvement in the Vietnamese war beginning to accelerate, Andrea confessed that "the thought of returning home poses nothing but terror for me." She did intend to return, but "the Vietnam war rips me in vital places, and America's values . . . make me angry and defensive . . . what troubles me most is that I am not fearless. . . . I have a measure of personal peace here and it will cost dearly to give it up. Which I must do when I return home . . . the fight for freedom in the U.S. is the essential fight of this age . . . my flesh crawls at the thought of what this war demands, for, as I think you know, it demands prison cells, the danger of assassination, and a great deal of public wrath . . . when I return I will still have to act out what I believe. . . . I wish that I loved America the way these people love Crete."

As contented as she felt on the island, it hadn't escaped Andrea's notice that "the church controls just about everything," and she in large measure blamed it for the endemic poverty, though few people went hungry. Nor did most Greeks, in contrast to most Americans, tend to blame their own personal shortcomings for their failure to prosper; they did *not* believe that "where there's a will there's a way," that if you failed in life the fault was entirely your own. "In America," Andrea would later write, "everything is new, like hemp before the rope is made. On Crete the rope was used, bloodstained, it smelled of everything that had ever touched it."

The plight of Greek women in particular moved Andrea. She learned that only nine out of every hundred women on Crete had completed secondary school and only two out of a hundred had ever attended college; that women had only gotten the vote in 1952 and still could not legally be the guardian of their own children, even when the father had died. Greek women were generally treated as work horses, incapable of independent and intelligent judgment. They "do everything," Andrea wrote home. "They work twice as hard as the men (who are only concerned with whatever their pro- fession is) and then have to conform to a whole litany of idiotic rules designed to 'protect' and shelter them. They do everything from heavy manual labor, to office work . . . then they go home and work some more." Mrs. Katsirdakis "keeps house for her family, plus runs the pension which entails cleaning two other houses, plus sews 10 to 12 hours a day . . . which she sells in the weekly village bazaar . . . and this is seven days a week." Yet Mr. Katsirdakis calls himself an "ardent democrat," Andrea pungently added, and was a kind man of whom she was genuinely fond. Her anguish over the plight of women—of women everywhere—was on the rise, though she still lacked some of the consequential analysis and vocabulary, plus a like-minded community, to mature her concern and bring it to political centrality.

———

The drive to become herself, which included opening up fully to the plight of other women, was paradoxically accelerated by falling entirely in love for the first time with a man. Neither in letters nor in her published writing does Andrea ever refer to him as other than "E" (though we now know that his name was Manolli), even though she wrote quite a bit about her love for him, including one long piece entitled "First Love."[23]

But not even in that article do we get more than a few bare bones, abstracted particulars: "I had been on Crete maybe three months when I first saw you. Glorious, golden moment. I was drinking vermouth at an outdoor cafe. The day was dark and drizzly. You stepped out of a doorway, looked around, stepped back in out of sight. You were so beautiful, so incredibly beautiful, radiating light, yr eyes so huge and deep and dark. I don't remember how we began to talk or when we first made love, but it really did happen that way, I saw you and the earth stood still, everything in me opened up and reached out to you. Later I understood that you were too beautiful, that yr physical beauty interfered with yr life . . . that it created an almost unbridgeable distance between you and others, even as it drew them to you."

We learn a few further details, but are given no information about how long the affair lasted, how it proceeded, or how it ended. E's own history and personality are provided only to the extent that we subscribe to the words Andrea puts in his mouth: "I (that is, E) was a member of the young communists, an illegal group in Greece since the Civil War; there was a woman comrade, and we had all done actions with her, and slept with her, and then she had a political difference with the others and they, who had been her lovers, refused to speak to her or to associate with her, she was ostracized and cursed; and I quit because I thought, *if these are the people who are making the revolution and if this is the way they act, then I don't want to live in the kind of world they would make.*"

At the time, Andrea tells us, "I didn't understand E's story. . . . I had seen many women used then abandoned, I had been used then abandoned myself; still, I could not make sense of what I had seen or of my own experience, I did not make sense of it for several more years." At the time, E's account even "embarrassed me somewhat because I didn't entirely understand what [he] . . . had done or why [he] . . . had done it." Still, she knew that she liked him for objecting to the woman's treatment.

Nothing about the behavior of the woman in E's story seemed to Andrea imprudent or ill-advised. She considered herself, with more than a touch of theatrical exaggeration, as destined to be used, dominated, discarded. She was a woman who believed that life was "what Miller and Mailer and Lawrence had said it was. I believed them. I thought that they were creative and brilliant truth tellers." Only later, after a feminist consciousness had taken hold, did she see her experience with E with different eyes: "my body [had been] . . . colonialized [sic], owned by others, imperialists who robbed it of its richest resources—possessed, taken, conquered, all the words those male writers use to describe ecstatic sexuality."

Even later, she would never be entirely sure why she decided to break away from E. She thought the underlying answer lay deep in history and applied to all women: "Our bondage is so ancient, so absolute, it is every inch of the past that we can know. So we cannot reclaim, because no memory of freedom animates us. We must invent, reinvent, create, imagine the scenarios of our own freedom against the will of the world. At the same time we must build the physical and psychic communities that will nourish and sustain us." In 1965, she later realized, she was still living out what she then had few words for, other than the myths of "romance" and sacrificial nobility ("A woman who loves a man accepts the pain"). She'd grown up with myths whose effect, she later understood, was to deprive her "of my bodily integrity, to cripple me creatively, to take from me myself."

All she knew at the time was that she and E had begun to have "monstrous wordless fights," which she found inexplicable: "What does it mean that two people, a man and a woman, who require each other for the sake of life itself . . . who do not share a common language . . . but know each other completely . . . begin to tear and rend each other's insides? . . . I swear," Andrea would later write, "I don't know, all these years later I still don't know."

She never fully claimed to understand why she broke away from E, "what in me [as she put it years later] stronger than my love for you—what nameless drive, in me but not claimed by me as part of me, moved me to decide to leave you, to walk to the boat, to get on the boat, to stay on the boat even as you called to me from the shore." She did, through the fog, remember one thing: "You hated it that I was a writer . . . you were jealous as you never would have been of another lover." She also remembered that once he knew about her writing "yr anger took explicit sexual forms. You began fucking me in the ass, brutally, brutally. I began to have rectal bleeding. I told you, I implored you. You ignored my screams of pain, my whispers begging you to stop. You said, a woman who loves a man stands the pain . . . to refuse was, I thought, to lose you, and any pain was smaller than that pain."

It got worse. On a trip to Athens, E got "the clap from some young man" and passed it on to Andrea. Whether from the gonorrhea or the rectal rape, surgery became necessary, and she lay wracked with pain in the hospital. He wrote her letters that she felt "were completely indifferent to my physical condition." Somehow they "became tender with each other again . . . made love again, with such great sadness and softness that it was new." He suggested they marry, but she refused. It was then that she realized she could leave him, that she *would* leave him.

The decision, made with apocalyptic bravado, "was not rational. . . . It was a feeling, an impulse, that inhabited my body like a fever. Once I felt it I knew that I would leave no matter what." E was sure that he knew why—it was because of her drive to become a writer, that part of her that (in Andrea's words) "could not be subsumed by seduction or anal assault or any sort of domination. It is that part that could not even be conquered, or quieted, by tenderness. It is that part of me that was, even then, most alive, and that no man, not even you, who was for me the air I breathed, could ever take from me. . . . I wanted to make Art, and I had a passion for life, and I wanted to act in the world so that it would be changed, and I knew that those things nourished one another but I did not know how. I did not know that they could be the same, that for me they must be the same, for they all had to live in this one body as one or they could not live at all."[24]

2

Marriage

Shortly before returning to the States on the freighter *Hellenic Glory* in May 1966, Andrea warned her parents that although she'd decided to come home, "I don't really know to what or for what," since she still "loved Crete, the only place that I really love," even if "it is too small, too limiting now. Perhaps," she warned, speaking somewhat more plainly, "my newest wounds will be visible, perhaps not. They are deep, but they are private. I ask you to love me, to respect my solitude, my attempt to share with you what is important to me, but do not make judgments where judgments are of no value." Still fresh in her mind, Andrea wrote her mother, is the way "you rejected and almost crucified me" during the House of Detention episode. It had taken her, she said, "a whole year nearly to heal."[1]

A recent exchange with Sylvia had made Andrea even more wary than usual. With great pride in the accomplishment, especially in the midst of the turmoil with E, Andrea had succeeded in self-publishing a chapbook of her poetry and in letter after letter had excitedly alerted her parents to the imminent arrival of an "Extraordinary Surprise." When Sylvia finally read the chapbook, her response was less than gratifying: she didn't like the poems, she wrote Andrea, thought they were difficult, their meaning hard to decipher. Andrea, in turn, adopted a stance of stoic indifference, writing Sylvia that her reaction had neither angered nor upset her, and then promptly belied the claim with a wounded admission that henceforth "it means that most of me is closed to you." Shifting to a somewhat loftily instructive tone, she explained to Sylvia that "modern poetry is complex and difficult," not "immediately accessible"; she herself had never found a poet worth reading who'd initially been "easily available; it was only through persistence that she'd been able "to break through my limitations and [have] revealed to me a new dimension of thought or life." In sum, Andrea wrote, "if this poem, or any poem, excludes you from itself, it is not necessarily the fault of the poem."[2]

Further revealing some of the anger she claimed not to be feeling, Andrea made a point of reporting that she'd also sent chapbooks to her two favorite professors at Bennington, and their response had been glowing, as had that of her classmate Anne Waldman, who was starting a new literary magazine in New York (and who would herself later become an admired poet closely connected to Allen Ginsberg). Never mind, Andrea wrote Sylvia: "One does not ask for your approval, one asks for your love. I must function with your approval or without it and indeed, from the jail experience, I learned how to contain myself without it. I am sorry for that, but I suppose that it was necessary." She assured Sylvia that she'd learned "a certain measure of wisdom, and that measure says that one simply lives one's life. Making do." She was anxious to return to Bennington and hoped that she "will find new horizons" awaiting her. But she added a warning: "I cannot return and become blind"; America's values, whether being played out in Vietnam or in Mississippi's "dismal swamps," were vile, "and when I return I will still have to act out what I believe."[3]

Andrea would, in retrospect, regard her return to Bennington as a waste of two years: "Most of us, as the mostly male faculty knew, would fall by the wayside into silence and all our good intentions and vast enthusiasms had nothing to do with what would happen to us" after we graduated. Yet at the least, Andrea formed a number of close friendships at Bennington, and a few of them would prove lifelong.

Among them were the incipient filmmaker Gretchen Langfeld and Kathleen Norris, a shy, sheltered adolescent from the Midwest who initially seemed wholly out of place in the racy, drug-and-sex-fueled turbulence said to characterize the quintessential Bennington undergraduate. It did typify more than a few, including, to some extent, Andrea herself. Yet if she and the reserved Kathleen diverged in manner, they shared a deep intelligence and a reverence for literature (both would go on to achieve considerable acclaim as writers; among Norris' best-known works are *The Cloister Walk* and *Dakota*). Had they not lived in the same dorm, they might never have been drawn to each other, but the raucous intimacy of dorm life brought them together (at one exuberant dorm party Kathleen was christened the Pope, and Andrea the Oracle); the friendship would last. Kathleen would in later life credit Bennington with her social and literary awakening, whereas Andrea—already an experienced sensualist and a devout reader—thought it had been mostly a waste of time.[4]

As a budding feminist, Andrea also resented the lack of any such consciousness on campus. Most of the consequential works of second-wave feminism—Millett's *Sexual Politics*, say, or Shulamith Firestone's *The Dialectic of Sex*—still lay in the future, but not even *first*-wave feminism was on the Bennington agenda. In the American history courses Andrea took, neither Susan B. Anthony nor Elizabeth Cady Stanton were so much as mentioned. Perhaps worse still, her mostly male professors all but uniformly exuded an air of confident superiority over their "weak-minded" students. "I left Bennington," Andrea would later write, "ignorant of what it means to be a woman in a patriarchal society—that is, in a society where women are systematically defined as inferior, where women are systematically despised."

When her brother Mark, verging on a decision of his own about college, turned to her for advice, Andrea formulated a carefully considered, even wise, set of observations that secondarily helped her to sort out her own next step as well. The first thing she wanted to tell him, she wrote, was that "no-one will ever give you freedom . . . whether by that one means freedom of action, freedom of life-style, or the more 'political' kinds of freedom, [it] is never <u>gratis</u>. . . . The price is sometimes measured in alienation from one's friends, or family, or society; sometimes it is measured in guilt; sometimes in fear; sometimes in regret. No one will ever tell you, except abstractly, that you should <u>really</u> live the way you find most livable . . . the main condition or reservation is usually [that] you should always live the way which is best according to your judgment, <u>until it differs from mine</u>."[5]

Turning specifically to their parents, Andrea acknowledged to Mark that it wasn't easy "to insist on yr privacy, on yr independence in a home which appears to grant you all of that <u>a priori</u>. Let me put it this way: no matter how close you are with Mommy and Daddy, there are things about you that they should not know; that they have no right to know. This is not only because there are many things which they do not understand, or because they are easily hurt, or because they tend to be over-protective. It is because you have places to go (both geographically and in your head), people to see (people whom Mom and Dad might abhor), and things to learn (things that a previous generation is not open to, things that are waiting especially for you). . . . To leave one leg at home is not to be able to move very far."

Sharing her own experience, Andrea told Mark that until she went to Greece "I didn't really know what it was to enjoy something, had never relaxed, not for a minute. In Greece, finally long separate from home, from the pressures of conformity, from many of the very destructive values of American society, I finally did experience joy and tranquility, not with any consistency, but sufficiently to know that they are part of the human condition, accessible to all humanity, and hidden by a catlike maze of laws, rules, fears, etc." She confided to her brother that she might very well leave the country again. "That won't be easy," she predicted, but she was willing to bear "all the fear and all the guilt that others will try to impose on you for being an aberration—for not doing things their way."

She supposed that finally "it's a matter of faith . . . faith in your own instincts . . . one can put off living, and thinking, and doing, and being (freedom) until one is dead, and win prizes all the way . . . but the real prizes are what happens inside of you. It will be very hard at home if you decide to do anything but go the straight and narrow diploma route: mother and dad worry, oppressively . . . [but] what they do not realize is that fear (generated by them) will compromise your manhood before any other thing, and that fear will destroy both your independence and your humanity. . . . I can't give you very much comfort, except to say that you are not alone—that I both love you and wait for you—that I will help you in whatever limited ways that I can."

Heeding her own advice, Andrea joined the struggle to challenge "the authoritarian structure at Bennington." As it had done earlier with the undergraduates, the administration instituted a kind of "loyalty oath" for those faculty members who wished to remain on staff; and when almost all of them complied, Andrea felt so enraged "at the incredible cowardice and hypocrisy of those arch-liberals" that she once again took a leave of absence and decided in the late summer of 1968 to return to Europe. This time she went to Amsterdam, having decided, with a touch of youthful grandiosity, that her dedication "was to the planet, not to one country on it"; besides, she'd heard about the exciting gains in popularity of the Dutch anarchist movement called Provo then convulsing Amsterdam.

By the time she arrived, the movement had already declined in influence, though only a few years earlier Provo, seemingly overnight, had made a wide-ranging challenge to what its adherents viewed as the smug, middle-class social democratic government in the Netherlands—its failure to disavow the U.S. involvement in Vietnam, its refusal to deal with environmental issues of automobile congestion and air pollution, or to accept (as most of Scandinavia had) the current drug and sex revolutions. The Provo "manifesto" denounced as well "this bureaucratic society . . . choking itself with officialdom and suppressing any form of spontaneity . . . [and] digging its own grave by a paranoid arms build-up." Provo felt a choice must be made: "desperate revolt or cowering defeat," and it saw "anarchism as a well of inspiration for the revolt."[6]

Provo's leading theoretician, a university student named Roel Van Duyn, defined what he called the "provotariat" as members of an "anti-class . . . an anonymous group of subversive elements . . . the outsiders, the kids who don't belong to the proletariat or the bourgeoisie or the squares, but do belong in a big rebel group." With inventive, even witty bravado, Provo for a brief period in 1965–66 succeeded in placing antic performance art in service to social revolution. Among its most constructively playful-yet-serious projects was the so-called White Bicycle Plan, designed all at once as both a serious alternative to the air-choking automobile and a provocation aimed at duping the police into a disproportionate response, thereby creating for Provo a mass of new sympathizers.

Provo concocted the White Bicycle scheme as an appropriate symbol for their goal of converting Amsterdam into "Playtown"— painting the bikes white was designed as a synonym for the "purity" of freedom. Billed as "the first free communal transport" and "a protest against private property," the white bicycles would, it was agreed, never be locked, could be used "by anyone who needs it, and then must be left for someone else." Embodying "simplicity and cleanliness," the white bicycle stood in contrast to "the vanity and foulness of the authoritarian car" and, it was predicted, would soon multiply and replace it. Multiply it did, but replacement proved elusive.

Provo's actions peaked in the early months of 1966, when five thousand young protestors took to the streets to denounce the wedding of Princess Beatrix, heiress to the Dutch throne, to Claus Von Amsberg, who'd served in the German army during World War II. Provo delightedly characterized—and denounced—Von Amsberg as an ex-Nazi well-suited to become part of the "parasitical" royal family, and set off smoke bombs to illustrate its disgust. In response, the Dutch police brutally beat the demonstrators, and thereby generated, just as Provo had hoped and predicted, considerable public sympathy for them. So much so that one of its members won election to the Amsterdam City Council.

That proved to be the high-water mark for the Provo movement, though not before it had succeeded in enlisting a disaffected segment of the working class, thereby outlining, to its satisfaction, future possibilities for coalition and for "spontaneous revolution" that ran counter to the traditional Marxist emphasis on disciplined, hierarchical cadres. The Provo prototype was precursor and archetype for the dynamic explosion that subsequently rocked France in

May 1968—a two-month period of civil unrest marked by general strikes that brought the French economy to a near halt.

In the post-1966 period, as Provo's energies began to wane, its leading figures decided that they themselves would announce the movement's demise, would make the best of a deteriorating situation by declaring itself (in the anarchist tradition) bored with the drudgery of political organizing, dismayed at the decline in inspired capers, and convinced that radical change was impossible as long as the masses remained oblivious to their own exploitation. Provo simply closed up shop, though its remnants lingered on.

Enter Andrea. From the first, she found Amsterdam very "livable . . . both cosmopolitan and provincial . . . sophisticated but simple," and the Dutch people, as she began to meet them, "full of intelligence." Before long, she was writing her parents that "I am for now any way genuinely more happy on European soil than on American." The United States "is my <u>home</u> (no question), [but] it is not a good place to live one's life. For me, right now." Her initial plan was to stay in Amsterdam only for a few months—enough time to investigate and write about the Provo movement—and then to proceed on to Paris, settle in for a longer stay, and devote herself to writing. It would not work out that way, for reasons both political and personal.

Wandering the streets of Amsterdam in search of a Provo meeting place, she soon found herself in Leidseplein Square, staring up at a large but decrepit wooden church, antithetically adorned in splashy blotches of psychedelic orange, red, and green paint. Moving closer, she saw that the church front was covered with announcements for jazz concerts, light shows, and movie festivals, along with assorted graffiti in various languages. The name of the place, she learned, was the Paradiso (sometimes called Project Paradiso), and it currently served not as a church but as the government-subsidized institution designed to pacify and render sterile the remnants of the Provo movement. Having already planned to write about the movement, which was all but unknown in the States (though closely allied in spirit with the Yippies of the late sixties), Andrea decided to investigate further.[7]

Entering the Paradiso, Andrea saw that the interior walls were also covered with paint, along with a number of erotic photos, including a picture of a man and a woman having sex that covered one entire wall. Following a sign pointing to "Cafe," she climbed the stairs to a landing, where a man was selling books; he turned out to be Hans Tuynman, a well-known Provo figure who'd earlier been arrested and given a three-month jail sentence for handing a policeman a pamphlet protesting the existence of police. After chatting with him, Andrea climbed up another flight and found herself in a large room, bordered with benches and pillows; a few people were scattered about, passing pipes to one another, and there was a bar toward the back.

Suddenly breathing in the familiar "sweet smell of hashish," Andrea learned that all sorts of drugs were freely used and distributed in Paradiso—and with the full knowledge of the Amsterdam City Council (she herself laid out ten guldens, about $2.80, for "a square of Red Lebanon"). She did regret, though, as a good anarchist would, that it was the government, not the people themselves, who controlled the rules regarding the availability and use of drugs in the Paradiso—an enforcement carried out with the help of on-site "karate experts." Andrea took a clear-eyed view of the situation: "The archetypical welfare state does not like mess. So you . . . find yourself a building, one that nobody is using, a fire hazard, inadequate toilet facilities, and you tell all of the freaks that it is their building for them from you . . . the administration comes from your people and not from theirs—a model of sociological efficiency."[8]

The authoritarian trappings hardly matched her version of a true open society; Paradiso seemed to her more like a "Potemkin village," a false front hiding the damaging reality—one that Andrea readily saw through. In her view, the people milling around inside the building were being deplorably discreet—"very quiet and very careful." She drew the unhappy conclusion that the Provo movement she'd so admired had degenerated into a scene of suffocating passivity.

Yet she still wanted to write about the movement and, with that end in mind, began seeking out and interviewing some of Provo's leading figures. One of them told her that the movement was best viewed not as a failure, but rather "as a stone that is thrown into

the water, and the water is getting higher and higher, overflow-
ing onto the land. The war is between the water and the land, not
between the stone and the water." When Andrea interviewed Roel
Van Duyn, considered the movement's leading theoretician, he put
it somewhat differently to her: "I see Provo as an element of a whole
series of historical events—a line, a line of revolt." But—"stimulated
by automation—I see too the growth of powerful states. I believe
that the provotariat [sic] will fight against that line of bureaucratism,
but I'm almost certain that we will lose. . . . We must have only very
modest ideals, very modest. We cannot any longer say, 'We want
a new world.' Let us say, 'We want to be good people, each of us.'
But it is not any more the time for big social ideals." Questioning
Van Duyn about the growing use of drugs within the movement,
Andrea was surprised when he denounced them as bad; "it was not
possible," he told her, "to be both a 'head' and a revolutionary. One
starts to smoke—and soon one can do nothing else."

Though profoundly impressed with Van Duyn—"my first completely enlightened human being"—Andrea did not, at twenty-two,
subscribe to his modest pessimism. Provo's stance of anti-
authoritarian activism remained for her a valid legacy (one to which
the international youth rebellion of 1968 would closely adhere). Her
defiant temperament made her keenly sensitive to the grotesque
inequities of the current social order. "I have met," she wrote home,
"some brilliant people" among the rebellious young, "some really
first rate minds and spirits." Van Duyn would re-emerge in 1970
with a plan to set up an alternative society—the so-called Kabouter
("dwarf" in Dutch) movement—focused on environmental issues
and tactically non-confrontational, and Andrea would write about
it sympathetically. But Kabouter's comparatively mild reformism
failed fully to engage her intense nature, her sense of the magnitude
of social change that remained necessary.[9]

Besides, her personal life quite suddenly pre-empted her focus
on politics, and soon took on a force that for a considerable time
would monopolize her emotional energy. Andrea had only been in
Amsterdam for some two months when in one of her letters home
she referred for the first time to someone named Iwan de Bruin.
He was, she reported, "a very close and growing closer friend here"

who'd taken her to the doctor when she developed a bad sore throat. A shot of penicillin cured the sore throat; not so the relationship with Iwan.[10]

His full name was Cornelius Dirk de Bruin, known to everyone as Iwan, and Andrea had initially met him one day at the Paradiso. She'd never seen him there before, but everyone seemed to know him. Andrea thought him strange-looking—very tall, blonde, with a receding hairline and a mobile, chiseled, face "capable of the subtlest modulations." Andrea found him difficult to get to know well: "he played the role of the great joker, and was always on the move, from person to person, from situation to situation. . . . His speech was punctuated with dramatic silences and convolutions of his entire body."

Though Iwan had been a prominent member of the Provo movement, he initially refused to let Andrea interview him for the article she was preparing. He spoke some English but would speak none to her, and it was only on a second meeting at Paradiso, after he and Andrea smoked hash in an empty cloakroom, that he began to open up, his English "garbled but expressive." To Andrea's surprise, he reacted to the hash atypically: he became "hyper-tense, nervous . . . tight with tension [he] talked rapidly and non-stop, seemed reluctant to pause even long enough to take a breath."[11]

Formally uneducated, Iwan told Andrea that he was currently thinking through various plans; one idea he had was to create an employment bureau for long-haired men, another to persuade the government to finance a "Speed Kills" campaign—money he would then use to buy amphetamines. "Corruption," he explained to Andrea, "is the basis of life." Through patience, Andrea was gradually able to extract at least *some* basic information about him: he was twenty-one, had served in the Dutch Marines in Surinam; wanting a discharge, he'd constantly disobeyed orders, spent time in the brig at hard labor as well as in a psychiatric hospital, and had finally been discharged early. He'd gotten involved in the Provo movement almost from the start, took part in any number of spontaneous actions, and had "bombed a public monument" (namely a statue of General Van Heutsz, the imperialist governor general of the Dutch East Indies at the turn of the twentieth century who had pacified—i.e., killed off—the Aceh natives).

When Andrea asked Iwan his opinion of the role that drugs played in the movement, quoting to him Van Duyn's contention that their easy availability at the Paradiso had "destroyed the revolutionary potential of the provotariat," Iwan disagreed. People who'd been scared, he insisted, joined Provo only after they started smoking. "Then they became braver. And of course many plans would not have been found [sic] if the people involved had not been stoned." Had the police, Andrea asked, become less brutal as a result of Provo? No, Iwan responded, the police were no softer, nor any looser.

Andrea persisted. On the plus side, she asked, what had Provo accomplished? "Provo accomplished nothing," Iwan snorted. "It was just a passing of time, just a happening." Then, either joking or in stoned earnest, he amended his judgment: "There is now a speakers' corner in Amsterdam; it is now possible for people to sell newspapers on the street. So some things have changed, and that's very important." "What will happen," Andrea asked him, "if the Paradiso ever closes?" Iwan was quick to answer: "Then we will make Provo again. The cops don't like that. They must decide what they don't like more."

The cops *did* close Paradiso, though only briefly. As Iwan had predicted, the closing set off street demonstrations, some of them larger than any seen since the Provo movement had officially shut down several years before. Andrea joined Iwan on some of the demonstrations, but he protectively warned her "that if the police come you must leave. Promise me. They will deport you." Andrea promised, and on the very next demonstration the police, on horseback, charged into the crowd; when one horse brushed close to Andrea's side, Iwan yelled out to her, "Get away from here, *get away*! . . ." Touched at Iwan's concern for her safety, Andrea ran to the sidelines, though she lingered to see if anyone needed her help.

In the weeks that followed, she and Iwan saw each other with increasing regularity. In letters home, Andrea left Iwan unmentioned and focused on how much she was learning. She described her "political-social experiences" in a kind of shorthand, as if to stress their urgency: "I think that you would be distressed . . . but am determined to analyze the American situation mercilessly and thereby to arrive at my necessary life-role and to live it, pay the cost—too many murderous annihilations in this world to do otherwise." She urged her parents to read the "brilliant psychoanalyst" Franz Fanon, and from the African poet Aime Cesaire passed on one of her favorite quotes: "And then, one lovely day, the middle class is brought up short by a staggering blow: The Gestapos are busy again, the prisons are filling up, the torturers are once more inventing, perfecting, consulting over their workbenches . . . and they wait, and they hope; and they hide the truth from themselves . . . [and] that Nazism they tolerated . . . it drips, it seeps, it wells from every crack in western Christian civilization until it engulfs that civilization in a bloody sea."[12]

The housing shortage in Amsterdam was acute, and Andrea, who had little money, kept shifting from one run-down rented room to another. Iwan, too, was nearly penniless, and sometimes the two of them, cold and hungry, would wander aimlessly in search of shelter. Iwan did odd jobs, including part-time work at the Paradiso, and through his contacts with fellow Provo-ites helped Andrea gain access to people she wanted to interview. She continued to work on her article, still hoping that she'd be able to sell it to a mainstream American publication and thereby augment their fragile finances. It was a time of deep frustration: she felt "extraordinary creative energy and desire to work" yet wasn't able to afford a decent room where she could settle down and concentrate. Living on the margins began to take a toll on her health, and she again fell ill. This time, Iwan brought her to his sister's house, where she was made welcome and nursed back to health.[13]

By the end of the year, Andrea and Iwan had decided to marry. In breaking the abrupt news to her parents, she emphasized that "we have spent much time together in the last three months, love each other beautifully and for real," and yet "we are in no great hurry, so don't you panic. . . . Things will happen as they must happen. Everything could change in an hour, and if it does, it does. Slow and easy. Everything. OK?" Though it was true that Iwan, too, had little money, Andrea confidently predicted to her parents that since the Netherlands was "pretty totally a welfare state" they'd have no trouble "subsisting" (which wasn't exactly the kind of reassurance likely to appease Sylvia and Harry).[14]

Soon after they decided to marry, Andrea finally finished her article on the Provo movement and sent it to Grace Paley, who'd offered to serve as an intermediary in shopping it around to an appropriate outlet—and in the meantime she sent Andrea $25 to hold her over (her parents also followed through, as they did from time to time, with an additional hundred). Andrea worried that the article might not be good enough for publication, especially since "most of the people I wanted to talk to I couldn't because I was sick." (In the upshot, a greatly shortened version would appear a year later in the *Village Voice*.)

Andrea was also counting on the completion of a short film that she and her Bennington classmate Gretchen Langfeld had off and on been trying to complete. At one point she turned to Allen Ginsberg for help in finding the needed funding. Andrea's relationship with him, peripheral though it was, went back several years. As a teenager she'd loved Ginsberg (in her words) "with a wholly passionate and sensual love, with poetry the medium of touch. He was the lyric poet I wanted to be, the visionary prophet. He lived in a world of creation I could barely imagine—somewhere inside God, not as His handmaiden. I wanted that luminous world."[15]

Reading Ginsberg's *Howl* during high school, Andrea had (as she put it) "been made . . . mad with ambition and anarchy." She confessed to her best friend that she'd been dying to send Ginsberg her own poems, but felt too shy. One night the friend decided to take the initiative; she "made a raid" on Andrea's storehouse of poems and mailed a bunch off to Ginsberg, Andrea herself contributing to the package a page she ripped out of William Carlos Williams' *Paterson* in which Ginsberg had announced in a juvenile letter to the older poet that *he* was destined to be "the next one." Andrea wanted Ginsberg to know that it was now her turn to be next.

She checked the mailbox day after day, looking in vain for a response. Finally, when about to give up hope, the desired postcard arrived and it contained (in Andrea's later words) "concrete, surgical remarks on my poems." She good-humoredly added that "he didn't anoint me, which was troubling, but I knew it would be harder than that. I carried that postcard with me in hovels and alleys, running from brutes and demons, in many countries over the many years." While in college she'd started to attend some of Ginsberg's poetry readings. "I begged money and traveled by bus for hours to get to them," she later explained, "and found them amazing communal celebrations. . . . To me it was truth and ecstasy but also a geography of how to risk everything, mess with language and life as if they were the original clay."[16]

At a Ginsberg reading in 1967 at St. Mark's Church in the Village in New York, Andrea risked all and introduced herself ("I thought the earth would open up and swallow me. I was awestruck, could barely speak or move"). Ginsberg took a liking to her and gave her his unlisted phone number. It took some time before she could screw up the courage to use it, but when she did, Ginsberg gave her his address and told her to come over. The acolyte swooned appropriately—and proceeded to have what she called "the most important, exquisite night of my life: we talked about poetry, yes, and people we both knew [Anne Waldman], and he made me tea and showed me things ('Bob Dylan bought me this tape recorder')." Then he walked Andrea to the bus, told her eleven times (she counted) that he loved her—and that was that.[17]

At least for several years: Andrea decided to stay away—"to write, not worship." Then, in 1968, she again contacted him, asking for help in raising money to complete the film project she and Gretchen had started on as far back as Bennington. She'd heard that John Lennon was coming to Amsterdam, and she hoped Ginsberg would introduce her to him. He did put her in touch with someone at Apple, the Beatles' corporation, in January 1969; she and Iwan borrowed money from friends, hitchhiked to Ostende, took the ferry to Dover, then the train to London—only to be told that Apple was "close to bankruptcy" and unable to contribute to the movie project. They did at least get to see *Hair*, and Andrea thought it "really fine, very pretty, much too commercial but some of it had sting." Some five years later, Andrea and Ginsberg would re-connect, though their relationship, the second time around, would prove hurtful and ugly.[18]

In her letters home over the next few months, Andrea, little by little, told her parents more about Iwan, carefully emphasizing (except for an occasional slip) his positive qualities. The overall message was clear—"I love Iwan, he is part of me, my life now is with him"—and she emphasized the attributes that best fit the message: Iwan "used to be in Provo, spent much time in jail for political activity, has not been married before, is 22 (one month younger than me), comes from a Catholic family [and] . . . has had much trouble with his family over his political opinions . . . is a kind and gentle man, [and] principled."[19]

Andrea acknowledged that Iwan had had little formal education, but he was "well read, especially in politics," and he and Andrea communicated in half-English and half-Dutch. Over time, Andrea went on, Iwan had held down various jobs, including driving a truck; currently he was collecting welfare and working at the Paradiso Wednesday through Saturday nights. He "wants desperately to be an actor," Andrea reported, and she was planning to write a play for him that they could put on at the Paradiso. They had recently, she wrote her parents, unexpectedly landed jobs as extras in the Jacques Tati film *Play Time* at "marvelous pay," which had further incited Iwan's dream of acting.

As for his deeply religious family, Andrea acknowledged that the picture was a bit less rosy. Iwan's brother Martin had been particularly incensed over his involvement with Provo, and his parents had thrown Iwan out for several months. His four sisters ranged, in Andrea's view, "from open-minded . . . to suspicious rigid Catholic paranoid," and Andrea found his father the most difficult of all. He had worked for the Nazis as a boat captain during World War II, and Andrea confessed that she "found it hard to be in the same room with him." She also mentioned, parenthetically, that Iwan was a heavy smoker and sometimes coughed up blood, and that he had a *somewhat* volatile temper.

By February 1969, Andrea and Iwan had finally managed to find an affordable place of their own, which was truly fortunate, she assured her family, since even married couples in Amsterdam often had to live apart for years in the homes of their respective parents.

True, their apartment had "no floor in places," but they borrowed enough money from a friend gradually to put in new planking. The space, Andrea confessed, *was* a bit "raw," which turned out to mean it had no stove for cooking, no refrigerator, and no heater. But (Andrea cheerfully added) "that is usual here and all over Europe." Besides, the rent was only $20 a month.

Having secured a place to live, Andrea and Iwan decided that for the sake of their families they would formally marry, though she cautioned her mother: "I must live as I see fit, I always have and always will. . . . I am living my notion of an honest life." They set the date for March 11, 1969, and insisted on a small, secular civil ceremony—and one as inexpensive as possible. They mostly got their way: a ring and new clothes marked the outer limits of their bow to tradition. Andrea wore a wine-red Turkish robe and Iwan a Tibetan one with Moroccan pants, there were only two formal witnesses (*not* a matron or best man), and the ceremony was kept simple, short, and bilingual ("not so bad after all," Andrea concluded). Her immediate family wasn't present (she'd encouraged them to save the money for a later trip), and Iwan's parents hosted at their home a cake and coffee reception—which Andrea and Iwan paid for. Most of the gifts were in cash and they used it to buy some much-needed items: a new toilet, a new bed, a refrigerator, and a record player. One mystifying gift from the States was finally identified from the customs declaration as fondue forks. Andrea declared herself "happy and fulfilled."[20]

The item that she wanted above all others, a typewriter, her father provided soon after the ceremony. Andrea hated writing longhand—it was too slow for her impatient flow of thoughts (plus her handwriting could be borderline illegible—and she was hugely grateful to at last turn her primary attention to writing. Of late, she'd been getting some encouragement. She finished and sent off her final senior thesis to Bennington, where it received much praise, and her close friend Kathy Norris wrote to say that a young instructor was including some of Andrea's poems in his course on American literature. The *International Times* (IT), with a circulation of forty thousand mostly leftwing readers, published an article of hers on Amsterdam and made positive noises about commission-

ing other pieces. And Grace Paley—that genius of generosity—let
Andrea know that she'd continue to try and place her article on Provo, despite both *Esquire* and the leftwing *Liberation* magazines having turned it down. Grace was also able to report that she'd given
Andrea's poetry chapbook to Ted Wilentz (the influential co-owner
of the Eighth Street Bookstore, at the time a famed literary hang-
out in Greenwich Village), that he'd been impressed and had asked
Grace to let him see anything else Andrea wrote.[21]

By 1967 the U.S. war in Vietnam, which by its close would take
more than fifty thousand American lives, and three to four million
Vietnamese ones, was costing some $25 billion a year. During his
successful campaign for the presidency in 1968, Nixon had strongly
suggested that he would begin to withdraw American troops from
the conflict, yet after taking office he not only reversed himself but
announced that on December 1, 1969, the Selective Service would
conduct two lotteries to determine the order of call for military service. In parallel, increasing numbers of Americans were becoming
persuaded that the war was both futile and immoral, and November 15, 1969, saw the largest antiwar protest in U.S. history in
Washington, DC.

Andrea had been passionately against the war from the beginning,
but by 1969 it had come much closer to home: her brother Mark
stood in jeopardy of being drafted. When he turned to Andrea for
advice, she carefully mulled over his options and in several thought-
ful letters shared her views; her detailed advice tells us a great deal
more about Andrea—much of it central to her character—than
about either Mark or the war. Her first attempt to write, she later
told him, with a scrupulosity that by age twenty-two had already
become a hallmark, had failed because "I became lost in some dis-
solution of image, not certain of yr adult identity, unable to find an
honest voice to address you in." When she began again, she felt the
need to warn him that "I am not one any more to comment on personal philosophies." She'd learned, or hoped she had, that "theories
composed in a warm room have very little to do with what is actually happening out on the streets." She was interested not "in ide-
ologies but much more in actions, relationships, experiences." What

she'd come to value most in others was simply their effort "to live honestly in the world."[22]

The rueful fact, she continued, was that "the war has finally come, uninvited, to the Dworkin family and there . . . [are] no pleasant or easy decisions to make . . . I am afraid, Mark, that there is no obvious way out," though she maintained the hope that his recent decision to pursue a career in molecular biology might have "military value . . . [and] you may have some special opportunities to save yourself from all ugly choices." The challenge, as Andrea saw it, was "to figure out which way you lose least."

What it came down to, she wrote, is that "you serve, you leave the country, or you go to jail." She placed no hope in one other possibility, the one that Mark himself was apparently expecting—a medical deferment, based on his needing glasses and on an unspecified "rectal thing." Andrea warned him that "your infirmities are not sufficient in war time to get you rejected." If, on the other hand, he knew himself to be homosexual, she continued, that would increase the odds, and he "should say so without shame or guilt or fear." But if he was heterosexual (as indeed he was) his only hope for a medical deferment was to establish a history of painful, incapacitating back trouble, which wasn't true, and lying about it would involve endless physical tests and play-acting; Andrea believed "it is probably the worst alternative."

Another option, which Andrea considered somewhat more plausible and a good deal more honorable, was to refuse to serve and to go into exile, a felony punishable by five years' imprisonment. The only two non-communist Western countries without an extradition treaty with the United States were Canada and Sweden. If he changed his citizenship to either, he'd remain on the FBI's wanted list and could never return—or rather, as Andrea put it, not "until amnesty is declared, which will probably be after we're all dead, and history has vindicated those who would not serve." Exile would also mean—and here Andrea cited her own experience—"that wherever you go, you will always be a stranger. . . . I will not lie to you about the sometimes terrible isolation and loneliness that is inevitable in such a situation." Like it or not, one is "born of a country the same way one is born of a womb. One develops cultural attitudes, assumptions, that are part of you organically."

In saying that, Andrea added, she wasn't speaking "from a sentimental love of the land . . . or from any precious emotional attachment to patriotic principles and the mother country—it comes (and perhaps one must be away to realize it) from the recognition that my mind was formed there, is intimately involved with what becomes of individuals there, with what society does to them, with the recognition that in my identity, in who I am, wherever I go, my roots are in America. The tree stands here," she eloquently added, "and it drinks other water and that is why it lives, but the roots reach far beyond where the tree stands." Her own bouts of loneliness, she pointed out, were mitigated by her "intellectual recognition that America at this moment is poison for me," plus "the absolute knowledge that I can return whenever I want."

She thought Mark ought to consider one other option, and offered it not "glibly or smugly or self-righteously": he could "face his day in court and go to prison." He could, in other words, simply refuse to be drafted, remain in the United States, and accept a jail sentence of probably three to five years in a federal penitentiary. She was well aware, she wrote Mark, that if he chose that route he'd stand convicted as a felon, which meant among much else (including their parents' likely feeling of shame, though they both repudiated the war) that on release he'd have considerable difficulty in finding employment. Yet she felt that "what stands out positively about this option is that it is direct, it is honorable in the most rigorous way, and it leaves you free after the sentence is over to move about as you wish." She'd known men, she told Mark, who'd taken the route of going to jail and had found that federal prisons were not nearly as brutal as city jails (case in point: the Women's House of Detention), and they'd found "good work to do," like setting up libraries and teaching. She believed that the national mood had shifted and that "there is more chance of growing acceptance for the man who goes to jail than for the man who leaves the country." Most important, it "leaves no blood on your hands, no mourners at your funeral."

Mark had mentioned in his own letters that he might simply allow himself to be drafted, on the assumption that his scientific training would all but guarantee he'd end up in a lab somewhere. In arguing against that prospect, Andrea's tone became more strenuous: "If you are drafted, you do not make conditions or propositions." Mark should remember, Andrea added, that army scientists "work on war, they make it technologically more perfect . . . and you have some responsibility for the things that you knowingly unleash on this world." She implored Mark to come to Amsterdam for a visit: they could talk over his options at leisure, and he'd get some taste of what it was like to live abroad. When Mark resisted the suggestion, Andrea assured him she "stood behind . . . [him] solidly no matter what you decide."

In the end, Mark would receive a deferment for graduate studies in molecular biology, for which Andrea all at once felt relief that he'd be spared along with anger (which she was wise enough to repress) that the country's wars would continue to be fought by its least privileged citizens. Having received his deferment, Mark felt free for the first time to vent annoyance with his sister for what he viewed as her attempt to lead him down the conscientious objector path. He also expressed disdain (which is how Andrea characterized it) for mass movements of all kinds, including the antiwar movement. He didn't believe, he wrote Andrea, in "going to meet enemies before they come to you," in "looking for trouble." In responding, Andrea dropped her previous attempts at neutrality and warned Mark directly that in his scorn for mass protest he was refusing "responsibility for crimes that jeopardize civil liberties" and was instead "continuing to look the other way because your fellow beings' business is not, in your mind, your own."[23]

Such indifference and apathy, she emphasized, were a form of self-deception. Mark needed to recognize, she wrote, "that if you permit certain life principles to be eroded . . . it takes no visionary powers to understand, to see very, very clearly, that what happens to the cat standing next to you will inevitably, today or tomorrow or next month, also happen to you . . . if the police come to take him away, you can ignore his plight but don't be surprised when they show up at your door too." In her opinion, now freely stated, Mark had let his scorn for "the masses" separate him "from the injustices of our time." In deciding on a dose of "tough love," Andrea risked alienating Mark, but—to both their credit—they remained close through most of their lives, despite some periods of estrangement.

As the first anniversary of their marriage approached ("I don't think any single event ever meant so much to me," Andrea wrote her parents), she and Iwan still found themselves beset with problems relating to daily life. Iwan worked days as a truck driver, as well as four nights a week at Paradiso. Andrea got a part-time job in a boutique, and then the two of them opened a small counter-cultural shop of their own, selling beads and the like; it was an almost instant failure. Andrea then tried to get a license as a public school teacher, but the bureaucratic hurdles defeated her. A group of Dutch women asked her to privately teach them about American literature, but the lack of books stymied that prospect (shipping her own from the States would have been too expensive, and a tight budget prohibited buying new ones). The next brainstorm was to buy a stencil machine to print and sell collections of poetry, but that too proved stillborn. Some stubborn health problems added to the dystopia: Andrea had bouts of spastic colitis and Iwan, unable to quit smoking, had periodic coughing fits that left him "nervous and tense." The accumulated stress produced in Andrea a kind of listless inability "to harness my energies . . . to rouse myself to begin a new project."[24]

It was at just this low ebb that two unexpected developments helped, at least temporarily, to restore their spirits. Andrea had become close friends with another young American, Ricki Abrams, who'd dropped out of Barnard and was currently the lover of Thatcher Clark, yet another American, who ran an experimental theatre unit. Through that connection Iwan landed a part in one of the troupe's productions (though as it would turn out, the role would not mark the onset of the acting career he longed for). As well, another friend, an Israeli painter close to the director Jacques Tati, again got them walk-on roles in Tati's latest film, *Trafic*. The work itself proved tedious ("long hours doing nothing") and Andrea found the people in general unpleasant, with the sole exception of the movie's star, Maria Kimberly, who Andrea thought the nicest person of the lot. The pay, in any case, was terrific ($1,800 for twelve days of work) and made it possible for them to afford tickets on a student-chartered plane to the States, where Iwan met Andrea's parents for the first time, with no recorded repercussions on either side.[25]

In early April 1970, just as the cold weather started to recede and their spirits to improve somewhat, the rotted floors in their house began literally to give way under their feet, and for two weeks they had to stay with Iwan's family. Rotting wood was common in many of the old houses in their district, and traditionally most people ignored the holes in the floor and were grateful for the roof over-head. But "Iwan and I are not known traditionalists," Andrea wrote her parents, and Iwan threatened to strong-arm the landlord if repairs weren't made. He finally agreed to patch up the flooring, but it then turned out that the paper thin walls were also in a state of decay, and that in turn led to nearly rebuilding the place from scratch. What followed was several months of "complete chaos"—everything packed away in boxes, workmen under foot, and nails, tools, and wood scattered across the floors.[26]

The unremitting chaos had at least one gratifying result: Andrea lost twenty pounds. Even as a young girl she'd been a bit chubby, but she now decided to consult a doctor about losing still more weight. "I'm doing it very slowly and realistically," she wrote her parents, "with lots of relapses." Iwan, she emphasized, "is being very help-ful because he loves me unconditionally, and more I can't ask for. Not that I'll ever be thin," she added, but she wasn't at all sure "that is such a desirable goal (I don't like the tyranny about how people are supposed to look), but I am quite sure that I will be thinner, and quite thin enough to please myself." She was embarked on what would be a lifelong struggle.

With repairs on their home finally completed early in the sum-mer of 1970, Andrea could no longer blame the seemingly endless disorder of their living situation for the problems that had begun to surface in the marriage. Her earlier experience with men had included molestation—twice in fact, once as a nine-year-old sitting in the dark of a movie house, and the second time as the victim of an acquaintance rape. She not only remembered the molestations but would later write about them; in her 1995 essay "My Life as a Writer," she describes her nine-year-old self as having internalized the rapist's view of her as "a breachable, breakable thing any stranger can wipe his dick on."[27]

Though politically sophisticated and radical in her sympathies, Andrea had grown up imbibing the middle-class belief in romantic love and the bliss of wedded life; as she would later write, "wife-beating is not on a woman's map of the world when she marries. It is, quite literally, beyond her imagination." Marital rape (and, implicitly, violence) was in all fifty states in 1970 *not* legally regarded as a crime. Perhaps because of the strong influence of Christianity (Corinthians 7:3–5) in the United States, it was only in the mid-seventies that marital rape *started* to be treated as actionable; till then it was a non-issue—a husband, after all, was entitled to satisfy his sexual appetite. Like many women at the time, Andrea regarded matrimony as a world apart, an arbor garlanded with roses, a cocoon of uncontaminated love.

Because she didn't believe it could happen, when Iwan lashed out at her physically for the first time, she told herself that it was "an accident, a mistake," the result of the accumulated hardships of his life. When it happened again, she blamed "the terrible hurts and frustrations" of his job search and vowed—to herself *and* to Iwan—to find a better way to comfort him. When it happened a third time, she blamed herself. Andrea, the Bennington rebel, gave way to the self-doubting little girl who Sylvia had consistently criticized for her shortcomings. Andrea vowed, as she'd done so many times before as a youngster, to "be better, kinder, quieter."[28]

In a mid-August letter to her parents, she made reference for the first time to "a big fight with Iwan," which Andrea ascribed to his "anger and shame" at Andrea's having asked Sylvia and Harry to make them the gift of some magazine subscriptions. He felt his manhood at stake, Andrea explained, his ability to be a good provider. In telling her parents about the fight, Andrea begged them—*twice* in one letter—not to make any mention of it when writing back, otherwise Iwan "will get more upset than you can imagine."

From the beginning Andrea had been aware of Iwan's volatile nature, but it was only now, a year and a half into their marriage, that it began to center directly on her. In letters home Andrea continued to dismiss their difficulties as simply the kind that "every married couple has," whereas in fact Iwan's enraged outbursts had started to escalate. By September, the situation had worsened to the point where Andrea could no longer contain her fear or deal with it entirely alone; she confessed to her brother—her language still vague, the revelations abstract—that "this summer has been very difficult and chaotic for me, a lot of mental changes . . . we have terrible fights sometimes . . . we worry a lot about what we're doing with our lives, separately and collectively." Perhaps to spare Mark (or in acknowledgment of his known limitations) she claimed, unpersuasively, that she was continuing to work on "getting my books published," even as she contradicted that claim with the acknowledgment that she mostly "thinks about it a lot, but am singularly lazy"—not an adjective either Andrea or anyone who knew her had ever used when describing her temperament.

In truth, much of her energy seems to have centered on performing traditional housewifely tasks—"simple, everyday things," she called them. She went back and forth to the vet with the dog and two cats they'd acquired along the way, bought and cooked food, dealt with tradesmen of all kinds, cleaned the house, scrubbed the floors—and slept for long hours ("I'm dead tired," she explained to her parents, "from shopping and cleaning"). Under the double burden of domestic chores and Iwan's burgeoning mistreatment, Andrea's sense of self-worth declined in tandem. Iwan, in contrast, became increasingly insistent that his exceptional potential as an actor was being thwarted by the lack of "opportunity at all for him" in Amsterdam. By the fall of 1970, Andrea's doubts about her own gifts had intensified to the point where she agreed with Iwan's estimate that his was the superior talent. She became (as she later put it) "slavishly conforming to every external convention that would demonstrate that I was a 'good wife', that would convince other people that I was happily married. And as the weight of social convention became insupportable, I remember withdrawing further and further."

She dutifully came up with a plan that gave absolute primacy to Iwan's needs, even suggesting that to enable him to take private acting lessons, they move to the States for at least a year; Andrea would take a teaching job to support them both, and would continue "of course" to remain primarily responsible for "running the house" (she was even learning how to sew, which she considered "a drag," and to make patterns, which proved *somewhat* engaging). In regard to her scheme to take up teaching, she insisted to her parents that she was "quite able and willing to deal with the turmoil of the public schools," but her parents knew better than to think that their once highly ambitious daughter would find anything remotely like fulfillment in a secondary school environment.

Andrea had earlier made it abundantly clear to them that her own years as a student in a traditional high school had been hellish: conformity had been the rule, with everyone expected to fit into the "little boxes" assigned them, their time "programmed and controlled like in [George Orwell's] *1984*." Such places, she had written, "create people who can't think for themselves, and such people always let a Spiro Agnew think for them." School had been "a very real imprisonment for me and the people I valued" and had very nearly destroyed her spirit. She *did* admire "non-authoritarian" education. Teaching in a school such as A.S. Neill's Summerhill could conceivably have held her interest, but to teach in the States she would have to rely on her father's teaching connections, and those were all with traditional-minded administrators.

Harry did his best to round up opportunities and did send her a substantial list of schools either in New York City or close enough to it to allow Iwan easy access to acting classes. Andrea *did* realize that "the strictures of a public school system might be impossible for me—but at the moment I feel so confined here, so at a dead end, that I don't know what to do." She sent off literally dozens of letters, but with a B.A. from "suspect" Bennington and no degree or certification in education, she got not a single interview (only five schools even bothered to send her an application form). The total lack of interest added to her sense of being a "devastating" failure. By mid-March of 1971, she confessed to her parents that "we are both very tense and very tired"; to her brother, Mark, she admitted that she and Iwan were "mightily depressed right now . . . I am doing no work of my own . . . it is an appalling dead end."[29]

As far as Iwan was concerned, Andrea's failure to find a job and her ensuing lethargy were the result of a willful refusal to activate herself. How was it possible for a young American woman with a college degree *not* to find employment? "Obviously" she was *deliberately* sabotaging his prospects; if they were unable to move to America, he would be unable to take acting lessons, unable to become the world-famous celebrity he felt certain was his designated destiny. As Iwan's rage built, his controls ebbed. He'd light a cigarette, smack his forehead in feigned remorse ("Aiii!, I *must* give up smoking!"), and then triumphantly ground the butt out on Andrea's body.

The abuse—the battery—had deep roots: for all his bravado, Iwan had entered into marriage as a virgin, and one with an impotency problem. Only years later, through the proxy of a purportedly fictional character, did Andrea manage to write about how his sexual and her psychological issues had meshed into at least a temporary "solution." "I teach him, slowly," the character "Andrea" writes in her 1986 novel *Ice and Fire*. "I have understood. He has too much respect for women. I teach him disrespect, systematically. I teach him how to tie knots, how to use rope, scarves, how to bite breasts: I teach him not to be afraid: of causing pain. It goes slowly. I teach him step by step. I invent sex therapy in this one room somewhere in the middle of Europe. I am an American innocent, in my fashion. . . . I fellate him. I teach him not to worry about erection. I tie him up. Dungeon, brothel, little girl, da-da. I ask him what he wants to do and we do it . . . I teach him everything about his body, I penetrate him, I scratch, I bite, I tie him up. . . . He does each thing back to me. He is nearly hard." The real-life Andrea, ironically, never found S&M practices erotic and would later speak out forcefully against them, characterizing sadomasochistic roles as masks adopted to avoid intimacy.[30]

Yet in *Ice and Fire* the sex therapy continues: "I do everything I can think of to help him: impotent and suicidal: I am saving his life. . . . He is nearly hard. . . . He needs some act, some gesture, some event to give him the final confidence: to get really hard. Reader: I married him. . . . He got hard, he fucked, it spilled over, it was frenzy, I ended up cowering, caged, catatonic. How it will end finally, I don't know. I wanted to help: but this was a hurricane of hate and rage let loose: I wanted to help: I saved him: not impotent, not suicidal, he beat me until I was a heap of collapsed bone, comatose, torn, bleeding, bruised so bad, so hard: how it will end, I don't know." Later, to a confidant, Andrea summed up her own situation—hardly dissimilar from the "Andrea" in *Ice and Fire*—in a single line: "I released a sadistic monster in him."

The beatings escalated to the point where Iwan was kicking her in the stomach, banging her head against the floor, even hitting her with a beam of wood that bruised her so badly she could hardly walk for days. She managed, once, to get herself to a doctor; he told her he could write her a prescription for Valium or have her committed; she chose the Valium. Sometimes Iwan beat her into unconsciousness. Her pain and fear became so great that she would scream out in agony, but no neighbor appeared to check on her. "If you scream for years," she later wrote, "they will look through you for years." They "see the bruises and injuries—and do nothing. . . . They say it's your fault or you like it or they deny it is happening . . . you begin to feel you don't exist . . . you begin to believe that he can hurt you as much as he wants and no one will help you. . . . Once you lose language, your isolation is absolute. . . . I wanted to die. . . . When I would come to after being beaten unconscious, the first feeling I had was a sorrow that I was alive." At age twenty-five, the brilliant, dynamic Andrea had become (as she subsequently described it) "a woman whose whole life was speechless desperation. . . . Smothering anxiety, waking nightmares, cold sweats, sobs that I choked on were the constants of my daily life. . . . I was nearly dead, catatonic, without the will to live."

As she later put it, "I felt entirely shrouded in a loneliness that no earthquake could move . . . imprisoned alone in a nightmare . . . the worst desolation I have ever known. I remember the frozen muscles of my smile as I gave false explanations of injuries that no one wanted to hear anyway." She lost track of time, was unable to sleep; she dropped and broke things; she couldn't remember what had happened yesterday, or what day it was. Sensing that Andrea was in more serious trouble than she was letting on, Sylvia and Harry decided on a trip to Amsterdam in July 1971.

The visit did not go well. When the four of them went to a movie one evening, Iwan abruptly told Andrea that he was leaving to go somewhere else. She begged him to stay, pleaded with him not to embarrass her in front of her parents. He told her that she was a nagging bitch and stormed out. When Andrea went after him, followed by Sylvia and Harry, he flew into a rage and struck her. When the beating continued, the police intervened and held him back; one officer told Andrea to press charges—"Your husband was trying to kill you"—but she refused. As the crowd dispersed, Andrea, in a stupor, started to walk away, not knowing where to go, barely able to stand. Iwan caught up with her, began beating her all over again, then abruptly disappeared. Back home, she couldn't stop crying and begged her parents to take her with them back to the States. Sylvia told her that her place was with her husband.

When Iwan returned home, he expressed "great remorse" about what had happened, acknowledged to the Dworkins that he alone was responsible, and asked them to give him a chance to redeem himself. Sylvia said something along the lines of Andrea's having made her own contribution to the upset (blaming the victim was an attitude the neighbors had already made familiar). Soon after, Harry and Sylvia returned to the States. Writing to her mother, Andrea expressed the sorrow she felt over the way Sylvia seemed always to "think the worst of me." In response, Sylvia reminded Andrea that she was the one who had said she didn't wish to discuss her situation with Iwan any further. To which Andrea replied with unexpected vigor: "I'm not one for fixing blame," she wrote her mother, "but any way you look at it what happened rests on Iwan's shoulders."[31]

That stark assertion was unexpectedly bold coming from a woman who'd been beaten into literal insensibility, and aggressively standing up to Sylvia may have been the psychological turning point for Andrea. It marked a clear shift from her previous torpor. But her recovery would be in fits and starts, and would last for years. No sooner had Andrea momentarily stood up to Sylvia and placed the blame squarely on Iwan's shoulders than she immediately retreated, devoting the rest of her very long letter to excuses for Iwan's violence: "he was under enormous pressure"; he'd learned that Paradiso was going to close for four to six weeks, and he'd be without income; "he did not sleep well or enough"; "he was upset and confused enough to see everything I said as provocation"; his "temper is a terrible thing . . . [but] that is his nature"; and finally, in a mournfully sad absolution: "he never hits the dog in anger."

But the spark had been lit; Andrea had managed, however fleetingly, to shift the blame from herself to Iwan. Why then didn't she simply leave him? Because, traumatized, she was still beset by periodic confusion, physically weakened, and uncertain where to go—let alone able to muster the *sustained* will to get there. Her parents hadn't offered a refuge, no alternative shelter was immediately available in Amsterdam, and she had no independent income. Besides, she was terrified of Iwan. Even if she could find a place to live, wouldn't Iwan learn of it, demand that she return, beat her for refusing? More women, Andrea learned, are killed *after* fleeing from their husbands than when still living with them.[32]

Yet somehow, against the odds and within only two months of her parents' visit, Andrea decided to make the break and face the consequences. She thought immediately of her close friend Ricki Abrams, a fellow expatriate and part-time prostitute, and her partner, Thatcher Clark. They agreed to take her in, but only temporarily, given that she'd arrived with her adored menagerie of dogs and cats, and space was limited.

Besides, fear followed her everywhere: "Escape is hell," she wrote, "a period of indeterminate length reckoned in years not months." Walking on the street, Iwan would suddenly appear out of nowhere, fists flying, "a lightning flash followed by riveting pain." Each episode put her mind "on the edge of its own destruction. Smothering anxiety, waking nightmares . . . were the constants of my daily life." The fear ensued "every minute of every day. One does not sleep. One cannot bear to be alone."

In desperation she did turn to her parents. Her funds were so low that instead of writing to them for help, she put in an urgent phone call. Their response (at least as she perceived it) was to tell her (in Andrea's later words) that they "consider their whole lives failures, etc. because of the delinquency of their big, bad daughter." But they did respond, and continued periodically to send small sums, for which Andrea was deeply grateful (and apologetic): "Please forgive me for being this awful drag on you," she guiltily wrote. "I am more pained & sorrier than you can imagine that I make you so unhappy. But then sometimes," she poignantly added, "I make you happy too don't I?"[33]

Gradually, very gradually, the forgotten emotion of anger began to resurface. And "the anger of the survivor" (as she later wrote) "is murderous. It is more dangerous to her than to the one who hurt her. She does not believe in murder; she wants him dead but will not kill him. She never gives up wanting him dead."

Clarity also began to return, and with it the knowledge that in the future (as she wrote) "it will be very difficult to lie to her or to manipulate her. She sees through the social strategies that have controlled her as a woman, the sexual strategies that have reduced her to a shadow of her own native possibilities. . . . The emotional severity of the survivor appears to others, even those closest to her, to be cold and unyielding, ruthless in its intensity. She knows too much about suffering to try to measure it when it is real, but she despises self-pity. She is self-protective, not out of arrogance, but because she has been ruined by her own fragility."[34]

3

Joining the Fray

Living in Europe, Andrea missed the first few years of the women's
liberation movement. None of its dramatic early events are referenced in her private correspondence or connected by word or deed
to her own political sympathies. A whole string of remarkable events
registered, if at all, only subliminally: the disruption of the Miss
America Pageant in 1968; the emergence of feminist consciousness-
raising groups like the Redstockings and New York Radical Women;
the takeover of the New Left's newspaper, *Rat*; Chicago's pioneering collective, The Westside Group; the demand for legal abortion;
the 1971 New York Radical Feminist Conference on Rape; the birth
of *Ms.* magazine in 1972 under the editorship of Gloria Steinem
amid a host of new feminist newspapers, newsletters, and pamphlets;
and—the event most germane to her immediate plight—the
formation, in 1971, of the first rape crisis center in the United States
(followed three years later by the first battered women's center).

Yet in December 1971, her strength returning and her concentration no longer wholly focused on the fear of Iwan's abrupt, violent
reappearance, Andrea and her friend Ricki began sporadic work on
writing a book together that related directly to the feminist movement then gathering force. As they planned it, the book would

explore certain historical practices that both directly reflected Andrea's own experience as a battered wife and placed it in a historical context of male brutalization of women through time.

Ricki helped along Andrea's political education by introducing her to some of the crucial radical feminist writings that had recently been appearing—and proving unexpected bestsellers: Kate Millett's *Sexual Politics* (1970), Shulamith Firestone's *The Dialectic of Sex* (1970), and Robin Morgan's anthology *Sisterhood Is Powerful*. Reading Millett's 1970 book had an especially profound effect on Andrea. "Something in me moved then," she later wrote, "shifted, changed forever. Suddenly I discovered . . . what I had felt somewhere but had had no name for, no place for. I began to feel what was being done to me, to experience it, to recognize it, to find the right names for it. I began to know that there was nothing good or romantic or noble in the myths I was living out. . . . I began to change in a way so fundamental that there was no longer any place for me in the world—I was no longer a woman as I had been a woman before."[1]

Another friend helped ease Andrea's economic plight by putting her in touch with the editor of *De Groene Amsterdammer* (the Green Amsterdammer), a paper popular with leftwing intellectuals. Andrea gave him samples from her small pile of published work and he reacted with enthusiasm, inviting her to write for them. That meant a press card, a flexible schedule, and even a tiny expense account; she immediately set to work researching conditions among "delinquent" girls in Amsterdam's women's prisons. By the end of November, Andrea was able to reassure her parents that "everything is falling into place." She had even become part of "an alternative Academy" housed in the drug-free basement of the re-opened Paradiso, where she assisted people for whom English was a second language, and where they could learn skills like weaving "to help free themselves from the whole consumer-production process."[2]

Andrea had her own space in the basement—that is, a desk and two chairs—"a sort of small studio *inside* a community of people I like, so that I am not so isolated." It was quite a turn-about, and a significant measure of Andrea's innate resilience and resourcefulness; "don't worry about me," she wrote her parents, "I am very strong." Above all, she consciously worked on "trying to free myself of any recriminations I may feel towards Iwan—to live in the present and towards the future, which looks to me positive and inviting." Iwan, though, wasn't making it any easier; he was, she wrote home, "being pretty evil." He reclaimed the dogs and cats, refused to let an anguished Andrea see them, and in general gave her "much difficulty." But she continued to "work hard, very hard, to try to get myself set up and be productive."

In order to put together enough free hours to work on their book, Andrea and Ricki both took jobs filling perfume bottles—injecting synthetic oil with a syringe, screwing on plastic caps, and then affixing labels: patchouli, musk, amber, jasmine, rose, etc. The work paid well but was dull and unrewarding—"shit labor," as Andrea put it— and toxic as well: they could only work three hours at a stretch without the fumes making them sick. Still, it was necessary if they were ever to clear enough time to make progress on the book. They set their immediate sights on completing the background research and preparing a working outline which, along with two sample chapters, they could then bring to a well-known London literary agent, Deborah Rogers (she represented Baldwin, Roth, and McCullers), who yet another friend had recommended.

Though Andrea took comfort in the fact that she was living with two "warm and supportive" people, she was still searching "desperately" to find an affordable place of her own. Since Amsterdam was impossibly expensive, she toyed over the next few months with various ideas for finding somewhere to live. For a time she thought of renting a small farm on the outskirts of the city and breeding dogs. She felt it was "something that I would love and that I could do really well"; it could be a source of income and as well satisfy other needs, "like working for myself, on my own terms, and doing something that I feel is really positive." Alas, even a small, rundown farm, she quickly learned, could cost around $10,000, which made it utterly out of the question. A temporary solution for her housing problem emerged when friends who lived on a boat and were planning a trip to North Africa let her house-sit free of charge for several months.[3]

Through all these wanderings and worries, Andrea continued to work with Ricki on the book. By February 1972, they'd completed two chapters, which they sent on to their new agent, in London, hoping for a quick sale and a desperately needed advance; once secured, they felt, "then these days of homelessness and begging will truly be over." Though living on the edge, Andrea assured her parents that "I am where I want to be, doing what I want to do, and am quite happy. I love the work I am doing, think it is excellent, that we are doing something valuable and original." She wished she could count on some sort of steady income and thought she could get by on $100 to $150 a month. She felt able, despite the past difficulties between them, to ask her parents, with trepidation, if they might be willing to provide a monthly check for that amount, adding that she "appreciates your help more than you can know."

The request annoyed Sylvia, and she conveyed her displeasure directly, telling Andrea that she should simply "come home to safety." In response, Andrea acknowledged that "there are many reasons to come home, but safety surely is not one." She apologized for having been "such a heavy financial strain," and expressed her gratitude "for what you've done for me," adding that she'd only asked because "you always led me to believe it was all right. Now that I know what a burden it is, I won't ask again." But that wasn't the end of it—neither of sending Andrea money nor of the ongoing tension between mother and daughter.[4]

At one point, Sylvia complained that her constant worrying about Andrea was due in part to not knowing more about what was going on in her life. To which Andrea replied that "I really don't know what you want. You know that you shouldn't ask questions that you don't really want to know the answer to—I won't lie." She didn't "much like being the source of all that worry" but didn't know "what to do about it—except not to share my problems. Some of them are unsharable, private, I've always had a very strong sense of privacy. Some of them are so transitory that they're not worth mentioning. Some are so continuous that they're also not worth mentioning. So that doesn't leave much over, except for emergencies." Above all, she wrote, she needed Sylvia to "respect the fact that I'm not looking for an easy life but for one which is creative, active, growing: I'm a writer and this book I'm writing is going to cause an explosion. Be prepared for it."[5]

In the meantime, Andrea heard that Iwan had quickly remarried—again to an American—and gone to the States, taking everything with him, except for the dogs and cat, down to the last dish. Still, Andrea was thrilled. Some legal hassles would have to be cleared up, but she was quick to move back into the apartment they'd shared, along with a Dutch filmmaker with whom she was having an affair. The apartment had no heat, and it was a chilly spring, but Ricki managed to locate an old coal stove, and friends helped to install it. "Things are falling into place one by one," she wrote optimistically to her parents, and "I'm really relieved." Even the dogs were well: "I'm so happy that through all this I've managed to keep them. . . . It seems like a cosmic turn."

Iwan, thereafter, vanished from her life—though for years she remained periodically haunted by him, terrified that he might reappear. As late as 1995, Andrea would hire a private investigator, Jim Hougan, to track down Iwan's subsequent history and whereabouts, and set her mind at rest. The investigator in turn utilized the services of a well-regarded British solicitor, and together they were able— before finally hitting a dead end—to piece together a hair-raising story. Iwan never became an actor, but he did become a major success as an underworld figure specializing in fencing diamonds and laundering large sums of money. He was wanted by American, British, and Dutch authorities, and his police files in Holland were found under the rare designation of "Class 1—Dangerous Individual." In the eighties alone the Dutch police charged Iwan with thirty-eight offenses, including "Causing grievous bodily harm" and "Malicious wounding." And yet Hougan and his British counterpart could find "no record of any disposition of any of these charges"; apparently, Hougan concluded, Iwan had "never been sentenced for anything that he's done." The British solicitor added that he'd "never encountered anything like it before" and had to conclude that "someone's protecting him. Someone in authority." We have no record of Andrea's reaction to Hougan's report, but it's a fair guess that it was chilling.[6]

In the immediate aftermath of Andrea's escape, she and Ricki continued to work intensely on the book, and continued to worry about how to earn just enough money to preserve a maximum amount of free time for writing. The American Library in Amsterdam invited them at one point to give a talk, but rather than stand in a room that featured a picture of Nixon, they refused the invitation. They kept expecting good news from their agent Deborah Rogers, along with the precious advance that would (in fantasy) solve all their problems. But as winter passed into spring, Rogers remained unable to arouse interest in the book; claiming to still be optimistic, she decided to send it to America.[7]

Unexpectedly, Ricki suddenly announced that she'd become disenchanted with the book project and wanted to withdraw, her decision based more on personal than on literary or financial considerations. What had happened was that nearly from the start of the undertaking, Andrea and Ricki had become lovers. The sexual part lasted eight months, a time (as Andrea characterized it) of sharing "space, bed, food, other lovers," and concentrated work on the book. Over a period of many months they'd had to surmount "arguments, traumas, material deprivation, introspection and confrontation"—in sum, "the hardest work either of us have ever done." The intensity gradually took its toll. After what Andrea called two "nightmare months" of "paranoia, not speaking except to exchange accusations or hurt," Ricki decided to call it quits. She'd determined that, after all, she did *not* want to sleep with women, that she "could not handle it."

For a time, she and Andrea tried reverting to friendship and continued to work on the book together. But then Ricki became "mightily depressed" and decided not to pursue co-authorship either. Her withdrawal upset Andrea, but she felt that not to finish the book would be "unthinkable." Ricki went off to Australia, and then India, and Andrea made the reluctant decision, after four years in Amsterdam, to return to the States, determined to complete the manuscript on her own. She felt "bloody exhausted from the 10,000 hassles of the last months" and intended to live quietly and inexpensively, perhaps in upper New York State or New England.

She summed up her comprehensive reasons—they were not simply literary—for returning: "I am coming back," she wrote her parents, "because being born in America means that it is there that what one refuses to do and what one insists on doing has the greatest significance. I am coming back because I know now that I will not pay taxes—any taxes; that the government does not represent me at all; that Nixon and his bunch are gangsters; that I cannot sit and smoke dope in Amsterdam, while brothers and sisters are being persecuted, imprisoned, killed in the States. I am coming back because I have lost my terror of prison and consequences, i.e., my bourgeois notions of respectability. I am coming back because George Jackson, the annihilation of the Panthers, the newest Vietnam theatre piece by Kissinger et al. have convinced me that the time is short, and that the time is now. I know now that the measure of a just society is its prisons and mental hospitals: we cannot tolerate either, anywhere. I'm coming back to fight."[8]

To afford a plane ticket, Andrea made a deal with a junkie friend to carry a briefcase (which she knew to be filled with heroin) through customs in exchange for the ticket and $1,000; the heroin deal fell through, though the generous junkie gave her the ticket (not the $1,000) anyway. She arrived back in the States in the immediate aftermath of Richard Nixon's 1972 landslide victory. In the weeks preceding it, he'd told the country that American and North Vietnamese representatives had begun meeting in Paris to hammer out an agreement for ending the war, that negotiations were proceeding smoothly, and that "peace with honor" was imminent. He did not tell the country that South Vietnam's president, Nguyen Van Thieu, strenuously objected to a ceasefire that would leave thousands of North Vietnamese soldiers in the South and thus well positioned to sweep to victory after the Americans departed.

Nor did he tell the country that five months before the election, a Nixon loyalist, Gordon Liddy of the Special Investigations Unit, had with four accomplices attempted a secret break-in at the office of the chairman of the Democratic National Committee in the Watergate Hotel in order to steal documents, and had been arrested. Nixon soon learned of the incident and with the help of his conscience-free secretary of state, Henry Kissinger, successfully covered it up. (Nixon's eventual downfall would be set in motion three months after the election when the Senate voted to convene a special committee to investigate the Watergate burglary; ultimately he'd be forced from office.)

In the November election, Nixon carried more than 60 percent of the popular vote and won every state except Massachusetts. Five days before his inauguration, he declared that the war in Vietnam had ended and that a formal peace treaty would shortly be signed in Paris. In truth, Thieu's opposition to the peace talks soon led to the collapse of negotiations. The war entered a more covert but hardly less murderous phase. At the point of Andrea's return to the States, the Nixon administration was dropping two tons of bombs every sixty seconds—three thousand a day—over North Vietnam, with fully one-half of the United States' entire B-52 bomber fleet taking part in the ferocious operation. The Pentagon claimed that its "smart bombs," guided by sophisticated new technology, were able with pinpoint accuracy to limit the strikes to military targets alone, yet multiple eyewitness accounts made it clear that civilian areas, including schools and hospitals, were being systematically and *deliberately* bombed. Still worse seemed imminent: the destruction of the dikes of North Vietnam's Tonkin Delta, which would set off floods leading to a catastrophic loss of life, and a "sagging of morale," in the North.

The savage air campaign achieved its purpose: North Vietnam was "persuaded"—over the bodies of tens of thousands—to resume talks, and a peace agreement was signed on January 27, 1973. It neither ended the war nor restored the peace; clandestine American bombing raids over Laos and Cambodia continued, the horrors of which soon began to leak out, and it was only in 1975, after the North Vietnamese had conquered the South through force of arms, that hostilities finally ended.

The 1972 election results had come as no surprise to Andrea. While still living in Amsterdam she and Iwan had helped to hide deserters from the U.S. military on their way to refuge in Sweden, and even as an undergraduate at Bennington, she'd tried to keep a marginal counseling center open "to keep the rural-poor men in the towns around the college from signing up to be soldiers. . . . Vietnam was the equivalent of welfare for them." By 1972, her opposition to the war had become red-hot; as she'd written her parents shortly before returning to the States, "when I return I will have to act out what I believe as the opportunity arises." She'd earlier abandoned any hope that electoral politics could ever produce the sweeping social changes she thought necessary; Nixon's demonstrated "might and wrath" (as she put it) only further convinced her that "struggle, personal struggle, collective struggle" had become a profound necessity.[9]

After stopping off to see her parents in New Jersey, she went to stay briefly with Grace Paley in New York City. The economic downturn that was beginning to engulf the country was already evident in the city: "the filth of the streets" (as Andreas described it), "the human beings sleeping in doorways, heads resting on empty beer cans . . . the lack of interchange between strangers because the danger is real and ever present." Old friends she visited seemed subdued and introverted, "wounded and very near despair" at Nixon's electoral triumph. She realized "that the next years . . . will be lived in conflict and struggle . . . at war not only with the American war machine, or the American government, but with the American way of life, which is the heart of the problem."

Somehow Andrea had to find a way to earn a living, locate affordable housing, live out her politics, find enough time to write—in short, to put down roots in what no longer quite felt like native ground. The price of everything astounded her. She wasn't able to afford a movie or come up with $2 to attend a poetry reading, or even buy necessities; she'd ignored dental problems for years, and a cyst on her breast now *had* to be dealt with. She was reluctantly forced to turn yet again to her parents. As always, they did help her but—as always—Sylvia's preaching accompanied the support. When Andrea, overwhelmed with juggling the difficulties of getting settled, failed to attend a family wedding, Sylvia declared herself ashamed and embarrassed and labeled Andrea selfish. The charge left Andrea feeling "very depressed, very unsure of myself, of whether I had the ability to do what I had set out to do."[10]

The parental storm eventually passed, and the multiple upheavals attendant on establishing a rudimentary new life slowly began to subside. By March of 1973, Andrea had managed to find enough part-time work to accumulate the needed $300 ($100 for rent, $100 for security, $100 for the agent) to rent a two-room, five-flight walk-up tenement apartment at 336 East 5th Street in the East Village. It had the *de rigueur* bathtub in the kitchen and a shared toilet down the hall. A beanbag chair, a $12 foam rubber mattress, a manual typewriter, a small table and chair—was pretty much the sum of her furnishings. Plus her beloved dogs, Gringo and her mother, Velvet, the two female German Shepherds she'd somehow managed to have shipped from Amsterdam (soon, painfully, she had to give up Velvet for adoption, having no money to support two animals). Every other day Andrea would take $7 out of a meager bank account she'd opened, haunt "happy hour" at various bars to cadge free food—and dutifully tithe herself with a small (though not to her) contribution to the Black Panthers' breakfast and literacy programs.[11]

Her part-time work consisted of running errands ($25) one day a week for the well-known poet Muriel Rukeyser, and $75 a week serving as the staff for the anti-Vietnam war group REDRESS (of which I was a member—it was how Andrea and I first met and became friendly). In between part-time jobs, Andrea found time to join a demonstration during Nixon's inauguration, and also helped organize the Bernstein Peace Concert in January 1973, which raised money for the Bach Mai hospital Nixon's bombs had all but destroyed.[12]

Through her political work, Andrea started to meet a number of what she enthusiastically called "really wonderful people." Rukeyser, who had impeccable leftwing credentials that went back to her early involvement with the Scottsboro Boys and the Spanish anti-Fascist struggle, was particularly energetic in introducing her around, as were Julian Beck and Judith Malina of the Living Theater, whom she'd met earlier in Europe. They put her in touch with a number of politically active members of the theater community, and Andrea formed a particularly close, though stormy, friendship with the then-celebrated Joe Chaikin, founder of the Open Theater, the widely admired and influential experimental group.

She and Joe rapidly became close friends. "You mean a great deal to me," Andrea wrote him at one point. "We have touched each other so deeply. . . . I was so moved by what I experienced as yr gentleness." The trajectory, and ultimate souring, of their friendship tells us a good deal about both their characters. Joe was a lively companion—warm and direct—as well as politically astute, though his animated charm, his abrupt and sprightly shifts in topic, blue eyes ablaze with cherubic "innocence," sometimes seemed to mock his own seriousness.[13]

After the friendship ran into trouble, Andrea summed up in a letter to Joe the basic cause of her disengagement: "It is an old story, a sexist scenario. The man says, Share my pain. The woman feels honored." Joe's "pain" sometimes centered on his tempestuous romances, but the steadiest source of his difficulty lay with lifelong medical issues. As a child he'd contracted rheumatic fever and over time had to have three open heart surgeries—the third one leading to a severe stroke and aphasia. One of the operations took place during the time when his relationship with Andrea was in crisis. After getting a letter from her, which essentially indicted him for narcissism, Joe angrily told her over the phone that he "would not turn to you in need or suffering, as I had." Andrea felt he had misunderstood her and overreacted; she wrote again, insisting that she'd merely meant to say that despite feeling hurt, "if you needed something concrete that I could do I would certainly do it."

But she reiterated her basic complaint: the underlying issue between them, she wrote, was "between a victimizing love and non-victimizing love. I have accused you of living off of the former in a series of relationships with women. It is, I know, a terrible accusation, and I believe it to be true. . . . It is, in my view, not a malicious charge but a just one. . . . I do not feel that it is crucial to my life to make you understand. . . . Every day I am sickened and debilitated by what happens to me as a woman and what happens to women around me. I know that if it matters enough to you, you will see and act; and that if it doesn't you won't. That's the truth of it." Andrea's transition from abused *hausfrau* to formidably independent feminist, had been rapid—and astonishingly absolute.

Joe responded with considerable (and atypical) heat: "I have . . . had profoundly mutual growing relationships with women which I continue to cherish. . . . Now I number among the male oppressors—featureless. And with no part of our friendship to value over a classification you have impaled me in. You speak of 'truth and honesty' as one who is immune to self-delusion. If so you would be the first . . . you have closed contact and communication. You have. Not me . . . [though] I would not want a friendship with anyone who would have me patterned and determined." Andrea had earlier told Joe that she intended to make him the co-dedicatee (along with Ricki Abrams) of her forthcoming book. He asked not to be included, and she complied—though they later had a guarded reconciliation.

The book itself, meanwhile, was nearing completion, though Andrea had still not found a publisher. Her London agent had given up, and she and Andrea had parted company. Forced to seek out a publisher on her own, Andrea wasn't having an easy time of it. She sent out the nearly completed manuscript to the three likeliest candidates for a work of combative radicalism: Grove, City Lights, and New Directions. All three turned her down. By this point, Andrea and I had become somewhat friendly, and I thought my own editor, the brilliant Hal Scharlatt at Dutton, might be more sympathetic. This time the dice finally rolled in Andrea's favor: Hal thought the manuscript needed work, but was willing to offer a contract. With publication now all but assured, Andrea turned her full energy to completing the book and to beginning the editorial process with Hal.[14]

In April 1974, *Woman Hating* appeared in bookstores—or, more accurately, was *due* to appear. *off our backs* (*oob*), the Washington, DC, feminist publication, reported that not a single bookstore in the DC area carried a copy. Dutton had originally planned a first printing of 7,500 but then lowered the print order to 5,000; *oob* accused John "Jack" McRae, the head of Dutton, of feeling that "the book was far too extreme" and deciding not to promote it. Yet the firm insisted that it had sent out 344 review copies to various outlets and publications, even if only three reviews appeared during the remaining eight months of 1974. One of the three, remarkably, was in *The Black Panther*—and thereby hangs a curious tale. Andrea had been regularly contributing small sums of money to the Panther organization over the previous few years, and she sent a copy of the book to its co-founder Huey Newton in appreciation for his work. He responded with a personal letter—"I have enjoyed reading it"—and also enclosed some of his own writing, which, he added, "I call insights (rather than poems)." There were six "insights" in all, these two being a fair sample:

> *The sun rises in the East*
> *We will make it set in the West*
> *And it will also be red*

> *The only difference between the capitalists*
> *the socialists and the communists*
> *is that the communists potentially*
> *have a bigger army.*

Later, when Huey was accused of shooting and killing a teenage prostitute in Oakland, Andrea (without saying why) "didn't believe that the police had framed him."[15]

Andrea was convinced that the lack of press coverage for *Woman Hating* was due in part to the steep price ($7.95) of the hardcover; few leftwing women, she felt, could afford it. To counteract the problem, both she and her newly acquired agent, Elaine Markson, lobbied hard and successfully to bring out a paperback edition quickly. In the meantime, at least a few speaking invitations—a badly needed supplement to Andrea's limited and irregular income—began to arrive. Andrea initially set her fee at a modest $200 plus expenses, but as word of her dynamic platform performances began to spread, she raised it to $500—which back then was quite a healthy sum.[16]

It helped, too, that support for the book came from some of the most prominent feminists of the day. Glowing testimonials came in from, among others, Gloria Steinem ("the book is fast, pure, and angry"), Audre Lorde ("much needed and long overdue"), Phyllis Chesler ("bold and visionary"), Kate Millett (a "testimonial . . . I'm delighted to give!"), Barbara Deming ("Andrea Dworkin speaks deep truths—both painful and healing"), and Marge Piercy ("brilliant"). By the end of 1975, Andrea, in something of a meteoric rise, was being included in the roster of speakers for several prestigious lecture series, along with such established figures as Millett, Scott Nearing, Margo Jefferson, Michael Harrington, Betty Dodson, Robin Morgan, Grace Paley, Morton Sobell, and Ti-Grace Atkinson.[17]

Andrea had long been an instinctive radical, and as her involvement in the feminist movement increased, her sympathies migrated *not* to Betty Friedan's liberal organization NOW, with its primary emphasis on integrating women into public life, but to those feminists calling for a more profound re-examination of issues relating to gender. Nor had Andrea ever been strongly attracted to Marxism or to a politics primarily rooted in economic issues, though unlike some middle-class feminists she was deeply aware of and concerned about divisions relating to race and poverty. As for the current turn to Eastern mysticism, she had zero interest in and considerable disdain for the Maharaj Ji, the Divine Light, and Flower Power.[18]

From this point on in her life it would be the issue of gender that would most passionately engage her sympathy and activism. Speaking to a women's sexuality conference late in 1974, she characterized the male sexual sensibility—culturally, not biologically determined—as "aggressive, competitive, objectifying, quantity oriented." Many feminists, she continued, "would like to think that in the last four years, or ten years, we have reversed, or at least impeded, those habits and customs of the thousands of years that went before . . . but there is no fact or figure to bear that out . . . women are poorer than ever, [are] . . . raped more and murdered more." She went on to characterize the "revolutionary kernel" of the feminist vision as "the abolition of all sex roles—that is, an absolute transformation of human sexuality and the institutions derived from it."[19]

In *Woman Hating*, Andrea spelled out at length both the history of women's debasement—using in particular the examples of the ancient Chinese practice of foot-binding and the widespread burning of alleged witches in Europe during the Middle Ages—and her visionary hopes for the future. Utilizing the considerable scholarship (the work of Mircea Eliade, for example) that had recently emerged on "primitive" and archaic societies, she concluded that all people are composed of properties and capacities currently parceled out to one *or* the other traditional gender. "The original myths," she wrote, "all concern a primal androgyne" (a creature combining what were later called feminine or masculine traits)— "an androgynous godhead, an androgynous people," as opposed to the modern gender model of two polar opposites, male and female. Her own guess—she rightly characterized the available evidence as too sparse to allow for certainty—was that "the first division of labor based on biological sex originated in a fundamental survival imperative. In the earliest of times, with no contraception and no notion of the place of the man in the process of impregnation, women were invested with the magical ability to bear children, a capacity that engendered 'awe and fear in men.'" Additionally, women—often pregnant and unable (though *not* weak and passive) to run and hunt—developed planting skills that led still further to their identification with fertility and generation, and to the division of humanity into two polar opposites.[20]

As for the demonstrably different biological equipment of men and women, Andrea argued against the common notion that two distinct and discreet *behavioral* patterns necessarily followed, that structural genetic and hormonal inheritance mandated different and complementary social roles for each gender. In arguing instead that maleness and femaleness are cultural—not biological—constructs, Andrea drew on an impressive variety of historical and scientific studies to justify her conclusion that there are not merely *two* genders ("We are a multi-sexed species," she wrote in *Woman Hating*), and was far in advance of what was then the commonplace dismissal of "trans" people as "freaks of nature." As well, she cited a variety of sources to reach the heretical conclusion that "conventional heterosexual behavior is the worst betrayal of our common humanity."

Andrea had been having sex with women since her teens, and had as well a long history of passionate and physical involvement with men. That didn't, however, incline her to adopt the label "bisexual"; she found both the notion and practice conceptually dualistic, in conflict with her own vision of "the multi-sexual nature of people . . . pansexual and role-free." Bisexuality, she insisted, was *not* the equivalent—and could even serve as a fortification against—androgyny. That is, to have sex with both genders (as the binary then had it) in the same way—for example, to be *always* dominant, never passive—could keep us, in her view, from the realization that we all have a potentially broad range of sexual desires and gender fantasies.[21]

One evening in 1974, during a very long dinner conversation, Andrea and I discussed some of the ramifications of the androgynous view of gender. We agreed that in at least one essential way all women and gay men share a common struggle: namely, rebellion against straight male dominance *and* our own deep-seated wish to offer ourselves, thrillingly, to his macho mistreatment. Andrea distinguished between our sense of the need for a feminist/gay alliance and the then-current ideology of the "Revolutionary Effeminists," as exemplified in the writings of Kenneth Pitchford (married at the time to the feminist Robin Morgan). In Andrea's view, Pitchford tended to see female traits as inherent and fixed, and she deplored his insistence that homosexual men should copy those traits, as well as subordinate their own needs in order to bring "womanhood" to power. Andrea saw the Pitchford model as static and tyrannical, a disguised imitation of the limited sexual imagination it purported to be in rebellion against.

She further argued that we needed "to break down the dichotomy between how we talk to ourselves and our closest friends, and how we present ourselves in our formal, social roles." That impulse could—and would—be belittled as mere exhibitionism, but the risk would have to be run. To decide to talk openly and in detail about our private lives represented—when not done merely to secure notoriety—an impulse to understand our feelings honestly and to share them honestly. It would mean trying to use words as genuine instruments of communication rather than, as currently, a means of self-inflation or a tool for deception—that is, a device for *preventing* communications that might threaten to upend accepted definitions of human-ness *and* relationships of power. The attempt, especially in the beginning, we agreed, *would* often fail; the words would come out as a grab-bag of postures, indulgent distortions, unfelt, arch formulations—in other words, what we were already used to. But the impulse behind those missteps, if it remained authentic, could represent the buried wish to break away from the exchange of bogus messages, to bridge the gulf of separation.

We assured each other that it didn't matter if our initial attempts fell lamentably short. That would only mean the performance was deficient, the communication incomplete. How could it initially be otherwise, coming from people schooled in defective integrity and truncated testimony—trained, in other words to maintain the traditional taboos. We needed at least to make a start toward what many of us were beginning urgently to feel: that people have to talk to each other in different ways about different things. A start is a start—not a completion. The need is there: to universalize, but not homogenize, freakiness: to allow people to see that what they've been taught to hide as individual shame could be converted into bonds of commonality.

Andrea had been living in Europe when the 1969 Stonewall riots erupted, and had no involvement in the radical Gay Liberation Front, which formed in their immediate aftermath. By the time she returned to the States, GLF had morphed into the single-issue organization Gay Activists Alliance, which centered its identity and politics on sexual orientation. That was not Andrea's central concern; for her, the primary emergency, far and away, was the plight of women—*all* women. By 1973 two additional gay organizations had emerged in New York, the Gay Academic Union and the National Gay Task Force, but neither showed much interest in feminism. At my urging, Andrea did get briefly involved with GAU, but soon left, convinced—as were a number of other women who tentatively affiliated—that gay men were *nearly* as sexist as straight ones.[22]

Yet she did now and then give a speech or write an article centered on LGBTQ issues. Possibly her most notorious was "Why Norman Mailer Refuses to Be the Woman He Is," which in 1973 appeared in the first issue of a new gay magazine *OUT* (it lasted for only two issues). The editor put the title of Andrea's article, along with a cartoon of Mailer dressed (à la Marilyn Monroe) in a windblown skirt and blouse, on its cover. "It used to be," Andrea began the article, "that one looked to Norman Mailer for energy, integrity, vision. . . . It used to be that where he walked, at least there it was dangerous to go, at least there one found battle worth doing." No longer, Andrea wrote. In *Marilyn*, his latest book, he turns out to merely be "a very sophisticated hack" using "all of his talent and energy to build a mystique of HIMSELF THE HERO AND HIS MANLINESS . . . creating the character he now plays in life, which is one-dimensional, rigid, and reductive." Marilyn Monroe "was fucked over in life—victimized, objectified, diminished, used, exploited," Andrea concluded, but "it took Mailer to do the definitive job in death."[23]

In the spring of 1974, John Stoltenberg walked out of a poetry reading in Greenwich Village to protest one of the readers' hateful words about women. On the sidewalk he ran into Andrea, who'd left the reading for the same reason. The two had been briefly introduced a few weeks earlier, at which time Andrea, at a glance, had dismissed John, who was tall, broad-shouldered, and with long locks of blond hair, as "a rather dim beach bum." For his part, John was struck by Andrea's blue denim bib overalls—her wardrobe of choice throughout her adult life—the "wild outgrowth" of black frizzy hair above a "warm, kind face" that was (and would remain) wholly "uncosmeticized." On this particular evening, they fell into deep conversation, and decided to see each other again. The meetings kept multiplying, and at one, Andrea gave John an author's copy of the just-published *Woman Hating*. He read it immediately, "enthralled and laughing out loud with joy" (as he describes it), especially impressed with Andrea's declaration that "'man' and 'woman' are fictions, caricatures, cultural constructs . . . we are . . . a multisexed species." As he would say in his own first book, *Refusing to Be a Man*, published many years later, "that liberating recognition saved my life."[24]

"Who can explain," John has written, "how anyone recognizes that they have fallen in love and that life apart is simply unthinkable?" Andrea, as she later wrote, "wasn't looking for a partner of any kind," which she thought was "fairly rare in women," and had been pleased that she *wasn't* in a "very emotional and vulnerable" state. Yet like John, she felt that their connection was immediate and deep, and within a very short time they made the decision to live together, which raised many a set of disapproving eyebrows. Andrea, along with her cat George and her German Shepherd Gringo—she was an animal lover all her life—left her fifth-floor walk-up on the Lower East Side and moved into John's spacious three-bedroom apartment half a block from Riverside Park. And they would stay together. Though frequently pestered (and just as frequently parried) for details about their intimate lives, "compassionate companions" was a formulation John once used, even though their relationship *was* intermittently sexual—that is, they "made love" but always without intercourse. By 1974 Andrea had decided to self-identify as lesbian, for his part, John had a brief heterosexual marriage behind him. Yet whether with his wife or with male sexual partners, he had never "fantasized fucking anyone. I'm not sure why. Maybe because I was always lacking in the physical aggression said to be 'normal' for boys." He enjoyed being *penetrated* anally, but was totally disinterested in *doing* the penetrating.[25]

In the early days of their relationship, they would lie together fully clothed; then, over time, they gradually got naked. "I remember lying on top of her," John recalls, "rubbing the base of my semi-erect penis against her pubic mound, rubbing my penis against her clitoris, rubbing our whole bodies together, kissing everywhere, sweating, breathing heavily, writhing, moaning, then cumming and cumming and holding each other tight. . . . I didn't yet know there was a word for this: *frottage.*" In John's experience, orgasm and ejaculation were not the same; the orgasms were "without effort and tension. I do not 'make them happen' nor does my partner. They seem to occur naturally in the general interflow of erotic communication."

Neither John nor Andrea exerted sexual pressure of any kind on the other. Neither wanted a "husband/wife" relationship ever again. Neither of them believed in monogamy, though both felt that lying about sexual contact with a third party amounted to betrayal. Should the desire arise, they agreed to feel entirely free to have sex with other people. Andrea had only one condition: no overnight houseguests, not even family members (or perhaps she meant *especially* not family members); John agreed, though reluctantly.

Neither John nor Andrea wished to share a bedroom at night—their body rhythms were directly opposite: John slept at night, and fell asleep easily; Andrea worked during the night and during the day slept fitfully, awakening frequently with intense nightmares. Above all, they felt safe with each other, felt free of demands and expectations. John recalls Andrea as a superb listener: she would "pay full attention, tell me exactly what she thought, never feign anything. I never had to lie to her about anything in order to please her . . . [we] could talk about anything and everything."

In many respects, they were very different people. Andrea was interested in horoscopes, tarot cards, and I Ching as "ancient forms and techniques [that] offered ways of conceptualizing and framing aspects of experience, character, and behavior that otherwise elude our attention or understanding"; John dutifully listened and became mildly interested, but no more than that. Whereas Andrea—seemingly from birth—had always been intensely political, John had only been "vaguely aware" as an undergraduate what SDS stood for; even then he was into theater, not civil rights. John *did* become interested somewhat in the developing political movement designed to combat discrimination against gay people, but he opposed the rapidity with which it narrowed its agenda. He gradually came to challenge, too, the widespread assumption of gay men—rife as well among their earlier radical straight counterparts in SNCC and SDS—that aggressive male behavior was "natural," was rooted in biology. By the mid-seventies John firmly believed, on the contrary, that such behavior was "entirely learned" and culturally dictated. Too many gay men, he asserted, are primarily interested in securing for themselves male privilege and power, and paid only lip service to the feminist struggle to end discrimination against *all* women. He knew that some gay men were sensitive to feminist issues—a group of them within the Gay Academic Union (and even earlier within the Gay Liberation Front) had started a consciousness-raising group to explore their own sexism—but he chose to believe (and perhaps exaggerate) that "they would sooner die than relinquish the prerogative that they got by being born male."[26]

They differed in how—or even if—they talked about work in progress. John liked to exchange views on what he was at work on; Andrea preferred to discuss the *feelings* that her work was evoking in her. Their career backgrounds also differed. Andrea had always wanted to be a writer. John—twenty-nine when they met (Andrea was twenty-seven)—had already earned an M.F.A. in theater arts at Columbia and a Master of Divinity from Union Theological Seminary. Fresh out of graduate school, he'd been hired by Joe Chaikin as administrative director of the highly respected Open Theater and for a time was "madly in love" with Joe, who didn't share his feelings; for a brief period John felt he was in love with *both* Joe and Andrea—and they themselves were at the time loving friends.[27]

At the time they moved in together, John had some savings from his Open Theater paychecks as well as a small amount left over from a playwriting grant. Once a week they'd go to the bank and withdraw $100—for Andrea that was a big step up in income—which they lived on until the following week. For a brief time he and Andrea actually started to write a verse play together, but the effort soon petered out; John would slowly start to shift to writing non-fiction, and would long remain amazed at Andrea's "writing discipline." Within a few years, when their limited funds ran out, he would find employment in the publishing industry, initially as a copy editor and then as the managing editor of various magazines.

Among the prominent women activists who admired *Woman Hating* were the poet Adrienne Rich and the longtime antiwar pacifist Barbara Deming. Both had reservations about the book, though Adrienne was the more critical of the two. Possibly with Carolyn Heilbrun's heralded 1973 book, *Towards a Recognition of Androgyny* in mind, Adrienne felt that *Woman Hating* had "little [that was] new or original in it." "I kept waiting for you," she wrote Andrea, "to get down into the question of masochism, which seems to me a crucial problem—how do we distinguish between masochism and the suffering which characterizes vital processes of change? How *do* we purge ourselves of masochism?" Overall Adrienne felt "little that is substantive in disagreement" with Andrea, but she urged her "to go deeper than you are going, beyond the broad critique and attack on patriarchy."[28]

Deming, a revered figure in leftwing circles, had originally and briefly met Andrea back in 1966 when both had appeared on the *David Susskind Show* to talk about jails (Deming had recently published *Prison Notes*). This was the show on which Andrea had described her nightmarish experience in the Women's House of Detention, including comments, which she later deeply regretted, about the "rampant" lesbianism in the prison and her terror at being sexually assaulted. Meeting again in 1975, Barbara told Andrea how anguished she'd felt during that Susskind show listening to Andrea's account of the "brutish, threatening" lesbians—feeling, as a lesbian, maligned and misunderstood. In those pre-Stonewall years Barbara had been afraid that revealing her lesbian identity on national television would compromise her political work as a civil rights pacifist.[29]

Andrea had deeply admired Deming from a distance and was mortified to learn that as an eighteen-year-old she'd inadvertently contributed to Barbara's chagrin as a woman "unable to live fully and openly in the world, robbed of pride and selfhood, robbed of a sexual identity which is nourished by visibility and dialogue." But Barbara fully understood Andrea's state of mind at the time and exonerated her from any deliberate malice. Indeed, after reading *Woman Hating* she wrote Andrea—who she hadn't seen since the Susskind show—to say that she found her book of "immense interest." She shared Andrea's vision of an androgynous humanity—every individual combining all the traits currently and artificially parceled out *either* to men *or* women. Yet Barbara, too, was somewhat critical of *Woman Hating*: in particular, she lamented the lack of any discussion in the book of how to implement and encourage the transition from institutionalized misogyny to a society free of stereotypic gender roles (Deming seems to have missed Andrea's admittedly limited references to transgender people as being a potentially valuable model). Barbara was also somewhat more leery than Andrea about separating herself from her long-time male associates in the non-violent peace movement, though she was no longer sure that they could continue to "struggle side by side. . . . It is going to take non-cooperation with them to make them change."[30]

A case in point soon arose, with Andrea herself directly implicated. When the collective that ran *Liberation* magazine—which had a readership of about ten thousand and was a leading leftwing publication—turned down one of Andrea's articles, Barbara, in protest, asked that her name be removed from the masthead as an associate of the magazine. She remained as vigorously attached as ever to the philosophy of radical non-violence for which *Liberation* stood, but felt that the journal wasn't sufficiently receptive to feminism— the rejection of Andrea's "invaluable" work being the most recent example.[31]

The dispute quickly became entangled and extended. When *WIN*, another leftwing collective-run publication, also turned down a piece by Andrea, Barbara, who frequently wrote for the publication, protested that "you take men more seriously than you take women—in spite of yourselves"; Barbara's nature being essentially conciliatory, she added: "I would *underline* 'in spite of yourselves.'" When Andrea, more obstinate, declared that she would never again submit anything to *WIN*, Barbara expressed the hope that she would reconsider: "We are, so many of us who *are* changing so fast these days that I think it a mistake to count any of us who *are* changing hopeless." In that regard, she singled out Maris Cakars, a leading figure in the *WIN* collective, "as really struggling to treat us [women] without difference."

One of the women (there were several) connected to the *Liberation/WIN* collectives, in a gesture of goodwill, asked Andrea to read and critique the mock-up of the next issue of *Liberation*, but then dismissed the critique Andrea sent in as "accusatory and hostile," even while expressing agreement with Andrea that "the concerns of women are not adequately reflected" in *Liberation*—nor, she added, were those of "blacks and other minorities." She solicited Andrea's further help in producing a publication "committed to an integrated political vision which sees the connection between different kinds of oppression" (what Kimberle Crenshaw would later name and theorize as "intersectionality").[32]

Two weeks later, *WIN*'s Maris Cakars notified Andrea that the collective had again voted against publishing an article of hers—this time it was her twenty-two poem cycle, "VIETNAM VARIATIONS"—as well as a piece by John entitled "Toward Gender Justice." That put a temporary end to their willingness to submit articles either to *Liberation* or *WIN*, but decidedly *not* an end to a correspondence that at times grew acrimonious, at other times achingly reflective, typifying the uneasy turmoil of quarrelling siblings (with mother, in the person of Barbara Deming, wretchedly wringing her hands on the sidelines).

The back-and-forth continued for some time, with periods of reconciliation alternating with "final" renunciations. For a brief time in the spring of 1975, downright harmony reigned: "I feel," Andrea wrote the *WIN* collective, "that *WIN* has made some sort of commitment to my writing"—they'd just accepted a new piece of hers, "Redefining Nonviolence"—"and I am quite prepared to make some sort of a commitment to *WIN*." She and John even visited the collective's farm near Woodstock (New York City had become too expensive) and had a "lovely dinner."[33]

Yet once again congeniality gave way to displeasure. "My quarrel with what you are doing," Andrea wrote at one point, "is not that it is not feminist enough but that it is not feminist at all." To which the editorial board of *WIN* replied that Andrea was "unable to forgive," even when past errors of judgment had been acknowledged. True, Andrea admitted: "I find it difficult to agree to anything that threatens to compromise the integrity of my work." At one point during the prolonged and hurtful counterpoint, Andrea described the agony of her process in words that are likely to resonate for any serious feminist writer (and perhaps for a few other kinds as well):

> Doing feminist work requires a surfeit of nerve and stamina. At first one works on an energy generated by sheer conviction. So one lays it out—about sex roles, about marriage, about sex, about misogyny, about lesbian identity, whatever. But as one sends out work and meets with constant editorial abuse, and then slowly as one's work gets printed here and there and one experiences the anger and vilification so often directed at feminist work—then, even sitting down to work at all becomes more and more difficult. One knows that there is no place to publish; one knows the rejection letters that will come before they are written; one knows the abuse that will come if the work is printed. Ironically, as one learns more and more about the nature of women's oppression through one's work,

it becomes harder to work. One's work in the world meets the same kind of abuse of one's body.[34]

Then, late in 1975, yet another squabble led to a definitive rupture (as it was, *WIN* would only survive for another two years). Andrea's understanding was that the editorial board had agreed to a series of discussions to determine common ground, but before those could take place the board voted unanimously *against* devoting special issues of the publication to "feminist topics." Meaning precisely *what?* Andrea wanted to know: have you voted against a special issue on rape? on abortion? on health care for women? on female sexuality? "Too bad," an angry Andrea responded, "especially since, among other matters, half a million women were *known* to have been raped in 1973 alone." It incensed Andrea that radical feminists like herself and Barbara Deming "are, whether you like it or not, experts in our field; we study these questions full-time; we know the writers writing on them and . . . have access to the work of women in all fields related to women, which you do not. What a gift of time and work you have voted unanimously against." Furious, she announced that "I can no longer tolerate the bad faith, malice, and manipulations of those who determine *WIN*'s policy and morality." A permanent break had been made.[35]

While *Liberation* and *WIN* had resisted throwing open the gates to radical feminism, they remained among the few outlets available for serious leftwing writing, and parting company with them reduced Andrea's options—though it didn't affect her income, for the simple reason that neither publication had ever been able to afford paying its writers. As a matter of sheer survival, Andrea had to figure out a way to supplement her meager income. When she somehow learned that a one-year teaching post in Literature/History had opened up at Hampshire College in Amherst, Massachusetts, she submitted an application—and even got Mary Daly, the well-known feminist theologian and author of *Beyond God the Father,* with whom she'd been corresponding but hadn't personally met, to write a letter of recommendation.[36]

The search committee that interviewed Andrea for the job

reported to the dean that she'd shown "wide reading" and had demonstrated "real profundity of analysis and intellectual power." The dean was unimpressed and turned down the search committee's recommended appointment. He characterized Andrea as "a clever self-publicist" and dismissed the committee's opinion that she was "widely read" as "unproven from her papers or presence"; he characterized *Woman Hating* as a mere "text book." Hampshire had opened its doors in 1970, proudly touting itself as an experimental college open to radical views on education—though not, apparently, on womanhood.[37]

As early as its preview edition in 1972, *Ms.* magazine reached a large audience and, unique among feminist publications, actually paid its authors well. During the first three years of the magazine's existence, Andrea wasn't asked to contribute, nor had she met its editor, Gloria Steinem. Yet in the spring of 1975 she took it upon herself to write to her for the first time—not to suggest an article nor a meeting, but rather to present her with a set of questions about a matter that at the time was profoundly upsetting Steinem: the public brouhaha over her purported involvement more than a decade earlier with the CIA.[38]

Some months earlier, the radical feminist collective Redstockings had issued a lengthy press release accusing Steinem of having been, back in 1959, a willing accomplice of the CIA's secret anti-Soviet intrigues and, in particular, attending the 1959 Youth Festival in Vienna. We "have become convinced," the Redstockings press release of May 9, 1975, added, "that *Ms.* magazine, founded and edited by her, is hurting the women's liberation movement." They spoke, the release continued, "as the originator of *consciousness-raising* and the Miss America Protest, as the women who were the first to talk in public about their abortions and the need for women to control their own bodies, who coined such slogans as *sisterhood is powerful* and *the personal is political* that launched the movement." Redstockings claimed that Steinem had worked for the CIA-financed Independent Research Service from 1959 to 1962, and under its auspices had infiltrated the 1959 Vienna Youth Festival in order to spread anti-Communist poison. The collective further charged Steinem and *Ms.* with "working against the development of a truly mass women's movement" even as it reoriented feminism away from its radical roots.

The Redstockings' attack on Steinem for a time caused a serious split in the movement. When Andrea and Barbara Deming (neither of whom was involved with Redstockings) were asked to sign a statement in advance of a confrontation with Steinem at an international conference in Mexico, they decided to write directly to Steinem instead, "hoping it would de-escalate the whole thing in a responsible way." Andrea wrote most of the letter, and it was decided that she alone should sign it. She posed a number of questions to Steinem, all of them relating to the accusations that the Redstockings press release had posed. For example: "Did you have an association with the C.I.A. from 1959 to 1969? If so, have you purposely misrepresented, concealed, or lied about that association? Were you, during that time, involved in collecting information on political activists?"

Steinem's answers were honest and (for the fair-minded) absolving. Yes, she wrote, the CIA had been among her sponsors, but the CIA was then among the few government agencies that had *protected* its employees from Senator McCarthy's harassment; the CIA of 1958–60 was not the CIA we currently knew—the one that had toppled the leftwing Allende regime in Chile and helped mastermind the hideous war in Vietnam. As for the 1959 Vienna Youth Festival, she'd never given much thought to its funding; her primary purpose in attending had been to deepen understanding between different peoples and cultures, and she'd come away "full of idealism and activism."[39]

Having posed the necessary questions to Steinem about the CIA, Andrea then proceeded in her letter—her basic sympathies, after all, were with *radical* feminism—to sharply criticize *Ms.* as "often mediocre and the level of thought, analysis, and ambition seems not only inadequate but corrupt. . . . We know that many fine feminist writers are regarded contemptuously by the editors of *Ms.* We know that the survival of radical feminists is more and more endangered by the worsening economic situation; *Ms.* will not help us to survive by buying our work." Nonetheless, Andrea wrote—in defiance of the Redstockings—"these facts alone do not warrant, in our opinion, a judgment that *Ms.* magazine is part of a government conspiracy to destroy the women's movement."

Andrea's questions regarding Steinem's past CIA affiliation in fact helped mark out a path designed to soothe the division within feminist ranks. She essentially handed Steinem a rationale for having accepted CIA funding: "A former association with the CIA," Andrea wrote, "would not make you *per se* an enemy in our eyes, and we caution our sisters against forgetting how people, especially women, change alliances and values as feminist consciousness grows." Many male radicals, Andrea went on, "have been members of reactionary and malicious institutions. They have renounced those institutions and have gone on to do important political work." Andrea even provided examples: Philip Agee and William Sloane Coffin had once worked for the CIA, and Daniel Ellsberg had once worked for the Rand corporation.

In her letter to Steinem Andrea went still further: "We reject some of their [Redstockings] tactics and values as inappropriate at best and shabby at worst . . . quoting out of context, generalizing where the facts do not warrant generalization, making vast political condemnations . . . we hope that in your own response to the Redstockings press release you will speak to the totalitarian character of many of the methods used and charges made. In ending we want to say that women, all of us, have been contaminated and polluted by the male associations forced on us for the sake of survival. We do not stand in judgment on you."

Sympathy gradually shifted toward Steinem, and then died down. When Redstockings a few years later allowed Random House to publish an expurgated version (which some read as borderline homophobic) of their book *Feminist Revolution*, it led to a renewed flare-up of antagonism that again found Andrea vocally siding with the anti-Redstockings contingent. In a letter to *off our backs*, she criticized the collective for allowing "a censored version of their book to be published." Kathie Sarachild, a leading Redstocking, scornfully admonished her for being "ignorant of the realities of publishing." Not one to be silenced, Andrea promptly raised additionally embarrassing questions: "Why did Redstockings think that

Gloria's corporate connections as they had construed them were more powerful or evil than their own, e.g., RCA's ownership of Random House, their publisher? Why did they allow passages that they considered essential to be deleted from their book rather than fight Random House or take the book to another publisher? What were their positions on rape, pornography, and lesbianism as feminist issues?"[40]

In riskily joining the fray as a comparative newcomer to feminist in-fighting, in remonstrating with Redstockings even though sharing its commitment to radical feminism, Andrea exhibited the unshakeable integrity that would in the future bring down on her own head so much venomous wrath. On the plus side, in siding with Steinem during one of the most charged confrontations of her career, Andrea made an influential friend and a potential ally.

4

The Mid-Seventies

By the time Jimmy Carter took office in 1977, a considerable economic downturn had taken hold. Heavy industry, and in particular the steel mills of the Midwest, had increasingly closed up shop or moved overseas. The unfamiliar malaise of "stagflation" gripped the country: a mystifying mix of sluggish economic growth, high unemployment, and rising inflation. Real wages for the average male worker dropped by an alarming 10 percent, and the gap between rich and poor began to accelerate.

In direct parallel to a faltering economy, tolerance within the country for social justice movements weakened considerably. In Boston, whites rioted against mandatory school busing, attacks on affirmative action programs and social welfare legislation grew, and the popularity of "right-to-work" laws made rapid headway in sapping the strength of labor unions. At the 1976 Republican National Convention, the ERA plank made it onto the platform by a bare four votes—and a horde of new converts joined Phyllis Schlafly's anti-abortion, "pro-family" crusade.

Simultaneously, Anita Bryant began her Save Our Children campaign against gay rights, and in *Newsweek* the widely read columnist George Will questioned the wisdom of the American Psychiatric

Association's having removed homosexuality from its list of mental disorders, calling it a direct threat to the traditional family unit on which "much else depends." The backlash extended to the Supreme Court when in 1976 it voted six to three in *Doe v. Commonwealth* to let stand a statute punishing sodomy between consenting adults. The New York City Council made its own contribution to the rightwing turn by defeating a gay civil rights bill, with the Catholic Archdiocese proudly leading the fight against what it called the "sexually disoriented."

Within social justice movements themselves, the forces of liberal assimilationism had pretty much routed the radical firebrands. Membership in the Black Panther Party peaked in 1970, then gradually contracted; the Latino Young Lords, similarly, had been effectively crippled by 1973. Radical feminist collectives like the Redstockings and the Furies increasingly gave way to cultural feminism, which rejected androgyny and emphasized the *innate* differences between males and females. And left-oriented gay organizations like GLF and GAA, which had been broadly critical of the country's embedded inequities, would soon give way to single-issue centrist groups like the Human Rights Campaign Fund that stressed increased access to membership *within* current institutional structures.

Many movement radicals like Andrea had been able to get by—barely—by taking on part-time paying jobs with sympathetic employers. But with the economic downturn, many of the employers had to take on these jobs themselves even as the competition for part-time work rose in tandem with mounting unemployment. In one sense Andrea was among the more fortunate: word had begun to spread that she was a charismatic speaker, and invitations to lecture had increased. That meant more traveling—which ate into her writing time—than she would have wanted: dreary bus rides, primitive accommodations, insomniac nights. Yet along with earning badly needed money, Andrea did get to meet a countless variety of women, who opened their homes and hearts to her, sharing their stories of fear and desperation.

She put a great deal of care into her talks, reading widely and carefully rehearsing her text. Passionately engaged with the topics on which she spoke, she was blessed too with an inherently theatrical nature and an imposing, forceful physical presence. One woman who heard her speak at a Washington, DC, NOW event captured what many felt was her powerful impact on an audience: "The speech dealt with her theories on the historical oppression of women and was extraordinary—'*Our foremothers believed that they had given us the tools which would enable us to transform a corrupt nation into a nation of righteousness. It is a bitter thing to say that they were mistaken*'—I was riveted in my seat, my body felt suspended. I wanted to turn around to see how other people were reacting but I was unable to move . . . the passion was so strong that when she finished speaking Andrea herself was in tears and much of the audience was close to crying. . . . The room trembled when the speech was finished."[1]

As Andrea herself put it, her public speeches were "not the extemporaneous exposition of thoughts or the outpouring of feelings, but crafted prose that would inform, persuade, disturb, cause recognition, sanction rage." Responding to an admiring letter from another fan, Andrea wrote back, "I know that I respect my audiences and never condescend to them. I try to tell them the truth as I understand it and I try to say it as honestly as I can . . . it is taking communication seriously and thinking you had better say what you mean, now not later, because this is the only chance you may ever have."

Thanks to the thorough forethought Andrea invested in preparing her talks, they were able to serve a double function as readable essays, and in 1976 she published a collection of them under the overall title *Our Blood*. The essays were markedly different one from the other; Andrea wasn't the sort of lecturer who went from place to place repeating the same speech on different occasions with barely a change in commas. Her scrupulous attention to the needs of a given occasion, and audience, is part of the reason for the powerful impact she had.[2]

But scrupulosity doesn't sell books, nor convince publishers to sign them up in the first place. Andrea, with good reason, saw the publishing establishment in the 1970s as dominated by "timid and powerless women editors, the superstructure of men who make the real decisions, [and] misogynistic reviewers. . . . I was too naive to know that hack writing is the only paying game in town." She was once offered $1,500—then a huge sum for magazine writing—to do an article about the hedonistic use by suburban women of barbiturates and amphetamines. Though living on the margins, she told the assignment editor that she thought "women used amphetamines to get through miserable days and barbiturates to get through miserable nights." That may sound (as she wrote in the preface to *Our Blood*) "like great rebellious fun—telling establishment types to go fuck themselves with their fistful of dollars—but when one is very poor, as I was, it is not fun. It is instead profoundly distressing." She turned down the assignment, and did so "with considerable indignation."

That in turn got her increasingly marked down as "a wild woman," an "incorrigible," a reputation that haunted and hurt her—"not hurt my feelings, but hurt my ability to make a living." Being "blunt and not particularly polite" was not what magazine and book publishers expected or wanted, at least not from a woman. On reading a draft of a few chapters of *Woman Hating*, one editor had told her, "You write like a man. When you write like a woman we will consider publishing you." Her ambition was perceived as megalomaniacal, and she herself was seen as "a bitch" for harboring a goal so unfeminine.

According to Andrea's values, writing and lecturing should never replace political activism but rather alternate with it. Instinctively, she preferred solitude, with social contact held to a minimum. But her ideological fervor, and her conscience, insistently brought her back into the fray, dragging her away from the isolation needed to write. Yes, she derived sustenance from public applause, yet was never entirely comfortable with it—nor, for that matter, with prolonged isolation. It was a constant balancing act for her, a steady source of internal conflict about where her time and energy were most needed and best invested (an unsolvable conundrum, of course, for any writer/activist).

For Andrea, the conflict suddenly intensified when the controversy with *WIN* in 1976 all but coincided—collided, really—with the commercial release in New York of *Snuff,* the notorious film that purported to show the rape and dismemberment on camera of one of its actresses. Andrea and John first learned about the film from seeing a poster for it in the subway ("Made in America where life is cheap"). As early as October 1975, the *New York Post* had carried a story about snuff films being shot in South America that had begun to circulate on what the *Post* called the "pornography-connoisseur circuit," where a wealthy clientele paid $1,500 to purchase eight reels of film. Four months later, on February 11, 1976, *Snuff* opened in New York at the National Theatre at 44th Street and Broadway.[3]

The film's commercial release hit Andrea hard, doubtless dredging up all too vividly her earlier life with Iwan. As she bleakly wrote her friend, the playwright Susan Yankowitz, "I'm upset in such a terrible way that I can't keep my eyes closed, nothing comforts me. . . . I just can't stop crying. . . . Part of the trouble is that I'm afraid to try to organize because I'm afraid to discover that there is widespread indifference. I just couldn't bear it, I'd rather try to put it into the perspective of, well, this is but one instance, and not the worst one by a long shot, of that which my work reveals"—like the thousands of years of Chinese foot-binding or the widespread burning of "witches" that she'd described in *Woman Hating*.[4]

Yankowitz, who was currently on the West Coast, encouraged Andrea to get active: "media attention is, I think, essential. . . . And of course there must be demonstrations and pickets at the theatre . . . knowing you, I know that you will find the strength to do whatever you can, in your own way, out of your own energy, however depleted." Grimly, Andrea took up the challenge. She circulated a lengthy summary of what was known to date: "Those who have viewed the film consistently report that . . . [it] is a clear hoax designed to capitalize on the morbid titillation provoked by news reports of the existence of real 'snuff' films. They also say that the film is insufferable trash. The apparent phoniness of the death at the end of the film is not in any sense the issue"; fake though the film was, by its very existence it "suggests that sexual violence against women as entertainment and for profit will be condoned by a callous community and protected by corrupt law."[5]

Andrea helped to round up signatures from both men and women petitioning District Attorney Robert Morgenthau to close down the theater showing *Snuff*. The petitioners called upon the DA "to prosecute and prevent the presentation, distribution, and advertising of the film," and among those who signed were Susan Brownmiller (author of the 1975 bestseller *Against Our Will*), Ellen Burstyn, Joe Chaikin, Dave Dellinger of the War Resisters League, Barbara Deming, Grace Paley, Muriel Rukeyser, Donald Shriver (president of Union Theological Seminary), Susan Sontag, and Gloria Steinem. The signers were described by Nat Hentoff in the *Village Voice* as a "posse." Morgenthau's response further enflamed them: even if an "authentic" snuff film was shown, he said, closing it down would probably not be actionable since the murder would have been committed outside his jurisdiction. His reply fed the view that snuff films constituted "an intolerable danger to women."

Andrea saw the danger of *Snuff* as three-fold: the film would prove an incitement to violence against women; it presented the dismemberment and murder of a woman as sexual entertainment; and it would lead to a demand for *real* snuff films. A sizeable number of women agreed with her. Demonstrations at the National Theatre began on February 15 and continued nightly, and on at least one night drew some five hundred pickets to the theater (John and several other men joined the protesters). There were also demonstrations at the offices of the film's booking agency and distributor, as well as boycotts when the film opened in Los Angeles, Boston, Philadelphia, Denver, and Rochester. The protestors in Philadelphia, exercising what they called their "First Amendment rights of picketing," succeeded in closing down the theater.

Andrea also wrote for support directly to Congresswoman Bella Abzug, who responded that she supported picketing, a letter-writing campaign, and "all efforts to stop the showing of this film." She herself wrote a letter of protest to Allen Shackleton, president of the company that distributed *Snuff*: "Has it occurred to you," it read, "that this film may encourage others—and our society has many sadists who will do anything for money—to actually murder a woman and show it on film? Do you want that on your conscience?" Shackleton remained unfazed. In supporting the picketing, Abzug did draw a line: she refused to sanction outright legal suppression, because, as she wrote Andrea, "I am concerned about protection of the First Amendment" guaranteeing free speech.

Abzug was not alone. A fierce, prolonged debate over what the

First Amendment did or did not permit was right around the corner and would become central to a decades-long, and still unfinished, argument about the definition of pornography and its effects on viewers. Could *Snuff* best be described as a commercial for violence against women, and if so, wasn't that just as objectionable as a commercial for genocide? Anti-pornography feminists would answer with a resounding "yes" and would mount an unrelenting campaign that insisted porn constituted an "action" and was tantamount to encouraging violence and rape against women.

That debate would soon heat up, but it was the opening of *Snuff* in New York that marked its inauguration. A few early cannonades in the press—mostly written by men, mostly persuaded that feminist objections were a function of prudish morality—laid out some of the basic contentions that would later inform the full-blown argument. One (male) columnist thought it obvious that the "depiction or description of murder is not considered obscene—just read your Bible or Shakespeare. Or turn on your TV set." Another (also male) quoted the "King of Smut," Al Goldstein, to the effect that the protest against *Snuff* was "bullshit created by the morals squad to give pornography a black eye." One of the firmest denunciations of the feminist protest came from the Bloomington, Indiana Gay Rights Coalition: "What many of these women fail to realize," the gay group claimed, "is that their support of 'censorship' only lends fuel to the enemies of feminism and gayness. Even the stupidest of prosecutors, police, or anti-porn campaigners realizes that serious gay and feminist publications and books pose a much greater threat to their traditional view of society and family than does the hardest of hard core porn."

In the 1976 *Snuff* debate, the two polar positions that would represent the decades-long debate to follow were laid out by Nat Hentoff, who described himself as a First Amendment purist, on one side, and the feminist writer Leah Fritz on the other. Hentoff insisted that "cutting off thought, cutting off expression, for the greater good of us all, only results in the cutting off of more thought and more expression. Where does one stop after one has begun snuffing out expression, however repellent and frightening?"

In response, Leah Fritz pointed out that First Amendment

rights have never been absolute—"threatening letters, blackmail [and] ransom notes" are among the many acts *not* protected. More broadly still, she argued, "the First Amendment doesn't belong to everybody—not equally. . . . [it belongs to] the men who control the economy, make the wars, and fund the media . . . only those words which please the sponsor, or the publisher, or the producer, are heard with any clarity." Andrea, too, stressed what most of the mainstream leaders of the women's movement too often ignored: the lack of access among *poor* women to the rights purportedly available to all in a democratic society. In her speeches she frequently spoke of how racial and ethnic prejudice was integrally related to sexism and male domination. The poor and minorities of every stripe, she wrote at one point, have been "devastated by male-enfranchised portraits of ourselves as docile, semi-paralyzed, infantile, stupid, grinning victims. . . . The censorship of our own visions of ourselves—of what we might become—has been nearly complete." You can print your own pamphlet or preach from a soapbox, but your "free speech" will reach few listeners. The terms of the antagonistic positions had been set—with multiple adjustments and modifications in the years ahead.[6]

The controversy centering on *Snuff* itself had pretty much played itself out by the spring of 1976, but during the preceding three months the issue, as Andrea wrote a correspondent, "wacked the life right out of me, many weeks were spent in fevered organizing, desperate ploys, and futile meetings. . . . It's been a really hard time. I hope that Saturn or whatever has moved on, hopefully out of the universe altogether." In combination with the immediately preceding controversy with *Liberation* and *WIN*, the struggle over *Snuff* made her feel pretty much drained of energy.

There was scant time for recuperation. Her essay collection *Our Blood* was due for publication in the early fall of 1976. Fearing that it would suffer the same fate as *Woman Hating*—that it would get a few reviews in out-of-the-way places and none in the mainstream press—Andrea decided to become her own press agent. She contacted nearly a hundred feminist activists and editors and also wrote personal (and shyly embarrassed) letters to various feminist eminences soliciting blurbs. Her agent, Elaine Markson, meanwhile, approached virtually every known paperback publisher, but failed to get a single offer; it was only five years later, in 1981, that Perigee—the only unionized publishing house in New York—bought the rights, belatedly allowing Andrea to feel "a shaky sense of victory."[7]

The feminist eminences, on the other hand, came through in style. Gloria Steinem hailed *Our Blood* as performing "the special miracle of writing from great anger but never from vengeance"; Kate Millett characterized it as "a fierce book. . . . The fury of generations of silent women is in it"; and her loyal mentor Muriel Rukeyser saluted *Our Blood* as a "brilliant and important book . . . ferocious in its truth."

Of the nine essays in *Our Blood*, at least six had originated as speeches, and each was markedly different from the others. Andrea's own favorite was "The Root Cause" (as a speech she'd called it "Androgyny"). Her argument in essence was that when discussing gender, a distinction had to be made between what is *real* and what is *true*. As the current reality had it, there were two and only two genders, male and female, and they were polar opposites that at the same time were complementary: each gender, as Andrea put it, "is supposed to have the dignity of its own separate identity," its own distinctive and consequential sphere of influence, while both were necessary to "a harmonious whole"—a view still widely held forty years later.

Such a claim, Andrea insisted, had nothing to do with truth: there was no such egalitarianism. The male gender was defined as possessing the positive qualities of high intelligence, daring, strength, and courage, while the distinctive (and biologically determined) features of the female were the lesser qualities of dependency, passivity, emotionality, and masochism. Yet other cultures, Andrea pointed out, assigned quite different qualities to the genders (and made room for more than two); cultural variations were so pronounced that they could only be understood as the product of an inherent androgyny, with social norms defining what was or wasn't acceptable gender behavior. Women, in Andrea's formulation, "will never be free until the delusion of sexual polarity is destroyed. . . . This is the revolutionary possibility inherent in the feminist struggle."

She called for "the abolition of all sex roles . . . an absolute trans-

formation of human sexuality and the institutions derived from it."
That social revolution, she argued in the essay "Renouncing Sexual
Equality," could never be achieved by working within the system.
In her view, the effort to win "equality" within established social
institutions was in fact "a commitment to becoming the rich instead
of the poor, the rapist instead of the raped, the murderer instead of
the murdered." She asked instead for a different commitment—to
the abolition of poverty, rape, and murder; that is, a commitment
to ending the system of oppression called patriarchy, to ending the
male sexual model itself.

Our Blood fared no better with the mainstream press and public
than *Woman Hating* had. The three pre-publication journals were
mixed: a favorable notice in *Library Journal* was over-balanced by
pans in *Kirkus* and *Publishers Weekly*. Six months after the book's
appearance, it had gotten a glowing review from Andrea's friend
Leah Fritz in *City Women*, and a few—a very few—other notices in
Gay Community News, *Sojourner*, *The Villager*, *off our backs*, and *Pacific
Sun*; the only review that reached a mainstream audience was in *Ms.*
Robin Morgan, editor of the pathbreaking anthology *Sisterhood Is
Powerful*, spent three weeks leaving messages for Harvey Shapiro,
head of the *Sunday New York Times Book Review*, offering to do a
review, but never got a return call. Gloria Steinem also struck out
with Digby Diehl at the *Los Angeles Times*. Andrea herself succeeded
in getting through on the phone to Marianne Partridge, managing
editor of the *Village Voice*—yet nothing appeared in its pages. Given
the limited coverage, the sales figures for *Our Blood* were dismal,
and the prospects of finding an interested publisher for her future
work bleak. She decided to try her hand at writing fiction and began
work on a novel she called *Ruins* (the story of a woman's life told in
letters), to which she'd periodically return but would never manage
to sell or finish.[8]

Her spirits took a decided downturn, in seeming parallel to the
miasma that had settled over the city at large. New York in 1976 was,
quite simply, on the verge of bankruptcy. The apartment building
she and John were living in on West 97th Street had sixteen bur-
glaries in the previous year, and social services—hospitals, street
cleaning, garbage collection—had become *occasional*. "It is some

incredible nightmare," Andrea wrote a friend, "and the rest of the country just turns its back while New York dies."

She and John, Andrea wrote Kathy Norris, her still-close friend from Bennington days, "have been so happy together" and have shared "a joy beyond anything I knew to be possible." Yet as living conditions continued to deteriorate, Andrea felt caught in a vise of poverty, extreme fatigue, and heightened anxiety. For a time she feared a nervous breakdown and described herself as being in a state of "deep confusion and strange displacedness . . . everything seems fragmented and disjointed . . . there is nothing left here to make it worthwhile to be here."[9]

An attempted rape in the lobby of their building proved the final straw, and when Barbara Deming—to whom Andrea had dedicated *Our Blood*—invited them to join her and her partner Jane Gapen in relocating to Florida, they decided to accept.

Andrea realized that "Florida is a strange place for me to go," since she disliked heat, yet she felt her "imagination is exhausted" and it was "time to change everything"—at least for a few years. For Barbara the warmer climate had become a necessity: she'd had a calamitous automobile accident in 1971 from which she would never fully recover and could no longer tolerate a Northern winter. She and Jane had found a tiny, isolated island called Sugar Loaf Key, some twenty miles from Key West, with three separate detached units on the property. Andrea and John decided to give it a try.

The move itself proved arduous. It took almost a month of nonstop work to empty and clean the apartment they'd been living in—all during an excruciating September heat spell. The rented truck finally loaded, they looked forward to a leisurely, recuperative trip, full of "exciting adventures." Instead, the truck's lights kept going on and off, and in order to rendezvous on time with the men Barbara had hired in Sugar Loaf to help with the unloading, John had to drive long, hard hours (Andrea having never learned). The negative omens were compounded on arrival: the men failed to show up, and they had to start unloading the truck themselves in subtropical heat. The men did appear the next day and finished the job.[10]

The situation thereafter sporadically improved, but Andrea was at first despondent. "It is not exactly what I expected down here," she wrote, struggling for understatement: "a subtropical climate is unbelievably different from a temperate climate—especially the wild life, the bugs, the reptiles . . . [the] scorpions, rattlesnakes and other poisonous snakes, many large and fearsome spiders." Their cottage, moreover, was (in Andrea's words) "grimy and grim, filled with dirty, awful furniture, filled with huge cockroaches which came out of every corner or lay dead in such places as the refrigerator or came lunging out of cabinets as I was cleaning them. Nothing here consoled me. Everything was foreign, utterly strange and bizarre." Trying for humor, she wrote a friend that she was "the killer without peer, anything moves, it dies one way or the other. John tries to kill, but his heart isn't in it, so he misses. He's good at carrying out the carcasses though. From each according to her ability, to each accordingly." The situation had its comic side but, for a city girl, was also genuinely unnerving.[11]

They began to make the cottage habitable by emptying it of all its shabby furnishings, taking down the filthy curtains, throwing out the dirty linens and stained dishes, painting the entire house in flat white, repairing the stairs, fixing doors, building bookcases—and then refurnishing sparsely. Andrea was learning how to do many things "I didn't know how to do, but still, it bores me." She was "very prone to sudden shifts of mood, extreme shifts, cataclysmic shifts. I also imagine running away quite frequently. Usually in the middle of the night I want to get on a plane back to New York."

Andrea had never lived in a rural environment, and Sugar Loaf Key was closer to jungle than suburb. "Everything is nature," she wrote a friend. "*Father* Nature, unsentimental, malevolent, or at least indifferent to the presence of a frail, frightened creature like myself." The local men were "part of nature too—they kill for pleasure or sport." There were only twenty-five houses on the entire island, the sunlight a glaring "heavy yellow," the dense foliage often impenetrable and, to Andrea, the green color so deep that it was "absolutely vulgar . . . there is nothing delicate or subtle here, nothing consoling, no place anywhere for a human sensibility. It is all wild, exquisitely beautiful, but entirely forbidding." Though her mood sometimes brightened, more typically she felt overwhelmed and frightened. "I find myself," she wrote a friend, "no matter what

I'm doing, looking around suddenly to see if I am alone, or if some creature has climbed up a wall beside me or behind me. I hope I can conquer my fear, because the seeds of madness in it are real. . . . I have warned John that I don't know if I can bear it or not."

Mixed in with the dread were occasional good days, especially when she went swimming ("It is the whole Gulf of Mexico which stretches before one, dramatic, exquisite"). She even tried snorkeling, though as she drolly put it, "my major goal is not to see the sea life but to avoid it. . . . John goes snorkeling to see things under water; I go snorkeling to make sure that nothing is there." After a few weeks, she also began to notice a marked improvement in her health; she stopped eating sweets, ate "well and moderately," felt less exhausted, and now and then even sunbathed nude on Barbara and Jane's deck. When she confessed in a letter to a friend that she had the beginning of a suntan, the friend responded: "I'll never recognize you unless you promise to come holding a can of Tab in one hand and of course wearing your overalls. And please don't tell anyone else you've gotten tan. . . . Next thing you know people will no longer think you're . . . that weird witch who collects limp peniseses [sic]. . . . After all, they think you only read the complete works of Emma Goldman in braille."[12]

But Andrea's good cheer was shallow and unreliable, subject to sudden evaporation. Venturing off the property now and then into Key West, she was appalled by the local human population. On the surface all was "southern courtesy, so pleasant, so superficial. Underneath, the murderous truth . . . the klansman, the hangman . . . the tangled knot of lies, the evangelical baptists, the red-necked (literally), red-faced, muscled men. . . . The women are virtually invisible, shadowed presences who accompany their men on boats but have never been taught to swim, who live in rattlesnake country wearing fragile shoes (the manly men wear impressive boots)—one never sees two women together without men, rarely a woman alone."

She also felt a decided undertow of local anti-Semitism, virulent if unspoken: there was a "Pirate and Torture Museum" in Key West that prominently displayed a large newspaper headline: "ALL THE WORLD WANTS THE JEWS DEAD." On the surface, she found the town "quaint for tourists, pretty little shops . . . overpriced cute-sy things." Yet a kind of "male vagabond culture" prevailed—"all on the road but without the energy to move an inch. . . . '60s imitators, but very cynical. . . . There is also a very hard and decadent gay male culture, as in New York. . . . Blacks and whites seem to stay sepa-rated, live in different areas . . . the black areas are poorer [and] . . . with little economic viability . . . a few lesbians drift among the men in the gay bars, are distinguished from the female impersonators because they don't wear makeup or dresses." Andrea vowed to go into Key West as little as possible—only for the most necessary chores.

She longed to be writing again but couldn't get comfortable enough; she had "this strange alien feeling," she wrote a friend, "this lack of safety . . . I feel myself a prisoner." She berated herself for a lack of willpower in simply getting down to work: she'd man-aged to, she reminded herself "in smaller, grimmer rooms, in wilder cement jungles." But the pep talk didn't work, the dejection too pervasive—"miserable is too weak a word," she wrote Kathy Norris. Other than to write an occasional letter, Andrea couldn't summon up her usual discipline, and she tormented herself with the convic-tion that when the discipline to write goes "with it goes sanity." The longer she stayed away "from the work I want to do," she wrote Susan Yankowitz, "the more disoriented I feel . . . I find my resolve wavering, and my belief in myself quite weakened, fractured. . . . I miss New York dreadfully."

Feeling "trapped and desperate," she discharged some of her pent-up anger outward onto Barbara, which may have saved her from a complete emotional collapse. When Barbara repeatedly expressed concern over Andrea's unhappiness, holding herself responsible for having brought her to Florida in the first place, Andrea told herself that Barbara, being rich (at the moment she was in fact in debt, having refused to pay taxes during the Vietnam War), couldn't pos-sibly understand the hopelessness of someone entangled in poverty, incapable of leaving a place and situation she hated. When Barba-ra offered to reimburse her and John for the cost of a move back North, they accepted on the assumption that it was a gift; when it arrived in the form of a grant from Barbara's tiny Women's Fund,

Andrea angrily turned it down on the grounds, possibly realistic, that they couldn't afford to pay the taxes.

Andrea decided that Barbara "is very manipulative, and when manipulation doesn't work, resorts to lies"—not an estimate commonly shared; many regarded Deming as a secular saint. Throughout her conflict with Barbara, Andrea's mother, Sylvia, may or may not have consciously popped into Andrea's head but surely she lurked close nearby. Back in September, on their way to Sugar Loaf, Andrea and John had stopped in to see her parents at their home in Camden, New Jersey, and later Andrea described the scene in a letter: "Things have been very bitter with my mother . . . she wouldn't even look at me or sit at the same table with me . . . on the trip down, I did cry and cry for the way she treated me, and what she thought of me, and, truly, how she despised me. I can't even say the kind of misery it's caused me . . . I have felt this misery over and over again in my life."[13]

Barbara herself became deeply upset over Andrea's unhappy state. Sleeping badly, her stomach upset, she held herself responsible for not having sufficiently prepared for Andrea's needs; she felt certain that she'd "grievously let her friend down" (Barbara's partner, Jane Gapen, scornfully disagreed, describing Andrea as "a 2 year old . . . with murder in her heart"). Before coming to Sugar Loaf, Barbara felt that she and Andrea "had been in such very deep communion," and Andrea had felt the same, writing to a friend that Barbara was a "magnificent" person. She tried to talk with Andrea about what had gone wrong between them, and revealed her own "anguish at having hurt" her. But Andrea seemed "traumatized," sullen, and unreachable.[14]

Perhaps the friendship, which had meant so much to both women, could have been saved if Andrea had more fully shared with Barbara the series of devastating blows that had recently befallen her, almost simultaneously, severely jeopardizing her self-image as a writer and making her (in her own words) "crazy and strange and cantankerous." What had happened was that her agent, Elaine Markson, relayed word from *Ms.* magazine that its December 1976 issue would include both an article Andrea had submitted some months earlier *and* a positive review of *Our Blood*. The news had made Andrea briefly euphoric. "Yes, it's finally happened," she wrote a friend. "I have cracked" (*Ms.*, that is). Andrea and John haunted the mailbox, nerves on edge, awaiting imminent deliverance.

And then the news arrived: the December *Ms.* did contain Andrea's article, but not the review. When Elaine made inquiries she was told the review was now scheduled for the February issue. Andrea was "heartbroken"; by February, she knew, *Our Blood* would no longer be in bookstores; besides, the actual appearance of the review, known to be positive, was crucial to a pending paperback sale. Before Andrea could absorb the bad tidings, they deepened: rereading her article in *Ms.* she discovered it had been printed with *the wrong ending*, "a clumsy, discarded one." She felt violated—and enraged. The only possible explanation, Andrea decided, was deliberate sabotage.

She put in an angry call to Letty Cottin Pogrebin, one of the founding editors of *Ms.*, who was horrified, and had no explanation. Then it got still worse: when Andrea calmed down enough to read the piece carefully she discovered that someone had added a few words to the wrong ending "to improve it"—but which in Andrea's view didn't. Her contract with *Ms.* had guaranteed that nothing could be added or deleted without her written permission (Andrea was always a stickler on this point). Why hadn't the contract been honored? No one could provide a satisfactory answer. "I'm enraged and powerless," Andrea told her sympathetic friend Leah Fritz—"thoroughly screwed once again by my darling sisters at *Ms.*" The magazine, she concluded, was "a pestilence."

"I am deadly down, I don't know what to do," Andrea wrote another friend. For weeks she felt "bitter and demoralized," staring at the walls, going "slowly mad with choked up rage." Then she remembered—or in her desperate state invented—the sardonic advice Muriel Rukeyser had given her when *Woman Hating* was about to be published: "If you want Hal Scharlatt to push your book, you'd better sleep with him." A Eureka moment (if more than a bit bizarre). And who would that "right person" be? She came up with an answer, bitterly ironic, perhaps deadly serious: "Well, frankly, Joe [Chaikin—who was gay] who could then call his friend Susan Sontag and his friend Martin Duberman and his friend Elizabeth Hardwick and his friend this one and his friend that one. A few dinners, a few parties, a few whorish adventures. Oh, I'm sick with the fury of it."[15]

John pushed hard for "an emergency trip to New York"—not, obviously, to sleep around, but rather, more realistically, to meet with various feminist friends, tell them the truth of her plight of being penniless and worn down, and ask for help, especially in trying to rescue *Our Blood* from near oblivion. Andrea agreed to go and—quite miraculously, given her state of mind (and lack of funds)—actually made the trip, met with various friends and admirers, and discovered—and it was this, not the attempted salvaging of *Our Blood*, that would prove her real deliverance—that "many people seemed willing to do what they could. Every one greeted me in a way I'm not used to . . . like Someone Important. There was much genuine affection and genuine respect."

The trip produced no tangible result—no promise of additional reviews, no paperback sale for *Our Blood*—but, more important, it did raise Andrea's spirits: after a long, obliterating silence, people had praised her, told her that her work mattered, made her feel that she *did* exist as a writer. Returning to Sugar Loaf, she now found enough energy to send off a few cautiously timid letters to well-placed feminist writers like Louise Bernikow (who edited the 1979 anthology *The World Split Open*) and, at the suggestion of *Ms.*'s Pogrebin, Ellen Goodman, the syndicated columnist at the *Washington Post*, asking if they might consider doing a review of *Our Blood*. She even managed to start writing again and by mid-January 1977 had completed a new article, "Why So-Called Radical Men Love and Need Pornography." She sent it off to the *Village Voice*, and dared to tell herself that it stood a good chance of being accepted. The *Voice* didn't want it, but the *Soho Weekly News*—then a popular counter-cultural publication—was pleased to publish it; and from there *Gay Community News*, the most influential of the left-leaning gay papers, reprinted it.

It was an imposing piece, thunderous in its dissection of the murderous interface between fathers and sons, and satisfyingly pierced with some stunning, haunting phrasing that lifts it above the crustacean bed of psychoanalytic theory. The article was apparently designed to serve all at once as a commemoration of the rebellious sons who'd refused service in the Vietnam War, who'd rebelled against their fathers' celebration of murder as "solace . . . stilling their sobs as they mourn the emptiness and alienation of their lives." Simultaneously, the piece was a lament for what had become of those rebellious sons in the aftermath of the war, when they were "no longer carefree boys, wildly flushed by the discovery of their penises as instruments of pleasure." As they'd aged, as impotence and loss replaced exuberance, they turned back to their fathers' world, "bonded with the fathers who had tried to kill them," rejoined the male culture in which "slow murder is the heart of eros, fast murder is the heart of action, and systematized murder is the heart of history." And in that return, the once-rebellious sons necessarily rejected "the revolutionary militancy of the women" who had supported their struggle, re-allied instead with the "institutionalized brute force" wielded by their fathers and discovered that "the perfect vehicle for forging this alliance was pornography," a realm where "male virility never waned" and where "images of rape and torture" were the reliable instruments "to terrorize women into silence."[16]

For a time, it looked as if Andrea's larger work-in-progress, her novel *Ruins*, would also find a home. A small feminist publisher on the west coast, Moon Books (whose distributor was Random House), expressed enthusiasm for the manuscript. Having worked on the book off and on for three years, Andrea was delighted at the interest, and yet suspicious of it, sensing—accurately, it would turn out—the phantom nature of Moon's resources and its unlikely staying power. Soon after, June Arnold, who ran the much more prominent feminist press, Daughters, Inc., asked to see the novel— and then also turned it down: "Our old-fashioned preference [is] for novels with story-line and characters," she wrote Andrea. In other words, Andrea thought, I'm not "old-fashioned."

Arnold, who was rather widely seen in feminist circles as more than a little tyrannical, had earlier rejected *Woman Hating*, informing Andrea at the time that she couldn't publish her because she "wrote like a man." Then, in the fall of 1976, Arnold wrote an article in the feminist journal *Quest* denouncing women writers who published with establishment—which is to say, male-dominated—presses, and advising readers not to buy or review *any* book written by such a woman. The article deeply upset Andrea, and she held Arnold at least partly responsible for the fact that *Our Blood* was largely ignored in the feminist press. She wondered how Arnold rationalized the fact that she herself advertised in the mainstream, male press—including, recently, a very expensive full page ad in the *New York Times*.

It took many months before Andrea's anger subsided to the point where she was able to write Arnold directly, telling her that she felt the article in *Quest* had personally maligned her; "You yourself," she wrote Arnold, "have economic resources on which to draw"— indeed, Arnold was an independently wealthy woman—"while others, like myself, have lived lives of economic misery and desperation . . . It is very terrible for me . . . to be undermined by you." Frankly, she wrote Arnold, "I have had many second thoughts about whether you and I could ever work together. I've decided that, for myself, the only way to find out would be to get together and have a conversation and see whether the mutual respect that would be necessary to such an undertaking does exist." Arnold wrote back to say that it had never been her intention to cut off potential publishing possibilities for Andrea; the thesis of her *Quest* article was that women who published "with male controlled presses" did so to win "male esteem." Andrea replied that what she desired wasn't "male esteem" but rather "food and shelter, the resources to go on writing"; she looked forward to the day "when survival is secure enough that I can do anything for the esteem of anyone."

The two women did finally arrange a meeting to talk over the issues between them and during it Arnold remarked that Andrea was (as Andrea quoted her to a third party) "one of the writers she is building a feminist press for." Andrea immediately sent her a revised copy of *Ruins*—and then waited. It was not until May 1977 that Arnold finally responded, but with the old familiar message: "although our respect for you as a writer remains high, we are turning down our chance to publish *Ruins*. . . . I know that many women prefer to write and read letters, journals, diaries . . . [but] we still find those forms (or unforms) lacking in something for us—tension, dramatic interchange between women, publicness . . ." (Arnold didn't pause to define those vaporous terms).

She did feel sure, Arnold added, that "most other presses don't have our hang-up and furthermore we know that anything you write will sell well"—though in fact she knew that the opposite had thus far been true—"so I don't think you will have any trouble finding a publisher—if it has to be the boys, that's that." ("I think it's called being thrown to the dogs," Andrea remarked.) To June Arnold, she wrote, "Turn down the book if you must, but don't give me glib, meaningless assurances based on a complete misunderstanding of my situation." Well, Andrea decided finally, Arnold's reaction wasn't very surprising: the feminist press was "too small not to have its own orthodoxy." She felt the "male" presses—meaning all the big ones—were "out front: they have power and they use it—they are the guardians of proper thought, proper expression." Sadly, so were the feminist presses, but "they gloss it over, aren't honest with writers or themselves."

Andrea recounted all this to Gloria Steinem in response to a letter from her asking if Andrea had any unpublished work that *Ms.* might consider. "The question," Andrea wrote back, "brings me to tears." Yes, she gratefully replied, though "not a very prolific writer—I write very slowly and do only one thing at a time"—she had several pieces that she'd be glad to show Gloria, including a speech she was preparing on pornography. They made plans for dinner.

Thanks to Steinem, and a few other loyal friends and admirers, the smooth disdain of a June Arnold didn't lie like a rock in Andrea's gut, incapacitating her. The dead end that had made Andrea feel entrapped gave way to renewed energy, allowing her to entertain at least marginal optimism that new prospects would open up for her in the near future. Her increased vitality helped to make her again more available for deeper intimacy in her friendships, and particularly with Joanne Kastor.[17]

The two had initially met at a Gay Academic Union meeting a few years earlier, and for a time in 1977–78, the friendship passed over into something more like a romance, with, for a brief time, a rather skittish sexual component. "I want to be yr lover, now, for as long as I can imagine. I want you very much," Andrea wrote to

Joanne at the insecure high point of enthusiasm—one that Joanne seems never to have reached: "I don't think I could have 'casual sex' with you once a year and want you the rest of the year." Both women seem to have been ambivalent from the start about broadening the friendship into a full-blown affair. The very qualities that Joanne most admired about Andrea—"the purity, clarity, and tenacity with which you have clung to your beliefs"—weren't likely to make her available for the kind of daily compromising essential to an ongoing relationship. On Andrea's part, her ability fully to trust another person with her well-being—John was the one exception—had as a result of her ruinous relationship with Iwan been markedly damaged: she was quick to anticipate being hurt or misled in advance of any actual threat, or to magnify deception if it did appear.

Besides, as she warily reminded Joanne, both of them "are overcommitted and single-minded about work" and unavailable for the frequent get-togethers of a "normal" affair. Joanne agreed: "I can't deal with a sexual relationship now . . . [though] I don't want to close the door forever." Their friendship remained close through the seventies, dwindled in the eighties to a more casual and occasional connection, and then petered out. In Andrea's case, there's no more than the barest hint in her later correspondence of any other sexual encounter or dalliance; the absence of reference in her letters to female lovers doesn't mean that none existed; she may simply have opted for discretion. Still, her highly charged erotic youth seems in adulthood—perhaps as a result of trauma from Iwan's brutality—to have primarily given way to periodic *frottage* with John (who, unlike Andrea, *did* remain sexually active with his male partners).

Shortly after the encounter with June Arnold, a quite unexpected sort of offer came along. Andrea's agent, Elaine Markson, who would prove phenomenally active on her behalf, decided to encourage a close friend to start a lecture booking agency, and offered up Andrea as the friend's first client. It really was (as Andrea called it) "a magnificent stroke": Andrea was a superbly dynamic speaker, and within weeks she had two speaking engagements, one at the University of Massachusetts as part of International Women's Week, and the other "a partial benefit" for a woman's restaurant. The latter netted Andrea a paycheck of exactly $81.45, but the UMass talk "Pornography: The New Terrorism" drew about a hundred people, and Andrea's fee came to a substantial $250. It marked a promising new start, and in several directions: her speech so energized the audience that women came up to hug and kiss her at the close, and the following day forty-five people who'd heard her talk successfully prevented a porn film from opening at a local movie house.[18]

By this point, Andrea and John had finally managed to leave Sugar Loaf Key, and had relocated in Cummington, a small rural community in western Massachusetts. During Andrea's trip to New York some months earlier, John had taken on the selfless, tedious task of sending off applications for residency in one of the well-known writers retreats—MacDowell, Yaddo, or the Millay Colony. That first tier hadn't been receptive but, lowering their expectations, John and Andrea had somehow managed to locate a Community of the Arts in Cummington (billed as "an environment congenial to creative activity") that put out the welcome mat; they accepted in a flash. *Getting* there, however, proved no easy feat.

Though by this time inured to hardship, the trip to Cummington took on a dimension all its own. About twelve miles out from their destination, the used car they'd bought for $200, along with a rented U-Haul, started to slip and slide on the snow-covered, icy roads. They had to stop and hire a tow truck for the last part of the journey—except the truck itself got stuck on a hill, and they spent hours digging it out. The U-Haul then promptly buried itself in yet another snow bank and couldn't be pried loose. They were forced to abandon it until the next day. Only one woman from the Cummington community offered to help them unload, and the three laboriously carried the U-Haul contents, one piece at a time, up a precarious snow-covered hill.[19]

Andrea quickly sized up the place: "a lot of ignorant, sadistic males and their colonized docile women." It was an inauspicious but accurate forecast of what lay ahead. The refusal of help, it turned out, had been deliberate: the men in the community—and it was composed primarily of men—had read both Andrea and John (who'd also begun to write) prior to their arrival and been incensed. Though the community advertised itself as a place where artists could stay for a few months, in practice it had become a permanent home for a bunch of what Andrea called zombie men, "mean dead-heads." One of them, a relatively young man, "punished"—hit, beat, and kicked—a cat in front of Andrea, an animal lover, for the "odi-ous crime" of having gotten into the beans.

For Andrea, the worst of it was that the few women in residence proved obedient allies of the men, dutifully serving their needs and keeping their mouths shut. Even had Andrea been willing to try, there was no way she could make herself innocuous. And she wasn't willing to try. Going into the bathroom one night, she found a mag-azine called *Cheri*, "disgusting from beginning to end," which high-lighted a series of photos of a woman mutilating herself—cutting off a nipple with scissors, cutting into her breast with a long knife, and finally putting the knife into her vagina. Shaking with rage, Andrea and John burned the magazine to ashes.

Since everyone in the community had to volunteer for certain tasks, Andrea and John took it upon themselves to reorganize the community library, and did so by dividing it into books by men and books by women; the end result was 273 shelves devoted to men, and 29 to women. Andrea and John decided to leave nearly a full wall labeled "Reserved for Books by Women to Be Acquired." The men in the community freely vented their anger over the episode, and Andrea felt their situation had become precarious. They made a hasty exit, heading straight to Northampton, home to Smith Col-lege, which they knew was a safe haven for outspoken women and their allies.[20]

5

The Gathering Storm

"The months of difficulty," Andrea wrote her friend Elsa Dorfman, the photographer, "are being shed, bit by bit," though for the first two weeks of living in Northampton she had "nothing but nightmares." Even after becoming more acclimated, the lack of money remained an acute worry. They had just enough for a deposit on a place to live, though not enough to afford any furnishings other than mattresses to sleep on the floor—not even chairs, not even a decent pair of shoes (Andrea had to stuff Ace bandages in the old pair, and her feet were "in awful shape"). She and John promptly applied for food stamps. On top of all that, she was ridden with guilt about still being deeply in debt to various friends. "I'm absolutely raw with worry," she wrote a friend, "worry that's gone on over years and years, worry that never stops."[1]

She and John thought that by living "with absolute niggardliness" they could survive for two months. In the interim, they hoped to find *some* new source of income, though Andrea couldn't bear the idea of going back to menial work like typing. Over the past few years, John had become increasingly involved in helping other feminist-minded men set up supportive organizations and publications ("Men Against Pornography"), and had begun as well his own career as both speaker and writer; he also worked briefly for Northampton's Family Planning Council as a rape prevention educator. Yet the point finally arrived when he and Andrea ran out of options for earning money. Andrea held out hope that she could find some kind of teaching job, but soon discovered that nothing was immediately available. Elaine Markson managed to arrange a meeting with Lewis Lapham, editor-in-chief at *Harper's Magazine*, to discuss a possible article on pornography. Lapham had earlier turned down Andrea's work as too feminist and "not civil libertarian enough," but Elaine thought he was simply confused by it and urged Andrea to make a quick trip to New York.

She did, but nothing tangible came of it. When, soon after, two friends of hers turned down her request to do a reading at their bookstore, her desperation peaked: "It turns out over and over," she bitterly wrote, "that one can count on nothing." Despairing, Andrea hatched a highly improbable plan. She took her "very last money," rented Harvard's Loeb Student Center for the single day of June 10, 1977, and gave a reading from her unpublished novel, *Ruins*. The hope was to do several things simultaneously: to raise a few hundred dollars for herself, a few hundred for her close friend Eleanor Johnson's new feminist theatre company, Emmatroupe, and, finally, to stir up some general interest in getting more of her work published. The plan for a reading, she wrote Gloria Steinem, "is kind of all or nothing."

It turned out to be nothing—or very nearly so. Despite putting out a press release and pasting up flyers, the turnout wasn't even large enough to pay for the hall, and Andrea ended up further in debt than ever. It left her feeling "bitter" and "confused"—"I don't know how to make money, I don't know what to do." Gloria Steinem did. She was so alarmed at Andrea's plight that she came through with a personal loan of $2,000. Acknowledging it, Andrea told Gloria that "a terrible and terrifying pressure" had been lifted for at least a time: "yr. kindness means to me—everything"; and to a third party Andrea described Gloria as "just such a fine and generous woman." (Among others who "loaned" money to Andrea at various times were Letty Cottin Pogrebin and Shere Hite.)[2]

Gloria's loan raised Andrea's spirits, energizing her enough

to do some renewed political work. She joined Gloria and Adrienne Rich in preparing a statement meant to spur a new initiative
regarding pornography. The plan was to form a national Women's
Anti-Defamation League and to drum up support for it through
a full-page ad in the *New York Times*. Andrea prepared most of
the text for the ad. They circulated it to a number of prominent
feminists for comment and possible amending. The purpose of the
League itself, as the cover letter described it, was "to bring pressure through exposé reporting, legal action and civil disobedience,
until the popular images of violence and humiliation now directed
against women of all ages, races, and groups are tolerated no more."

Steinem, Rich, and Dworkin spelled out as well their wish "to
encourage, not suppress, accurate reporting on sexual expression,
sexual options, and sexual freedom. We want children to grow up
without the threat of being exploited and abused as sexual play-
things and sexual entertainment. We want a world in which men
can live without the pornographic incitements to 'masculine' violence that now saturate male-controlled media. We want women to
live without the fear and rage that come from seeing our humiliation sold as entertainment."[3]

The statement put particular stress on what had long been the
most prominent argument *against* placing restraints on pornographic imagery: the First Amendment's guarantee of free speech. The
League statement did affirm the amendment's cardinal importance
but insisted that it be weighed against pornography's "threat to our
physical safety and emotional well-being": the amendment "was
never intended to protect pornographic images: the rape, humiliation, torture and murder of women for erotic entertainment. . . . We
would draw the line wherever violence or hostility toward women
is equated with sexual pleasure. We would draw the line wherever
children are sexually exploited. We do not oppose sex education,
erotic literature or erotic art." Nearly all those sonorous declara-
tions, seemingly obvious on their face, required further definition.
How does one measure humiliation? When we mention children,
precisely what age do we have in mind? Can violence itself be caus-
ally isolated as the source of sexual pleasure? And so forth. As would
quickly become apparent, every attempt to clarify and define would

involve a host of subjectivities, and in the years ahead debate over "where to draw the line" would produce rancorous contention within the movement and antagonistic opposition from without.

By inviting open comment and criticism on the ad, they produced a mini-flood of letters and phone calls suggesting alternate wording, the inclusion of *this*, and the exclusion of *that*. All of which was probably expected, even viewed as inevitable: political action groups, notoriously, often have to tread water while "the fine points"—the wording of a manifesto, the color of a banner, the designated line of march—are hashed over, then rehashed again and again until finally nailed down. Which is sometimes never.

And so it was with the Women's Anti-Defamation League. "Conflicts . . . are tearing us all apart," Andrea wrote the early lesbian activist Martha Shelley, who'd seen her share of contention in the post-Stonewall Gay Liberation Front. To some extent divisions within a social justice movement are part of the process itself— they give legitimate expression to the diversity of backgrounds and values of the individuals involved. But when divisions are too prolonged and deep, or become too personalized, protracted negotiation can prove destructive.[4]

After the first full exchange of opinions over the Anti-Defamation League's intentions, Adrienne Rich, for one, was feeling more than a bit deluged: "To date I have received comments from Barbara Myerhoff and Susan Brownmiller (their rewrite of the statement); from Barbara Deming and Jane Verlaine [Gapen], both of whom feel they can 'live with' the original statement; a phone call from Robin Morgan in Chicago promising minor written comments on her return but saying that essentially she thought it a good statement; a promise from Jane Alpert, who is moving house, that she'll send written comments soon; ditto from Grace Paley; two negative reactions to the Brownmiller-Myerhoff rewrite from Karla Jay and Leah Fritz. Also a note of legal advice from Jan Goodman." Andrea also objected—"adamantly"—to the Brownmiller/Myerhoff rewrite of the original statement, and said flat-out that she "won't go along with it."

Conflict was further heightened when the novelist Lois Gould published a "HERS" column in the *New York Times* calling for flexibility and compromise even when dealing with women who opposed the ERA, abortion, and gay rights. Susan Brownmiller came out in support of Gould's stance, but she was nearly alone, though Leah Fritz characterized Gould as having meant no harm. Yet Fritz, too, thought Brownmiller's response "slightly screwy" and for good measure wrote Andrea that Susan was "jealous of you because she knows everyone respects your work on an artistic level." Andrea herself wrote to the *Times* denouncing Gould for ignoring "the threat of the [Anita Bryant's] Save Our Children campaign to the civil rights and safety of all despised minorities as well—male homosexuals, Blacks, Jews."

At another point, Leah Fritz brought up the fact that there were no black women at their meetings, which caused considerable consternation, but no plan of action for remedying the situation. The internal debate went on for so many months over so many doctrinal differences and so many stylistic quibbles that Andrea later characterized the attempt to organize as "a study in powerlessness . . . their inability to take a stand because of all the things they think they're taking into account." Ultimately burn-out set it, and the Women's Anti-Defamation League proved stillborn.[5]

During the prolonged round robin of letters and phone calls Andrea had sometimes sounded sternly resistant to changes in the original statement, yet her mood throughout was decidedly upbeat: active engagement—no matter its controversial nature—was precisely what she'd needed to pull out of the doldrums. During the course of debating the purpose of the Women's Anti-Defamation League she'd gone from isolation to multiple meetings, spirited exchanges, and in some cases new friendships—Susan Brownmiller, with whom she'd have considerable interaction in the near future, was among the prominent feminists she met for the first time.

Andrea's improved state of mind showed itself in various ways. Strictly a night person all her life, she started to get up at 5:30 in the morning in order to go running (which she'd first picked up, briefly, in Florida; it was the only exercise she ever enjoyed). She was also able to come to a firm decision that her next book would be on the subject of pornography, and promptly sent off a proposal to Elaine, who set up several meetings for her with New York publishers.

They didn't go well. Accused of advocating censorship, Andrea ran into "persistent political opposition . . . so rude and so blatant to upset me very deeply." She tried explaining that she was not advocating the repeal of the First Amendment or an end to free speech, but was instead pointing out that the vast majority of women did not, in their daily lives, have that right, that they'd been conditioned to internalize without complaint male values and domination. The result, Andrea argued, was that some of the main motifs of the heterosexual pornography industry—its torture chambers, whips, and chains—designed to please and entertain men (or a considerable subset of them) in fact terrified women, though they were afraid to say so. What about *their* right not to have to live in fear and remain silent? In 1977 the questioning—and the raging discord it engendered within feminist ranks—was in its infancy.[6]

Andrea had for some time been proposing to *Ms.* that she do a piece on "the female supremacy part of lesbian separatism," formulating it as a challenge to the whole notion of biological determinism. The idea for the piece had originated in a panel she'd participated in a few months earlier—her fellow panelists had been the high-powered trio of Betty Powell, Ginny Apuzzo, and Bertha Harris, and the topic, "Lesbianism: A Personal Politic." At the time, Andrea had made it clear to the audience that she was speaking distinctly as a Jew and as a woman who denied any biological basis for the supremacy or inferiority of any single group of people. Her views were not well received, and she was "hissed, booed, and called a slut," which convinced her more than ever that she had to take on the mythology that had been developing among lesbian separatists that "men are a different species, inferior to women."[7]

Andrea was also deeply sympathetic to the heightened complaint of women of color that their special perspectives and needs were being consistently ignored by the mainstream feminist movement. They'd become used to white feminists declaring, even fervently, their anti-racism, all the while ignoring how their racial privilege skewered the way they shaped the feminist agenda. In 1977 the Combahee River Collective issued its now-historic "A Black Feminist Statement," calling upon women of color to organize around their own agenda, one that acknowledged the interlocking oppressions of gender, race, and class unfamiliar to middle-class white feminists. Rejecting separatism as a strategy, the Combahee Collective affirmed their alliance with black men in the struggle against racism.

At the same time, yet for different reasons, Andrea stopped working in combined lesbian and gay male groups (like the Gay Academic Union in which she'd earlier been briefly involved) because of the "psychic" bullying that she'd seen gay men exert not only over lesbians but also over gay men with feminist convictions (like John Stoltenberg). She was also repelled by the common if unspoken view that "it's unmanly to be influenced in any way by these women"—to her that implicitly echoed the insult of being called "a mama's boy."

Her longstanding antipathy to the view that maleness or femaleness were biologically determined categories led her to withdraw from "mixed movement gay work" altogether rather than lend even a semblance of encouragement to an ideology based on a belief in innate gender traits and capacities. It had been somewhat different and better in the early days of the post-Stonewall movement, but she no longer felt that gay men in general were currently much interested in winning equal rights for women; they seemed to her far more intent on aping the macho behavior of straight men. When the Equal Rights Amendment was defeated in Florida, Andrea acidly noted that "enraged male mourners did not flood the streets with either shouts or tears."

A particularly nasty skirmish erupted when John Mitzel, a prominent member of the radical Boston collective Fag Rag, attacked anti-porn feminists as being anti-sex. Andrea believed Mitzel's article had decidedly anti-Semitic and "boy-lover" overtones, and she rallied a variety of her feminist cohorts—including Gloria Steinem and Susan Brownmiller—to respond to his "vile" piece. Whatever Mitzel's individual sins, when Andrea characterized "boy-love" as "the new cause to which radical male homosexuals are devoting themselves," she was generalizing too broadly. There were precious few gay male radicals still around by the late seventies, and the Fag Rag collective wasn't representative of their views and activities.[8]

She of course acknowledged that there were exceptions—Allen Young (who co-authored a number of LGBT books with Karla Jay) was among her reliable friends—but Andrea felt that they were in a small minority. Though she continued to criticize mainstream gay male attitudes, she did occasionally publish in leftwing gay outlets, where feminism was at least somewhat understood and honored, and particularly in Boston's *Gay Community News* and Toronto's *The Body Politic*. In her article "The Power of Words," originally given as a speech but then published in *GCN*, Andrea argued that hatred of homosexuals permeated our society, but emphasized that contempt for lesbians "is most often a political repudiation of [all] women who organize in their own behalf to achieve public presence, significant power, visible integrity." The word "lesbian" was commonly used "to focus male hostility on women who dare to rebel, and it is also used to frighten and bully women who have not yet rebelled."[9]

"The Power of Words," representing as it did a form of lesbian activism, didn't typify Andrea's engagement with the large lesbian community in Northampton. Early on in her stay, she made the conscious decision to absent herself from participation in local politics. She did so reluctantly: she was in need of friends—all of her closest ones lived elsewhere, mostly in New York—and besides, there had locally been a series of vigilante attacks on lesbians by groups of men (one of them identified as the son of a prominent judge): eight lesbians had been raped within a short period of time, and the nearby Everywoman Center had been receiving threatening phone calls warning that "No woman is safe in Northampton." Andrea was not only indignant but fearful.

Yet she held back from involvement. She and John met people who individually they liked very much, but they *dis*liked the "separatist" overtones in general of the lesbian community in Northampton; Andrea believed in communication with the larger world and felt that ghettoization of any kind was misguided. The "ghetto," she wrote, "has always been a very unhealthy place—for Jews, blacks, etc.—and I don't think it's any healthier for lesbians. Voluntary association of people with like social problems is different than a fortress mentality born out of victimization." She felt that in meeting after meeting, separatists had "stopped discussion, the flow of

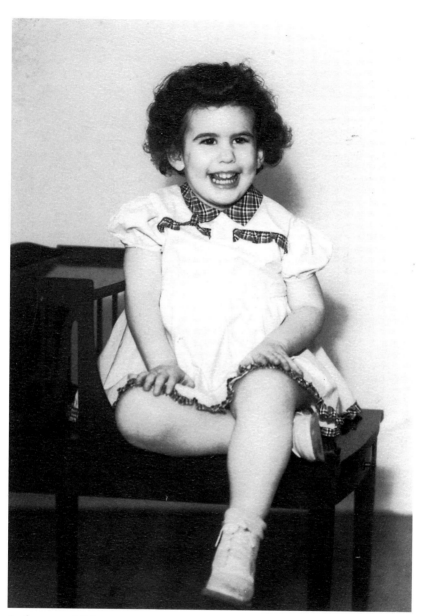

Andrea as a child

Andrea with her mother, Sylvia

Andrea with her father, Harry

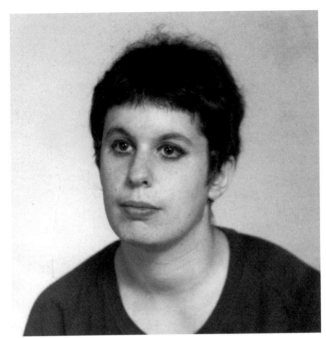

Andrea at
Bennington

At Iraklion, Crete, 1966

Iwan and Andrea's wedding, Amsterdam, 1969

Barbara Deming at a civil
rights demonstration (War
Resisters League Archives)

Andrea speaking in
Woodstock, 1974 (Diana
Davies Papers, Smith College
Special Collections)

With John Stoltenberg and
Gringo, Sugar Loaf Key,
Florida, 1976

Andrea with Grace Paley (to her right) at a "Snuff" protest in front of the
National Theater in Times Square, New York, early 1976

Andrea beside Bella Abzug at the October 20, 1979, WAP march. To Bella's
right is Robin Morgan, with Gloria Steinem right behind her

Robin Morgan, Susan Brownmiller, and Gloria Steinem at Women Against Pornography march in 1979 (Photo courtesy of Schlesinger Library, Radcliffe Institute, Harvard University)

Andrea demonstrating against pornography in the French Quarter, New Orleans, 1984, with John Stoltenberg (in white pants)

WAP storefront, 1980, announcing the national boycott of *Deep Throat* (back row, left to right: not identified, Valerie Harper, Catharine MacKinnon; front row: Linda Marchiano, not identified, Andrea Dworkin)

Gloria Steinem in the *Ms.* office, 1980 (Gloria Steinem Papers, Smith College Special Collections)

Andrea testifying before the Attorney General's Commission on Pornography in 1986

Andrea with Allen Ginsberg at godson Isaac Dorfman Silverglate's bar mitzvah, April 21, 1990

Andrea with her brother Mark in Vienna shortly before his death from cancer, 1992

Andrea with her father, 1992

Andrea seated at her desk, October 2003 (Copyright © 2005 by John Goetz and The Estate of Andrea Dworkin)

Andrea and John Stoltenberg, October 2003 (Copyright © 2005 by John Goetz and The Estate of Andrea Dworkin)

Andrea Dworkin. December 12, 2003

Dorfman

Andrea post-surgery in 2003 (courtesy of Elsa Dorfman)

Andrea alone on a park bench (Copyright © 2005 by John Goetz and The Estate of Andrea Dworkin)

ideas, by intimidation of the meanest sort . . . hisses and shouts and clenched fists does intimidate people into conformity of both belief and action"—it was a case of "hurt and damaged people (which all women are) taking it out on each other."

The feminist community in Northampton also had a large contingent of therapists, but they, too, in Andrea's view, weren't sympathetic to "the kind of work I do, or its demands . . . it's like having to translate everything. There is no common vocabulary of work or work-related problems." In New York City, many movement people were themselves in the arts or had friends who were—they were "people who have some kind of audience or public presence" and didn't regard artists as "notably 'special.'" The feminist group in Northampton, being small, was "fairly incestuous"—meaning that anything one did rapidly became public knowledge, especially "if there is curiosity about the person." Andrea recognized that she was perhaps being "too self-protective," but she and John decided to remain pretty much apart from the local gay community. "The quiet consoles me," Andrea wrote a friend. "It's the only way I stay vaguely balanced."

By the end of the year, Andrea wrote her brother Mark, who was living and working in Europe, that "things are looking up, slowly, looking better than they have in quite a while." Reduced financial strain was part of the reason: the lecture bureau was having some real success in getting Andrea bookings. By early 1978, she was giving speeches roughly once a month, mostly on pornography, the venues varying as much as the fees: the University of Massachusetts gave her what was then the whopping fee of $1,000, the Valley Women's Martial Arts, Inc. came through with $800, the New Haven Women's Liberation Center with $500, and Yale $300. As always, Andrea prepared thoroughly, spoke with contagious passion, and left behind a newly converted group of admirers and feminist activists.[10]

With money issues less acute, renewed energy surfaced for writing—as did the hope, on which they'd kept a tight lid, of ending their isolation and moving back to New York City (though how they would survive once there still held them back). Andrea had known for some time that the next subject she wanted to write about was rightwing women. She wanted to explore at length her thesis that social conservatism "convinces women that they have protection from male assault, which is, according to this view, an *outside* danger. . . . The right wing presents the family as the only safe enclave. . . . What is wrong with this frame, of course, is that it is untrue, in that women are more often threatened by men of their own family . . . [and] by men of their own racial and economic groups."[11]

Working steadily, Andrea had a draft of an article in hand by late March 1978 and sent it to Gloria Steinem for possible publication in *Ms.* "With this piece, I feel I've found my wings again," she wrote Gloria in a covering letter. She undiplomatically added—feeling that she could speak frankly without risking their mutual regard—that "*Ms.* itself seems to want to clip writers' wings." Her article, Andrea acknowledged, was *very* long and unfortunately—as she wrote Gloria—"*Ms.* seems to be going in an entirely different direction . . . to my distress, the last issues seem to me so bland stylistically—even when the content is good, the writing is too tame, too all the same. I don't like it, and I don't want to fit into it . . . my writing won't amount to shit if I don't do it my own way, and that's just a fact."

This wasn't the standard prescription for buttering-up a potential publisher. Yet Gloria took it in stride, as Andrea probably knew she would—even though she added a provocative coda: "Gloria, I found myself thinking of giving up writing because the thought of conforming to demands of length and style that I don't like so depressed me." Gloria's integrity was a fair match for Andrea's own; she advised her to "stop thinking that I can somehow solve your reluctance [to accept cuts] with magic editing." Ultimately, Gloria stressed, "your commitment to me and to us is to *write*, and to do it exactly as it feels best and most possible." In regard to the article at hand, she confirmed Andrea's assumption: *Ms.* could only publish it "in a very much shortened form." But she enveloped the bad news with overall enthusiasm for the material: she found it so rich that she seconded Andrea's urge to expand the article into a book about rightwing women—and indeed within a few years Andrea would do exactly that, in the interim publishing an edited article-length version ("Safety, Shelter, Rules, Form, Love: The Promise of the Ultra-Right") in the June 1979 issue of *Ms.*

This wasn't the last time that Andrea made Gloria, in her position as editor-in-chief of *Ms.*, the target of complaint—though what Andrea called the "tenderness" she felt for Gloria to some extent stayed her hand. Over the years their run-ins were few, especially when put in the context of the trench warfare that periodically engulfed the feminist movement. But on at least one other occasion a serious conflict arose over what Andrea regarded as a breach of contract; she went so far—in a letter to Robin Morgan—as to accuse Gloria of "dishonesty" and "repeated lies." Having learned better over the years than to tamper with Andrea's prose without her express consent, Gloria—facing an eleventh-hour deadline, and following legal advice—rewrote a sentence in one of Andrea's articles, and for the word "Porsche" substituted "auto."[12]

It deeply upset Andrea. Ferdinand Porsche, head of the auto company, had been imprisoned for twenty months after World War II for war crimes (though never brought to trial), and in her *Ms.* article Andrea had deliberately called the firm out for its complicity in cooperating with the Nazis. To Andrea, establishing the linkage between the name "Porsche" and anti-Semitism was profoundly important. In response, Gloria implied that Andrea's extreme distress about the changing of a single word was disproportionate—which upset Andrea still more.

"If you believe that it is all trivial and that I wasted time and energy on something not very important," Andrea responded, "then I simply don't know how to be clear and understood, and I can't operate in a context that reduces my deepest concerns to a misguided personal overzealousness. I am absolutely lost . . . how can I hope to be understood and respected if you don't understand the issues involved here?" Gloria pleaded ignorance of the Porsche connection to the Nazis, and Andrea in turn repeated that "I care a great deal for you, as I told you. . . . Surely you must know that I have been a loyal friend, and that, while I must protect my work and my ethics, I do not want to harm either you or the magazine." Gloria never again touched a word of Andrea's prose without prior consultation, and Andrea never again found fault with her standards, either ethical or journalistic.

It was one thing to be writing again, but quite another to get the work published. Feminist outlets, except for Boston's *off our backs*, tended to follow June Arnold's dictum to turn down the work of those women who'd published in "male" media—a position that had infuriated Andrea, having been many times rejected by feminist outlets, including Arnold's own Daughters, Inc., leaving her no option other than turning to mainstream outlets. The situation was compounded in the late seventies by a pronounced nationwide shift to the right—including, it could be argued, the straight male left: with the Vietnam War behind it and the New Left no longer viable, the left shifted its primary energy not to supporting movements for racial, sexual, and gender equality but to nuclear disarmament, a struggle against right-to-work laws, and a commitment to "democratic socialism." The chief organizational exception was the New American Movement (NAM), which focused on community organizing and was somewhat receptive to feminist and black issues—though less so to gay rights. NAM's membership peaked in the late seventies at about four thousand (and in 1983 it would merge with Michael Harrington's Democratic Organizing Socialist Committee). The few independent journals on the left—*Radical America*, *The Guardian*, *In These Times*—had limited subscriptions and focused primarily on economic issues.

Ever since her negative experience with the *Liberation* and *WIN* collectives, Andrea had given up hope of interesting the male left in feminist issues. By 1976 the situation in the Middle East had given her an additional set of grievances; as she wrote a friend, "I feel rage at the male lefties who support the Arabs—who support social orders in which women are denied all rights and all dignity. I am also enraged by the Israelis, who betrayed basic social ideas . . . of gender equality and justice. . . . When I look at the Mid-East, I see what the Israeli women and the Arab women share, their common reality—poverty, crimes of violence (rape and wife-beating most particularly) . . . committed against them . . . not by men on the other side, but by husbands, fathers, brothers, and sons . . . I hate the left, which doesn't give a fuck about women, never has, and probably never will."[13]

Phyllis Schlafly's rightwing Eagle Forum and Anita Bryant's anti-gay campaign, Save Our Children, far more typified the national mood and agenda. The rising tide of social conservatism in the late seventies saw the defeat of the ERA, widespread assaults on affirmative action and social welfare legislation, and the nearly uniform rejection of gay civil rights ordinances—often by crushing margins. In California the so-called Briggs Amendment calling for the expulsion of gay teachers (and of any straight ones who presented homosexuality in a positive light) did eventually go down to defeat, but not before gathering some half-million signatories. Those who supported anti-gay initiatives also believed that God (or biology) had ordained separate spheres for men and women. They flooded into evangelical churches, whose pastors—Jerry Falwell most prominently—denounced homosexuality and feminism from the pulpit as threats to the nation's moral fiber, to traditional family values: the homebound woman and the patriarchal male.

Andrea may have recovered her vigor, but she was in a political landscape far more hostile than it had earlier been to radicalism of any sort. One case in point was the enflamed critical reception of *The Hite Report: A Nationwide Study of Female Sexuality* when it was first published in 1976. A revealing study of women's widespread dissatisfaction with the male view that vaginal penetration (rather than clitoral arousal) was the source of female sexual pleasure, the *Report* was roundly attacked—purportedly for its sampling errors but more fundamentally for its implied attack on male sexual competence.[14]

Andrea published a long letter defending Hite in *off our backs*, and she was appalled when the leftwing magazine *Seven Days* trashed Hite's book. She took it, justifiably, as yet more evidence of the general hostility to feminism among men on the left: "antifeminist and unrepentant. Callow. Hard. Against tenderness and questioning. Everything from a predetermined and rigid ideological viewpoint." She took exception to the increasing number of feminists who seemed to think (as Andrea put it in her own interview with Hite) "that if we don't frighten men, the opposition to social and sexual freedom for women will dissipate or lessen. Whereas, I think that opposition has to be described fully, confronted head on. . . . The left is . . . still as misogynistic as ever . . . [Some feminists] are concluding that if only we were *nicer*, the opposition would be nicer too. Militancy of spirit and action is [in fact] crucial in regaining lost ground . . ."

About the only leftwing male-dominated publication Andrea trusted was *Mother Jones*, which had first appeared in February 1976. She felt it had consciously decided to allocate "a definite amount of space for feature articles that are feminist, feminist-inspired, or feminist related," and she couldn't "think of another left magazine that has." Andrea's opinion of *Mother Jones* was further bolstered when they accepted for publication her article "A Battered Wife Survives" (though she thought silly the title they used, "The Bruise That Doesn't Heal"). In it, she recounted her own history—"On my twenty-fifth birthday . . . I was nearly dead, almost catatonic, without the will to live"—and then used her personal story to describe "the anger of the survivor" and her ability to "see through the social strategies that have controlled her as a woman, the sexual strategies that have reduced her to a shadow of her own native possibilities. She knows that her life depends on never being taken in by romantic illusion or sexual hallucination."[15]

She wrote, too, about the devastating isolation she'd felt when those closest to her had refused to believe the transparent evidence of her battering, "turning away" from her, "pretending not to see the injuries," including "my parents, dear god, especially my parents." Andrea had seen very little of her immediate family of late, and hadn't sent them most of the recent articles she'd published. But she felt she should forewarn her parents about the *Mother Jones* piece: subscriptions to the magazine had recently risen significantly, and it was available on mainstream newsstands. Rather than risk someone else telling them about it, and knowing it would upset and pain them, she decided to do so herself. In her letter to them she repeated what she'd often said before: "Whatever courage I have, or ability to realize my talent," she felt was due to them and she hoped they would appreciate her honesty in the article.

Her hope wasn't realized. Her parents, understandably enough, regarded the article as (in Andrea's words) "a slander against them, and have accused me of committing a 'foul' act." Her mother sent her a four-page letter denouncing her as "sick" and "rotten," and the incident may have contributed to Sylvia's hospitalization soon after for surgery—"My fault," Andrea wrote, "or is intended to seem, or has seemed so often that no one need hurl the accusation explicitly anymore. . . . So we are torn asunder, and I am drowning in the blame." It was "a replay of much that has happened other times, but this time I can't take it, and it has really devastated me. . . . Can't take this kind of punishment anymore. The ties are being cut, finally, by me. But the pain is excruciating."

In her determination to end contact, she included her brother, Mark. "I really do not want to be part of our family any more at all," she wrote him. "I am sick of being mistreated by mother and more recently, re my piece on being a battered wife, by father. Yr silence was eloquent too, especially since according to dad you read the letter mother sent me. He conveyed to me yr opinion that mother had a right to write what she wanted. Her right to do that was never in question. That was all I heard about you or in reference to you. Nothing from you . . . it doesn't mean much to me now. It can't be undone." In time, though, she and her brother did manage a somewhat circumscribed reconciliation, made easier by Mark's having settled in Vienna.[16]

Along with increasing attacks on feminism in the late seventies, there seems to have been a parallel rise in recrimination within the women's movement itself. Andrea, for one, had a particularly nasty falling out with Phyllis Chesler, the author of *Women and Madness*, who'd earlier gone out of her way to break the silence that had greeted *Woman Hating* by soliciting letters from prominent feminists praising the book. The flare-up between the two came after Phyllis told Elaine Markson—who was also Phyllis' agent—that Andrea had plagiarized her work. Elaine promptly told Phyllis to find another agent, and passed on the accusation to Andrea, who was hugely upset by it. Anyone who knew Andrea at all well was aware that she prided herself on her integrity. Possibly she did, unconsciously, elaborate on an idea that had originated with Phyllis, but any intentional plagiarism would have been so far out of character as to constitute a personality transformation. It was precisely Andrea's stubborn refusal to prevaricate—to dilute the absolute truth as she saw it—that often aroused resentment among those who preferred a more "judicious" approach.[17]

Andrea put the matter plainly in an unambiguous letter to Phyllis: "I am very distressed and very angry. . . . I did not steal yr ideas . . . I care about both yr life and yr work. I have tried to be a true friend to you in both areas. But there is a strain of emotional tyranny from you to me that I cannot stand . . . our friendship is, in my opinion, entirely betrayed by yr behavior. . . . In the future, in every feminist struggle, I will support you in every way I know how. Beyond that, I can give you nothing, I can promise you nothing."

Phyllis' response was to object to Andrea's "tough" tone, and to deny that she'd ever accused her of plagiarism. What she had said, Phyllis claimed, was that in her article Andrea had used images of Abraham and Isaac and of King Midas that she had herself laid out in a manuscript that she'd given Andrea to read. In any case, Phyllis insisted, she had made no *public* accusation, but had merely mentioned the peculiar similarities to a few mutual friends, like Eleanor Johnson and Elaine Markson. "I only wanted a tiny footnote of credit," Phyllis claimed. She was not, in any case, prepared to grant Andrea's wish that she "post a Papal Bull on some wall in your mind" absolving her of the plagiarism charge.

Andrea was having none of it. She pointed out to Phyllis that images of Abraham and Isaac and King Midas "are in the consciousness of everyone who has read or thought or been told stories as a child"—they were "part of our common cultural heritage, from which we all work"; she'd first written about Abraham and Isaac when she was ten years old! She was happy to learn that Phyllis had "never accused" her of plagiarism, though that "will possibly be news to Elaine and to Eleanor." Andrea got a terse response: "Let this be the last word. (Yes, let me have it if you can). I don't want to correspond with you."

Andrea sent her reaction instead to her friend Leah Fritz: "Phyllis's good qualities I have always seen. I wanted very much to be a true friend to her and was—part of being a true friend is not to let somebody walk all over you. . . . Phyllis seems to see 'friends' (allies) as ones who will do what she wants when she wants. She can't recognize other women as peers, only as needy ones who need her help (testimonies to her worth and power), and who, as a consequence, owe her obedience. She seems to me incapable of reciprocity. It's exactly *friendship* that she seems incapable of. Friendship, it seems to me, means that you recognize someone else as equal to but different from herself—that you respect not only their strengths but also their weaknesses, being cognizant of yr own." And there the matter heavily lay; there would be renewed contact in the years ahead, but never closeness.[18]

Thanks to an advance for a planned book on pornography, Andrea and John were able to return to New York City on July 1, 1978. She felt that they would "miss the roses, lilacs, and mountains here—the general peace. . . . But I have been intellectually very isolated . . . isolation from peers who are engaged in the same kind of struggle is particularly difficult." Luckily, she and John found "a very beautiful" old building at 231 Second Avenue, the neighborhood "rife with prostitution, pornography houses, pimps, and the like," but their own street well-lighted and with easy access to good public transportation. It had, too, many remnants of "the old Jewish lower East Side culture, and an honorable if very poor concentration of old people who never moved up and out. Of course, all sprinkled with the obligatory poor artists. And the black and Puerto Rican poor, stuck in a bankrupt city." John and some friends built some basic furniture out of "found" materials, and "worked their asses off" to turn what had been a "pigsty" into a comfortable apartment; for the first time in quite a while they actually had chairs to sit on. Andrea was home.[19]

6

Pornography

From nearly the start of the second-wave feminist movement in the late sixties, the issue of pornography as an expression of male sexism had been *an* issue; ten years later it had, in various incarnations, become *the* issue—and for Andrea herself a consuming one.[1]

Her own views on the subject underwent considerable revision over time. When in high school, she told an interviewer, she'd associated pornography with sexual rebellion against prudery, part of the counter-cultural assault on all vestiges of righteous propriety. Learning that many of the writers she most admired, ranging from Baudelaire to Mailer ("I defended Norman Mailer longer than any living human being on the face of the earth."), had been dismissed as pornographic only further convinced her that pornography, as she put it, "contained special, important, elite, pioneering knowledge—that it showed sexuality the whole conventional world had to keep from everyone." Since pornography seemed to have powerfully influenced many great male writers, it appeared to have "a very special value."[2]

The first time she'd devoted an entire speech to the subject was at UMass–Amherst in late 1977. She entitled it "Pornography: The New Terrorism," and it became a staple of her cross-country speaking tours, usually eliciting a fervent response in her audience. It was a short speech, but it embodied most of the themes that Andrea would henceforth emphasize: "women are a degraded and terrified people"; "the ideology that energizes and justifies this systematic degradation . . . is the ideology of biological inferiority"; "when pornographers are challenged by *women*, police, district attorneys, and judges punish the women, all the while ritualistically claiming to be the legal guardians of 'free speech.'" In fact, according to Andrea, the judiciary had become the legal guardians of male profit, male property, and phallic power: "what does it mean that yet again—and after years of feminist analysis and activism—the men (gay, leftist, whatever) who proclaim a commitment to social justice are resolute in their refusal to face up to the meaning and significance of their enthusiastic advocacy of yet another woman-hating plague?"[3]

In December 1978, Andrea gave a version of the speech at a day-long colloquium, "Obscenity: Degradation of Women Versus Right of Free Speech" at the New York University Law School. The *New York Times* covered the event, which consisted of a series of panels and individual presentations, and accurately summed up the occasion as "fierce." It followed hard on an exhilarating three-day conference in San Francisco in November 1978 that Andrea had kicked off with a stirring speech and which had culminated in five thousand women from thirty states marching through the city's "red light" district. Seeing Andrea in action for the first time, Susan Brownmiller promptly dubbed her "Rolling Thunder"; Brownmiller admitted that Andrea's "dramatized martyrdom and revival-tent theatrics never sat well" with her personally, but she deeply admired Andrea's courage.

The intoxicating emotion of the San Francisco event carried over into the colloquium at NYU only a few weeks later. It started at a high pitch—and remained there. The heightened emotion was established early on with a slide show prepared by a female NYU law student of women in chains, being mutilated, battered, and sexually abused; it drew gasps from the audience. The San Francisco group Women Against Violence in Pornography and Media (WAVPM), put on a comparable display in the lobby that featured sexually explicit and grotesque photographs of women from the pages of such best-selling magazines as *Playboy*, *Penthouse*, and *Hustler*. Yet another group of photographs was on display from a European magazine of a woman having sex with a pig.

In her own speech at the event—which according to the *New York Times* was "highly passionate"—Andrea characterized the current epidemic of images of women "bound, bruised and maimed" in movies, magazines, record jacket covers, posters, and books, as amounting to nothing less than "death threats to a female population in rebellion"; in her view men were meeting that rebellion—"now a reality throughout this country"—with "an escalation of terror." Yet women, she predicted, would not be silenced; they were instead developing a range of strategies to resist the further spread of sadistic pornography, including petitions, picketing, boycotts, "organized vandalism," speak-outs, teach-ins, and "campaigns and harassment of distributors and exhibitors of 'woman-hating films.'" Her speech drew a standing ovation.

Not everyone was smitten. Paul Chevigny, a well-known leftist lawyer, walked out in protest in the middle of Andrea's talk. He represented a number of First Amendment "absolutists" at the conference—not all of them male—who insisted (to quote one of them, Herald Price Fahringer) that although he "found pornographic material most distasteful personally," the Constitution's First Amendment guaranteed free speech, and he thought people "should have the right to see and read what they please."[4]

Fahringer's view was widely shared by those who were displeased with the hateful imagery in pornography but could see no way of mitigating its adverse effects without seriously compromising the sacrosanct First Amendment. When another, more sanguine male lawyer at the NYU conference confidently predicted that no action need be taken because "bad pornography will perish, and only good pornography—if there is such a thing—will survive," his remarks drew hisses from the audience. Yet another lawyer simply insisted that "obscenity is not free speech, so it's not protected by the First Amendment," though he neglected to define "obscenity" or to spell out how it differed from both "erotica" and "porn."

At this early stage in the decades-long struggle over pornography, some of the argument centered on the rather nebulous, even confusing, guidelines that the Supreme Court had laid down in its 1973 decision, *Miller vs. California.* In attempting to adjudge whether material was obscene, the Court had offered a three-part test: is it "patently offensive," "hard core" sexual conduct?; does it lack serious scientific, literary, artistic, or political value?; and does it appeal to the "prurient interest" of an average person, as defined by current community standards? The search for definitions of "offensive," "prurient," and the like produced considerable head-scratching and few firm answers.

Anti-porn feminists claimed that what *was* clear was the mounting consumption of pornography: in 1979 some 18 million men regularly bought soft-core pornography (it constituted 30 percent of all newsstand sales), and the adult movie industry drew three million viewers a week. What was also clear was the rise in violence against women: in the first four months of 1977, the number of *reported* rapes was up 60 percent over the previous year, and the number of battered wives seeking protection jumped 40 percent in a single year. Whether the rise in the consumption of pornography was linked to the comparable rise in violence against women would be a major ideological battle in the years ahead.[5]

Feminists concerned about the effect of pornographic imagery insisted that the First Amendment had been originally designed to protect the right of *political dissent* from governmental censorship. Besides, they added, neither the founders nor subsequent legal precedent had ever concluded that free speech was an *absolute* right; in a host of litigated cases, a number of restraints had been applied, including false advertising and public defamation. As Susan Brownmiller wrote in a 1979 column in *Newsday*, "We are not opposed to sex and desire . . . and we certainly believe that explicit sexual material has its place in literature, art, science and education. Here we part company rather swiftly with old-line conservatives who don't want sex education in the high schools, for example. . . . [Nor are we] saying 'smash the presses' or 'ban the bad ones', but simply 'Get the stuff out of our sight.'"[6]

Andrea, for her part, pointed out that "the government in all its aspects—legislative, executive, judicial, enforcement—has been composed almost exclusively of men. . . . Women have had virtually nothing to do with either formulating or applying laws on obscenity or anything else. In the arena of political power, women have been effectively silenced" (a charge accurate enough when made in 1979, though less so now). "We have even been criticized for picketing, the logic being that an exhibitor of pornography might cave in under the pressure, which would constitute a dangerous precedent. The men have counseled us to be silent so that 'freedom of speech' will survive. The only limitation on it will be that women simply will not have it—no loss, since women have not had it. Such a limitation does not 'offend' the First Amendment or male civil libertarians."[7]

Up to this point, the West Coast had taken much of the lead in anti-porn organizing. But Susan Brownmiller became convinced that New York City—"the home," as she put it, "of both Times Square *and* the national media"—was the only place to launch a national feminist anti-pornography movement. She took the initiative in inviting Lynn Campbell, a prime organizer on the West Coast, to relocate to New York and help launch the organization that became known as Women Against Pornography (WAP). In fairly short order, money was raised for Campbell's salary (Brownmiller and Adrienne Rich were especially generous contributors), an apartment for her was found, and a number of well-known feminist activists lent their support.

Andrea wasn't among them. "I just couldn't stand any more meetings," she said, nor any more of the intense back-biting that had characterized recent events (like the extended discussions for what ended up as the dead-in-the-water ad in the *New York Times* for the Women's Anti-Defamation League). That effort had consumed most of her energy, which she now wanted to devote to her new project—a full-length book on pornography. She also felt some philosophical differences with the WAP organizers. As she put it, "I had a problem with suggesting that erotic literature was a pure form of pornography." When Brownmiller insisted that WAP was strictly devoted to educational activities about porn and its impact, Andrea retreated to a different reason for not joining up: "I am not somebody who goes into a group and makes a place for myself," she truthfully told Susan. "I'm much shyer than that, which people don't know and that's true."[8]

Despite Andrea's occasional misgivings about WAP—and she didn't participate in any of its now-famous "porn tours" of the (pre-sanitized) Times Square area—she did take part in selected WAP events, including its two national conferences in the fall of 1979. The first, the East Coast Feminist Conference on Pornography, was held on the weekend of September 15–16, and a host of prominent feminists appeared. Among the conference highlights was the youthful legal-aid lawyer Wendy Kaminer's lucid presentation of what she believed should be WAP's relationship to the First Amendment: "We respect First Amendment strictures against the imposition of prior restraints on any form of expression, and we do not wish to deprive pornographers of their due process rights. We do not advocate the summary closings of businesses that deal in pornography. . . . We respect the right of all adults to read or view what they choose in the privacy of their own homes. We have not put forth any repressive legislative proposals. . . . The Supreme Court has traditionally held that 'obscenity' is not protected speech, but the Court has struggled with the formulation of a fair and workable definition of obscenity. . . . We want to change the definition of obscenity so that it focuses on violence. . . . Pornography is not a harmless outlet for sexual fantasies. It is fascistic, misogynist propaganda that fosters acts of violence against women." Kaminer, in her brief presentation, had both outlined WAP's current position on pornography *and* forecast the divisions that would arise among feminists over very nearly every assertion in her statement—and would in short order fiercely divide the movement.[9]

For the time being, Andrea was willing to participate in both of the two WAP-sponsored conferences, but was suspicious of aspects of both. A lot of the money that WAP had thus far raised came from the generosity of individuals, but some of it had come from sources whose primary interest in supporting the group's activities had little or nothing to do with feminism. Among the contributors were Off-Track Betting, the League of Theater Owners, and, most controversial of all, the 42nd Street Redevelopment Corporation (the latter also provided WAP with free office space in Times Square). The main concern of such "benefactors" was "cleaning up" the Times Square area—closing down the massage parlors, porn theaters, and street prostitution that dominated the district and made its commercial redevelopment—otherwise known as the advance of capitalism—more difficult.[10]

An additional point of controversy was the $10 charge WAP levied for getting on its mailing list. For some women—certainly for Andrea—$10 (the rough equivalent of $100 today) was not their idea of loose change. WAP recognized as much and waived the fee for those willing to do volunteer work for the conference. But that smacked of "work in exchange for welfare"; combined with the absence at the conference of literature available in Spanish and the mere scattering of black and Third World women in attendance (or on WAP's mailing list, which by the time of the second conference had grown to some nine thousand), it gave alarming credence to the charge that WAP was an organization for middle-class whites.

Another point of controversy was WAP's position—or lack of one—on prostitution. Having prostituted herself from time to time as a young woman, Andrea was sympathetic to those forced to sell their bodies out of economic necessity. Several prostitutes and topless dancers gave testimony at the NYU conference about their lives, and there was a common thread in their stories: prostitution was a job for women who had few other options. One attendee insisted that some women like being prostitutes; another said it "isn't all that different from marriage"; a third added—to appreciative laughter—that "when you're talking about pimps, some are nice—just like there are some nice husbands." WAP had taken no official stand on prostitution one way or the other, but several women at the conference warned that it should be treated not as a question of morality but of economics, and that if WAP wanted to get women out of prostitution they would have to provide immediate practical aid, like housing, job training, employment, food, and money.

The central source of contention revolved around the issue of censorship. WAP had received overtures from various rightwing anti-porn groups that also had on their agendas a determination to fight abortion and homosexuality. One speaker at NYU cautioned the attendees that "the enemy of our enemy is not our friend" and warned WAP to think carefully about advocating any position that hinted at attempted censorship. Bella Abzug spoke to the issue with her usual confidence: "My position on pornography is not contrary to my lifetime position as a civil libertarian. I do not believe it is necessary for us to interfere with anyone's constitutional right to produce pornography. But that doesn't require us to encourage and assist in the proliferation of pornographic materials on the streets and in the stores."

What about pornography that portrayed *violence* against women? Did it not thereby encourage rape and battering? Dorchen Leidholdt, a former rape crisis counselor and one of WAP's founders, presented the conference attendees with specific data linking porn and violence: some one hundred psychiatrists, she noted, had reported to the 1967 Commission on Pornography that in their practices they had male patients who felt strongly that pornography *had* incited them to heightened aggression against women. She quoted as well the work of two academic psychologists, Ed Donnerstein and Neil Malamuth, whose research suggested a connection between the viewing of violent pornography and the triggering of "real-life" physical attacks against women. But others in the audience challenged that connection and criticized WAP for failing to offer a concrete definition of "pornography"—and jumping off from that, a coherent policy statement on the issue.[11]

In one of the many NYU workshops, the respected political essayist Ellen Willis vigorously insisted that pornography and violence were *not* interrelated: "You cannot define pornography," she said, "as any eroticism you don't like." In an influential article she wrote for the *Village Voice* immediately after the conference, Willis spelled out her views: "There are many varieties of porn, some pernicious, some more or less benign . . . nearly all porn is sexist in that it is the product of a male imagination and aimed at a male market. . . . If feminists define pornography, per se, as the enemy, the result will be to make a lot of women ashamed of their sexual feelings and afraid to be honest about them. And the last thing women need is more sexual shame, guilt, and hypocrisy—this time served up as feminism."[12]

WAP organizers, Willis went on, maintained that pornography is not really about sex but about violence against women, and made much of the fact "that Charles Manson and David Berkowitz [Son of Sam] had porn collections. . . . But if *Hustler* were to vanish from the shelves tomorrow, I doubt that rape or wife-beating statistics would decline." Willis recounted the distinction Robin Morgan and Gloria Steinem had made at the conference between pornography and erotica. Porn, they'd argued (in Willis' words), "reflects a dehumanized sexuality based on male domination and exploitation of women," whereas erotica expresses "an integrated sexuality based on mutual affection and desire between equals."

In Willis' opinion, the distinction failed to hold up: the erotica-versus-porn approach, in her view, "endorsed the portrayal of sex as we might like it to be and condemned the portrayal of sex as it too often is, whether in action or only in fantasy. But if pornography is to arouse, it must appeal to the feelings we have, not those that by some utopian standard we ought to have . . . the view of sex that most often emerges from talk about 'erotica' is as sentimental and euphemistic as the word itself: lovemaking should be beautiful, romantic, soft, nice, and devoid of messiness. . . . This goody-goody concept of eroticism is not feminist but feminine."

Furthermore, according to Willis, "in the movement's rhetoric pornography is a code word for vicious male lust. To the objection that some women get off on porn, the standard reply is that this only shows how thoroughly women have been brainwashed by male values." The crusade against pornography, Willis predicted, will bolster "the good girl–bad girl split." She accused Susan Brownmiller and other WAP organizers as endorsing the Supreme Court's contention "that obscenity is not protected speech," a position that Willis and others regarded "as a clear infringement of First Amendment rights." Brownmiller [according to Willis] insisted "that the First Amendment was designed to protect political dissent, not expressions of woman-hating violence. But to make such a distinction is to defeat the amendment's purpose, since it implicitly cedes to the government the right to define 'political' . . . it makes no sense to oppose pornography on the grounds that it's sexist propaganda, then turn around and argue that it's not political."

Andrea indirectly replied to Willis' critique in a response she wrote to two *New York Times* editorials that had denounced WAP's "strident and overwrought" attempt to undermine the First Amendment, and which had quoted from Andrea's earlier article, "Pornography: The New Terrorism." The *Times* refused to publish her response, as did a number of other publications, including the *Washington Post*, *The Nation*, the *Village Voice*, and her own touted *Mother Jones* (it was finally published in the 1980 anthology, *Take Back the Night*). In her letter to the *Times*, Andrea contrasted the paper's defense of "freedom of speech" in regard to pictures that showed "women sexually violated and humiliated, bound, gagged, sliced up, tortured in a multiplicity of ways" with its failure to speak out against "the enforced silence of women through the centuries."[13]

She further pointed out that the Constitution had been written "exclusively by white men who owned land and black slaves" and who denied the vote—the right to be heard on political issues—to all women. Both the law and pornography, she insisted, "express male contempt for women: they have in the past and they do now." Rape and battery were widespread, but "there is not a feminist alive who could possibly look to the male legal system for real protection from the systematized sadism of men." Women who protest pornography as both an expression of male sadism and a further incitement to it were once again being counseled to remain silent—in the name, bizarrely, of freedom of speech.

Andrea joined WAP's October 20, 1979, "March on Times Square" and gave one of the speeches at the subsequent rally in Bryant Park. She spoke out forcefully—and got a tumultuous response when she insisted that women "will never again accept any depiction of us that has as its first principle, its first premise, that we want to be abused, that we enjoy being hurt, that we like being forced." Those are *male* assumptions about *women's* lives. "Some people say that pornography is only fantasy. What part of it is fantasy? Women are beaten and raped and forced and whipped and held captive. The violence depicted is real. The acts of violence depicted in pornography are actual acts committed against real women and real female children. The fantasy is that women want to be abused."[14]

———

Subsequent to the Bryant Park rally, Andrea decided that she needed, above all else, to return to sustained work on her book, to be
free for a time from the maelstrom of "the war against pornography" and to devote herself to isolating and analyzing the underlying
issues and assumptions at stake. Her sense that *that* would be her
major contribution to the politics of pornography had been earlier
reinforced when she'd met a young law professor named Catharine
("Kitty" to her close friends and family) MacKinnon, who'd contacted her after reading *Woman Hating* and invited her to speak to
one of her classes at Yale on pornography. "It was wonderful for
me to have you here," Kitty wrote after the Yale event. "I feel good
about the slow-moving, careful way we are with each other, the gentleness, the regard, the exploration, the caution." It was the beginning of what would be a lasting friendship, and a collaboration of
profound consequence. For Andrea, the cordiality—though she and
Kitty would have their disagreements—was a great relief after what
she called "the exhausting fighting among feminists . . . strange,
divisive, huge melodramas. They get to me."[15]

Kitty was the gifted, attractive daughter of a Republican con-
gressman from Minnesota. Tall, decisive, and stylish, Kitty cut an
imposing, dramatic figure in her severely elegant suits, reinforced
by the energetic clarity of her mind and manner. In the early stages
of her career, when she and Andrea first met, Kitty was already
immersed in fighting for the recognition of sexual harassment as a
form of sex discrimination. By the end of the decade, in a celebrated
1979 book, *Sexual Harassment of Working Women*, she originated the
legal claim for sexual harassment as sex discrimination, which in
1986 the Supreme Court would affirm under Title VII of the 1964
Civil Rights Act.

Though MacKinnon would eventually have a long and distinguished academic career, the controversial causes she espoused
and the intensity with which she uncompromisingly pursued them
proved a predictable liability in the struggle to gain a tenured law
school appointment. She spent a dozen years "living on the road,"
with occasional appointments as a visiting professor, pegged to a
low salary. Her political collaboration with Andrea proceeded at a
gradual pace, as they both during the seventies became increasing-

ly immersed in the issues spawned by the pornography debate. By the summer of 1978, they were sharing and critiquing each other's manuscripts, and as they did so their mutual admiration grew: "The intellectual acuity and rigor of yr arguments are illuminating and challenging," Andrea wrote her at one point.[16]

Andrea and Kitty felt secure enough in their relationship to read each other's work with an eye toward *improving*, not simply admiring, it (though they usually did). When Kitty, for example, read Andrea's book *Pornography* in manuscript, she pulled no punches: "You take certain things on the level of their own self-presentation, which is myth, and hold them to that standard, rather than criticizing deeper realities, which in each case are even more open to attack. Example . . . where you say 'the objective scientists' find such and such, it is not clear whether you are faulting their objectivity or questioning objectivity itself. It seems more like the former, and I think the latter is more devastating and telling." Conversely, though Andrea praised Kitty's speech "Violence Against Women—A Perspective" as "wonderful," she felt free to tell her that "I think it is just patently wrong to say that 'lesbian eroticism' per se is not from the male standpoint, and also that therefore from the male standpoint it is the most obscene. . . . *The Well of Loneliness* is I think saturated with the 'male viewpoint.'"[17]

That mixture of admiration and admonishment is every writer's definition of an ideal editor, and both women knew they'd been lucky to have found it in each other. Still, a loving friendship no less than a loving marriage is inescapably subject to periodic misunderstandings. Not all of them, in the case of Andrea and Kitty, came under the rubric of intellectual disagreements. A dozen years later, Andrea (in a letter to a third party) referred to the "many differences" on "many things" that had developed between them. She put them down to their dissimilar backgrounds: "I am Jewish from an East European family decimated by the Holocaust and she is . . . Anglo-Saxon and privileged . . . I find her ignorance about the history of Jews and the Holocaust upsetting and difficult." (Kitty's family background was in fact Celtic and on her father's side working class).

Most people, unlike MacKinnon, seemed unable to understand

why writing a book about pornography would drain whatever energy Andrea had, but as she explained to a friend, "women tied to
cars, in spiked heels, asses exposed for fucking, and the like"—these
"are photographs I can't recover from. . . . I get physically sick, and
have to work in a state of nausea. . . . When I can't communicate
how terrible it is—for instance, to all the liberal-leftists who can't
understand what's so terrible—I get so angry I could explode, and
it wastes me, so I stay isolated." On top of the anguish of constantly
staring at and writing about women being degraded and abused, she
was feeling desperate again about money: "*how* to finish the pornography book is the question."

Just then—after some twenty or so publishers had rejected the
manuscript at various stages—Doubleday, to everyone's considerable surprise, decided to option it; yet when Andrea again ran out
of money in the spring of 1979, she was turned down for a further advance. A book of her previously published essays that she'd
somehow managed to put together had also been turned down
everywhere, and the paying magazines, with the exception of *Ms.*,
remained closed to her. *Mother Jones* did accept the chapter on the
Marquis de Sade from the pornography manuscript, but when they
edited it in such a way as to make (in Andrea's phrase) "pop-bad-
hamburger of it," she—characteristically—threatened to withdraw
it. Elaborate negotiations followed and *a* version was finally put
together that met Andrea's formidable standards.

She'd learned early on in her career as a writer that editors "made
changes in my work without my knowledge," sometimes changing
the content ("knowingly or without realizing it"), and she became
a stickler for reading final proofs. None of which meant that she
would automatically refuse critical input (indeed, she accepted them
"many times and very gratefully"), but she would always remain
determined to protect the integrity of her work; even when her need
for money was acute, she'd withdraw a piece if she felt it had been
editorially mangled. "I live in a fairly hostile world," she once wrote
the features editor of *Gay Community News*, and "don't like being
vilified for things I don't believe or things I didn't actually write,
which is what happens more often than not."[18]

It came as a surprise to Andrea when Adrienne Rich "insisted" on seeing the three chapters of her pornography book that she'd already completed. Surprised because a certain amount of ill will, its origin somewhat obscure, had recently developed between the two. Toward the end of 1976, Andrea had enigmatically written Kathy Norris, her friend from Bennington days, "Adrienne just managed to injure me too, again. She has the power to review *Our Blood* in the Times Book Review, but won't, cause she hates it, or objects to it, or something. Her manner is very hard to take, she radiates a disapproval, self-righteousness, that injures."[19]

Nor did matters improve. Six months later, in another letter to Kathy, Andrea wrote, "I can't deal with her [Adrienne] at all. She has a small, strange, totalitarian mind . . ." Six months after that, Andrea complained to Robin Morgan that Adrienne continued to treat her with a "condescension" she found "entirely inappropriate," since she had "honored and defended" Adrienne's work "so different from my own, often and long." She didn't mean to imply, Andrea explained, that this "in any sense obligates her to reciprocate," but she remained "mystified" at "the reasons for this entrenched antagonism."

Despite the accumulated antipathy, Adrienne read the three chapters rapidly and called Andrea to say "how powerful" she found them. They made an appointment to talk further about it, though Andrea, perhaps gratefully, doubted "that we will ever discuss the past. I need every bit of strong feminist support I can get, because this [the pornography book] is the hardest thing I have ever done." She was soon happily reporting to Robin Morgan that Adrienne "has been warmly supportive of late."

The early months of 1980 proved a difficult time for Andrea, perhaps because they followed hard on a period of intense public activity and nearly daily engagement with other people, all of which got in the way of completing *Pornography*; besides, her preferred state was isolation. This time, even with John's support and encouragement, she felt "extremely discouraged," even going so far at one point as to write Kitty MacKinnon that "my spirit is broken." Yet she'd finally found a publisher for a slender forty-eight-page collection of short stories (full of the warmth and humor Andrea was widely thought to lack) entitled *the new woman's broken heart* that Elaine Markson had previously been unable to sell. The buyer was a tiny feminist house in California called Frog in the Well. Up to that point it had published only pamphlets, including those by Andrea, John, and Barbara Deming. Andrea's short stories would be the group's first "book-length" work, and her hope was that "at this time of extreme economic hardship for feminist writers we can establish a viable, interesting, and important new feminist publishing house."[20]

The hope, as would soon become apparent, wouldn't be realized—neither for the press in the long run nor for Andrea's stories in the short. There was no money for ads, and Andrea turned to directly soliciting reviews for the book from writers and friends who'd earlier expressed admiration for her work. But they, too, shied away. Leah Fritz, who'd long been a staunch supporter, typified the reaction: the manuscript "disturbs me too much. Perhaps it is because I am so close to you that I feel its despair so keenly. . . . Please forgive me for failing you in this instance."[21]

Mother Jones did nothing to improve Andrea's spirits when it published a piece about what it called the "New Victorian prudes"—i.e., anti-porn feminists. In protest, Andrea sent the magazine a long response and a short private one to its editor, Deirdre English, who she knew and respected. Her letter to English was in essence a lament, her anger and misery pouring out over the longstanding misinterpretation of her own position: "I am so tired, especially of being called a prude for working on the issue, not to mention a fascist, not to mention a censor, and last but not least, I have been screamed at by so many lawyers in public places for being a threat to free speech when I just want it for myself and for other women." Every feminist involved in discussions of pornography, Andrea went on, "who can't leave it alone, even if they don't quite know why . . . has to keep conquering the effects of these epithets and attributions, the chilling effect, as the lawyers would say." Deirdre English responded with openness and grace: "I welcomed your letter and your reactions, critical as they were, and understood them to come from a spirit of honest and open communication." She did not, however, respond to the substance of Andrea's complaints.[22]

In her long letter to *Mother Jones*, Andrea reined in her sense of personal exhaustion and wrote a tightly controlled, lucid response. "Every attempt to discuss the meaning of pornography to women," she wrote, "has been treated as an assault on free speech rather than an exercise of it." Every insult is hurled at feminists attempting to point out that the central themes of male pornography are "forced sex and insatiable sluts": the woman is forced to discover "that she loves abuse"; that pretense ended, she then enthusiastically delights in male domination. Contrary to *Mother Jones*, Andrea went on, feminists are not "retreating into an old-fashioned moralism" but rather insisting on leading "sexually self-determined lives." Besides, Andrea insisted—and this would subsequently prove the most contentious point—pornography *does* influence sexual behavior; it is not, as is often declared, mere entertainment or fantasy. She wasn't claiming that the relationship between pornography and sexual abuse was simple, but only "that pornography effectively promotes abusive sex as viable, exciting, and properly within the scope of normal male sexual behavior."[23]

Yet another source of demoralization during the opening months of 1980 centered on lecture fees, on which Andrea relied for economic survival. She wasn't getting as many invitations to speak as earlier, and when she did, the financial terms offered were low, haggled over in a humiliating way, and not always honored after the event was successfully concluded. One case in point was an invitation to speak at the rally preceding a large "Take Back the Night" march down Hollywood Boulevard in Los Angeles. Given the disastrous state of her finances at the time, Andrea could only accept a speaking engagement if all her expenses were paid along with the lecture fee. Andrea asked the L.A. sponsors for $500, but the organizers bargained her down to $300; she was so poor at this point in her life that she had to accept. On top of that humiliation, she was told after the event that her airfare and other expenses would be paid once the necessary funds were raised, though her understanding had been that the money was in hand from the start. After months of charges and counter-charges, and heartsick at the debasement, Andrea decided to end the hurtful squabble and set-tled for a check that failed by a considerable margin to meet her expenses. "Situations like this," Andrea wrote one of the organizers, "make it impossible for any but the rich to participate as I did in your march—don't you understand that?"

Then came the worst blow of all: Anchor/Doubleday rejected the nearly completed manuscript, *Pornography*, in which she'd invest-ed three years of work—and at the same time, weirdly, refused to release her from the contract. This gave sadism a whole new dimen-sion; the traditionally genteel world of publishing chose one of its prime critics for an undisguised display of the power imbalance between author and editor. The "horrible blow" deepened Andrea's depression and led her, in desperation, to do what she most hated: ask friends to loan her money.[24]

Hearing the rumor that Doubleday was busy assigning blame for the rejection of *Pornography* on the deficiencies of the manuscript itself, Andrea, determined to at least salvage her reputation, wrote a long letter to her Doubleday editor carefully outlining the his-tory of the project: "I am told that the book I submitted to you, from yr point of view, is not the book I promised you. . . . I showed you chapter by chapter what I was doing. I don't think I exaggerate when I say that you encouraged me at every turn, seemed to love the work, encouraged the direction I was going in. . . . I changed the nature of the project and its projected length several times with yr complete approval and encouragement. You told me—and these are words I treasure—that you thought it the greatest book you had been involved in publishing." The letter may have been necessary balm for Andrea's state of mind, but, predictably, it had no effect on Doubleday's decision. It did, however, finally agree to release her from the contract.[25]

It had been a dreary six months, suddenly broken by the news early in August that Wendy Goldwyn, an editor at St. Martin's, wanted to pick up the contract. Andrea learned that the president of the firm, Tom McCormick, "hates the book and has done every-thing possible to discourage Wendy from acquiring it, and me from accepting the offer." McCormick reluctantly agreed to a contract that Andrea described as "foul—one that no self-respecting writer would sign" (the loss of British rights, for example); but she did, desperate for the small advance and comforted by the fact that Wendy "has put her job on the line for the book" and that St. Martin's "is small and ambitious with an interesting list and good relations with small, independent booksellers."

Knowing *Pornography* would definitely see the light of day gave her spirits a needed boost. She vowed, as she wrote Gloria Steinem, "to outwit and get past the male critical establishment, to get the book out and read, not to let it die . . . I feel very aggressive about the book—scared, very scared, but very aggressive." She called on Gloria for help, and other friends too, in advising her where to send the manuscript or galleys, how to "place parts of it in mass market women's magazines that reach different readers than *Ms.*," and how to reach a male audience "who are or who pretend to be feminists." Andrea wrote as well to thank Adrienne Rich for what she learned had been her "incredible support" in persuading St. Martin's to do the book, and asking for her comments on the manuscript. "I cannot tell you how much happier I am now," she wrote Adrienne. "I actually smile. My dreams are only moderately terrible. Feeling is beginning to enter my body. Sometimes hours pass and I am not in knots. It's wonderful."

A mere two weeks later, it all came crashing down. Again. Andrea had agreed as part of the deal to reorganize the material in the book—to put the chapter on the Marquis de Sade, for example, up front—and to write both a new afterword and an introduction; on her own she'd also intended another go-round on the entire manuscript to sharpen and clarify some of her arguments. She had never agreed, as her editor, Wendy Goldwyn, suddenly claimed, to write another *ten* chapters. That demand, coming out of the blue, floored her. Wendy also claimed that St. Martin's had only recently discovered that *Woman Hating* had sold badly (it had, in fact, sold nine thousand copies—quite good for a serious, "mid-list" book).[26]

The truth of the matter was that St. Martin's had gotten cold feet (with Tom McCormick, no doubt, pouring on ice cubes in a steady stream). Andrea knew she was powerless to change his mind, but bitter and disheartened, she was determined on sending Wendy an *accurate* account of what had transpired: "My integrity forbids me accepting yr bullshit version of the story. . . . I did everything I agreed to do. Elaine and I were completely upfront with you on every level about everything. . . . I have absolutely no respect on any level for what you have done to me; but don't blame me for it—and don't think for a minute that I buy it." For good measure, Andrea sent copies of her letter to Gloria, Adrienne, Shere Hite, and Robin Morgan. Wendy did not respond, though St. Martin's let Elaine know that they were canceling the contract. As Andrea wrote Adrienne, "On the one hand, I am completely confident and militant inside; and on the other, I keep crumbling. . . . I'm sorry to sound so melodramatic but I am getting tired and impatient and with that goes both arrogance and self-pity. . . . If I could take all the editors in the world and put them in a bottle and throw them into the sea, I would I swear."[27]

In the meantime, she continued to make the publishing rounds; Elaine managed to set up a number of meetings with editors at other houses, and Andrea, feeling vaguely punch-drunk, continued to attend them. "And so it goes," she told Adrienne, "long intense conversations with editors who love the book but essentially want everything different, and even if someone were right I am afraid that I have endured so much pure stupidity that I have become stupid and would not know it. Now I'm dealing with a lot of male editors and am seeing incredible gender-polarized readings of the book that astonish: they keep looking for the woman's voice in the book that pleads, begs, apologizes—."

Meanwhile, at home in their fifth-floor walkup at 231 Second Avenue, a hamburger joint had recently opened on the ground floor and was continuing to send up the dumbwaiter shaft a steady stream of noxious fumes that permeated the apartment and made them feel headachy and nauseated much of the time. As Andrea later described it, "the gas could pass through anything, and did: a clenched fist; layers of human fat; the porous walls of this particular slum dwelling; the human heart and brain and especially the abdomen, where it turned spike-like and tore into the lower intestine with sharp bitter thrusts." John had recently gone to work at *Essence* (from 1981 to 1985 he'd become its managing editor) and was out of the apartment during the day, when the fumes were at their worst. Andrea had to keep the windows open "no matter how cold or wet or ugly or dusty or hot or wretched," and for relief she'd take long, long walks through the city, then crawl back home "like a slug, dragging the day's fatigue behind me." They stopped paying rent and would ultimately bring a lawsuit against the landlord.[28]

Then out of nowhere an editor at Perigee named Sam Mitnick expressed interest, and after what Andrea described as "excruciating negotiations re content, which I won," decided to offer her a contract for *Pornography*. Andrea described Mitnick to Gloria as "tense, neurotic, Jewish, 36, two heart attacks, open heart surgery, very smart, very driven—thrives on the opposition to the book in house." He was, she decided, "a gay Jewish prince," and she liked him: not only was he "very bright" but he "actually likes to read—a superior virtue, and an unusual one, in an editor." Working with Mitnick, Andrea felt she finally understood why the manuscript had "contaminated" its earlier female editors: "they were perceived as one with it, as if it was their opinion. With a male editor, no one even thinks to make that assumption of association."[29]

True or not, meeting Mitnick marked a genuine turning point. Not only did he publish Andrea's book on pornography in 1981, but that same year he got Perigee to put out the paperback edition of *Our Blood*—a goal that had eluded Andrea and Elaine for five years. Still further, Mitnick was able to get Andrea a contract for the next book she wanted to write—a study of rightwing women. "So things are looking up for the first time in a long time," Andrea wrote Robin Morgan. She added, humorously, that henceforth she might even have to give up referring to her writing career as "in the Greek tragic mode," which John had naturalized into the phrase "the House of Camden."[30]

On completing *Pornography*, Andrea, in relief, set down her thoughts: "I had never expected the process . . . to be, in a sense, so ruthless and awful . . . if this is what it does to me, and I know all the material that isn't here, all that is left out, what will it do to others? . . . I don't know, except that I wrote it as truthfully as I knew how—except the last sentence, where I told what might be truth, what might be a lie, knowingly: 'The boys are betting. The boys are wrong' ['The boys are betting on our compliance, our ignorance, our fear. We have always refused to face the worst that men have done to us. The boys count on it.'] Are they [wrong]? Maybe. But about three weeks ago I came across this excerpt from a Kafka letter . . .

"'If the book we are reading does not wake us, as with a foot hammering on our skull, why then do we read it? . . . what we must have are those books which come upon us like ill fortune and distress us deeply, like the death of one we love better than ourselves, like suicide. A book must be an ice-axe to break the sea frozen inside us.' I will probably keep wondering if I have managed something like what Kafka meant, because I think that if it is less, it isn't justified."[31]

Having spent some four years researching the subject—and the text of *Pornography* attests to the depth of that research—Andrea now knew a great deal more than she had as a younger woman, and the new knowledge had transformed her views. She no longer saw pornography as benign—let alone as providing liberating inspiration for the artist, which she *had* thought as a teenager. She'd long since faced "what the content of pornography actually is and how the acts of forced sex in it correspond to the reality of women's lives." In her opinion, even the pornography that could be described "as not being violent, objectifies women in a way which" she now believed "is the precondition for violence . . . dehumanizing someone makes it a lot easier to hurt them." The most pervasive scenario in both written and visual heterosexual pornography, she'd come to believe, centrally involved scenes of (male) dominance and (female) submission. Nor, she now belatedly realized, should that have come as a surprise. How could it be otherwise?

In *Pornography*, Andrea argued that the destructive "metamessage" of most porn, reflecting the society in which it was created, "is that the female in her pure sexuality is sadistic, a conviction articulated not only by the pornographers but also by the enlightened philosophers on all levels. The Christians called women carnal and evil and killed nine million as witches. The enlightened thinkers secularize the conviction, turn faith to idea." Thus Havelock Ellis, in his classic 1933 work *Studies in the Psychology of Sex*, justified "the male force used against women in sex by positing a more fundamental female sadism." Half a century later, Georges Bataille's

1928 *Story of the Eye*, proclaimed profound by a host of contemporary pundits, including Sartre, Foucault, Roland Barthes, and Susan Sontag—particularly Sontag, who Andrea decided "is an honorary man and doesn't intend to give it up"—argued "that pornography of high quality—gracefully conceived and written—is art." "High quality" because, according to Bataille's intellectual admirers, he has revealed "the authentic nexus between sex and death." What his admirers have failed to notice, Andrea believed, is that Bataille has "obscured the meaning of force in sex . . . as the essential dynamic."[32]

"This is 'big news,'" Andrea mockingly writes, "to women whose lives are circumscribed by the sexual sadism of males; but it is good news to those males who justify their abuse of women by believing that women are sexually sadistic at heart and that the sadism of women is formidable despite the fact that it is not socially or historically self-evident. The cage is justified because the animal inside it is wild and thus dangerous. . . . As long as this alleged female sadism is controlled by men, it can be manipulated to give men pleasure: dominance in the male system is pleasure."

Andrea's treatment in *Pornography* of the Marquis de Sade's intellectual admirers is no less pungent. She mocks the claims of his then most recent biographer, Donald Thomas, that "the cruelties of his fiction are quite at variance with almost all of Sade's conduct" and that his sexual desires were "indulged largely in his fiction." Such characterizations are not merely false history, Andrea charges, but they also serve "to trivialize Sade's brutalities against women." What such a defense amounts to, she tellingly charges, is that "the victims of Sade's sexual terrorism are less important than 'philosophical disquisitions.'" To demonstrate that Thomas' apologia typifies the approach of Sade's biographers, Andrea quotes from another: "He [Sade] had given a few girls and women a little pain, but not so much really. . . . Most of the women he had used in his orgies had come to him willingly enough, for payment, or, oddly enough, because they liked him." Tellingly, Andrea makes one of Sade's victims, Rose Keller, the co-dedicatee (along with John Stoltenberg) of her book.[33]

In *Pornography* Andrea also takes on—and eviscerates—almost along the way, such present-day admirers of Sade's as the literary

critic Richard Gilman and the cultural historian Christopher
Lasch. She dismisses Gilman's "banal prose" rather quickly, with
a quote from his 1980 book *Decadence*: Sade "is the first compelling
enunciator in modern times of the desire . . . to act otherwise than
existing moral structures coerced one into doing." Substitute the
name of any villain—Hitler, Stalin—for Sade, and the absurdity of
Gilman's admiration becomes apparent. Andrea was only slightly
more respectful of Lasch. She cites his statement that Sade anticipated a "defense of woman's sexual rights—their rights to dispose of
their own bodies, as feminists would put it today"—though he did
so, according to Lasch, "more clearly than the feminists." Andrea's
response is scorching: "The notion that Sade presages feminist
demands for women's sexual rights is rivaled in self-serving absurdity only by the opinion of Gerald and Caroline Greene, in *S-M:
The Last Taboo*, that 'if there was one thing de Sade was not, it was
a sexist.'"

To the assertion of some of her critics that "women do have
more freedom than they had, say, a hundred, 150 years ago," thus
demonstrating that change is possible, Andrea's response was that
"the kind of change I'm interested in is when women are no longer
defined in relation to and by contrast with men. And the kind of
change I'm interested in has to do with an end to a gender system
that I think is specious, that I think is not . . . [an accurate] catego-
rization of human beings . . . a woman is born into this system and
her destiny is predetermined from birth. The coercive nature of
that predetermination is what we're struggling against . . . one of
the reasons that we don't have answers is that we have refused to
describe the sexual system in which we live accurately." She felt that
to the extent she'd made a contribution, it was in "describing this
system the way that it is. . . . We're going to have to find a way to
organize an economy from the ground up that is not based on the
sex-class labour of women, including reproductive labour. Socialist
or Marxist societies have not done that. . . . What I believe we have
to do is everything. I know that ends up sounding like no answer,
but it is what we have to do." It wasn't a job, in her view, that the
intellectual left was prepared to take on. It had, as Andrea saw it,
"*advocated* pornography as crucial to liberation," and an endless line

of prominent left supporters, from Ramsay Clark to Dick Gregory to Paul Krassner and an "unbelievable array of leftist newspapers and writers," had actually claimed Larry Flynt, publisher of *Hustler*, as a working-class hero.

With the publication of *Pornography: Men Possessing Women*, Andrea got back as good as she'd given out. Her legion of critics were quick to tell her that she had not managed much more than a screech in the night. Fortunately, Kitty had read the book while it was still in manuscript, had recognized it as Andrea's most important work to date, and had told her so before the critical deluge descended. "This is just an incredible book," she'd written Andrea, "and fundamental to all of our work on every level." Kitty singled out as "overwhelmingly excellent" Andrea's discussion of fetishism and objectification and her arresting treatment of racism—namely, that "poverty forces . . . [the black woman into pornography], but it is the sexual valuation of her skin that *predetermines* her *poverty*."[34]

A few other assessments appeared that grasped the significance of *Pornography*, including Leah Fritz's three cheers for Andrea's deft skewering of the reigning male cultural gods, including Norman Mailer and his "essentially racist" work, *The White Negro*. And when Dorothy Allison wrote what was at least a mixed review, Andrea wrote her to say that "after the vicious stuff I've been getting on my book, I was pretty grateful to you because you granted me something, quite a lot actually." But those few friendly voices aside, Andrea took a severe critical drubbing; it was almost as if the deeper her perceptions went, the louder the shrieks that rent the air.[35]

Many of the reviews of the book were woundingly personal: as a lesbian she hated all men; her rage distorted her judgment; overweight and "unsightly," she invited male rejection. She was accused as well of a host of intellectual crimes: that she'd created a dualistic system—abusive men, submissive women—that was not only ahistorical, but philosophically sterile; and, some of her critics charged—quite misreading Andrea's utopian side—that she believed that male supremacy would, necessarily, *always* be in the saddle, with only momentary glimpses of freedom possible for women. As Andrea's friend Leah Fritz put it, "The rage spewed forth by these critics, both male and female, can only be compared to the riots that occurred when Picasso's paintings were exhibited at the famous Armory show in 1913."[36]

One of the most negative reviews came in the most important press outlet: the *New York Times*. Ellen Willis, the reviewer, acknowledged that pornography, like "all cultural images influence behavior . . . they articulate and legitimize feelings that already exist." Pornography, in other words, was a symptom not a cause of the violence endemic in the culture. What Ellis omitted and implicitly denied was in fact at the heart of Andrea's argument—that along with *representing* the amount of violence in the culture, pornography also *amplified* that violence. In place of acknowledging the breadth and sophistication of Andrea's analysis, Willis settled for calling it "a book-length sermon, preached with a rhetorical flourish and a single-minded intensity that meet somewhere between poetry and rant."[37]

Andrea had a long history behind her of being ignored or belittled or misunderstood, and she tried to be philosophical about Willis' put-down even though she was aware that a pan in the *Times* all but guaranteed truncated sales. As she wrote her friend Ellen Frankfort, "If the book were in cloth that would be the end of it. Since it's in paper it has a chance . . . [though] the reviews around the country, with about two exceptions, have been absolutely devastating: 'the book is sexual bigotry, hatred of men', etc. Nothing about what I actually did. Nothing about what pornography actually is . . . it's a crazy kind of hostility, completely out of control on every level." When Andrea sent the book out to "lots of feminists of many different kinds," the response was different—was "overwhelmingly enthusiastic."

Being human, Andrea suffered from the reception. "I am having a hard time with it," she wrote a friend. "I had no idea it could affect me this way." Yet she stood her ground. She insisted that she had *not* chosen "out-of-the-ordinary" examples of pornography but rather representative ones: "I did not weight the argument," she told a reporter from the feminist publication *Sojourner*, "by picking anything that was particularly bizarre"; to begin her chapter on "Force," for example, she purposely chose a picture "that most people would not view as violent"—and then persuasively dissected its essentially ugly misogyny. The overall message of *Pornography* was clear-cut: the industry directly and accurately reflected social psychology—the existing *power* differential between men and women.

7

Lovelace; Trans; and Right-Wing Women

Andrea's dismay over the reception of *Pornography* was a match for the negative mood of the country as a whole in regard to the issues relating to gender and sexuality about which she most cared. One key development in the late seventies and early eighties involved the transformation of both national political parties: in accelerating numbers, the Southern Democrats shifted allegiance to the Republican Party, which simultaneously began to purge itself of its own pro-choice minority. In the 1980 election, reversing a long-standing historical trend, more white women (by a margin of nearly 10 percent) voted Democratic than voted Republican. The parties were becoming more polarized, and the Republicans decidedly more conservative. In his inaugural address, Ronald Reagan spoke of the need to "protect the unborn" and, in a transparent attack on racial busing, pledged to "end the manipulation of schoolchildren by utopian planners."

The backlash against the women's movement was palpable. Attacks on abortion rights steadily mounted, spurred on by pressure groups like the Eagle Forum and the Moral Majority. Poor women suffered most: when the Supreme Court, in *Harris v. McRae*, confirmed the constitutionality of the 1976 Hyde Amendment (which banned the use of federal funding to pay for abortions through Medicaid), it greatly increased the odds that some 45 million low-income women would lose access to *safe* abortions. The Reagan administration heightened their plight when it shifted responsibility for a host of other social service programs—rape crisis centers, food pantries, battered women's shelters, etc.—from the federal government to the states or to the private sector, neither of which had the resources to meet the demand.

Meanwhile, the demise of the Equal Rights Amendment looked assured as the right poured money and troops into the struggle to kill it on the state level. In another, quite different sign of the times, the books of George Gilder began to grace the *New York Times* bestseller lists. Especially popular was his *Sexual Suicide*, which stressed the biologically determined differences between men and women and denounced feminists as a profound threat to the "natural" unit of the nuclear family (which Gilder further glorified in *Wealth and Poverty*, a book that sold over a million copies).

The radical feminist movement itself was in considerable disarray, with the issues of pornography and sadomasochism increasingly dividing it—abetted, on a more elevated plane, by the division between feminists committed to the view that men and women were biologically different (and complementary) and those like Andrea, who saw gender as socially constructed. Deflated expectations took hold across the board; as Andrea herself predicted soon after Reagan's triumph, "We lost an awful lot in this [1980] election and most of us are in a state of anguish. We face a loss of abortion rights [and] the defeat of the ERA is assured." Legal protection for rape within marriage was still on the books in all states but three, and "we have 28 million battered wives."[1]

In an interview with *Feminist Studies* in 1981, Andrea told the interviewer that the feminist movement had been helping women, "saving their lives," but "we're not changing the institutions that keep the women getting hurt. . . . We're sitting here talking about some improvement in some laws . . . [but] we have to use pornography as a tool to understand the system in which we live, and to change it. We would be fools," she said, "to think that we would have inner lives that are entirely dissociated from the actual system in which we live. . . . I think that men commit acts of forced sex against women systematically" and that was precisely what the women's movement had begun to realize.

Not Betty Friedan's movement. Not the leadership, as opposed to the grassroots membership, of NOW. Not the brilliant *Village Voice* columnist Ellen Willis, who derisively insisted that "in Andrea Dworkin's moral universe the battle of the sexes is a Manichaean clash between absolute power and absolute powerlessness, absolute villains and absolute victims." Barbara Deming pointed out to Willis that Andrea "considers male sexual aggression not innate, but learned." As she'd written in *Pornography*, such aggression is "institutionalized in sports, the military, acculturated sexuality, the history and mythology of heroism, it is taught to boys until they become its advocates . . . advocates of that which they most fear." Barbara herself differed from Andrea in thinking "that men are more divided in themselves than [she] allows"; when boys "abandon their mothers, learn contempt for them," Barbara wrote, "a *part* of them regrets the choice, sees it as a lying act, and always will. This regret [is] rarely conscious of course."[2]

In regard to Friedan, Andrea was scornful. Friedan "has been insisting for several years now," Andrea wrote late in 1979, "about how to maintain our wondrous equality which we have already achieved according to her. *We* are concerned about wife battery, marital rape, incest, and the many forms of child abuse. We are concerned about the poverty of women as a class. . . . We are concerned about the sexual harassment suffered by working women and students. We are concerned about the rights of lesbian mothers and homosexual children. We are concerned about the proliferation of woman-hating propaganda. . . . We are concerned about the reproductive rights of women and girls. . . . We are concerned about the most basic issues of material survival. Friedan is concerned about issues of privilege and comfort. Most women do not have that luxury."[3]

The closest thing to a publicity campaign for *Pornography* resulted not from favorable reviews or Perigee's ads for the book, but from the accidents of friendship. Andrea's close friend, the photographer Elsa Dorfman, was married to the liberal lawyer Harvey Silverglate, and he in turn was friendly with the lawyer and academic Alan Dershowitz. From that string of connections emerged a Dworkin/Dershowitz debate at Radcliffe's Longfellow Hall on May 13, 1981. The place was packed, with people sitting in the aisles and standing along the walls. The pending event, according to one reporter, "was the hottest topic in town, and most local newspapers and radio stations carried stories on it." In an interview she gave the evening before the debate, Andrea explained her own reasons for accepting the invitation: "He offered me access to his institutional power, and I had to accept. It hurts me terribly to be so powerless in this society that I have to accept his chivalry." Doubtless, too, she viewed the debate as a chance to counteract the landslide of negative reviews, and to spread word of the book's *actual* contents.

Andrea opened the debate in a tone that a reporter described as "soft-spoken and very eloquent." (People meeting Andrea for the first time and having only read her vehement prose were often shocked at how gentle and "nice" she was on a personal level, and what a generous "good listener"; her private voice was kind and empathetic.) Julie Bindel, for one, loved her "dry humour, unwavering integrity, and shy vulnerability . . . [she was] warm, open-minded . . . with feminists from all sides of the debate, Andrea would patiently and respectfully listen."[4]

On the platform, she did often sound fierce, and her soft-spoken speech that night at Radcliffe wasn't typical. She did, though, successfully convey the essence of her defense against the standard charge that curtailing pornography was an affront to the First Amendment's guarantee of free speech: "women as a class are excluded from being able to exercise speech—rape, battery, and incest all being ways of keeping a class of people from being able to speak at all." The overflow crowd remained hushed throughout her talk—and gave her a standing ovation at its close.

Dershowitz, for his part, was apparently not having one of his "chivalrous" evenings. Instead of using the podium and microphone, as Andrea had, he remained seated (translation: "this was not an occasion one was required to 'rise' to"). According to a reporter from *Sojourner*, he "almost immediately alienated the audience by calling Dworkin and her ideas 'dangerous.'" He then minimized the "fuss" over pornography by declaring that the women involved had "obviously" volunteered to be photographed. Was Dworkin suggesting that they be denied the right to do so? In answer to his own question, he opened a magazine that he said was written by a group of "S & M lesbians" and read a passage from it denouncing any and all efforts to censor pornographic material. If censorship came to pass, Dershowitz warned the audience—apparently assuming it was composed solely of gay people—"your own interests could be the first ones ruled out." He managed to antagonize the crowd to the point where several spectators angrily shouted out that he was a "sexist" and a "pornographer." Andrea declined to respond, other than to say that Dershowitz had misrepresented her views and turned the event into "a mind fuck."[5]

Simultaneous with the Radcliffe debate, Andrea and Kitty were gradually being drawn into a controversy that centered precisely on Dershowitz's claim that women voluntarily participated in pornographic productions. The dispute focused on Linda Boreman, the birth name of the woman who'd come to be known as Linda Lovelace, star of the hugely successful 1972 hardcore film *Deep Throat* (even the *New York Times* reviewed it). In 1980, Linda had published her autobiography, *Ordeal*, which described in convincing detail how her abusive manager, pimp, and husband, Chuck Traynor, had coerced her into prostitution and into performing in porn films ("My initiation was a gang rape by five men, arranged by Mr. Traynor. . . . I felt like garbage, I engaged in sex acts in pornography against my will to avoid being killed").

It was Gloria Steinem who told Andrea that she had to read *Ordeal*. She did, though no one had to convince her that such horror stories, which paralleled her own, *did* happen, and with some frequency. That Linda herself had been living a nightmare was supported by polygraph tests and by a professional psychiatric diagnosis of complex PTSD. Once having read *Ordeal*, Andrea was unable to stop thinking about it, and she began to wonder if Linda's grievances against the pornographers couldn't be brought as a civil suit for damages. At that point she didn't know MacKinnon well, but she invited her to a book party for her short story collection, *a new woman's broken heart*.[6]

They talked together in a corner about *Ordeal* and MacKinnon particularly remembers Andrea saying "We got the Klan, why can't we get the pornographers?" Intrigued, MacKinnon mulled the matter over and then phoned Andrea to say that she thought a civil suit against the makers of the porn film *Deep Throat* (in which Linda had been forced to perform prodigious feats of fellatio) might be a possible way to go. At a subsequent WAP event, to which Andrea had invited MacKinnon, they met Linda, then eight months pregnant with her second child. Gloria Steinem had already briefed Linda about a possible suit, and she told MacKinnon, "I hear you have some legal ideas about *Deep Throat*." When MacKinnon said she did, Linda suggested a meeting at her house on Long Island, where she lived with her second husband, Larry Marciano.[7]

The group that soon after drove out to Long Island consisted of Andrea, Kitty, Gloria, Stan Pottinger, a former Department of Justice Civil Division lawyer close to Gloria, and Kent Harvey, a colleague of Kitty's. As Andrea later put it, they spent "about six hours drilling Linda like banshies from hell. . . . I was very, very rough on her—much more than Kitty was. And I came out of it believing not only every word that she said but that she was tough enough to be able to do this. So we sort of set the parameters of basically making a civil rights claim that covered marital rape, abduction, rape, prostitution, and the making of pornography."

Through the auspices of WAP, a press conference was arranged that included Linda, Andrea, Kitty, and Gloria (and in supportive attendance, the ERA activist Valerie Harper, who during much of the 1970s had played Rhoda Morgenstern on *The Mary Tyler Moore Show*). From that point on, the case would absorb a fair amount of Andrea and Kitty's available time. A few additional people were gradually brought into the discussion, including Linda's husband and a lawyer who represented a number of Vietnam vets. What became clear early on was that the statute of limitations had already run out—a serious impediment to bringing the lawsuit (not to mention that as recently as 1975, marital rape had been legal in all fifty states). Eventually, they all put their opinions on the table, with the final decision left up to Linda. Andrea and Kitty wanted to go forward, but none of the men did, and Gloria (who Linda trusted entirely) sided with the men. Kitty came up with the unique theory that a viable way around the statute of limitations might be possible under a court ruling that declared sex discrimination a conspiracy to violate civil rights.

The risks for Linda were formidable, and (according to Kitty) for quite some time she held up "strongly under all of this." Kitty herself was prepared to proceed, though at the time she was an underpaid, untenured university professor who would personally—Andrea being too poor—bear the brunt of the considerable legal expenses entailed. As Linda mulled over the decision of whether to proceed, Kitty, through long letters, kept her thoroughly informed, never minimizing the risky consequences of a judge's ruling against them. Linda seemed to grow more determined by the day, and at one point Kitty triumphantly wrote Andrea that "every time Linda asserts herself . . . I am an audience of thousands of women's voices cheering . . ." Yet in the end, Linda—who now had two young children to take care of—decided not to go ahead with the lawsuit; it was simply too risky, both psychically and financially. Kitty remained her lawyer.[8]

In the fall of 1981, Kitty and Andrea planned to teach a graduate seminar on feminist theory together at Stanford, where Kitty was currently on a "hand-to-mouth" appointment. But as it turned out, the feminist studies department wasn't keen on inviting Andrea to the campus, and Kitty, though "livid and rageful," made the strategic decision to postpone submitting the course proposal. Andrea interpreted the temporary retreat as a permanent defeat and, deeply insulted at Stanford's cold shoulder, refused to pursue the project further. Kitty wittily noted that "we must have crossed some line from being friends into being a long-term relationship, in that you are having prideful explosions at me" (Andrea had hung up on her at one point). No, Kitty added, "I am not just like you—why does that mean I cannot be trusted?"[9]

Andrea apologized for hanging up, but otherwise (temporarily) stood her ground: when you told "me you had given up our course because of the threats in order to get a [university] contract, you also said this was something (a kind of thing, a category of act) you had never done before in yr life. You recognized the character of it, what it was and what it meant. I recognize what it was too. That's all. It shocked and hurt me terribly . . . giving up that proposal for a joint course was giving in to McCarthyism, political blackmail, and the ostracization of a radical, in this case me. . . . I don't like this kind of shit, Kitty. . . . I want to keep working together on Linda, pornography, the issues . . . but I do not want to come out there." And they did continue to work together, closely, on the issues—which in turn led to enough meetings and personal contact to rapidly reintroduce warmth and trust into the relationship.

During the early months of 1982, Andrea was absorbed in finishing *Right-Wing Women*. That consuming effort would alone have necessitated a considerable retreat from activism, but the divisions and denunciations that had increasingly marked feminist politics made the retreat something of a welcome respite. It was a time of disgruntlement in the nation as a whole, as well as in the feminist movement; despite a large tax cut and a steep rise in military spending, 10 percent of the labor force was unemployed. As for feminism, polarization on the West Coast was particularly pronounced; much of it focused on the public actions of Samois, a lesbian S/M group, and its publications (*Coming to Power* and Pat Califia's *Sapphistry*). Middle-of-the-road heterosexual feminists were appalled, and— somewhat to Andrea's surprise—Betty Friedan's NOW passed a resolution condemning S/M. The issue of race further divided the movement. African American and Hispanic women, feeling their special perspectives and needs largely ignored, formed their own publishing collective, Kitchen Table Press; its anthology *This Bridge Called My Back*, edited by Gloria Anzaldua and Cherrie Moraga, became an instant classic.

Andrea was feeling both the economic pinch and the escalating feminist warfare. Her East Village apartment building, already beset by noxious fumes, had also become overrun with rats. She and John were desperate to move but couldn't afford to, and Andrea settled into what she herself described as a "sullen, morbid, deathlike"

mood, finding reliable comfort only in John and in the absorption
of work. "It is impossible to be part of a movement," she wrote a
friend, "that embraces the swastika as sex toy" (a reference to the
symbol that now and then appeared on the leather outfits of S/M
dykes). "The courage required to face and change the real condition
of women under men is not here."

John shared Andrea's negative view of sadomasochism. In his
own 1980 article in *Gay Community News*, "What Is the Meaning of
S&M?," deploring its spreading appeal, he argued that its roots were
to be found "in the social structure of male-over-female domination"—in eroticized violence and powerlessness: "In order to believe
that relationships between sadists and masochists are 'liberated,'"
he wrote, "one would have to believe that contempt is caring, that
humiliation is respect, that brutality is affection, and that bondage
is freedom."[10]

Andrea recognized that her current pessimistic mood might be
exaggerated: "I think my limits are real—I think there is plenty I
don't see—I am sure of it." Still, it was hard not to be in what she
called "a misogynistic snit" when pro-S/M and pro-pornography
forces seemed to have taken over the movement and some of her
own basic beliefs had come under fire. In her view, feminists were
currently "underestimating the magnitude of male power" and, perhaps even more important, seemed increasingly wedded to what she
viewed as the mistaken notion that "gender" had a biological basis,
was an intrinsic given. "I don't believe in gender," Andrea wrote a
friend, "and for what it's worth, I hope I will die not believing in it,
whatever else I start or stop believing. I don't believe that gender
exists outside a social system of oppression . . . and female friendship
within this system has a revolutionary consequence that is intrinsic
to it . . . it can be as close to freedom as we can get—but it is also
as tattered and ragged and ruined as our various bodies and souls."

As the strength of the radical wing of feminism weakened,
Andrea not only held her ground, but extended it. In her very first
book, *Woman Hating*, published in 1974, she'd taken a firm and
positive view not only of the gender model of androgyny but also
of those who insisted on the integrity of a "transsexual" identity
(today more commonly referred to as transgender). Empathy in the

face of human suffering was a hallmark of Andrea's character, and as early as 1974 she insisted that "every transsexual is entitled to a sex-change operation, and it should be provided by the community as one of its functions." (Nor did she ever change her mind on the subject.) Back then she'd also been way ahead of the cultural curve in insisting that there were not two genders but rather many, predicting that "we will discover cross-sexed phenomena in proportion to our ability to see them." The "multi-sexual nature of people," she argued, must be "accepted into the forms of human community."[11]

Half a dozen years later, as the emphasis on male/female biological differences continued to gain cultural ground, Andrea stood firm on her earlier conviction that gender was fluid and multi-faceted. For a time in the seventies, she'd been somewhat friendly with Janice Raymond, whose transphobic 1979 book *The Transsexual Empire: The Making of a She-Male*, deplored the "medicalization" of gender that encouraged surgical intervention to create "a woman according to man's image." It was a view that Andrea deplored, and she let Raymond know it at some length: "I knew of transsexuals in Europe as a small, vigorously persecuted minority, without any recourse to civil or political protection. They lived in absolute exile, as far as I could see, conjuring up for me the deepest reaches of Jewish experience. They were driven by their ostracization to prostitution, drugs, and suicide, conjuring up for me the deepest reaches of female experience. Their sense of gender dislocateness [sic] was congruent with mine, in that my rage at the cultural and so-called biological definitions of womanhood and femininity was absolute. I perceived their suffering as authentic. . . . Looking back, I can see other, unknown at the time, sources of my own particular empathy. Male-to-female transsexuals were in rebellion against the phallus and so was I. Female-to-male transsexuals were seeking a freedom only possible to males in patriarchy, and so was I. The means were different, but the impulses were related. I haven't changed my mind." Kitty entirely agreed with Andrea: "Jan Raymond is wrong. . . . She is thinking that our problem is gender. I think that our problem is sexuality."[12]

Andrea felt, too—and deeply regretted—that so many political women now seemed to believe "that talking to all kinds of women

means abandoning their own style and their own principles. What
are they afraid of? Guilt by association? Is this what the feminist
movement has come to?—that women can be discredited, or fear
they'll be accused of sharing their politics if they *talk* to conservative women, or middle-class women, or women in high heels
or women in dresses or women who wear make-up." Any woman
who feels that "having a politically correct line" and associates only
with those who share it were, in Andrea's view, "hallucinating an
autonomy that women by definition in a male supremacist society
cannot have."[13]

In regard to men, Andrea felt that the women's movement as a
whole hadn't concentrated nearly enough on talking to and educat-
ing men—an opinion, had it been widely known, that would have
shocked those multitudes, then and since, who have cavalierly dismissed her as a man-hater, and probably a pathological one. The
feminist sociologist Michael Kimmel, himself heterosexual, has
been one of the few men to question the dogmatic view that Andrea
thought "all men are rapists"; Kimmel insisted that in fact "all manner of furious male-bashing, man-hating, and anti-sex ideas have
been projected onto her."

What Andrea actually felt was that among younger men especially (as she told an interviewer in 1982), "in the last four or five years
I've begun to see a substantial and vocal and active minority of men
that is profoundly anti-sexist. And I think we have to understand
that we've really made an impact there, it's one that we haven't even
recognized, we don't even know we've done it. . . . And 'educate'
is an euphemism for put pressure on, coerce, do activism around
everything, the whole spectrum of action from the most militant to
the most communicative."

Andrea completed *Right-Wing Women* in late March of 1982. Only
a few weeks later, in mid-April, more than eight hundred women
gathered at Barnard College for what would become a historic conference on female sexuality. Andrea wasn't there by choice, though
the invitation to attend had been an "open call." The conference had
a number of plenary sessions and some seventeen workshops devoted to a wide variety of issues (including abortion rights, psycho-

therapy, popular sex advice literature, and disability rights). WAP distorted the actual breadth of the conference in claiming that it was essentially about three issues only: S/M, lesbian butch/femme roles, and pornography (in fact, there was only one workshop on butch/femme, and none specifically focused on S/M, though that topic was often referenced in other workshops). WAP was closer to the mark when it insisted that no special effort had been made to enlist any of its members in the eight months of planning sessions that led up to the conference "to tell the truth about our politics," is how the WAP protest leaflet that they handed out at the conference put it.[14]

WAP and two other anti-porn groups staged a protest at the conference garbed in T-shirts that on one side read "For Feminist Sexuality" and on the other "Against S/M," and also circulated a two-page leaflet accusing the organizers of shutting out "a major part of the feminist movement" in favor of "the very sexual institutions and values that oppress all women." In response to a barrage of phone calls from women identifying themselves as members of anti-porn groups and critical of the conference for advancing "patriarchal values," the Barnard administrators buckled under the pressure and on the eve of the event confiscated 1,500 copies of the seventy-two-page handbook *Diary of a Conference*, which its organizers had put together as a guide to the event. Carole Vance, coordinator of the conference, subsequently ascribed the protest to the anti-pornographers' "loss of control over the discourse."

The arguments within feminism remained at fever pitch through most of the 1980s. When the journal *Feminist Studies* subsequently printed documents relating to the conference in its Spring 1983 issue (followed in its Fall 1983 issue by fourteen pages of letters denouncing WAP), that organization's steering committee sent *Feminist Studies* an eleven-page letter of protest correcting what it insisted had been the many distortions in the journal's coverage. *Feminist Studies* refused to print it.

The letter contained a concise summary of what WAP insisted were its *actual* positions, as opposed to the distorted versions (so WAP asserted) ascribed to it at the conference and repeated in *Feminist Studies*—and by a number of historians since. Though Andrea hadn't participated in the conference, and hadn't formally joined WAP, her own views adhered closely to those in the WAP steering committee letter. She wasn't "anti-sex"—she was against what she viewed as stereotypic role-playing (butch-femme) and rituals of dominance and submission (S/M). Nor had she "sought out" an alliance with the right ("Feminists who did anything against pornography were accused of being in bed with the right," Andrea insisted. "We have never worked with the right. . . . We have never wanted to and so we never have . . . part of the media coverage has been to create an alliance that has never existed"). The related accusation of "playing into the Right's traditional values," moreover, was the equivalent of saying that one should refrain from criticizing Israel for confiscating Palestinian land because it would feed anti-Semitism.[15]

Of prime importance—both to Andrea and to WAP—was what they insisted had been the conference's misrepresentation of their position regarding biological determinism. Throughout the conference, WAP members had been referred to as "cultural feminists"—that is, advocates of the view that women and men were fundamentally, innately, different from each other. So-called cultural feminists focused on their own subculture, art, and spirituality. And they insisted that male *values*—not *men*—were the enemy, and in particular, *machismo* and normative heterosexuality.[16]

The opposing forces within feminism weren't always clearly demarked, and many feminists went back and forth between the opposing camps. But at the unwavering heart of cultural feminism was the conviction that biology determined that women are fundamentally alike—and fundamentally different from men. Andrea's view, to the contrary, was that although sex roles *were* currently dichotomous, both the structure and content of those roles were culturally constructed; neither men nor women were naturally this way or that. Her vehemence in denouncing men as selfish, violent, and woman-hating could sometimes seem the echo of a determinist position, but her core belief was that a gender-just world *could* come into existence; nothing in our hormones or genes prevented it (though the oppressive weight and imprinting of historical *experience* might).

When John Stoltenberg took part in a panel on pornography at a different conference, he put the matter succinctly: "I want a world in which gender is not a battle for power differences. In fact, I could really do without gender"—that is, as currently defined. To achieve a social order free of female subordination and abuse, the epiphenomena—pornography, sadomasochism, and dichotomous sex roles (like butch-femme)—that reflected and deepened a split-gender view of humanity had to be uncompromisingly resisted. In Andrea's view, the defenders of porn, S/M, and butch-femme were deluded: they saw themselves as radical heroes, unconventional pioneers of sexual pleasure bent on rethinking feminist orthodoxy that viewed women as victims devoid of agency, whereas in fact, Andrea believed, they were profoundly conformist, offering strict allegiance to the *pre-existing* division of sex roles between those who dominate and those who submit.[17]

Right-Wing Women, released early in 1983, was by a considerable margin Andrea's most impressive achievement to date, though arguable in some of its particulars and necessarily dated in others (women today are not *as* segregated in "female job ghettos"; nor is politics any longer "an all-male clique of power"). The book's sustained tone is one of solemn authority—the sort of mature even-temperedness foretold but not sustained in her earlier books, which periodically succumbed to eruptions of thunderous moralizing. *Right-Wing Women* reflects more fully than any of Andrea's previous work the many-faceted strands of her temperament, ranging (without contradiction) from brooding desolation and gloom-ridden sooth-saying, to a sensitive receptivity, even tenderness, toward those she opposed politically—in this case, right-wing women, who most radical feminists of her generation contemptuously dismissed as ignorant puppets of their masters. Fittingly, Andrea dedicated the book to two other multi-faceted and generous women: Gloria Steinem and Muriel Rukeyser.

At the heart of *Right-Wing Women* is Andrea's obstinate insistence not only of their humanity, but also of their *agency*: they know what they're doing; their choices are deliberate, even shrewd. They're not stupid, they're not dupes, they're not unfeeling robots. They may have made their pact with the Devil, but as a survival tactic, and not as sacrificial lambs. The right-wing woman, in Andrea's view, conforms to a pre-assigned role, but does so as a necessary safety measure. "No one," Andrea writes, "can bear to live a meaningless life"; by attaching themselves to men and to "the values honored by men," these women "seek to acquire value." Which is what we all do, or try to.

The Right offers women (or claims to) valuable protection— from disorder, from homelessness, from shame. It abides by the rules of the game: domesticity and child-bearing; if adhered to, it guarantees protection from a dangerous outside world. Andrea illustrates the difficult trade-off with some surprising examples, pre-eminently the anti-homosexual crusader Anita Bryant, who in 1983, with AIDS now a full-blown catastrophe, would hardly seem a likely subject for sympathy. Andrea uses Bryant's autobiography, *Mine Eyes Have Seen the Glory*, to document the brutal poverty, material and emotional, of her childhood. When her father deserted the family, Anita blamed herself, in particular her "driving ambition." As an adult, guilty over her "abnormal" wish to win fame as a singer, she proved easy prey for Bob Green, a Miami disc jockey, who manipulated her into marriage and then took over her life. "One sees a woman," Andrea writes, "hemmed in, desperately trying to please a husband . . . whose control of her life on every level is virtually absolute" and sometimes violent. Torn between her desire for a career and her assigned role as a "good wife and mother," religion became Anita's only real solace, Jesus her "true husband." Her notoriously bigoted testimony against the Dade County homosexual rights ordinance was given, in Andrea's view, reluctantly—anything less, Bob Green had insisted, would be to condone sin, to fall short in her Christian duty. Eventually Anita succeeded in freeing herself from Green, and Andrea, in a final benediction, writes *"Pace,* sister."

Not all of *Right-Wing Women* is quite so benign. As part of her research, Andrea attended the National Women's Conference in Houston and tried to talk with some of the conservative women in attendance; she found their conversation "ludicrous, terrifying, bizarre, instructive"—and only intermittently moving. Many of the women refused to talk with her at all. Those who did told her that lesbians are "rapists, certified committers of sexual assault against women and girls." Nor were the women more kindly disposed toward Jews; she was told they were "Christ-killers, communists and usu- rers." Dialogue proved impossible: the women were impervious to counter-views. Yet Andrea—here *denying* them agency—placed the blame not on the women themselves but on the men who "almost totally" controlled the right-wing movement, and built it "on the fear and ignorance of women."

The women knew, as Andrea saw it, that "men hate intelligence in women," and in *Right-Wing Women* she indicts the men for bringing "home half-truths, ego-laden lies," which they then use "to demand solace or sex or housekeeping." The intelligence of the women had scant chance of being expressed, let alone nurtured: "without the light of public life, discourse, and action," intelligence dies. Yet women's innate *capacity*, Andrea stresses, is hardly in doubt: the three greatest writers in the English language were surely, she believed, George Eliot, Jane Austen, and Virginia Woolf.

Andrea makes it clear in *Right-Wing Women* that she isn't sug- gesting men employ overt force in reducing the women in their lives to submission, nor that most women are consciously discon- tented with their lot. Her focus is on how woman-hating has been institutionalized and how those institutions—like the law—serve to keep women in their place. Certainly in the 1980s, and even today, marital rape and battering are difficult to prove in court, even when women do find the considerable courage necessary to bring suit. Nor does Andrea put all the blame for women's unequal position on right-wing men; she's profoundly angry at men on the *left* for their opposition to abortion and their generally patronizing atti- tude toward their female compatriots. She even takes her lesbian sisters to task for their self-satisfaction in being cultural rebels when in fact all that they've done is to "break a few rules." And she has no patience for cultural feminists who portray themselves as *inher- ently* nurturant and closer to nature than men are. Nor, in fact, does Andrea see men as irredeemable; their smug sense of superiority is the product of a given set of social values, and society *can* be reno- vated, its values changed.

The only instance in *Right-Wing Women* where Andrea consistently loses her footing is when she leaves the contemporary scene and turns to historical examples to make her points—assuming, in the process, an unchanging continuity from past to present. She equates, for example, the obstacles and mockery that greeted the remarkable Victoria Woodhull in the late nineteenth century when she asserted her independence and "masculine" competence as directly relevant to the current plight of women. But Woodhull's arrest under the 1872 Comstock Law could not happen today, nor can her crusade "against the material dependency of women on men" be compared to the expanded economic opportunities today for women, even if access still falls far short of the ideal, especially for the many who lack access to a first-rate education.

When Andrea asks "Is there a way out of the home that does not lead, inevitably and horribly, to the street corner?" she means for us to treat the question as still being accurately descriptive of the either/or options available to women today. But if housewife or whore no longer covers the available range of options, the range for most women remains, especially working-class women, sharply limited. Still, it was probably an overstatement to say (as Andrea does) that "women's work that is not marriage or prostitution is mostly segregated, always underpaid, stagnant, sex-stereotyped." Nor is the ideological commitment of right-wing women sufficiently explained by the formulaic "they do what they have to in order to survive." Many, if not most, could survive even if they did not hate Jews and homosexuals. Similarly, Andrea's flat-out insistence that, as in the past, women today "cannot be responsible for pregnancy, in the sense of acting to prevent it, because women do not control when, where, how, and on what terms they have intercourse" is simply not an accurate accounting of the options currently available.

Fortunately, there is far more insight than hyperbole in *Right-Wing Women*. And the hyperbole itself is sometimes fetching, expressed with a power and certitude that prove captivating even when we blink in disbelief at the actual content. Some of the power of Andrea's prose comes from a free-wheeling mix of the sonorous sentence with in-your-face street talk. A sample: "In sorrow or not, bearing babies is what women can do that men need—really need, no handjob can substitute here . . ." What is so disarming about Andrea the human being is that, with all of her fears and fragilities, she could front on the world like a pugilistic tough guy.

A few years before *Right-Wing Women* was published, Andrea and John had finally been able to leave their rat-infested slum apartment and move to a fourth-floor walkup on Tenth Street in Brooklyn. She'd long wished for more space and a reprieve from the sordid surroundings of their tenement apartment on Second Avenue and 14th Street—the flashing lights, the ambulance sirens, the music blasting through the night, the screams from the street, the junkies blocking their doorway, the piss and shit, the rats. The new setting delighted them—birds, flowers, and just enough cement to forestall Andrea's terror of the countryside. They settled in and nervously awaited the book's critical reception; having been trashed so mercilessly in the past, and misunderstood so often, Andrea was understandably apprehensive. Then came the unexpected blurb from Alice Walker: "Simply brilliant, groundbreaking . . . extraordinary in its passionate lucidity." Andrea knew better than to think she was home free ("Whom the Gods Would Destroy, They First Make Mad with Power" could well have been her talisman).[18]

Then came the news that the Women's Press wanted to publish the book in England. Then came the reviews, many of them positive—a jarring surprise to Andrea, steeled as she'd become to hurtful dismissal. For self-protection (for confirmation that she was doomed to be misunderstood) she latched on to Elaine Markson's report that the *New York Times* had a feminist on staff read the book and she'd reported that it "had no new ideas and wasn't interesting." "The indignity of it," Andrea harrumphed, possibly with relief. Someone else reported that they'd heard Katha Pollitt at *The Nation* describe the book as "kill your husband feminism" and declare she would not be reviewing it. Now that was more like it—familiar territory Andrea knew how to navigate. "I am barely hanging together," she wrote an admirer.

But the Furies refused to run to type. Ann Jones, author of the much-admired *Women Who Kill*, praised *Right-Wing Women* as a "brilliant, compelling analysis." The influential leftwing magazine

In These Times ran a review praising Andrea for confronting a major question for feminists: "Why aren't all women feminists?" The Canadian cultural periodical *FUSE* ran a long review declaring flat out that "if you want to know about sexism and feminism, *Right-Wing Women* is a superb text" and describing Andrea's prose as "crisp and aggressive." And the well-known sociologist Pauline Bart, in a lengthy review in *New Women's Times Feminist Review*, declared *Right-Wing Women* "a brilliant book," not "judicious" and not air-tight in its arguments, but marked by "acute sensitivity."[19]

There were, to be sure, some dissenting reviews, and one suspects that these rang louder in Andrea's ears—confirming as they did her "fate" to be a misunderstood visionary—than their number warranted. At a guess, the unfavorable review that probably hurt the most was Jan Clausen's in *Womannews*. Clausen was an out-lesbian writer much admired for her 1980 book, *Mother, Sister, Daughter, Lover.* Her critique mattered, and it was wide-ranging. She rightly pointed out that Andrea had never paused to define which right-wing women she was analyzing and how they differed from women "who hold less extreme views." In Clausen's view, Andrea was best seen as "a premier rhetorician of female victimization" and thought she *did* "succeed brilliantly in conveying the emotional tone of *some* female experience." But she felt strongly that Andrea's critique of men on the left was over-drawn, and decried as not analytic her vision of "monolithic male power and universal female victimhood."[20]

8

The Ordinance

"A leak from the visiting professorship committee," Kitty
MacKinnon wrote Andrea from the University of Minneso-
ta, "has it that we/you have been awarded it"—that is, a jointly taught
course on pornography. All that was needed was "a letter in hand on
the precise financial terms." It was welcome news. Andrea's reviews
may have markedly improved, but her financial situation remained
precarious; a university salary, even for a single term, would be a
considerable bonanza. By mail the two friends began to plan the
course and debate the merits of whether to assign Henry Miller ("he
is the real pornographer," Kitty thought) or D.H. Lawrence.[1]

Then the plot thickened. Word came down to Kitty that the
Women's Studies faculty wasn't willing to invite Andrea for even a
part-time teaching job. Opposition to the course seemed tenacious,
and the resistance to it ugly—including graffiti scrawled on Kitty's office door. Though still not a tenured professor, Kitty riskily
refused to withdraw the course proposal, and eventually the opposition gave in and the joint course with Andrea was finally approved
for the fall term of 1983.

Yet the ugliness periodically resurfaced. A parody of the course
description began to make the rounds; it may possibly have been

intended as good-humored ribbing, but if so its misogynistic, anti-Semitic overtones fell far short of the mark. It upset Kitty so much that she was "unable to sleep or eat for four days." (When the term was over, a still indignant Kitty resigned from the university and went "back on the academic road"). Andrea, more inured to mockery, agreed to a student newspaper interview, but when the resulting article turned out to be full of misrepresentations, she wrote an angry rejoinder that may not have cleared the air but did state her views with notable clarity:[2]

> I did not say that Professor MacKinnon and I have been working for almost ten years to formulate an argument to make pornography illegal. *Banning* is not in my political vocabulary. . . . It is not *illegal* to seek the aid of government to "suppress" ideas one doesn't like, especially when those ideas amount to a systematic oppression of a group of people because of a condition of birth. . . . People have fought the idea of racism, for instance, by getting the government to outlaw segregation. It was not *illegal* for people to try to do this . . . I am distressed and disgusted by [the student's] . . . need to search out men to tell her that I am wrong on every score. Being an "objective" journalist might consist of getting what someone says right (being accurate), rather than trying to balance a view you don't understand with one that is reassuringly familiar even though staggeringly ignorant.

Then came the Andrea-esque closing line: "You do not have permission to abridge this letter." Period.

While teaching the course together (Andrea taught a second one of her own, on English literature), a citizen's group approached her for assistance in persuading the city of Minneapolis not to rezone their working-class neighborhood to allow for the sale of pornography, fearing they'd be "horrendously affected by it." Andrea consulted with Kitty, who proposed drafting a piece of legislation based on the ideas they'd earlier developed for the aborted Linda ("Lovelace")

Marciano case. The basic concept was that pornography was a sex discriminatory practice that violated women's civil rights through coercion, trafficking, and other sex-based violations. Appearing before the city's zoning and planning committee, Andrea elucidated the likely harms that derived from pornography, and Kitty addressed possible solutions—including a legislative ordinance.[3]

Their presentation was so effective that the Minneapolis City Council retained their services to hold public hearings on pornography and to draft a model ordinance for dealing with it. Avoiding hitherto standard (and contested) words like "prurient" and "obscene," they settled on defining pornography as "the graphic sexually explicit subordination of women" (Andrea sometimes used a shortened form: "the sexualized subordination of women"). She and Kitty viewed pornography (as Andrea had earlier put it) as "where all the nerve endings connected for the sexual abuse of women, and how it got legitimized and turned into a form of entertainment. . . . I thought it was a damn good way to continue to fight against rape and to begin to fight against prostitution."[4]

In ideologically grounding their project on the view that pornography violated women's civil rights, they were adopting a legal strategy that the right wing hadn't previously employed as part of its own assault on "smut." Andrea further distinguished between the two movements: "we are against hierarchy and for equality . . . against the sexual and civil subordination of women . . . that is why we are feminist, not right-wing." Even if pornography is viewed as a symptom rather than the root cause of women's oppression, "the fact that something is a symptom (as Andrea would later put it) does not mean that it's not crucial to the health of the organism"—if you're sick with a 104 temperature, "the first thing you have to do is to get rid of the temperature before you can get better."[5]

Recognizing that the definition of pornography as "graphic sexually explicit subordination of women" was an abstract umbrella term, they itemized the various specific acts it covered, like being "penetrated by objects or animals," or portrayed "as sexual objects who enjoy humiliation or pain," experience sexual pleasure in "rape, incest, or other sexual assaults," or are "presented in scenarios of degradation, humiliation, injury, or torture." The model legislative ordinance they drew up added the critical sentence—which opponents of the ordinance rarely acknowledged—that "the use of men, children, or transsexuals in the place of women is also pornography for purposes of this law."

Legally, the ordinance made pornography actionable: it allowed women who'd been its victims, through coercion, force, assault, or trafficking, to bring a civil suit, and for the first time to do so *not* under the previously used—and mostly useless—grounds of obscenity or zoning infractions. A civil suit had the additional advantage of requiring for conviction only a "preponderance of evidence," unlike a criminal case, where guilt must be proven "beyond a reasonable doubt." Under the model ordinance the burden of proof, as in all civil cases, would be on the plaintiff. To bring a successful suit, a "victim" would have to prove that pornography had harmed her in a specific way or—in regard to trafficking—had harmed women in general. After a plaintiff testified to injury, it would be up to the presiding judge to award damages or issue some other form of relief.

Though cries of "censorship!" immediately arose, the charge wasn't factually applicable, since no part of the ordinance involved prior restraint, nor was any reference made in it to obscenity law (which empowers the state to use criminal law to suppress speech, in contravention of the spirit of the First Amendment). The ordinance was (in Andrea's words) "a harm-based equality law, which derives its constitutional claim from the principles underlying the Fourteenth Amendment, especially the equal protection clause." Andrea wanted no part in censorship. She abhorred the idea of putting more power in the hands of the state, and Kitty entirely agreed. Later, Andrea herself would be a victim of censorship: customs officials in New Zealand would ban *Pornography* as obscene, and *all* of her books would be suppressed in South Africa.[6]

After drafting the ordinance, Andrea and Kitty began pressing for its implementation. They organized a set of hearings in Minneapolis and drew up a press release to publicize them (as they were dropping the release in the mail, Andrea laughingly—and prophetically—turned to Kitty: "We are about to become two of the most notorious women in America"). The initial hearings in what would be the first round of a protracted struggle took place before a committee of the Minneapolis City Council and were open to the public.

To substantiate their view that pornography both represented and further encouraged violence against women, they called on a host of both expert witnesses and individual victims to provide testimony. The witnesses included psychologists and therapists, adult individuals who'd suffered sexual abuse, social workers, and academic researchers from various fields of expertise. A string of women came forward to offer testimony about their own experiences, including Carol L., an American Indian who described being gang-raped by men who kept calling her "squaw"; Ruth, who described her husband as using pornography as a kind of textbook in demanding her compliance with his prescribed sexual experiments; and Rita, who recounted a Girl Scout camping trip during which, at age thirteen, she was gang-raped at gunpoint by a group of hunters aroused by a session with porn magazines.

Taken together, the witnesses embodied Andrea's claim that the split in the feminist movement, which would shortly become a chasm, over the issue of pornography was a *class* division. The ordinance, she and Kitty believed, made it possible for the first time for poor women who'd previously had no public voice, to present their grievances and to seek redress for them, even as it alienated the educated, academic elite of feminists already comfortable enough with power and privilege to consider themselves immune from sexual exploitation.

The Minnesota hearings also heard testimony—either cited or given in person—regarding what in 1983 was still an early stage of formal research into the effects of pornography on actual behavior. Much of the early work had been done by psychologists Edward Donnerstein and Neil Malamuth, which—though to some extent inconclusive—had led them to conclude that "violent imagery does change men's attitudes about sexual aggression towards women" (increasing, for example, the number of rape fantasies; Malamuth found that 30 percent of the men he studied who regularly used pornography admitted to "some likelihood" of raping women if they could be assured of not being caught and punished).[7]

A later update, published in 1990, would go still further: acknowledging that some studies more or less exonerated pornography from harmful effects on women, it would nonetheless conclude that "the weight of evidence is accumulating that intensive exposure to *soft*-core pornography desensitizes men's attitude to rape, increases sexual callousness, and shifts their preferences toward hard-core pornography . . . exposure to violent pornography [in turn] increases men's acceptance . . . of violence against women." Not all people, of course, will react the same way, whether seeing a depiction of women being bound and gagged or viewing Monet's water lilies floating serenely in an idyllic summer pond.

The Minnesota hearings were the opening salvo in what would be a long series of presentations, conferences, and debates—a general war of words marked by heated rhetoric and wounding accusations on all sides. In response to the ordinance, a number of prominent "pro-sex" feminists who'd earlier spearheaded the controversial 1982 Barnard Conference formed a new organization, the Feminist Anti-Censorship Taskforce (FACT), to work against the passage and implementation of Kitty and Andrea's model ordinance. Among the leading figures in FACT were Gayle Rubin, Pat Califia, Amber Hollibaugh, Joan Nestle, Dorothy Allison, Carole Vance, Nan Hunter, and Lisa Duggan. Not that they agreed with each other on all particulars. In a long letter to Nan Hunter, for example, Gayle Rubin conceded the need to "include people with a wide range of opinion on pornography itself," but underlined her wariness "of any tendency that includes the 'middle of the road' at the expense of those who have taken more radical positions"—those, for example, who demand open access to sexual materials for minors ("outlandish child porn laws continue to be passed at an appalling rate," Rubin wrote) and who are actively working to destigmatize S/M.[8]

The FACT forces filed an amicus brief in the U.S. Court of Appeals, 7th Circuit, that accused Kitty and Andrea of depicting men as "attack dogs" and women "as incapable of consent." The brief also cogently insisted that the language of the ordinance was "unconstitutionally vague and shifting," that its central terms—like "sexually explicit exploitation"—had no fixed meaning, and that sexually explicit speech "does not cause or incite violence in a manner sufficiently direct to justify its suppression under the First Amendment." It broadly claimed that "women need the freedom and the socially recognized space to appropriate for themselves the robustness of what traditionally has been male language."[9]

The foundational charge of a lack of sufficiently direct evidence particularly irritated Andrea. The empirical evidence that FACT demanded, Andrea argued, meant evidence produced in a laboratory—precisely the kind of causative proof that FACT had to know could never become available. Researchers can find, she argued, "that exposure to certain kinds of pornography will cause men to administer larger doses of and more electric shocks to women in a laboratory setting—[but] you cannot set up an experiment that lets men rape women. So the finding comes out like this: exposure to pornography . . . leads to greater aggression against women; or, pornography increases aggression against women. But there will never be a finding that pornography causes rape."

There *is*, she pointed out, empirical evidence in abundance from clinical psychologists or the police or battered women's shelters, but because such evidence "is based on the story of the woman," it "has the lowest legitimacy." The fact remains, Andrea insisted, that there is more correlational evidence that pornography causes rape than that tobacco causes lung cancer. The only way to produce direct evidence of the effect of tobacco would be to "take 300 kids, lock them in a lab, give some tobacco to smoke, some a placebo, and see which ones develop lung cancer. That is the way research into *causation* has to be modeled."

The various local battles that ensued would be hard fought in a number of separate venues, including Indianapolis, Los Angeles, Boston, Detroit, Des Moines, Omaha, Columbus, St. Louis, Cincinnati, and Madison, with FACT alliances in a number of instances barely winning out over the anti-porn brigades: in Suffolk County, New York, and on the Los Angeles County Board of Supervisors, the model ordinance was twice defeated by a single vote. Proof of injury—the whole question of the causal relationship of pornography to harm—was the most vigorously contested issue. By 1984, the anti-pornography forces were able to cite the research collected in Malamuth and Donnerstein's book, *Pornography and Sexual Aggression*, which reported a wide variety of studies affirming the desensitizing effects of pornography and claiming that men who watched violent pornography were more likely than non-users to hold attitudes about rape that primarily blamed the women involved: "she led him on"; "she got him sexually excited"; "she really wanted it but enjoyed pretending otherwise." Though Kitty and Andrea frequently cited Malamuth and Donnerstein, they were sometimes irritated at the wishy-washy, evasive testimony they gave: "They are holding back even on the results of their own work," Andrea commented to a friend.[10]

For much of the next two years, the ordinance struggle absorbed most of Andrea's time and energy. "I am travelling like a maniac, organizing," she wrote a friend. "We are pushing so damned hard on pornography and we are getting somewhere, though sometimes it isn't clear whether backwards or forwards." To another she wrote, "I am travelling all the time . . . and it makes me more restless, not less." Toward the end of 1984 she—all in the same week—gave a speech before some eight hundred people, testified before a Senate subcommittee, and spent three hours in the ACLU office in Washington, DC, trying to convince its head that she wasn't "a fascist censor." During one stretch she gave two to three speeches a day for eleven days in a row, and unlike her earlier experiences, they were filled less with applause and adulation than with a "quite considerable" increase in "anger and threatened violence."[11]

Judging from both media coverage and personal testimony, Andrea had grown into an extraordinarily charismatic public speaker—direct, authentic, emotionally powerful, thoroughly grounded in the relevant arguments and blessed with singular clarity in conveying them, even drily humorous occasionally, despite her antagonists' portrait of her as a dour curmudgeon. Though in many ways a natural on the platform—her command of language, her quick thinking, the emphatic boldness of her arguments, the potency of her personality—she was nonetheless often dissatisfied with her performance, and throughout the two years of continuous public debate she continued to hone her skills, often feeling shaky and vaguely nauseated before the curtain went up ("I always get very scared before I speak," she wrote a friend at one point, "knees knocking literally, trembling, cold sweats").[12]

After she and Kitty had completed their work drafting a model ordinance, and Andrea had something concrete to work with, she felt more at ease when speaking publicly, especially since she could find comfort in the tumultuous receptions she often got. But there were plenty of brickbats too. She was often denounced to her face as a fascist out to destroy the First Amendment, a prude who hated men *and* sex, a "hysterical dyke," a leftwing turncoat wasting her energy on a trivial issue like pornography instead of what really mattered: poverty or nukes. Through repetition the charges lost some of their sting, and through practice she learned to remain patient and calm in confronting red-faced verbal denunciation. None of it was easy, but most of it became possible—a considerable triumph in the face of what was often gross derision. "The more hostile they are," she advised a friend about to participate in a public event, "the quieter inside you have to be able to get . . . in addition to concentrating on what it is essential to say, one must also concentrate on staying absolutely centered, being able to withstand a host of onslaughts. . . . You have to remember that better people than you and I have been heckled, hurt, beat upon, etc. You have to see it in terms of a long time . . . you are going to have to talk to a hundred years' worth of room-fulls of people to make change."

It would all have been easier if she and Kitty had been able to fall back on institutional support. Fundraising was about as antithetical to Andrea's skill set as yachting, and for much the same reason: having been poor most of her adult life, she also felt "terribly humiliated" when having to solicit rich people for money. The ordinance issue *did* arouse considerable interest and widened access to a broad constituency, but it wasn't a particularly prosperous one. If more funds could somehow become available, Andrea dreamed of a two-person staff that could take on a host of needed tasks: organize training sessions for speakers around the country to argue in favor of an ordinance; set up workshops on the hundred or so legal issues that the pornography question raised; oversee grassroots work in support of the ordinances; set up events; do mailings, handle the press, arrange the thousand details of travel, etc. Andrea was well aware that conflict was an inescapable part of any movement for social change, and she knew "there was no smoother way." Still, she couldn't help longing now and then for some respite from the struggle, for the blessed isolation of reading and writing—her true sources of solace.

They did find an ideally qualified litigator in the person of Anne Simon, who'd been in law school with Kitty, had worked with the NOW Legal and Educational Defense Fund, and was currently working at the Center for Constitutional Rights. Anne became, as Andrea put, "a personal source of infinite information for me about law, which I have needed desperately" (though most of her tutoring came from Kitty: the two spoke on the phone virtually daily, much of the time about legal matters). Though Anne, who believed in the cause, worked pro bono, she had to attend to her full-time job as well and could make herself available for only some ten hours a month.

Coverage of the ordinance battles was widespread in the press, frequently harsh, and sometimes downright ugly. In Minneapolis, the very first site of confrontation, the ordinance passed the city council twice—and Mayor Donald Fraser vetoed it twice. In response, an angry and deeply disappointed Andrea, who'd lobbied Fraser in person several times, wrote him a lengthy letter castigating his decision:

> I understand that you give speeches around the country in which you say that politicians should do something about torture in the world. I understand that you were instrumental in developing the human rights guidelines that affected Federal funding to El Salvador. Yet in our conversations—and in conversations reported to me by other women—you are entirely indifferent to the torture of women in and because of pornography. . . . You offered the Minnesota Twins $400,000 to stay in Minneapolis, and you say you have no money to defend the civil rights bill from . . . threatened litigation. The Twins left. What will happen to the $400,000? Whose rights will it be used to advance? Can it be true that someone of conscience has

money for baseball, but none to stop a trade in torture? I do
not believe this of you. It cannot be possible.[13]

But it was. Mayor Fraser held firm, and the struggle to pass
the ordinance moved on to Indianapolis, where the bill was narrowed to overtly violent pornography—the kind, presumably, that
"everyone" was against. Yet when the ordinance passed the Indianapolis City Council, the ACLU—with whom Andrea had already
tangled—got into the act, filing a brief accusing Kitty and Andrea
of advocating censorship, even though the term technically refers
to government-sponsored control of speech. Andrea also had a particularly nasty give-and-take with the *Village Voice* columnist Nat
Hentoff. The two had tangled before about the sanctity (or not) of
the First Amendment (Hentoff proudly called himself a free speech
"absolutist"—though conceding that libel might not qualify). In
a *Voice* article headlined "Is the First Amendment Dangerous to
Women?" he denounced the ordinance, suggesting it was so broad
that the Bible itself would come under censorship, and labeled Kitty
"the Anthony Comstock of our time."[14]

Despite Hentoff, the procedure outlined in the Indianapolis ordinance for a woman to bring a civil suit was quite specific, though its
implications were broad. If, say, a sexually explicit magazine—such
as the *Hustler* cover photo montage showing a naked woman being
passed through a meat grinder—was used in an assault or attack on
an individual, that individual could file a complaint with the Indianapolis Office of Equal Opportunity, which would then investigate.
If the material met the statutory definition of pornography and the
assault or attack could be proved to be due to it, the case could go to
civil court, which could assess damages. Under the trafficking pro-
vision, a plaintiff was also allowed to sue the publisher and distributor of the discredited material for damages and for an injunction
forbidding its further dissemination.

According to Hentoff, the MacKinnon/Dworkin ordinance had
"contributed to a moral crusade that is threatening to expand to
other places on a wider scale" (indeed, it was already on the docket
in Detroit, Des Moines, Omaha, Columbus, St. Louis, Cincinnati,
and Madison). He singled out one such place, Suffolk County, New

York, where a right-wing Republican legislator had recently introduced a version of the ordinance that cited pornography as causing sodomy, the "destruction of the family unit," and in general
"crimes inimical to the public good." But what Hentoff failed to
mention was that Andrea and Kitty, on hearing the specifics of the
Suffolk County ordinance, immediately denounced it and successfully worked against its passage.

In a second article, Hentoff used Kitty's own mentor, the distinguished and progressive Yale Law School professor Thomas
Emerson, as a witness against the ordinance. He honorably noted
that Emerson expressed his *agreement* with MacKinnon that "pornography plays a major part in establishing and maintaining male
supremacy in our society," but Emerson also expressed the view that
her solution to the harm done by pornography was "nearly limitless"
in its scope and could theoretically "outlaw a substantial portion of
the world's literature." The ACLU agreed that such an outcome was
not farfetched. In an amicus brief, it argued that since "sexual subordination"—the key operative term in the ordinance—"is inherently vague," it opened up a can of worms. As did other terms in the
ordinance, such as "sexually explicit," "abasement," and "shown as
filthy or inferior."[15]

In "Equal-Opportunity Banning," Hentoff used one of Kitty
and Andrea's own chosen experts, Edward Donnerstein, to testify
against them. It was true, Hentoff argued, that current research
indicated that if men are shown movies containing a good deal
of violence against women, some of their attitudes toward wom-
en become more negative. But what Donnerstein's research did
not conclude, Hentoff argued, was that the *behavior* of those men
changed. He quoted Donnerstein himself to the effect that his
research had been misinterpreted; he had *not* found a connection
between violent pornography and actual violence against women—
nor had any other researcher. But this was, in fact, an instance of
Donnerstein reinterpreting his data—a tendency to obscure the
findings of his own research, about which Kitty and Andrea had
earlier complained.

In this instance, Donnerstein himself, in a letter to the *Voice* that
his co-researcher Daniel Linz also signed, insisted that Hentoff

had misrepresented their findings. "While it is true," they wrote, "that many zealous persons both of feminist and conservative political persuasions have attempted to overstate the conclusions of our research (claiming, for example, that our work demonstrates that exposure to pornography *directly* causes rape), *Dworkin and MacKinnon have not.* [their italics] They have consistently used social psychological research cautiously in their legal documents, and as only one form of evidence, linking violent pornography with violence against women. They have rightly placed the research in its proper perspective, saying only that the research shows that certain forms of pornography promote attitudes of callousness toward victims of violence and cause increases in aggressive behavior in a laboratory setting. . . . [MacKinnon and Dworkin] are the *only* individuals from among the many conservatives and feminists involved with this issue who have taken the time to check with us personally about what conclusions can legitimately be drawn from research in this area."[16]

Also present at the Indianapolis hearings was the young historian Lisa Duggan, who became a member of FACT. She, too, wrote a lengthy account for the *Village Voice* and, unlike Hentoff, spent considerable time interviewing the central figures in the dispute. Though the ordinance had passed the city council and been signed by the mayor, it was not yet in effect: a coalition of publishers, booksellers, and the like, joined by the ACLU, had immediately challenged the statute in federal district court as a violation of the First Amendment.

In her article Duggan took issue with the MacKinnon/Dworkin view, as expressed in the ordinance, that sexually explicit images subordinating women were "singularly dangerous, more dangerous than nonsexual images of gross violence against women, more dangerous than advertising images of housewives as dingbats obsessed with getting men's shirt collars clean." It was a clever thrust, yet not exactly accurate. Kitty and Andrea knew perfectly well that the over-riding culprit was the structural patriarchy, not one of its offshoots like *Hustler* or "snuff" films. They had never argued, as Duggan claimed, "that pornography is at the root of virtually every form of exploitation and discrimination known to woman."

Nor had they been calling for any sort of ban of sexually explicit material, though "ban" was the accusatory word Duggan used against them. What they advocated was not a ban but rather the creation of a legal channel whereby women who felt they'd been harmed by pornography could bring civil suit for damages. They had not called in the ordinance for prior restraint of any media outlet, nor had they advocated any enlargement of police or prosecutorial power; their emphasis was on the exercise of civil rights, not censorship. Nor—as FACT also charged—had they "allied" with the right-winger Moral Majority. They found themselves on the same side of the pornography argument, but not for the same reasons: the Moral Majority was against all non-traditional forms of sex and promoted traditional family life and gender roles; Kitty and Andrea were against the abuse and subordination of women and *for* the rights of sexual minorities and gender non-conformists.[17]

As a result of the widespread publicity generated by the ordinance hearings, Attorney General William French Smith resurrected on the federal level the Commission on Obscenity and Pornography, which had been moribund since 1970. Andrea herself testified before it on January 22, 1986, toward the end of the Commission's hearings in New York City. By that point, it had already become the object of a sophisticated, coordinated attack for what was perceived as its growing sympathy for Kitty and Andrea's civil rights approach. The pro-pornography Media Coalition had hired the largest public relations firm in Washington, DC, Gray and Company (with known ties to the Reagan White House), to come up with a strategy that would discredit the Commission. Working with a million-dollar budget, they organized a campaign that planted a variety of stories discrediting both committee staff members and witnesses, as well as debunking as fake any newspaper stories that reported various scientific studies linking pornography with harm to women and children.[18]

Andrea began her testimony before the Commission by spelling out some facts and figures: 65–70 percent of the women who worked in pornographic media had themselves been victims of incest or childhood sexual abuse. At least that high a percentage came from low-income homes, had had limited educational opportunities,

were themselves poor, and had few economic options. The younger ones were frequently runaways who'd been raped, filmed, and
exploited by pimps. The powerlessness of most of the adult women
in pornography made them, out of fear (and with frozen smiles),
involuntarily complicit with the brutality of the scene—including
overt violence.

Having painted the terrain with grim accuracy, Andrea moved on
to examine some of pornography's broader implications. She took
on the free speech issue directly. Precisely whose free speech is at
stake? she asked. Should we consider the presentation of a woman
bound and gagged as speech? "Who is that speech for? We have
women being tortured and we are told that that is somebody's
speech? Whose speech is it? It's the speech of a pimp, it is not the
speech of a woman. The only words we hear in pornography from
women are that women want to be hurt, ask to be hurt, like to be
raped, get sexual pleasure from sexual violence; and even when
a woman is covered in filth, we are supposed to believe that her
speech is that she likes it and she wants more of it."

Besides, Andrea argued, the absolutists righteously rising to
the defense of the First Amendment failed to note that it did *not*
license libel, slander, blackmail, bribery, so-called fighting words
(for instance, walking up to someone on the street and calling him a
fascist), incitement to violence, or—in a recent 9–0 decision by the
Supreme Court—child pornography. The Supreme Court itself had
on occasion refused to interpret the First Amendment as an absolute
bar on government regulation. Along with the well-known rejection of the right to shout "Fire!" in a crowded theater, the Court
had found that speech or action could be so harmful that it could
constitutionally restrict the expression. Similarly, it had found that
the standard remedy of encouraging more speech wasn't always
available or effective; the individual is seen as harmed by the *speech*
itself, not by subsequent or prior acts. And what of the history of the
First Amendment? To Andrea it was "a sick mixture of patriotism
and racism"—as if the Amendment "did not coexist with slavery or
segregation; as if it does not now exist with illiteracy, hunger, and
poverty."[19]

By the time of Andrea's testimony, the Commission members

had already stumbled several times through the thicket of conflicting terms and definitions that characterized obscenity laws and case decisions. It was a morass of contradiction and confusion. Was "indecent" the same as "obscene"? Should restrictions exist on the production and distribution of printed material as well as material with pictorial content? Where does erotica fit in? Didn't that term relate solely to literary merit—James Joyce, say, or perhaps Henry Miller? Did the so-called Hicklin test corrupt those whose minds are open to such immoral influences? But who did that leave *out*? In the *Jacobellis* decision in 1964, Justice Potter Stewart had settled for "community standards" as the best guide in determining obscenity, but opinions in even small communities varied; whose should get primacy? In 1973, the Supreme Court in *Miller vs. California* had established a three-tier test for determining what was obscene rather than merely erotic.[20]

The "Miller test" had invoked terms like "offensive sexual conduct" and "lack of serious value"—but who had the moral confidence (and legitimacy) to define such vague terms? Where did nudity fit in (was the film *Carnal Knowledge* obscene?)? Beside the intrinsic definitional problems lay the real-world issue of whether it was *possible* for a mere individual to win a lawsuit against a big-time pornographer. Even several corporations had failed in the attempt. The Pillsbury company had earlier brought suit against Al Goldstein and his publication, *Screw*, which had run a series of cartoons portraying the trademark Pillsbury Doughboy fucking—and had lost in court, mostly due to the testimony of an ACLU attorney arguing against any infringement of free speech.

In the whole tangled history of legal approaches to pornography, about the only definition that *hadn't* been suggested was precisely the one Andrea and Kitty introduced: productive of harm to women and children. As Andrea put it in her testimony before the Commission, obscenity laws were hopelessly vague; "prurient interest" (what gave an erection, say, to a male juror) "has nothing to do with the objective reality of what is happening to women in pornography"—to them as performers, and to them as the partners of men influenced by the endemic violence of pornographic depictions of sex. Nor, Andrea argued, was the standard of "community values" that some state obscenity laws had adopted any more satis-fying. What did it even "mean in a society when violence against women is pandemic, when according to the FBI a woman is battered every eighteen seconds and it's the most commonly committed vio-lent crime in the country? What would 'community standards' have meant in the segregated South? What would 'community standards' have meant during the heyday of Nazi Germany?"[21]

What *women* needed, Andrea told the Commission, is "the equal protection principle of the Fourteenth Amendment"; the "reality of pornography" was that it embodied "the subordination of wom-en. . . . I am here asking the simplest thing. I am saying hurt people need remedies, not platitudes, not laws that you know already don't work. . . . People silenced by exploitation and brutality need real speech, not to be told that when they are hung from meat hooks, that is their speech . . . the law that Catharine MacKinnon and I developed applies only to sexually explicit material that subordinates women in a way that is detrimental to our civil status." (Addressing an all-male conference in 1983, Andrea made a comparable, if still more eloquent plea: "Why are you so slow? Why are you so slow to understand the simplest things? Not the complicated ideologi-cal things. You understand those. The simple things! The cliches! Simply that women are human to precisely the degree and quality that you are!")[22]

Before the Commission, Andrea's words and manner were pow-erful to the point where several of the members—their awe of her performance palpable—thanked her for her contribution. They did ask for several clarifications, but did so with the utmost respect. One commissioner posed this question: "If we could find a man and a woman who totally and freely agree to sadomasochistic activities, would you think that should be prohibited, even though in itself it is a very degrading thing to occur to a woman and to a man also?"

Andrea, honorably, made it clear in her response that she opposed sadomasochism, objected to "the degradation intrin-sic to the acts" (though "degradation" would of course not be the description—certainly not a *sufficient, inclusive* one—that practitio-ners of S/M would themselves use to depict their acts). She did go on in her reply to raise the knotty, usually ignored question of the nature of consent. What in fact did that word mean? "The forms of coercion—including the reality of poverty, the vulnerability of child sexual abuse" make it "very difficult to understand" when something close to true volition is actually present.

Another commissioner followed up: "I take it from your response . . . that you believe it does not occur that a woman voluntarily poses for pictures for *Penthouse* or *Playboy*." No, Andrea responded, "I believe that it does voluntarily occur." But *Playboy* "is the top of the ladder . . . the highest amount of money that a woman gets paid for posing . . . [but] the fact that women sometimes voluntarily are part of pornography should not stop us from doing something about the women who are coerced . . . the fact that most women . . . sixty-five to seventy-five percent . . . who are in pornography are victims of child sexual abuse is probably the most telling point about what the pornography system is all about . . . we have to deal with pornography as a real system of coercion that operates both in terms of physical coercion and economic vulnerability."

Toward the end of her testimony, a question finally came up about men—about whether some men who performed in pornography couldn't also be considered exploited. Andrea's response was a decided "yes"—that is, "for young men, for men who are runaways, for men who are dispossessed in some sense from society; but men who don't die in it get out of it, usually . . . it doesn't become a way of life in the same way that it does for women. It's not a total dead end with no other options ever." In regard to black men, she thought the question had "tremendous implications . . . their constant, constant use as rapists in pornography is very [much] tied to their low civil status." She recalled as well that during the hearings in Minneapolis, "we had a great deal of testimony about the use of all-male pornography in homosexual battery; I believe that that is real . . . that under civil rights legislation, men who are battered in that way must have a right to sue."

It was at precisely that point, April 1985, that *Ms.* magazine entered the fray with a lengthy article, "Is One Woman's Sexuality Another Woman's Pornography?" The title alone hinted at how the article would be tilted, though trying all the while to appear even-handed. Given *Ms.*'s wide circulation and the large chunks of time and information that Kitty and Andrea had given to the article's author, Mary Kay Blakely, they were at first disheartened—and then livid. Andrea described the article to a friend as "a nightmare of malice and misogyny . . . and it hurts like hell. It's our political reality." In terms of incidence and length of quotation, the *Ms.* article featured MacKinnon and Nan Hunter, the ACLU lawyer and FACT member, about equally, with somewhat less space given to the two other leading antagonists, Andrea and Carole Vance. But the tone of authority in the article did rather subtly lean to the FACT side. All four women emerged as smart, committed, and well-informed—but Hunter at a bit greater length came off as a bit more trenchant. In some eyes, that emphasis reflected the comparative worth of the two opposing arguments; in others', the disparity resulted from the greater appeal to *Ms.*'s editors of FACT's arguments.[23]

Carole Vance, without challenge, was allowed to say in the *Ms.* article that "attitudes are very poor predictors of behavior." (But wasn't a rabid anti-Semite *more* likely to *behave* badly toward a Jew?) Kitty, on the other hand, was quoted as acknowledging that "the research can't tell on an individual basis which man will go and rape a woman after having been exposed to a certain amount of pornography," but she also said (which wasn't included) that the research showed "the rate of abuse of women will increase with the consumption of pornography." When *Ms.*, moreover, elaborated on the legal issues in play, opponents of the ordinance were given considerably more space, and filled some of it with dubious accusations—like the suggestion that the anti-porn forces were being hypocritical in objecting to violent sexual images while not protesting the violence in non-sexual war films (as if any movement for social justice has ever taken on all possible issues simultaneously). It was true enough, as another FACT member insisted, that "pornography is a part, but not all of a violent, woman-hating culture," but while awaiting the total renovation of that culture couldn't a bit of credit be granted to those taking on at least one aspect of the assault against women?[24]

Andrea wrote a furious, over-the-top letter to the managing editor of *Ms.*, outlining her and Kitty's grievances. *Ms.*, according to Andrea's indictment, had made "the sexual abuse of pornography invisible"; had "ignored the phenomenally invigorating" effects of the ordinance on women, even though it was not yet a working law anywhere; had made no reference to "the racist hatred in pornography," though she and Kitty had provided "a staggering amount of information" on the subject; had "given us no credit, no honor"—the only moment in her letter that Andrea let her personal hurt show— "for working on this issue in the face of unremitting hostility"; and had inaccurately portrayed the women in FACT, who opposed the ordinance, as "more than 50% of the women's movement, which they are not. You have made their criticism and solipsisms more important than the issue of pornography or the ordinance."[25]

Her summary was vintage Dworkin (when the wound was deep and she breathed fire):

> I don't want anything more to do with *Ms.* ever. Not ever.
>
> As a feminist courtesy, I have never made public my deep political objections to the way . . . [*Ms.*] trivializes feminism. That period of self-censorship is now over.
>
> We brought you extraordinary information . . . [and] you turned what we gave you into shit. This letter is not for publication.

———

The attorney general's Commission's final report essentially adopted Kitty and Andrea's civil rights approach, and called for direct relief to the victims of the injuries "so exhaustively documented in our hearings throughout the country." The Commission further concluded that since the harms "are real," "the need for a remedy for those harms is pressing," and it recommended that Congress consider legislation. Various bills did follow, including in 1994 the Violence Against Women Act, which provided for a federal civil remedy for gender-based violence attendant on instances of rape and battering.[26]

The ordinance that Kitty and Andrea had designed, however, did not become law anywhere. It did pass in Minneapolis, without any right-wing support, and by two city councils—though the mayor vetoed it. It also passed in Indianapolis, where the mayor signed it in April 1984. There, however, a media coalition backed by the ACLU sued, and a Reagan-appointed judge declared the ordinance unconstitutional on First Amendment grounds—a ruling initially affirmed in 1985 by a three-judge panel of the Seventh Circuit Court of Appeals and then "summarily affirmed" (that is, without argument) by the Supreme Court. Kitty and Andrea took some comfort from the opinion of one of the judges that "depictions of subordination tend to perpetuate subordination."

At the time, the highly regarded constitutional scholar Laurence Tribe wrote to the Minneapolis City Council in defense of the ordinance (though he later modified his views somewhat): "While many hard questions of conflicting rights will face any court that confronts challenges to the ordinance, as drafted it rests on a rationale that closely parallels many previously accepted exceptions to justly stringent First Amendment guarantees. . . . I urge you not . . . to prevent the courts from adjudicating what may eventually be found to be the first sensible approach to an area which has vexed some of the best legal minds for decades."

After the ordinance was defeated in Cambridge, Massachusetts, 57 percent to 43 percent—it won in the working-class wards, lost in the wards around Harvard—the game seemed played out. Or, to put it perhaps more accurately, for a time nobody seemed to know what route to pursue next, or even what the central issue was that remained in need of solution. Kitty and Andrea remained entirely committed to the broad goal of ending the subservient status of women and, as a part of that, the endemic violence employed against them. But despite all their ingenuity and perseverance, no legal solution seemed available. Arrayed against them was the same coalition of prominent feminists—"the Barnard Conference crowd"—determined to resist any effort that they felt jeopardized the rights of sexual minorities and the uninhibited exercise of free speech.

Legal scholars, down to the present day, continue to debate the interlocking issues intrinsic to the debate over pornography. A number of them still insist—as did Kitty and Andrea—that the right of free speech has never been considered an unencumbered liberty; as the First Amendment scholar Rodney A. Smolla has pointed out,

"Justice [Hugo] Black aside, the absolutist view has never been fully accepted by any member of the Supreme Court . . . absolutism proves to be too brittle and simplistic a methodology, and is simply not viable as a general working approach to free speech." The relationship between speech and harm has constantly shifted, and hard questions remain. To protect women from harm, are curtailments on the right of free speech acceptable? "Speech" has long been constitutionally confined to white males; to attain, or even to approximate, equality for women, is it essential to broaden the restrictions on pornographic materials that cause harm to women?[27]

In point of fact, religious beliefs still find much greater protection in the courts than does the argument for women's equality. Of course in the era of the internet, with mounting billions being spent on pornography, the entire notion of trying to curtail its potential harm becomes something of a fool's errand. What can be done, moreover, about the fact that U.S. jurisprudence continues to privilege the First Amendment's right to freedom of expression over the Fourteenth Amendment's right to equal protection of the law? The former favors those in power, the latter gives prime emphasis to the injuries of women and minorities; it remains true today that the unalloyed free speech of pornographers outweighs the civil rights of women. Allowing for the occasional pro-ordinance legal decision, the bottom line seems still to be that the harm pornography causes does *not* outweigh the harm that might follow from placing restrictions on it. As Andrea put it after the Supreme Court declared the ordinance unconstitutional, "Right now, we have nothing. We have bottomed out. None of us have money left; or time; or heart. We are tired beyond belief."[28]

The prolonged and angry debate took its toll on personal friendships. In Andrea's case, the chief casualty was her relationship with Adrienne Rich (which had never been untroubled). When Adrienne in 1985 signed on to a FACT amicus brief, the feminist publication *off our backs* asked her to write an article for them explaining her decision. Adrienne agreed, and the resulting piece led to a round-robin of recriminations. Earlier, Adrienne had participated in WAP meetings and events, but had grown concerned (as she put it) "that the affirmation of lesbian sexuality was being downplayed in the interests of reaching a wider constituency." She continued to have "no doubt" that "images of victimized women, purveyed as sexual turn-ons, serve both to suggest and to justify acts which are . . . causing extreme suffering and destruction to thousands of women." Adrienne also still had serious doubts about the efficacy of the First Amendment "in a society where the flow of information and access to mass media is controlled by those with access to wealth, over-whelmingly male and white."[29]

She had not been, in other words, a ready or easy recruit to the ranks of FACT; instead, Adrienne still believed that the organiza-tion underestimated "the actual toll taken on women's lives" and too easily dismissed "the coercive conditions which impel women into the pornography industry." Pornography, as she currently saw it, *did* have profound consequences for those women who worked in the industry, and on the men who used pornography as well.

What *had* changed in her position was that she felt "more and more loath to ascribe the subordination of women, the prevalence of male violence, and the stunning asymmetries of material power" between men and women to any one cause. Yet she had come to believe that pornography was *not* central "in creating and main-taining the civil inequality of the sexes." She believed misogyny was deeply embedded in the country's—and most of the world's—institutional structures. She now felt that the anti-pornography ordinance, "like the patriarchal family, offers false protections, at too high a price." In her *off our backs* statement Adrienne took spe-cific issue with one of Andrea's recent articles, "Against the Male Flood: Censorship, Pornography, and Equality"—but centrally misread it as a call for heightening the power of the police to control the pornographers: "I am less sure than Dworkin and MacKinnon that this is a time when further powers of suppression should be turned over to the State."

Neither Andrea nor Kitty had made such a proposal; indeed, it would have been anathema to their unequivocal rejection of police power or the use of "prior restraint" to curtail the effects of por-nography. Both were outraged at Adrienne's misrepresentation, and both wrote responses to *off our backs* that were howls of indignation. "The basic problem, as I see it," Kitty wrote, "is that you took your view of our work from the opposition—meaning your information was minimally one-sided, a lot biased, and some false."[30]

Kitty went on to explicitly state that the ordinance does not involve the police any more than, say, sexual harassment or race discrimination in housing does. "It does not empower prosecutors to initiate suits in the name of the state or to send police to seize materials." Moreover, Kitty added, Adrienne had misstated their argument about causality: "To find something [pornography] 'central' in sex inequality . . . is not to find it exclusively causal, or alone in its centrality. You assume both and we never said either. . . . I can't believe that if the issue were racism . . . you would go on about all the other things that contribute to the problem as a reason to do nothing about a part of it. Eliminating segregation didn't eliminate racism. Did you therefore oppose desegregation? Was it therefore not 'central'? . . . you say the harm of pornography is real to you. Yet you still side with the status quo, with letting it go on, with doing nothing."

If Kitty's response to Adrienne was a thunderstorm, Andrea's was a tornado: "The FACT women are the old S/M crowd," she wrote (in an inflated generalization). "The brief you (Adrienne) signed is woman-hating, antifeminist, racist, intellectually dishonest, and politically reprehensible. And that is kind." The ordinance she and Kitty had been proposing "is in behalf of powerless, poor, mostly women (though some young men, many gay), frequently illiterate, often refugees from incest and prostitution as well as pornography . . . the women who signed the FACT brief are . . . lawyers and academics for the most part . . . [they] don't have anything at stake except their privilege. . . . As you know, access to print is a form of wealth; and the academy is not a street corner. . . . It ends up being exactly this, dear sister: the comfy women, to keep what's theirs, are prepared to let the powerless women be hurt forever . . . most women are silenced through civil inferiority and sexual abuse and thus have no recourse to the protections of the First Amendment . . .

"If this is feminism, it deserves to die. I want nothing ever to do with it. I think, though, that feminism is in the aspirations and courage of those other women I mentioned, the ones I think you have forgotten about (if you ever knew them): the poor, the genuinely powerless. I think that there is a movement based on their experiences, many of which are also my own; and we are determined to change this system. . . . If this FACT brief really represents you, I am happy to sever all political affiliation with you. If the FACT brief does not represent you, you had better do something about the fact that you have signed it."

More than a decade later, Kitty and Andrea edited the hearings and testimony generated during the 1980s in four cities—Minneapolis, Indianapolis, Los Angeles, and Boston—into a thick volume, *In Harm's Way: The Pornography Civil Rights Hearings*. It was their answer, as they had frequently complained during the ten-year period preceding the volume's appearance, to the media reports recounting testimony at the various hearings that had often appeared truncated and inaccurate to them, and in some instances even rewritten by editors to conform more closely with their own subjective views.[31]

Kitty and Andrea wrote separate introductions to *In Harm's Way*, with Kitty elucidating the legal history, and Andrea—always somewhat allergic to theory—summarizing and commenting on the specific human stories (including her own) that illustrated the central issues aired during the hearings. In her piece, Andrea came down hard on the left, accusing its lawyers of buying into the argument—originating in the counter-cultural sixties—that pornography was merely an artifact of "liberated sexuality," no more, no less. They had labeled anti-porn agitators "right-wing collaborators" and described themselves as defenders of free speech (even though in the sixties, the left had flexibly rejected an absolutist adherence to free speech when faced with racist speech that incited violence). Andrea was less persuasive when accusing the left of equating rape with "free sex"—and not at all persuasive when accusing the left of defending rape within marriage. Kitty, in her own introduction to *In Harm's Way*, made it convincingly clear that she and Andrea regarded the right with abhorrence. She fully and persuasively rejected the widespread charge that they actively sanctioned an

anti-pornography coalition between radical feminists and conservative women, pointing out that with only one exception (a Republican woman who supported the ERA) *all* the sponsors of anti-porn
ordinances in all of the cities in which they had been introduced
self-identified as either liberal or radical.

Much still lay ahead, in regard to both the continued sparring
between opposing forces already on the scene, and the later entrance
of third-wave feminists, whose new voices would offer innovative
perspectives on issues that dated back to the 1980s, and in some
instances would introduce related topics (for example, the effects
of various forms of parenting on subsequent patterns of sexuality
and gender presentation) that had been unknown or ignored in the
earlier debate.[32]

There *were* a few voices raised as early as the mid-eighties that
pointed ahead to issues that would prove central to third-wave
feminism. The English media critic Richard Dyer was one. As a
pro-feminist socialist and a gay man who had easy access to porn
and acknowledged the pleasure he took in it, Dyer felt that some
aspects of the porn debate were being ignored or underplayed. The
role of capitalism, for one. Did capitalism provide unusually fallow,
or even unique, grounds for the production of pornography? For
Dyer, the answer was yes, yet at the same time he didn't believe
that "all capitalist cultural production always all the time expresses
capitalist ideology." He was interested in "moments of contradiction, instability and give in our culture"—those points, in other
words, "at which change can be effected." He believed, too, that the
MacKinnon/Dworkin side of the debate on pornography rightly
stressed "the degradation of women that characterizes so much heterosexual porn," and that they were right to emphasize such porn
as "woman-degrading representations of sexuality." Yet he thought
their arguments would have profited from paying more attention
than they did to gay porn.[33]

Kitty and Andrea's critique *had* focused on heterosexual porn
(with a largish sidebar disparaging lesbian S/M), yet in the few
places where Andrea chose to comment on gay male porn, Dyer
thought her characterizations were inaccurate. This was particu-

larly the case, as he saw it, in the way she depicted young, black men as primarily occupying "feminine" roles in gay porn. Her characterization was true enough in regard to scenes involving drag, Dyer conceded, but decidedly not true for those porn depictions of muscular, hyper-masculine black men dominating and penetrating feminine "little white guys" or (less frequently) those shown having sex with equally butch white men. The matter, he felt, was of some political import: though porn in general mostly reinforced "the worst aspects of the social construction of masculinity," the wider range of representations of gay male sexuality suggested a standard narrative that depicted a lifestyle as one combining "a basic romanticism with an easy acceptance of promiscuity." That dominant pattern of gay cultural production, egalitarian and non-familial, had a potentially valuable—and radical—story to tell mainstream viewers.

The media critic B. Ruby Rich is another example of a dissident voice in the mid-eighties that asked questions about some of the basic assumptions and absences that typified that decade's porn debate. Citing the Samois anthology *Coming to Power: Writings and Graphics on Lesbian S/M*, Rich questioned by indirection the unwavering anti-S/M position that Kitty and Andrea had adopted in their anti-porn writings. A more productive debate, Rich suggested, would be "honest enough to confront the continuum of sexual practice that links S/M to a more common experience." Drawing on Jessica Benjamin's essay "Master and Slave: The Fantasy of Erotic Domination"—notable, in Rich's view, as one of the few "to bring psychoanalytic theory to bear upon issues of sexuality"—she stresses in particular Benjamin's view that the erotic attraction of domination/submission scenarios rests on "the need for transcendence"; or, in Benjamin's own words, "the experience of losing the self . . . is increasingly difficult to obtain except in the erotic relationship . . . sexual eroticism has become the heir to religious eroticism." To which Rich adds, "It is indeed peculiar that the debate on sadomasochism should have arisen as a lesbian issue when the practice is so widespread among heterosexuals."[34]

In regard specifically to pornography, Rich points out that the debate remained inconclusively poised "between two inadequate definitions: either a conscious degradation of women, ideologically aligned with misogyny and psychologically linked to actual violence against women; or one of the few expressions of explicit sexuality in a repressive culture lacking in sex education and opposed to the taking of pleasure." In Rich's view, the debate had been severely hampered by the paucity of empirical studies in combination with "the lack of honest testimony" among the debaters—that is, their refusal to explore in depth how their own histories had been instrumental in placing them on one side or the other of the debate.

The example Rich gives is startling and refreshingly unnerving: in Scott MacDonald's article "Confessions of a Feminist Porn Watcher," he suggests (to quote Rich) "that pornography functions as a repetitive reassurance machine for a male psyche far more fragile than generally acknowledged—so tenuous indeed, that it requires a continual assertion of its powerfulness to neutralize incipient physical and spiritual impotence." Pornography's psychological function, in other words, is not—or not simply—to subordinate women, but to comfort men.[35]

Rich's review essay is studded with comparable provocations: "Do women not objectify men as well, albeit in a different manner? In fact, if the male form of objectification is degradation, then perhaps the female form, as demonstrated by the Harlequins, is idealization"; "All sexual relations seem to concern some kind of power disequilibrium, some kernel of psychic domination or surrender, some terror of dependence fighting a wish to depend, a simultaneous desire for—yet horror of—merging"; "The adoption of butch-fem roles or lesbian sadomasochism may well constitute an alternative remedy to the problem of merging identi[ties] . . . [in S/M] women are constructing and insisting upon the *otherness* of the partner."

Rich's intervention in what had become a somewhat claustrophobic debate, the two sides implacably opposed and hostile, is not in itself immune to challenge. But that isn't the point. What her speculations demonstrate—as early as 1986—is that closure is hardly imminent. Not only hasn't the issue of pornography been resolved, but the many side issues into which it opens out (ideologically aligned with misogyny, psychologically linked with the male fragility that secretly feeds it) have barely been explored. Kitty and Andrea had done basic spade work, and in the face of mockery and belittlement, but the soil they tilled may turn out to have additional layers, largely unexplored. A prolonged dig—downright archeological given its potential depth—remains on the calendar. What needs to be added, as the sun beats mercilessly down, is a modicum of compassion for all those sweating to get below the topsoil.

The MacKinnon/Dworkin ordinance stayed in play a while longer, until the Supreme Court in the spring of 1986 affirmed an appeals court decision that had declared it unconstitutional. That decidedly took the air out of the balloon, yet even then, for Kitty and Andrea, not decisively so. Retreat was inescapable, but surrender wasn't in their nature. They continued, though irregularly, to argue that the central issue was not censorship but harm to women. That harm in fact escalated—not only did VCRs and the internet lead to a still further expansion of sexually violent pornography, but some of the local women who'd testified at various ordinance hearings and remained in their communities became the subsequent subject of harassment. Andrea had come to know several of these women rather well and felt personally responsible when one of them actually committed suicide.

She and Kitty remained closely in touch, though they did disagree on the value of trying to redefine obscenity law; Kitty's position was that if a court decides that pornography is not as important as the pornographer's free speech, then you have a precedent that can be used to try and pass the civil rights law. Andrea felt—and so it turned out—that ultimately it's the police who decide what part of an obscenity statute will be enforced and what part won't. As late as 1998, when Susan Brownmiller was interviewing Andrea for a book she was writing (*In Our Time*) and casually said, "So you're out of the ordinance business now? You're back to just writing?," Andrea's response was, "I did get out of it to write" but "my own view is that [eventually] it's going to pass" and probably first in a foreign country, not the United States. "The U.S. is making a lot of money exporting sexual abuse."[36]

9

Writing

Andrea tried to get others active in the anti-porn campaign to take over a portion of her political work, but had only mixed success. In truth, she wasn't replaceable in most instances. A few (including MacKinnon) were equally brilliant, but no one else could match Andrea's oratorical skills, nor the incantatory power of her writing. Yet another drain on her time opened up when she decided that politically she *had* to file a lawsuit against publisher Larry Flynt and *Hustler* magazine; for some time it had been running a series of scatologically mocking cartoons depicting her in what she called "defamatory, vile, and obscene" ways.[1]

One of the cartoons showed two women engaged in a lesbian act of oral sex with the caption, "You remind me so much of Andrea Dworkin, Edna. It's a dog-eat-dog world." Another was a two-page spread of fifteen pictures showing women masturbating and engaging in sex with each other, with a caption that read "While I'm teaching this little *shiksa* the joys of Yiddish, the Andrea Dworkin Fan Club begins some really serious suck-'n-squat." The December 1984 issue of *Hustler* contained a photograph of a woman receiving cunnilingus from a man as he masturbates; the caption read "The woman in the throes of ecstasy is the mother of radical feminist Andrea Dworkin." Taken collectively, Andrea regarded the imagery as "a form of assault and as such an effort to intimidate me into abandoning my rights of free speech, assembly, and petition." Put another way, she was deliberately personalizing the issue at the heart of the anti-porn debate: Flynt's claim of free speech pitted against the personal harm, both psychological and professional, being inflicted on her—an assault, in short, on her civil rights, to "still and chill" *her* ability to exercise her First Amendment rights.

A recent Supreme Court decision had concluded that "an aggrieved party could sue the publisher of libelous materials in any jurisdiction in which the materials were distributed." Andrea's choice of venue was Wyoming—the first state to grant women suffrage, and so the most fitting place to air the case. The well-known lawyer Gerry Spence represented Andrea. He'd recently announced himself a convert to feminism and in 1974 had won the case brought by the family of whistleblower Karen Silkwood following her death. Spence expected Wyoming's courts to reject the case, but then planned to bring suit in a federal court. The *Hustler* legal battle would prove (in Andrea's words) a "hard and long" process.[2]

Another development—this one a *welcome* claim on her time—was the news that an English publisher had finally, after multiple rejection slips in the United States, agreed to publish a paperback edition of her proposed novel, *Ice and Fire*. The terms, though, were stringent: the contract stipulated that Andrea had to complete a chapter each month from May 1, 1985, to July 1986, or the contract would automatically become null and void. Such draconian demands may well have been unprecedented, but the publisher, the distinguished house of Secker & Warburg, felt it was taking a chance on a highly controversial writer whose earlier books had sold poorly. Andrea, for her part, had no other suitor waiting in the wings—though soon after Secker & Warburg's offer on *Ice and Fire*, the Free Press picked up *Intercourse*, her hefty non-fiction work that had been turned down by numerous houses. That left Andrea with a happily dizzying publication schedule, which saw, in the space of six months, English editions of *Ice and Fire* in hardcover (Weidenfeld and Nicholson) and paperback (Secker and Warburg), and the publication of *Intercourse* in both England and the United States.[3]

"It is all quite incredible," Andrea wrote, having marked 1986 her "now-or-never" fortieth birthday. Secker & Warburg proceeded to put icing on the cake by offering to bring her to England for a publicity tour. "I am dropping anything I have to drop to work on my book," Andrea announced in mid-July, 1985. To meet her assorted deadlines, she withdrew as much as possible from human contact into what she called "a kind of shabby solitude, not really real because I have so many political responsibilities that are tied to my relations with other people," including a number of pre-arranged speaking engagements.

As it would turn out, she wasn't able to sequester herself to the extent she would have liked; too many requests for her time seemed worthy and necessary. She felt obligated during her retreat to pass out anti-porn leaflets at the annual NOW convention in New Orleans and lead a march down Bourbon Street, bullhorn in hand: "Hey, hey, ho, ho, pornography has got to go!"; to fly to Wyoming for the opening arguments of the *Hustler* lawsuit (only to have the case postponed at the last minute); to testify before the Presidential Commission on Pornography; to picket a Republican gathering; and to fly over to England for ten days of editorial meetings and public appearances.[4]

Also, the Supreme Court's 1986 negation of the ordinance still lay ahead and it was due to be voted on in two different places that summer of 1985. As Andrea wrote to one friend, "The political pressure is still on—creating a lot of conflict and trouble, when peace and solitude are needed to write; money is awful, not much coming in, actually nothing over the summer at all. . . . I am very worried that the ordinance will fail legally and politically, partly because we are all so resource-less, so unable to mount the campaigns that need to happen." John, as before, became the sole breadwinner. He'd been working as managing editor at *Essence* magazine, but left in May 1985 in order to have enough free time to put together the book that became *Refusing to Be a Man*, as well as to continue working for passage of the ordinance. For roughly six months he subbed for the managing editor of *Working Woman* and then for years thereafter cobbled together various consulting jobs (only some of which provided a full-time-equivalent salary with benefits).[5]

As Andrea battled *Hustler*, John—through *Sex & Justice*, the newsletter he edited for the National Organization for Changing Men—protested the December 1984 issue of *Penthouse*, which had featured pictures of naked Asian women tied up with rough hemp ropes and hanging from trees. "In the ten or so years I've been an activist in the feminist anti-pornography movement," he wrote, "I have learned never to underestimate how much further the pornography industry will go in its sexualization of brutality and contempt."

The most consequential draw on Andrea's time was her appearance before the Attorney General's Commission on Pornography, the so-called Meese Commission—an eleven-member investigatory panel (seven men, four women) chaired not by Meese himself but by Henry Hudson, the commonwealth attorney of Arlington, Virginia, who, notoriously, had shut down every adult bookstore in his jurisdiction. Meese was widely viewed as the leading spokesperson for President Ronald Reagan in his determination to reassert traditional moral values—despite the supposedly sacred Republican tradition of minimizing the interference of the federal government in the lives of the citizenry. In the 1960s and 1970s, it had been the left pushing for government intervention to promote the black civil rights struggle and to end the war in Vietnam. But by the mid-eighties the pendulum had decidedly swung back, as it always had (the free-wheeling twenties, for instance, gave way to the buttoned-up fifties); this time it was the Right calling for the government to step in and regulate morality (or, in Jerry Falwell's deathless words, "to push pornography back to Sleaze Town to live amongst the roaches where it belongs"). In the midst of the ferocious AIDS epidemic, even Jesse Jackson spoke out against "sex without love."[6]

Nearly twenty years earlier, during a far more permissive period, Richard Nixon's presidential commission on pornography had recommended that a massive sex education campaign be initiated, that open discussion and long-term research should be encouraged on issues relating to sexuality, and that legislation "should not seek to interfere with the right of adults who wish to do so to read, obtain, or view explicit sexual materials." (Both Nixon and Congress turned down the permissive report.) By the time the Meese Commission began its hearings in the summer of 1985, the cultural climate had unmistakably shifted, and the Commission's executive director, Alan Sears, prematurely sent out a warning letter of notification to a number of companies that they were "dealing in pornography"; as a direct result, the 7-Eleven chain immediately stopped selling adult magazines in its 7,500 stores. A federal district judge soon ordered the Commission to retract Sears' threatening letter, characterizing it as constituting "prior restraint on speech."[7]

Still, the direction in which the Commission was headed was abundantly clear (prior to their appointment, seven of the eleven members had previously spoken out against pornography), passions on all sides were quickly enflamed, and pre-existing antagonisms within feminism were emphatically underscored. For a time the wounding accusations stayed relatively low key, but when the Meese Commission concluded its investigation and in July 1986 formally released its report—a staggering 1,960 pages—a cloudburst followed.

Of the Commission's multiple conclusions—and ninety-three recommendations!—a few proved particularly inflammatory. The rape of women, the report announced, was a prominent theme in pornography, and some of the women were depicted as *enjoying* the sexual violence done to them ("they say 'no' but really mean 'yes'"); further, the report insisted that violent pornography led directly to violence against women and that even non-violent pornography could be degrading when it depicted, as it often did, women "as existing solely for the sexual satisfaction of others, usually men," or when it showed "people, usually women, in decidedly subordinate roles in their sexual relations with others." Perhaps the Commission's most provocative statement was its flat-out assertion that "none of us believes" that "uncommitted sexuality . . . [is] a good thing," thereby implicitly condemning a considerable segment of gay male subculture that deplored monogamy and celebrated sexual "adventuring."[8]

The Commission recommended stricter obscenity laws but also endorsed the MacKinnon/Dworkin civil rights approach to pornography, characterizing it as "alternative and preferable." Andrea and Kitty applauded the endorsement: "For the first time in history," they wrote, "women have succeeded in convincing a national

governmental body of a truth women have long known: pornography harms women and children." Yet they also deemed the Meese
report flawed in its recommendation to strengthen obscenity laws
and extend their enforcement; they'd long denounced such laws as
dangerously irrelevant and as heightening the discretionary powers
of the police. As Dorchen Leidholdt, the spokesperson for WAP,
added, "Obscenity laws misconceive the harm of pornography as an
affront to sensibilities instead of an injury to women's lives."

Nan Hunter, a prominent figure in FACT, made a point sounded
by many: the conservative commission's true concern was not harm
to women's lives but rather the spread of sexually explicit material,
especially the part that represented sexual minorities; what truly
horrified most of the commissioners, Hunter convincingly insisted,
was homosexuality, abortion, and teenage, premarital, and extra-
marital sex. Nor was FACT alone in its opposition. The ACLU,
where Hunter was a staff member, tried to discredit some of the testimony given to the commission; *Playboy* and *Penthouse* threatened
lawsuits; and a National Coalition Against Censorship (NCAC) was
formed (its ranks filled with celebrities like the novelist Kurt Von-
negut and actress Colleen Dewhurst).

The dissenters all hammered home the view that there was a
direct link between the influence of MacKinnon and Dworkin and
the growing climate of suppression, despite the fact that they had
both frequently made it clear, and publicly, that they opposed any
sort of categorical ban on written or visual material. Their goal—
often repeated, just as often ignored—was to extend the recourse
of the courts to those women who could prove harm from materials (such as depictions of non-consensual S/M) that subordinate
them through words or pictures. If pornography, as the Commission insisted, did represent an assault against women, then why
wasn't it considered just as harmful as anti-black and anti-Semitic
material?

Should legal decisions under their model ordinance go beyond
awarding damages to individuals into a general proscription against
pornography that portrayed women as asking for and receiving
debased treatment, the result, Andrea and Kitty argued, would *not*
amount to an unconstitutional assault on the First Amendment. In
their view, the access of poor and marginalized women to speak (and

be heard) had long been obstructed, and to a more total extent than anything the ordinance threatened. As Andrea put it, "Pornography has precisely to do with the situation of poor women—which in my view is why we are getting so much shit thrown at us in the women's movement. People have no idea how middle-classed and privileged their liberal First Amendment stuff is—how power and money determine who can actually speak in this society." Besides, she argued, the First Amendment did not intend a free pass to any form of speech; both libel and perjury had never been forms of protected expression.

Perhaps in an imperfect world, Andrea argued, the best that could be hoped for would be to reach for the very first time something like a *balance* between the civil rights of pornographers and those of women; the former would lose some iota of the fullness of their freedom of (murderous) expression, and the latter would no longer have to remain *entirely* silent. Resistance to such a compromise would draw heavily for its justification from the uncertainty surrounding the issue of causality, the weakest link in the theoretical positions of both the pro- and anti-pornography forces. *Did* violent pornography increase violent behavior toward women? *Was* the graphic portrayal of male sexual aggression and female subordination responsible for (or merely reflective of) the wide gap in power between men and women—even to the point of some women accepting and *defending* their lesser status? Did depictions of violent sexuality *cause* rape and battering, or were both merely secondary symptoms of a male supremacist culture? Who would dare to deny, Andrea asked, that men ruled and that women were subordinate? Short of defending such an arrangement—as many did—as an inescapable feature of *biology*, what grounds *other than* an attack on pornography could be enlisted in the struggle to curtail the male propensity to domestic aggression and global war? Curtailing the contribution that violent pornography made to maintaining male dominance might be no more than a start in diluting—and ultimately ending—it, but who was offering a more substantive or better way?

When Andrea herself testified before the Commission, she spoke with such moving simplicity that one of the commissioners, Park Elliott Dietz, director of the Institute of Law, Psychiatry and Public Policy at the University of Virginia, later said that he'd been brought to tears. ("I am asking you as individuals," Andrea had said, "to have the courage, because I think it's what you will need, to actually be willing yourselves to go and cut that woman down and untie her hands and take the gag out of her mouth, and to do something, for her freedom.")

As it would turn out, most commentators expressed emotions quite distinct from Dietz's—closer to fury than tears. In a long article in the *Village Voice*, Walter Kendrick, a professor of Victorian literature (no less) at Fordham University, singled out Andrea for special excoriation, in his outrage all but condemning her to the witches' pyre. Linking Andrea to Anthony Comstock, who Kendrick saw as her nineteenth-century soulmate, he mocked her as "fat, humorless, and literal-minded." Then, for good measure, he announced that Dietz "would have made an excellent Nazi," which is more than a bit looney given Dietz's admiration rather than denunciation of Dworkin the Jew. Kendrick referred to himself as a feminist even as he insisted that "a woman can choose to make or view pornography" and denounced those who would "infantilize" them by treating them as victims by fiat of gender." To be sure, he loftily concluded, "pleas for reason" such as his, would be drowned "in the shrieks of phony do-gooders and disingenuous rabble-rousers"—people like Andrea Dworkin, who would continue to insist that Linda Lovelace represented many more battered wives and drug-addicted porn stars than did Kendrick's woman, who "can choose," who had a resplendent array of prospects and options from which to pick.[9]

Judging from the rage with which Andrea and Kitty were denounced—including a strenuous attack from the ACLU to the effect that no evidence exists (which wasn't true) for the claim that pornography sparks sexual violence—one might never have guessed that Andrea and Kitty had in fact greeted the Meese Commission's conclusions and recommendations with considerable caution. "The Commission's report is flawed," they stated publicly, "by recommending extension and escalated enforcement of obscenity laws." All that those laws, by their nature, could achieve was a male-dictated definition of what constituted "obscenity" and a male-dictated political decision as to where it should (and *could*) be made available in specifically designed zones.

The FACT feminists denied that pornography was central to the

oppression of women—certainly not to the extent that it caused
sufficient harm to justify any curtailment of free speech. On the
contrary, FACT argued, pornography actually served some useful
social functions of benefit to women. It magnified, according to
one of FACT's leaders, "the misogyny present in the culture" (but
didn't that mean it *did* further oppress women?) and even carried
the subliminal message that lifetime monogamous pair-bonding
and vanilla sex did not meet the citizenry's sexual needs, that what
also needed advocacy was sexual variety, non-marital sex, group sex,
homo-sex, public sex, anonymous sex. To all of which Andrea might
have said amen, but she would have been quick to add that what
poor women of limited education and options had a far greater need
for was to be free from beatings, rape, and general subservience to
the unpredictable whims of their male masters.

Though pleased with the Meese Commission's acknowledgment
that depictions of violent sexuality *did* harm women, Andrea and
Kitty decried its lack of certainty about the causal link—the *extent*
of the consequences of viewing sexually violent material. The Commission during its hearings relied on some of the same experts that
Andrea and Kitty had—in particular, Professors Donnerstein and
Malamuth. Andrea had earlier complained about the professors vac-
illating in laying claim to the findings of their own research, but that
irresolution accelerated when testifying before the Commission.

Both Donnerstein and Malamuth issued disclaimers after the
Meese report was published, claiming that it misrepresented at
least part of their research: they denied the report's assertion that
sexually violent materials had increased to such an extent in recent
years as to become the most prevalent form of pornography. In
fact, they argued, the empirical data was limited and contradictory:
depictions of violence seemed to show an increase through the late
seventies, but then a decline. Research on films showing women
enjoying and becoming aroused at scenes of sexual violence were
particularly "tricky to interpret." As for men, they found "no reason to think that exposure to violent pornography is the cause of
these [aggressive] predispositions," yet they felt as well that it was
counterintuitive to believe that even if not the cause of male sexual
violence, these films in all likelihood did reinforce those predisposi-

tions. What remained unclear was whether the violence itself provided the reinforcement, or the violence within a sexual context.[10]

The Meese Commission itself initiated no original research. However, it did sponsor one weekend workshop, headed by Surgeon General C. Everett Koop and confined to "recognized authorities" in the field. At its close, the participants announced consensus in certain areas; the two most crucial were that "pornography that portrays sexual aggression as pleasurable for the victim increases the acceptance of the use of coercion in sexual relations," and that "exposure to violent pornography increases punitive behavior toward women." Koop summarized the evidence as "slim," yet persuasive enough to conclude that "pornography does present a clear and present danger to American public health." To which Neil Malamuth, a participant in the workshop, objected: although he agreed that films portraying sexual aggression "as pleasurable for the victim" do increase the amount of coercion in sexual relations, he did not agree that such pornography was "at the root of much of the rape that occurs today." He offered no alternative explanation. And there the matter rested for a time.[11]

Andrea's novel, *Ice and Fire*, and her new non-fiction book, *Intercourse*, were published in England almost simultaneously. In many ways, *Ice and Fire* is a *tour de force*. In its harrowing theme of living on the margins, the austere, jagged prose mirrors the horrors it recites, and the novel achieves the kind of hallucinatory intensity associated with the work of William Burroughs or Hubert Selby: "the needle just gutted her with pleasure: so afterward, in retrospect, one inferred that there had been a lack, a need, before the needle: but in fact she had been complete before and heavy and thick like some distilled perfume, sweet to the point of sickness, a nauseating sweetness: something transporting and divine: something that translated into eyelids weighed down and swollen, lips puffed up, the cracks in them spreading down, the body suddenly soft and pliant, ready to curl, to billow, to fold: a fragile body, delicate bones suddenly soft, eyes hiding behind lush eyelids: the hard tension of her hips dissolved, finally. The way other women look when they've been fucked hard and long, coming and coming, is how she looked: the way other women look fucked out, creamy and swollen, is how she looked. The needle gave her that, finally: dissolved."[12]

Using initials ("N.") for the two protagonists in the novel under-scores the encompassing abstraction—anonymity, really—that simultaneously lifts the lives recounted to myth-like impersonality even while recording the inescapable individuality of suffering. The driven, relentless quality of the writing is for a considerable portion of the novel mesmerizing, as is the staccato tempo of the corrosive-ly macabre narrative. Ultimately, though, the repetitious rhythm turns irksome, the relentless, unwavering pace tedious, the desola-tion too unvarying to sustain its grip; we move outside the experi-ence, our nerve endings shut off; we refuse to participate further.

Intercourse is a very different kind of book. It's a work of intri-cate argument—and easily misinterpreted. If *Ice and Fire* testifies, finally, to the limits of Andrea's imaginative powers, *Intercourse* impressively demonstrates the range of her analytic skill. It is far too complex a work to lend itself to simplistic summary, and Andrea doesn't make it any easier for us by devoting the first half of the book to *approaching* her essential subject through the indirection of literary criticism. Taking on a panoply of male writers as diverse as Tolstoy, James Baldwin, Isaac Bashevis Singer, Kobo Abe, and Ten-nessee Williams, she ranges from the contestably abstract ("The normal fuck by a normal man is taken to be an act of invasion and ownership undertaken in a mode of predation") to the provocatively epigrammatic ("We are inarticulate about sex, even though we talk about it all the time to say how much we like it").

It's only in the second half of *Intercourse* that a less veiled political agenda emerges, even if, some thirty years later, it sometimes reads as timeworn: "Most women are not distinct, private individuals to most men. . . . Women live inside this reality of being owned and being fucked; are sensate inside it; the body learning to respond to what male dominance offers as touch, as sex, as love." Now and then, Andrea's essential combativeness takes on the elegant contours of aphorism: "The old virginity—with its real potential for freedom and self-determination—is transformed into the new virginity—listless, dissatisfied ennui until awakened by the adventure of male sexual domination: combat on the world's tiniest battlefield."[13]

More typically, defiance is upfront and foremost: "The political meaning of intercourse for women is the fundamental question of feminism and freedom: can an occupied people—physically occupied inside, internally invaded—be free; can those with a metaphysically compromised privacy have self-determination; can those without a biologically based physical integrity have self-respect?" Andrea makes it clear that in her philosophy "there is nothing implicit in intercourse that mandates male dominance in society." The various and "staggering" civil inequalities that characterize the culture are injustices *not* related to "the natural, healthy act of intercourse . . . this book does not say that all men are rapists or that all intercourse is rape"—a clear enough statement, though her critics, then and now, settle for the simplistic dismissal of her position as "a rejection of intercourse."

Relying heavily on the findings of Shere Hite—a personal friend (whose first two books, *The Hite Report* and *The Hite Report on Male Sexuality*, Andrea fully credits)—she proceeds to itemize the *context* in which intercourse generally takes place, a context that both expresses and extends male dominance: intercourse is "frequently performed compulsively," usually requires the female partner "to look a certain way, be a certain type—even conform to preordained behaviors and scripts," and a female who "cannot exist before or during the act as a fully realized, existentially alive individual." But current conditions can, in Andrea's view, be improved—even radically so. The circumstances surrounding intercourse could be made to include "more deference to female sensuality prior to the act; less verbal assault as part of sexual expressiveness toward women . . . less romanticizing of rape . . . strong, self-respecting role models for girls." Should such conditions be met, "intercourse could be experienced in a world of social equality for the sexes."

Not that Andrea was optimistic. She concludes *Intercourse* with the observation that "incestuous rape is becoming a central paradigm for intercourse in our time. Women are supposed to be small and childlike, in looks, in rights; child prostitution keeps increasing in mass and in legitimacy, the children sexually used by a long chain of men—fathers, uncles, grandfathers, brothers, pimps, pornographers, and the good citizens who are the consumers; and men, who are, after all, just family, are supposed to slice us up the middle, leaving us in parts on the bed."

Ice and Fire received handsome blurbs from Kate Millett ("one waits for years to hear a new voice like this!") and Robin Morgan ("a major book") but she wasn't successful—though she always took a personal hand in securing blurbs—with Susan Brownmiller. In response to Andrea's solicitation, Susan wrote back: "I thought you knew that I don't do blurbs anymore. . . . My life has been a lot more pleasant since." Not good enough for Andrea. She wrote again, icily: "I am glad yr life is more pleasant not doing them, but I think for most of us life as feminist writers is harder and harder . . . I think yr decision is wrong." Susan didn't budge.[14]

Both *Ice and Fire* and *Intercourse* received (in Andrea's words) "exceptionally contemptuous" reviews, with *Ice and Fire* getting the somewhat warmer reception.[15] Marilyn French (*The Women's Room*) praised the book in *Ms.* as "a serious novel, a *bildungsroman* that portrays vividly and intensely, with a strong sense of reality, the substructure of male-female relations." In *The Women's Review of Books*, Louise Armstrong hailed *Ice and Fire* as "absolutely first-rate, totally of a piece; it risks everything and triumphs." And Kitty, not quick with compliments, read the novel in manuscript and told Andrea it was "astounding, political, to the end . . . I am gripped and thrilled." Still, on the whole, a number of the reviews were, as Andrea accurately described them, "pretty consistently spiteful and awful."[16]

A number were downright harsh, and the worst were in the most prominent publications. The review by Carol Sternhell, at the time director of the graduate program for journalism at NYU, in the *New York Times* provided ample grounds for Andrea's fear that she was destined to be misunderstood. She (accurately) described Sternhell's review as "unremittingly depressing . . . foul, illiterate." Ordinarily an entirely negative review in the *Times* would have meant—such was the paper's power—that a book was dead in the water. But Andrea's English publisher, Weidenfeld, decided—quite miraculously—to fight back against the Sternhell piece; it took out a full-page ad in the *Times* strongly pushing the novel. That led to an appearance, along with Erica Jong, on the influential Phil Donahue television show, on which Andrea acquitted herself splendidly (as Jong confirmed in a gracious letter to her). The reviews for *Intercourse* were still worse. Sternhell, in the same review for *Ice and Fire*, simply trashed *Intercourse* as a "harangue." In the process, she got certain important matters quite wrong: Andrea did *not* believe in "(unchanging) biological design," nor did she "confuse our sexual organs with our social organizations"—another version of pre-destination.[17]

The Nation paired *Intercourse* with Kitty's new book, *Feminism Unmodified* and—though it should have known better—turned over the assignment to Maureen Mullarkey, a conservative Catholic associated with the Federalist Society. The result, predictably, was a slashing, vituperative attack reminiscent of the edicts of Torquemada. Mullarkey dismissed "Dworkin's lunatic *pensees*" as a "hate-mongering tantrum . . . shackled like an S/M bondage slave to a primitive abhorrence of men." She thought Kitty merely "intellectually sloppy," though bracketed both books as "playing Hitler." Hinting strongly that feminism was a lesbian plot ("Heterosexuality is on trial in a kangaroo court"), Mullarkey either didn't know or didn't care that Kitty was not a lesbian. Perhaps in atonement, *The Nation* subsequently ran a number of letters protesting the savagery of the review, but the damage was done.[18]

"I live in a world," Andrea explained to a recent acquaintance, the English science fiction writer Michael Moorcock (who, with his wife, Linda Steele, would become close and lasting friends), where a *Nation* review "represents the political consensus among intellectuals and so-called radicals. And so I don't know what to do. What is there to do? I keep trying to understand it, and I can't." The review, she added, "was not out of line with the way my work and I are treated here. Usually MacKinnon is treated better"—though only by a hair in the case of Mullarkey—"partly because she is more lady-like in some ways, partly because she is much-credentialed (lawyer, Ph.D., actually earns a living, publishes in academic journals, lots of footnotes). She and I do our best to discuss this all politically and personally, because otherwise there can be such bitterness on my part and such insensitivity on hers, and vice versa."

Even some feminist publications were savage. *Sojourner* headlined its review of *Intercourse*, "A Distorted and Anti-Sex Vision," though "distorted" more accurately applied to the review itself (matched by a nasty, condescending tone); it dismissed the book as "anti-sex" and even claimed that Andrea believed intercourse would always be oppressive to women. It's worth noting, given the dismissal of Andrea as a man-hater, that in a *Sojourner* interview Andrea gave this response to the question "Are there any good men?": "I probably see both the best and worst of men. I think when you deal with pornography, you see the worst of men, and when you deal with social change, you see the best of men." Negative reviews by feminists disheartened Andrea more than any others. To her they were a marker of the movement's decline: radical feminism, dominant in the early seventies and demanding a revolution in attitudes and institutions, had given way to a far more accommodationist attitude—namely, a bigger piece of the pie.

Sojourner, at least, gave Andrea a chance to respond and she seized on it, vigorously correcting the opinions fallaciously ascribed to her: she was not anti-sex, she was not anti-male, she was not anti-intercourse. She also took the opportunity to again point out—citing Shere Hite—that most women (seven out of ten) "just don't like intercourse very much" and do not reach orgasm from intercourse. If intercourse brings so few women pleasure, "the real question," Andrea said, "is why intercourse is the central sex act in our society." The answer, she suspected, is that "men only feel they've had sex when they've had intercourse."[19]

Her publisher, Secker & Warburg, failed to stand by her. Though they'd managed to make a quite handsome paperback sale of *Intercourse* to the Free Press in the United States, they disinvited Andrea from the planned tour in England for the hardcover. The Free Press treated her no better, telling her in essence that even having been on the Donahue show, watched by five million or so viewers—*and*, they acknowledged, having performed "superbly"—they had *still* been unable to sell out the 7,500 first printing (as if that was strictly *her* fault), and were damned if they were going to spend any *more* money on trying to promote the book. Not surprisingly, Andrea began to feel "a lynch mentality around my work" had developed and it was being treated like "deranged garbage."[20]

Andrea was a firm believer in fighting back. She not only wrote a blistering response to Sternhell, but the *Times*, for once, actually printed it. "I despair," she wrote, "of being treated with respect, let alone fairly, in your pages," but the Sternhell review had crossed the line—it was "contemptuous beyond belief," the work of someone "who seems to be functionally illiterate." *Ice and Fire* was a novel, not an autobiography (as Sternhell had called it), and it cannot resonate for anyone who refuses to acknowledge "the intersection of poverty and sexual exploitation. You needed to give a damn about that interconnection before the novel could mean anything to you. It is probably easier to celebrate prostitution as a so-called feminist option for women, the current liberal dogma in this country, than to read *Ice and Fire* and feel the cost of being bought and sold."

In her wounded pride, Andrea may have gone a bit overboard, but "going overboard," she would probably want to claim, was an essential ingredient of her persona. Though *Ice and Fire* wasn't a literal transcription of her own life, it came close enough for a reviewer who called it "autobiographical" to have reason. The book, after all, is written in the first person, doesn't contradict any of the known facts in Andrea's life, and seems at most to embellish them. Curiously, though, in an interview she gave at the time to *New Directions for Women*, Andrea insisted that "if I were writing about myself, I wouldn't want to see all the things that I showed you about this character that I've created." Perhaps, as someone with an inflated view of the sanctity of literature, Andrea was intent on claiming the exalted ground of "novelist" or, more simply, attempting to separate herself from some of the personal ramifications of what she included that were likely to follow. Along these lines, when Kitty dashed off her glowing praise after finishing the manuscript of *Ice and Fire*, she added, with palpable anxiety, a few nervous questions: "Will everyone know that it is literally accurate? Can you survive your portrait of the publisher at Perigee? . . . John has seen it?"[21]

———

Along with a rock-bottom, almost corporeal, commitment to telling the truth as she saw it, sugar-coating nothing, Andrea held a parallel conviction that women "can understand the truth"—can absorb it and fight back against it. Now she wasn't so sure. The double-downed denunciation—two books dismissed simultaneously—was, she wrote a friend, "the most awful publication thing I have ever been through. I am close to devastation most of the time." She told Elaine Markson that the ruinous round of reviews "feels like being gang-raped"; she felt "pretty much at the end of my rope." Hating the feeling of being "paralyzed and passive," she started to badger Secker & Warburg to bring her over to England to defend herself against the "bare-boned misogyny" assailing her. They finally gave in; the books hadn't been selling, and they may have become persuaded that Andrea's oratorical skills could turn the tide. Another boost to her spirits came from Germany. The well-known feminist theoretician, Alice Schwarzer, and the other women who put out the influential journal *Emma*, hearing that Andrea was planning a trip to England, invited her to add Germany to her itinerary. Yet another invitation arrived from Kvinnefronten, the Women's Front of Norway.[22]

That same month of August 1987, there was even a bit of good news on the home front. The novelist Erica Jong, who'd earlier appeared with Andrea on the Phil Donahue TV show and been deeply impressed by her, now let her know that she, Erica, had made a deal with the *Washington Post Magazine* to do a cover story about Andrea as an example of "how badly women writers are treated" and also stressing her own conviction that the women's movement had failed because it had lost its nerve and retreated from its radical origins. "This is all astonishing," Andrea wrote Michael Moorcock and Linda Steele, "and it comes on the back of another astonishing media event": she and Gloria Steinem had just done a 2 a.m. to 4 a.m. network show called *Nightwatch*, and Gloria had unexpectedly come out with a strong endorsement of *Intercourse*.[23]

That was all decidedly cheering. Yet Andrea felt a bit leery too. "It is hard because I don't respect Erica's work, but I do respect her sense of what doing work costs women. She wants her work respected and feels it is not." It didn't help that Erica had said she wanted to interview Andrea for a "psycho-history"; this, Andrea humorously commented, "she will not get, but I am pretty terrified of her because she is smart and I am a bad liar and don't lie and at the same time want to protect my privacy like I have never wanted anything in my life. So this is the current dilemma. The current cosmic joke, on me." Andrea was willing to hold out the hope that Jong's article "will actually do some good, not just for me but for the movement."

First, the interview had to get published. The *Washington Post* quickly turned it down, telling Erica that it was self-serving—"and so it is business as usual in the land of free speech," Andrea wryly commented. Not that she had held out high hopes for the piece: "Everything Erica has said to me has made me think she doesn't know the differences between us, and it is a very peculiar feeling . . . [Yet] she is . . . very nice and very smart. [Her] kindness is treasured. It's a little disgusting on my part: the cowering dog . . . her conversation [is] absolutely cliché-ridden. There is no new-age verity too bland, too dull, or too stupid for her." Yet Erica did mean well, and did come through: Jong's "Changing My Mind About Andrea Dworkin" appeared in the June 1988 issue of *Ms.*, was clearly meant kindly, and despite some unfortunate bits ("Andrea dresses to keep men and the world at bay; I [dress] not only to attract but also for my own delight in costume and color"), was not only clearly admiring but tailored to persuade others that Andrea was an important writer whose work should be held in serious regard.

Just a week before she was due to leave for England, Andrea got the news that her case against *Hustler* magazine over the sexually explicit cartoons they'd published had been thrown out of court on summary judgment ("there is no genuine issue as to any material fact"). The presiding judge ruled, bizarrely, that Andrea had failed to show "by clear and convincing evidence" that *Hustler* had "acted with actual malice" (which he defined as publishing a statement "with knowledge that it was false or with reckless disregard of whether it was false or not"—implying that he was a devotee of truth). The judge acknowledged that the likenesses in the cartoons were unmistakably Andrea and that her own name *had* been used, but nonetheless ruled that there were no grounds to move forward to trial.[24]

The judge acknowledged that the cartoons were vicious but (here his opinion echoed the intrinsic confusion of libel law) had not been presented as factual in form; they were *fantasy only*—satire and hyperbole—and therefore protected. On the grounds that "vicious and gratuitously personal attacks may well attract support and sympathy for their targets," he ruled further that "Dworkin cannot maintain a separate cause of action for mental and emotional distress." Andrea's translation: "A man's fantasy has legal protection; my life, which is real, doesn't. I mean, shit. I am so fucking angry." Her lawyer emphasized the positive: the judge hadn't punished her for bringing the suit—hadn't required that *she* pay *Hustler*'s legal costs. No, Andrea told him, she did not feel grateful: "I'm not going to lie back and enjoy it." She found it hard to believe that no precedent existed for holding a cartoon libelous. Both Gloria Steinem and Susan Brownmiller agreed to Kitty's request to write amicus briefs, and Bella Abzug also submitted one on Andrea's behalf. With those in hand, she insisted on proceeding with an appeal—though in the upshot to no avail.[25]

The following week, on September 15, Andrea flew to London, to stay only a few days, less than she'd hoped. The *Emma* feminists in Germany had fallen behind schedule in getting out an edition of *Pornography* in time for Andrea's arrival, so that part of the itinerary was put off for a later trip. In the meantime, the group had gone ahead and initiated a (bastardized) version of the model ordinance in West Germany against pornography; the SPD (Socialist Party) had pledged its support, and a political campaign for passage was underway.

The trip to England proved much tougher than anticipated and then, soon after Andrea returned home—and just before Christmas—John lost his job as editor-in-chief of a start-up publication, *Working Woman Weekends*. The magazine had in fact been his idea, and he'd been hired full-time to get it off the ground. The root cause of his firing, Andrea felt, was his active role on behalf of the anti-pornography ordinance. In her opinion, his job became overtly in jeopardy when the disastrous double review of her two books appeared in the *New York Times*: as she reported to Moorcock, "He [John] was made to account for his relationship to me, [and] to show his superior his deposition to *Hustler* about our relationship." All of which John too believed was contributory to his firing, but he felt the decisive reason had been the stock market crash and the decline in ad revenue.

Fortunately, no immediate financial crisis was at hand, thanks to the small amount of savings they'd been managing to put aside. Within a few months John landed another position, initially temporary, at *LEAR'S*, a magazine for women over forty that Frances Lear (ex-wife of Norman) was rather chaotically putting together with her thirty million in alimony. John reported that *LEAR'S* was "a madhouse," full of "knotty problems" in need of solving, but a challenging, creative one (he would stay at *LEAR'S* nearly three years). He also had good news from Elaine Markson about the collection of his speeches and essays that she'd been shopping around. The publisher was a small West Coast one, Beitenbush, but Elaine said they had an excellent reputation and would do well by him; as it would turn out, Meridian, a Penguin Group subsidiary, would reissue the collection in 1990.

On the whole, as Andrea acknowledged to Alice Schwarzer, "I have rare happiness in my personal life." Lately, with John unemployed and usually at home (and their apartment small), "it has been hard, and that takes its toll, which, I think, one cannot help." Yet overall, she added, at a certain point in life, "parts of you go dead, and things you could feel before you can no longer feel, and youth and hope seem further." She gave that sentiment a more humorous twist in a letter to Robin Morgan: "Love is strange (but not as strange as men in cars)."

Andrea was eager to start on a new novel that had been going around in her head for some time; she wanted, she wrote Michael Moorcock, to write about "what it's like being raped over and over and what it means and what it does. Most women are raped more than once and we don't even dare acknowledge it . . . because in this world it suggests the woman is at fault." Entitled *Mercy*, the novel would eventually come out in 1991, but initially Andrea had "great trouble slowing down and having patience after running so hard and so far these last years."[26]

She'd been running hard because she had to, driven by both temperament and political necessity. "I can stand almost anything when I am working," she once wrote. When not working, she was quite incapable of relaxing. At one point, she tried to watch television, but decided "I simply haven't got the discipline"—a curious explanation for someone whose tendency to self-castigation kept her bound to the obligatory grindstone. Her few attempts at a vacation simply confirmed her inability to enjoy one. Persuaded at one point to take a few days off in North Carolina, she drolly reported back that "the beach was beige. So was the apartment . . . I don't know how to rest."

Mostly out of financial necessity she again began, soon after the double publication in 1987 of *Ice and Fire* and *Intercourse*, to accept speaking invitations that kept her intermittently hop-scotching from place to place. Friends in various locales would offer her a bed, a guest room, a whole apartment. But she would rarely "inflict" herself; I'm an "impossible guest," she'd say, with restless tics and disruptive habits: preferring to write at night, she usually slept during the day—that is, when insomnia didn't interfere. "I'm always waiting for the Cossacks to come basically, ready to run, so it's absurd to even try" to relax. Nor did travel hold any appeal, unless connected to promoting a book or fulfilling a political commitment. "I've gotten bug-o-phobic," she reported to Moorcock. "It seems like some kind of metaphysical agoraphobia to me; my small and self-destructive recognition that the earth is not mine to live on in peace."

She would willingly, even eagerly, embrace travel when the need to promote—or more typically to try to *salvage*—one of her books arose. And that was decidedly the case during most of 1988. Her anger alone propelled her from place to place. At age forty-two, with five substantial books behind her, Andrea had become increasingly well known, thanks to a trail of brutal, demeaning reviews, more as a figure of derision than esteem. On one level, she had faith in the originality and acuity of her work and was able to ascribe

some of the belligerent derision which had greeted it to its innovative nature. But no one is *that* immune to persistent mockery;
besides, despite all her public bravado, she'd carried with her from
childhood the constant and torturous aspersions cast on her character by a distraught and ill mother. As she acknowledged to herself
early in the year, "I have never felt so little confidence in myself or
in my chosen way of life. It's gotten to me."

She wasn't desperate now for money, but she *was* feeling desolate—
and perplexed—about her ongoing difficulty in getting published
and, once published, finding an understanding, appreciative audience. She put together a collection of her articles and speeches,
entitling it *Letters from a War Zone*, and wrote introductions to
each piece, but Elaine was unable to rouse any interest at all among
American publishers. Secker & Warburg agreed to publish the collection, and it appeared in England in 1988, but Andrea had long
been unhappy with Secker's off-handed, we're-doing-you-a-big-
favor attitude toward her. At the same time, *Intercourse* had failed
to find a paperback publisher in the United States. To top off the
grim accounting, both *Pornography* and *Right-Wing Women* went
out of print, and *Ice and Fire* was remaindered. Andrea and Elaine
tried resurrecting as *Love Letters* her early, unpublished novel
Ruins, which after more than a decade had taken on the status of an
ancient artifact—but it failed to spark any interest. Andrea summed
up her reaction in two lines: "I am facing an overwhelming number of dead ends here and . . . I am sick of being marginal in every
sense."[27]

An offer eventually came in from a Secker & Warburg subsidiary, Arrow Books, to do a paperback edition of *Intercourse*. They
even offered to bring Andrea over to England to help promote the
book. Unalloyed good news was unthinkable; swift on the heels
of Arrow's offer came the Supreme Court's unanimous, broadly
worded decision extending First Amendment protection to pornographers for parodies—under which *Hustler*'s Dworkin cartoons
obviously qualified. The appeal she'd filed after *Hustler*'s initial victory went straight out the window. Andrea predicted to Robin Morgan, tongue in cheek, that "Pat Robertson is well on his way to being
president" (and Robin thanked her for her "wonderfully mournful

comments"). Andrea added, on a more serious note, that the Court's decision had simply exposed what she and Kitty had been saying all along: that the Right *defends* pornography. Obscenity law had previously served that function, but no longer did, forcing the Supreme Court "to go out in the open to protect the pornographers."[28]

The trip to England in May provided a boost, though a minor one. She did the requisite number of appearances, but was told several times that *Intercourse* was "a bit too radical" for English tastes. Certain English feminists didn't strike her as radical enough; at several dinner parties she met a number of the more prominent figures in the British movement: "Well, he's a fucking man, what do you expect?!" seemed the canned response to all issues relating to their lives. "I couldn't get them to listen to anything specific or anything that had really to do with social policy decisions. . . . I just cannot figure out how their politics don't add up to just being superior human beings. I can't locate where they see change; who changes and how. Anyway, it drives me nuts."

When *Letters from a War Zone* appeared in England, press coverage, though limited, was more positive than usual. The *Irish Times* even gave her a rave: "Dworkin is a passionate essayist, full of wit, morality and an acute sense of justice." The review was apparently enough to catch the ear of the powers-that-be at E.P. Dutton, Andrea's very first publisher, with whom she'd parted on less than cordial terms. Negotiations began for an American edition of *Letters*, which would appear the following year—at which point the *New York Times*, still hot on her trail, would publish yet another damning review ("rage and self-righteous indignation . . . vulgarity and crassness of language," etc.). "It is a very discouraging time for me," Andrea wrote Robin Morgan. "I am truly being buried alive."[29]

Back in 1978, Andrea uncovered, of all things, a knack for real estate. According to John, she had a nose for a bargain, a sense of timing about the market, and the eyes to envision how to remodel a livable home from its present decay. For a long time, financial stringency had made escape seem impossible. But then they had an unexpected windfall. After the fumes from the ground floor restaurant, which had long plagued them, grew unbearable, they went to court to try and force a recalcitrant landlord to take action. The case had dragged on—but then they suddenly found themselves on the winning side of a $30,000 court judgment. With those unheard-of riches in hand, they had begun house hunting, and Andrea's keen eye had spotted the fourth-floor walkup of a co-op on Tenth Street in Brooklyn's Park Slope, near Prospect Park. John was terrified at the prospect of giving up their affordable rental and taking on a mortgage, but Andrea was adamant, and for two or three days (according to John), they came very close to breaking up. Then, talking about his plight to a friend over lunch, John suddenly started sobbing, and realized he couldn't bear the thought of separating from her.[30]

And so, soon after Andrea's return from England in the spring of 1988, they slowly began to pack up their old apartment and begin repairs on the new one. It became a drawn-out process that lingered on through the early fall. But Andrea was cheerful throughout, joking about how she'd always "longed to have a sofa" and, more seriously, how she felt "an overwhelming sense of joy at having figured out how to have a sense of permanence." Though surrounded for months on end with the usual chaos of moving, she managed between chores to do serious work on her new novel. She called it *Mercy* in reference to the passage in Isaiah, 54:7–8. Andrea's exegesis turned the parable on its head: "God turned his head away for a minute in wrath, but when he turns it back you'll get all this mercy. Well . . . the question is, when women are raped is it that he turned his head away or that he's watching. Are we his pornography? It rather feels that way."[31]

There was better literary news as well. In the spring, *Intercourse* was published in a mass market edition in England and—quite a shock to Andrea—was actually on the *London Sunday Times* bestseller list, if only briefly. Her books also began to be translated: *Pornography* came out in Germany, and was both a critical and commercial success; *Ice and Fire* in Sweden, and *Intercourse* in both

Denmark and Norway. Secker & Warburg, moreover, bought *Mercy* on the basis of just three chapters, and for what Andrea called "a decent amount of money."

None of which, in her mind, was a substitute for an American market that continued in large measure to be closed off to her. No American publisher made an offer on *Mercy*. "If I couldn't publish in England," Andrea wrote a friend, "I would cease to exist as a writer." She added, the tone more bitter than humorous, that "virtually nothing of mine on pornography is available to an Amerikan [sic] audience, which is the freedom of speech that makes this country great, as people here tend to say."

Yet on still other fronts, there were positive signs. The anti-pornography ordinance continued to draw support in Germany; reports came in of its introduction in the Philippines and New Zealand; and Kitty even managed to get a commitment from a legislator (a gay environmentalist) in Tasmania to introduce it as a private members bill (when Andrea heard the news she expressed mock horror at the prospect of having to move to the South Pacific). The ordinance even showed renewed signs of life in the United States. In the small coastal city of Bellingham, Washington, known as something of an arts-oriented enclave, a local group, Civil Rights For Women (CROW), petitioned to put the bill on the ballot.[32]

The state ACLU initially opposed it, citing the now hoary grounds of free speech (though the organization had always defended the ballot as "speech"). That led a group of feminist lawyers to threaten to resign from the organization, and when the ACLU's national board came out in support of the right to put the ordinance on the ballot, the Washington ACLU reversed itself. In the balloting that followed, the ordinance not only garnered two-thirds of the vote, but carried 118 of Bellingham's 120 precincts—a stunning popular victory. Still, it proved a temporary one. Andrea herself went out to Bellingham to join the struggle for four days in October, right in the middle of the move to Park Slope. But when the ACLU again reversed itself and asked a federal district court to find the ordinance unconstitutional, the court complied.

———

Andrea loved their new home, though of course—those hovering Cossacks again—she managed to squeeze in a sidebar of guilt: "It's troublesome to me to move some place that has such an outward meaning of wealth; I've never done such a thing or had such an experience. . . . I'm not at ease with it at all. . . . I just mean that a house in New York City means wealth." The fact that repair work was still in progress when she and John moved into the apartment served the secondary purpose of easing her guilt: "I've been a captive here and my brain is pretty soggy from lack of sleep and sawdust and plaster dust. It's been a kind of a nightmare." She went off to do a week's lecturing in Michigan, and then, "terribly excited," attended an international conference in Israel, after which she planned to go for a few days' rest in Spain. But while in Israel she became "terribly sick and exhausted"—to her sorrow, she never got to see Vad Vashem—and had to return to the States.[33]

Once recovered, and with construction work on the Park Slope residence finally at an end, Andrea sealed herself off from public events for a number of months, determined on finishing *Mercy*. Now and then she'd let herself be pulled away for some uncommon reason or cause, and one in particular: the notorious, hideous revelation that a criminal defense lawyer named Joel Steinberg had over a period of time beaten to death his adopted daughter, Lisa, age six. Andrea's sometime friend, Susan Brownmiller, publicly blamed Lisa's death on her mother, Hedda Nussbaum, the battered woman who'd lived with Steinberg since 1976. Brownmiller's accusation stunned and horrified Andrea. She began to have flashbacks of her own earlier history as the battered wife of Iwan de Bruin, when no one heard her screams or believed her stories. She decided she had to write something in Nussbaum's defense; she hardly had a choice: flashbacks were worse than memories—"involuntary, outside time, vivid, almost three-dimensional . . . the air is the same—you are there and it is happening." Writing about it was the only way she knew to coax it back into the corner, to regain footing in the present.[34]

"My friend and colleague Susan Brownmiller," Andrea's article began, "does not want Hedda Nussbaum to be 'exonerated'—something no battered woman ever is, even if a child has not died." To those who agreed with Brownmiller that Nussbaum was legally and morally responsible for Lisa's death, Andrea's response was: "I don't think Hedda Nussbaum is 'innocent.' I don't know any innocent adult women; life is harder than that for everyone. But adult women who have been battered are especially not innocent. Battery is a forced descent into hell and you don't get by in hell by moral goodness. You disintegrate. You don't survive as a discrete personality with a sense of right and wrong."

She went on in the article to describe her own experience as a battered woman—the neighbors who hear nothing, the family members who look right through your bruises and injuries, the doctors who diagnose paranoia (or the kind ones who pat you on the head and prescribe tranquillizers). "You lose language, you want to die, you hope the next beating will kill you. You're present when he 'hurts other people'; you don't help them. 'Judge me, Susan.'" Even after escaping the marriage, for years you "wake up screaming in blind terror in the night. You're repelled by the hypocritical sentimentality that mourns the child Lisa but has no sympathy for her adult counterpart, for the battered wife you say 'wants it, she likes it, she chose it'. You conveniently forget that 'the only way to have helped Lisa Steinberg was to have helped Hedda Nussbaum.'"

Newsweek immediately accepted her article, but the magazine's lawyer intervened and halted publication on the grounds that it libeled (as Andrea put it) "the man who had battered me—unless I could prove through medical records or police records it had happened." Which of course Andrea couldn't; that was an essential part of the case at hand: doctors, police, even neighbors and friends, rarely credit a battered woman's story, let alone file formal reports. As Andrea would later write in the Dutton edition of *Letters*, "We learn fast that the system won't protect us—it only endangers us more—so we hide from the man and from the system—the hospitals, the police, the courts—the places where you get the proof. I still hide. It's not easy for a public person, but I do it. I'm a master of it." John vividly remembers that even years after they'd been living together, if he happened to enter Andrea's bedroom when she was asleep, she'd sometimes awaken and yell out in terror, thinking he was Iwan (both men were blonde and tall). Even after she realized it was John, shaken at the flashback, it would take time for her to calm down.

In any case, rather than alter her piece, as *Newsweek* suggested, Andrea withdrew it; the *Los Angeles Times* published it with only minor changes. Short though the article was, it had a powerful impact.

10

Mercy

Facing a March 1990 deadline from Secker & Warburg for *Mercy*, Andrea burrowed in, except for an occasional lecture to make some money. She was buoyed by the news that Dutton planned a print run of 25,000 for the American edition of *Letters from a War Zone*, and on top of that had agreed to publish *Pornography*.

As she worked on *Mercy*, at the forefront of Andrea's mind was her concern that many women who suffer rape are assaulted "more than once, and the way it hurts women—the way it slowly destroys us—isn't understood at all or felt at all." She wanted her novel to somehow succeed in conveying what that process of disintegration was like. It proved a painful book to work on because it brought her back "to some parts of my own life, and it's very hard. I'm sort of understanding that most of what I've experienced in fact isn't common—there's some stability there for most people that I don't have or some continuity or some respite. . . . The last 15 years with John and with my writing have been very different from all my life before that, which was very violent and vagrant."[1]

Yet, as always when consumed with the writing process, Andrea also felt profoundly at peace, in touch with her gifts, confident of making some contribution. In the case of *Mercy*, that peaceful period was brief, abruptly shattered by an attack so vicious that it left her feeling nearly unbalanced.

In the summer of 1989, as if out of nowhere, a book entitled *Burning Desires: Sex in America*, co-authored by Steve Chapple and David Talbot, appeared under the respectable auspices of Doubleday. The contents, though, read more like *Penthouse* magazine. The book—claiming to be drawn from interviews and other primary sources—contained a malign portrait of Andrea as a violent, hypocritical molester. Among the authors' specific charges—based, they claimed, on interviews with the well-known biographer Patricia Bosworth—was that Andrea had physically assaulted her in an attempt at rape. Andrea knew Bosworth, immediately contacted her, and learned that she'd never said such a thing and would gladly provide an affidavit to that effect should Andrea want one. She did— and Bosworth promptly provided it. *Burning Desires* rattled Andrea so badly that for a brief period she wasn't sure *what* she wanted to do, how next to proceed. "I can't talk about it without crying" she wrote to friends. "I am so tired, so upset in so many ways, so nervous, that my mind started getting *weak*, you know, buckling, my back has gone out again, and my periods gone bananas."[2]

But she did recognize that the book's accusations couldn't go unchallenged, and she enlisted both Elaine Markson's and Kitty MacKinnon's help in trying to get to the bottom of the whole awful business. Elaine discovered that the Doubleday editor of *Burning Desires* was Paul Bresnick, who'd previously been an editor at *Penthouse*. With that revelation, the plot began to unravel. Bresnick disclosed to Elaine that the two authors had told him that they'd interviewed Andrea herself—which they hadn't—and had taken careful notes. He further divulged that *Playboy* had paid "a ton of money" for four excerpts from *Burning Desires*, and had already started to run them in the April 1987 issue of the magazine.[3]

After further sleuthing, Andrea was able to discover that an interview she'd given to a woman who'd identified herself as an Israeli journalist—purportedly for a large daily newspaper in Israel—had in fact then been sold to *Penthouse*, where, partly cut and partly invented as an "exclusive"—it appeared in the magazine's April 1987 issue. Along with an introduction to the article that characterized

Andrea's recent novel *Ice and Fire* as pornographic, *Penthouse* printed a sidebar to the interview that set a new high in vilification: Andrea Dworkin, it read, is "a grotesque effigy of intellectual slime and hypocrisy . . . an inflexible, man-hating fanatic who cannot be taken seriously." The body of the "interview" was little better. It even had Andrea attacking feminism: "The problem with the women's movement," she's quoted as saying, "is that it hasn't significantly helped the advancement of women." To challenge her purported statement, *Penthouse* quoted two female professors to the effect that "women in America now enjoy an unparalleled measure of freedom."

Kitty urged Andrea to bring a libel suit against *Burning Desires*, and put her in touch with a San Francisco lawyer Kitty trusted. He—and several other lawyers as well—told Andrea that "as a public figure" she had "to accept any amount of insult, poison, distortion, and stupidity as a proper reward for having entered into the public dialogue." She could persist with a lawsuit, the lawyers told her, but the cost would run between $50,000 to $150,000—and she would lose. Andrea was understandably distraught. Without a verdict of libel to point to, the assorted accusations in *Burning Desires* would stand unchallenged—both her personal and professional lives put in jeopardy. What she needed was a court-mandated retraction and a public apology. Without those, she feared that the charges against her would become part of her biography and be used henceforth to destroy her credibility.

It was a fear she would have to live with. No lawyer would take the case; no legal judgment proved possible. The stalemate put her in touch with "a new aspect of powerlessness as a woman and punishment for having fought back." Short of continuing to butt her head against the wall—and wasting her life in the process—she had no choice but to pull back, had to try "to stay alive as a writer economically while being blacklisted and morally while being defamed and having the defamation being the only mirror and close to a major contaminant of self-consciousness." It all put her in "a rage about money," tormented about who has it and who doesn't: "it's not a new rage but the lawyer question brings it into high relief."

One added indignity now emerged from the wings: a detective story, *The Dog Collar Murders*, published that same year. It contained a fictionalized yet easily recognizable portrait of Andrea, strangled to death in a dog collar during S/M sex while attending an anti-pornography conference. Hearing about it, Andrea counted her blessings: "I don't have a copy, hallelujah!" Then for toppers came word that *Burning Desires* would have a paperback edition, with Doubleday reiterating its confidence in the integrity of the two authors and the paperback publisher, accordingly, announcing its refusal to remove the material about Andrea assaulting Patricia Bosworth. They suggested that if Andrea was upset, she could sue, apparently on the assumption that she'd be unable to afford the cost. Ordinarily they would have been right on both counts, but Elaine had recently succeeded in selling *Pornography* for a decent sum in Japan, and Andrea, feeling that her entire future was at stake, emptied her limited savings account, found a lawyer willing to accept a low fee, and did finally succeed in getting the material deleted from the paperback.[4]

And who was the paperback publisher? New American Library—E.P. Dutton in its new subsidiary guise, the same house that had published Andrea's first book, *Woman Hating*, and was currently publishing the U.S. edition of Andrea's *Letters from a War Zone*. The general mishmash got more disordered still when she received a phone call from her new (third) editor—currently at NAL—asking what she might know about an unexplained second printing of *Letters*. Nothing, Andrea answered. It seemed *someone* at NAL—it was all "a mystery"—had ordered a second printing of 4,300 copies of *Letters*; everyone professed ignorance, and no one knew what to do. "Well," Andrea laconically suggested, "you might try selling them."

Andrea had to lock herself away to finish *Mercy*. "Every bit of molecular energy," she later wrote, "was geared to writing it; I had terrorized all my friends such that no one dared call me for any reason; I had backed up mail and bills and so on for six months." But finally it was done, and she sent the manuscript off to her editor, Lesley Bryce, at Secker & Warburg; publication in England was set for October 1, 1990—just a few days, coincidentally, after Andrea's forty-fourth birthday. Knowing that *Mercy* had as yet been unable

to find an American publisher, and aware as well that the male president of one U.S. house had earlier vetoed a female editor's enthusiasm for publishing *Ice and Fire*, Lesley Bryce took it upon herself to
organize what Andrea called "an entirely female network inside the
company"; they managed to put *Mercy* into production without any
male editor at Secker having read it.[5]

In the meantime, John seemed to be in a good place—not that
he'd ever been demanding of Andrea's time; to the contrary, from
the earliest days of their relationship he'd put himself in service to
what he believed was her genius. But in the last few years he'd been
carving out a career of his own. Long active in the "male feminist"
movement, and speaking often at public events, he'd collected his
speeches in a book, *Refusing to Be a Man*. It was due out at roughly
the same time as *Mercy*. Secker suggested that John and Andrea
join forces in a combined promotional schedule; the underlying
assumption, as Andrea saw it, was that both books were works of
non-fiction anti-pornography, which she further took to imply that
both could be lumped into the over-arching theme of sexism. She
promptly hit the roof, refusing absolutely to join the planned duet.
She and John were distinctive individuals, she told Secker, as were
their two books. John agreed with her, and Secker mumblingly
backed off.[6]

"I don't expect good reviews" for *Mercy*, Andrea wrote Moorcock,
"or for it to be much appreciated," and in fact the book's reception would prove somewhat divided, certainly complex, mostly
negative. Which wasn't surprising: *Mercy* isn't a book one simply
likes or dislikes. It isn't a story, has no coherently laid-out narrative,
and most assuredly is not an entertainment; if anything, the book's
harrowing, imperious, and high-pitched repetitions more closely
resemble an anguished set of prophecies. *Mercy* has no fleshed-out
characters that one either does or doesn't identify with—or rather,
it's one leading character ("Andrea") and its other ("Not Andrea")
are so decisively *not* three-dimensional that one engages with them
(or doesn't) on an abstract rather than emotional level. The various
men who abuse and rape "Andrea"—starting at age nine—have no
identifying features, no explanatory histories or exculpatory psychology, not even names.

Collectively they are MAN, the violent, brutalizing force that condemns "Andrea" to an unending cycle of subordination and terror—molested as a child, abused as a wife, converted into a servant, raped at will, ultimately ignored and abandoned. She has two and only two options: to play out her prescribed social role and become a mute survivor, or to turn into "a body packed with rage," become an unforgiving "citizen of the night," accept no excuses ("he didn't mean it; or he didn't do it, not really, not fully, or not knowing, or not intending; he didn't understand; or he couldn't help it; or he won't again"), become her own judge and jury—and destroy the oppressor. Her piercing cry of pain unfolds into an apocalyptic retaliation that vengefully obliterates her torturers.

It can be argued that *Mercy* has a humanizing underbelly: "It's the Nazism," "Andrea" writes, that "you have to kill, not the Nazis. People die pretty easily, but cruelty doesn't." Simply murdering an abusive male, in other words, does nothing to destroy the structure of male complacency and power: "So you got to find a way," "Andrea" tells us, "to go up against the big thing, the menace; you have to stop it from being necessary—you have to change the world so no one needs it." Or as the real-life friend of Andrea's, Michael Moorcock, put it, she "still believes that most men could be both just and sensitive, that men and women are socialized into their roles and that legal reform and enlightened education together can change society, ridding us of inequality, providing genuine liberation for women and, incidentally, for men."[7]

That benign reading of *Mercy* hasn't persuaded most of its readers, either at the time of publication or since. The nearly uniform denunciations fell within a narrow range: a "mad, bad novel"; a "long, largely unpunctuated scream"; "grossly disgusting"; a "novel-length rape fantasy"; "*Mercy* left me feeling as if I had been carefully and thoroughly pulped with a verbal sledgehammer"; a "vulgar, reckless shout"; "sheer bad writing"; "grossly disgusting"; "Andrea isn't shocking us into truth. She is ranting"—and so on. In a stack of reviews, only two could be called well-disposed. One of the two was by a man, Frederic Lindsay, in the *Sunday Telegraph*, and not incisive: "the hypnotic power of her writing compels an empathetic sense of the vulnerability of women."[8]

Months, even years later, a few essay reviews appeared that were more nuanced and benign, and to some extent more positive. One of the more recent and probably the most incisive of them has been the critique of Martha Nussbaum, the cultural philosopher. In a lengthy analysis, published in 1999, Nussbaum makes clear that she regards *Mercy* as an important work: "it brings to the surface for scrutiny the strict retributive attitude that animates some portions of our moral and legal tradition and allows us to see this attitude as a reasonable response to terrible wrongs." Nussbaum emphasizes her agreement with Andrea's stress on "the pervasiveness of male violence against women," with her refusal "to deny and conceal these wrongs," and with "protesting loudly" against them. But Nussbaum rejects the view of *Mercy*'s narrator in the concluding section of the book when she refuses all sympathy with her tormentors ("None of them's innocent and who cares? I fucking don't care"). Though Nussbaum appears to agree with Andrea that "the social norms of the American heterosexual male are in some ways those of a rapist, and that . . . rape is not abnormal but 'normal' heterosexual intercourse," she nonetheless wants Andrea to acknowledge that there are individual exceptions. Vengeance, Nussbaum insists, is not the only alternative "to cowardly denial and capitulation." There is also the notion of clemency. If we are all products of social conditions that subvert justice and love—and we are—"slow, patient resistance" is the most reliable path to change.[9]

To which—I'm guessing here—Andrea might well have replied, "Thus have you liberals always argued, and with what result?—not the amelioration of injustice, but its steady advance." Anticipating such a response, Nussbaum repositions her argument: "if you really open your imagination and heart to admit the life story of someone else, it becomes far more difficult to finish that person off with a karate kick." The real-life Andrea's friends would argue that in fact she exemplified that humanistic approach—that she possessed precisely those qualities that Nussbaum urges on us all: sensitivity to the nuances of human suffering, calm, centered attention to what the Other is trying to say, a gentle and generous response (ordinarily) to human failings.[10]

Having known Andrea personally, if briefly, it came as no surprise when I read again and again in letters and interviews the often expressed astonishment at how, on a personal level, people found her "open," "quietly receptive," and "generous." One woman who heard her speak in 1993 wrote her to say that "what impressed me even more than the ideas you stated, was the way you put your ideas into practice . . . you responded more respectfully than anyone I had ever seen to women both whose ideas differed 180 degrees from your own and whose voices were filled with anger." Similarly, an interviewer wrote her to say, "Last night during the call-in radio show I was amazed at how patient you are even when a man says something truly ridiculous . . . how [do] you manage to do that? After hearing this shit over and over, year after year, that you don't want to just put your fist through the wall." To which Andrea responded, "Well no, not about that. I really have learned that it's mostly an opportunity . . . that this is my job, this is what I have to do, so I try to find better and better ways to do it."[11]

In her column "Between the Lines" in the *San Francisco Sunday Examiner and Chronicle*, Patricia Holt put it this way: "Andrea Dworkin writes very tough-minded books . . . but there is a sweetness about . . . [her] personality that always seems to light up an interview. She laughs, she listens; she never raises her soft, almost baby voice, never argues, never sounds polemic. She looks at you thoughtfully with wide and sympathetic eyes and explains her ideas with patience, even tenderness. Who can figure." Doubtless a detractor would use such material to describe Andrea as a dissembler, but no—she was simply multi-faceted, a person who saved her empathy for personal encounters and her fiery vehemence for the public platform.[12]

She sometimes *wrote*—especially in *Mercy*—in a "nightmarish and impolite" style, militantly on guard against sentimental sympathy. When she did so, it was in the name of the underdog, of those who, like her own younger self, had been silenced by the world's brutality. To confuse or equate the ferocious, morally problematic, ruthless harridan "Andrea" of *Mercy* with how the real-life Andrea actually treated people in everyday life would be to reduce a generous spirit to a murderous automaton.

Still, something more needs to be said about Andrea's rejection of Nussbaum's recommended stance of "patient resistance." In her private life, yes: Andrea would spend many a precious hour explaining to a friend or a neophyte feminist that when she wrote—in *Intercourse*, say—that "violation is a synonym for intercourse" she was *not* saying (though it was often and still is claimed) that she viewed all sex as rape—she valued reciprocity, not celibacy. Nussbaum's patient resistance may be a plausible tactic for dealing with moderate mistakes of ignorance and with negotiable adversaries. But the more massive inequities may require comparable resistance. Thanks to the recent emergence of the "Me Too" movement, it's once again understood that male privilege is more likely to yield to angry confrontation than to polite appeals to conscience. The collective anger of women has—some thirty years after the publication of *Mercy*—found new license and approbation. And as Rebecca Traister has recently reminded us, rage is not the opposite of rational: it can be—and in the past often has been—an appropriate response to appalling injustice; yes, the Jews of the Warsaw Ghetto were right to have taken up arms; yes, Toussaint L'Ouverture was right to have violently thrown off his chains.[13]

In the aftermath of finishing *Mercy*, Andrea felt "very detached, very remote"; she had "no ambivalence, no second thoughts"; "I don't quarrel with a tree, I don't quarrel with *Mercy*. It has that self-evidency, that simplicity, to me, now . . . a certain period of almost not existing at all for me." She felt something of the same kind of stasis in regard to the feminist movement. By 1990, in Andrea's view, violence against women and the weakness of the radical feminist movement had in tandem become "much worse." In part, she blamed the ever-expanding industry of pornography. She reiterated yet again that she saw no reason to preclude the existence of erotica, though she continued to feel puzzled as to why two people happy with each other would need it. She worried, too, that what the debate about the difference between erotica and pornography had come down to was that "erotica simply means pornography for intellectuals"—which meant (like so much else) that it was a class issue. For her, the difference between erotica and pornography was easy to ascertain: "look at the status of women" in the film, magazine, or book; if they're represented as subordinate, or if the threat of violence is present, then what you're looking at is pornography.

Ideally, Andrea believed that every movement should have a "whole spectrum" of people in it—"mainstream feminists, reformists, people who do different kinds of work and make a variety of contributions." She ascribed the "solid middle" of the feminist movement as having fallen away due to the "very serious and very systematic" campaign against women who protest. She believed that a number of feminists had "cut and run," fallen back on individual lifestyle goals. And she included in that indictment part of the lesbian community. She believed that in 1990 lesbians "are still responsible for a lot of the leadership" of the movement but that on the grassroots level "there is much more hiding and secrecy and duplicity again"—which she found "very frightening." There was also, she felt, an intensification of "male identification" among lesbians, as represented by the heightened prestige of a sadomasochistic lifestyle, which Andrea abhorred, and a kind of "self-referential clubhouse" tone: "we're special, we're different." She put her hopes primarily in the global spread of international feminism.[14]

One sign of the times had been the demise of *Ms.* magazine in 1987 (which Andrea had *not* lamented) and its purchase by an Australian media company. Two years later, concerned about the amount of "Cher-centered" content, a group of American feminists bought back the magazine and hired Robin Morgan as its editor-in-chief. That delighted Andrea. Her friendship with Robin went back some twenty years, and no serious quarrel had ever troubled it. The new male owner of *Ms.*, Dale Lang, guaranteed Robin a free hand for two issues, and in the run-up to her taking over, she and Andrea had several pow-wows about what the magazine's ideal reincarnation would look like, including a discussion of including the piece Andrea had been writing on Israel.

Robin ultimately decided that the new *Ms.* would be a bimonthly, run roughly a hundred pages per issue, carry no advertising or color—and *not* feature any mainstream celebrity on its cover. "A radical journal at last!" Andrea cheered. As the first issue neared publication, she glowingly reported to her London editor that "Robin has done an astonishing job in creating something worth publishing, worth reading." In her enthusiasm, Andrea's glum assessment of the feminist movement's decline went into abrupt reversal: "I think the zeitgeist really has changed . . . and millions of women can't stand it anymore—I'm saying there is a critical mass now in this direction, and I doubt that I'm misjudging it."[15]

Even in one of her rare upbeat states of mind, Andrea soon reverted to emphasizing instead all that remained undone. Her detractors liked to say that her bleak temperament made her incapable of sustaining a hopeful attitude—which has an element of truth to it. But far more intrinsic to Andrea's character was an inability to indulge for long in that chipper all-American boosterism so successful in blocking out reality. She put it bluntly in a 1991 speech to the Canadian Mental Health Association: "Violence against women is a major past-time. It is a mainstream cultural entertainment. And it is real. It is pervasive. It saturates the society. It's very hard to make anyone notice it, because there is so much of it."[16]

Several decisive events combined during 1991 to compound the sense of a passage, of a significant turning point. At the beginning of the year, after multiple medical crises, Andrea's mother, Sylvia, passed away. Andrea had been long estranged from her parents, but they had recently reconciled, preceded by renewed contact first with her brother, Mark, with whom she'd been in at least occasional touch.

But with her mother, Sylvia, the wounds had gone deep. From childhood on she'd hounded—not too strong a word—Andrea with accusations of inadequacy, of pointlessly, imprudently resisting established norms. Being made to feel profoundly deficient had contributed immeasurably to the underlay of masochism and anguish Andrea suffered as an adult. Sylvia, of course, was herself the product of a time when female dutifulness and conformity were standard measures of worth, and her ongoing bouts of serious illness did nothing to soften her wretched outbursts of wrath.[17]

Of late, though, the seventy-five-year-old Sylvia had become, in Andrea's words, "incredibly benign . . . she just seems to have realized (finally) that I am a separate person with a separate life." Sylvia had been going regularly for psychotherapy, and Andrea credited her mother's change with the simple fact of "having someone to talk to. . . . She's of that generation of women so completely isolated and yet responsible for everything the kids do, every failure, every act of non-conformity." The adult Andrea was able to empathize fully with how it had been for her mother: Sylvia had been unable to talk about the poverty of her life without indicting herself (rather than the culture) for its shortcomings, unable to explore impulses and interests considered "improper"—though she'd loved to read as a youngster, she felt she had to do it in secret. For Andrea, the "new" Sylvia came as "a great relief"—she was even able to tell Andrea how sorry she was that her daughter had had "such a hard life"; Andrea reassured her that "she shouldn't worry, because everything's fine, which it is."

Her father, Harry, had deeply loved his sometimes difficult wife, and he was bereft at her death; Andrea and John let him know that they would welcome his coming to live with them in Park Slope, but he decided to remain in Camden. "It seems very important to me," Andrea wrote her brother, Mark, "that in these last years he does what he wants for as long as possible. Whatever he wants."[18]

Soon after Sylvia's passing, her brother Mark revealed that he was about to be operated on for cancer of the esophagus. Though a stoic, it soon became clear that Mark was desperately ill, and on impulse Andrea flew to Vienna, where Mark lived with his wife, Eva, and worked as a scientist. Though at one point they'd been estranged, Andrea and Mark had a strong bond, and she wanted to spend time with him before his condition worsened, which he'd been told would be likely to happen soon, probably within the next few months. At the moment he was responding well to chemotherapy, though the cancer had already spread to his liver. It wasn't long after Andrea's visit that he suddenly took a turn for the worse.

The chemo abruptly stopped working, and the amount of pain markedly increased. Mark finally decided to tell his father that he was dying, and Harry and Andrea at once booked flights to Vienna; before they could arrive, Mark died. They reached Vienna immediately afterward and made arrangements for his burial. It was, according to Andrea, "physically demanding and emotionally deranged." Meeting Mark's friends and colleagues provided some solace, but

Harry was heart-broken. "I can't imagine his grief," Andrea wrote a friend. "My own is almost beyond my imagination. . . . It has been shattering." For a time after returning home, she became "very solitary. Can barely stand to speak to anyone," she wrote Michael Moorcock.[19]

For a while she was literally not earning anything. Then her father, in some unfathomable reaction to his son's death, started to send her substantial checks. They deeply upset her—she felt he was divesting himself of all earthly things, signaling his own imminent departure. "What I hate most," she wrote friends, "is that I need it and so I use it." To make herself less needy, she again started to accept invitations to speak.

Her prowess as a speaker and her prominence as a feminist nearly always guaranteed an overflow crowd and an enthusiastic reception. Gratifying though that was, traveling around the country did nothing to improve her mood. The AIDS crisis was at its height, with thousands dying and no miracle drugs on the horizon. Andrea wrote next to nothing directly on the crisis, in part because she no longer knew many gay men, in part because she saw her battles centered elsewhere. Yet neither she nor John thought they were immune to the HIV scourge. Quite the opposite. Since John enjoyed being anally penetrated and since he and Andrea continued to have occasional sex, they both assumed that they would test positive. When they finally took their courage in hand and got tested, they were astonished to learn they weren't infected.

Yet so much else remained depressing that their mood barely shifted. Yes, the Cold War had ended—the Berlin Wall had come down in 1989, yet Mikhail Gorbachev had been forced from office in 1991. Robert Bork's nomination to the Supreme Court had been defeated, yet the Right wing seemed stronger than ever, and gender discrimination, segregated schools, police brutality, rising global temperatures, and the heightened concentration of wealth continued to remain the dominant, and accelerating, patterns. "The general situation here is so corrupt, so degraded," Andrea wrote a Norwegian friend, "that it is hard to know how to anticipate the next blow, which always falls, followed by another one." Most of what she saw around her was "distressing, painful, or difficult."

Her spirits got something of a boost when she learned that *Mercy* had found translators and publishers in Germany, Japan, and— "can you believe"—Korea. But the United States? Not a nibble— not, that is, until the two young editors who'd recently launched the small house, Four Walls, Eight Windows (4W8W), expressed interest. It would not be a match made in heaven, though it started out well enough, with Andrea deliberately ignoring the obvious: that youthful ardor was usually a poor substitute for adult compe- tence. Mutual antagonism was almost immediate, and was all the more bizarre because it had absolutely nothing to do with Andrea's own book. To cut straight to the end point of a mountainous and excruciatingly extended thicket of controversy, the 4W8W editors solicited a blurb from Andrea for another book they were publish- ing. She graciously agreed, only to be brought up short by several paragraphs in the manuscript (written by two women) that seemed to suggest that lying about rape or incest was sometimes justified, even advisable, in order to obtain an abortion.

To Andrea, that was shockingly irresponsible. When she con- tacted various women who worked in rape crisis centers, they con- curred: "we do not make false charges of rape" and we "do not knowingly collude with anyone who does lie"—to do so would feed directly into the wrong-headed, popular stereotype that many women lie about having been sexually assaulted. The two female authors promptly accused Andrea of launching a campaign to pre- vent publication of their book; then an article appeared in the *New York Observer* ridiculing her as a "censor"—and on and on it went. Andrea accused the 4W8W editors of launching a whispering cam- paign to further discredit her; the ACLU named her Bigot of the Year; and in the agonizing upshot, the 4W8W editors canceled all publicity plans for their recently released paperback edition of *Mer- cy*. "I've just lost my very marginal publisher," Andrea wrote friends in England, "and am sinking fast."[20]

It soon got worse. After a period of relative inactivity, the "pornog- raphy wars" again heated up. One major catalyst was the nation- ally televised and wrenching 1991 Senate confirmation hearings of Clarence Thomas to the Supreme Court. Anita Hill's brave and damning testimony against her former boss, charging him with insistent sexual harassment, explosively reintroduced the specters of male entitlement and female endangerment. As several male members of the Senate Judiciary Committee—in particular Orrin Hatch, Alan Simpson, and Arlen Specter—piled on ugly innuendos about Hill's "stability," strongly implying that she was simply a spurned lover seeking revenge, many women across the country relived their own toxic memories of workplace harassment— and further conflated male sexuality with dangerous aggression. As for Clarence Thomas himself, Andrea felt utter disgust: she regarded him as "an incredible reactionary . . . setting a new record for judicial sadism. . . . Impeachment or assassination can remedy the appointment, nothing else. Natural death, but God is not on our side."[21]

That same year saw the introduction of a pornography "victim's compensation act" in Congress. The bill was narrowly written: one could only sue for damages if the material said to cause harm involved child pornography or obscene material, neither protected by the First Amendment. Still, criticism of the bill came from various directions, including from two hundred NOW chapters—and from the novelist John Irving. In an essay for the *New York Times* entitled "Pornography and the New Puritans," he expressed concern that if the bill passed—it didn't—"it will be the first piece of legislation to give credence to the unproven theory that sexually explicit material actually causes sexual crimes." He called the bill "a piece of back-door censorship, plain and simple."[22]

That phrasing conjured up porn wars past—and still present, if comparatively dormant. Andrea was among those who sent in letters protesting Irving's piece; uncharacteristically, the *New York Times* printed hers in its entirety. In it, she singled out as her chief concern Irving's blanket declaration that no proof exists for claiming that "sexually explicit material actually causes sexual crimes." Strangely, Andrea didn't cite the Donnerstein and Malamuth studies that she and Kitty had earlier used to back their claim that pornography *can* produce harm of varying sorts. She settled instead for an orphic declaration: pornographers "materially promote rape, battery, maiming and bondage; they make a product that they know dehumanizes, degrades and exploits women; they hurt women to make the pornography, and the consumers use the pornography in assaults both verbal and physical." But a pronouncement is not proof. By 1991 a significant number of confirming studies had already accumulated, and Andrea's failure to cite them in her letter to the *Times* may well have been a gauge of her having grown weary of the repetitive struggle—and her eagerness to shift focus to her new engagement with Israel.[23]

Whatever her wishes may have been, the Canadian Supreme Court's 1992 landmark decision, *Butler v. The Queen*, rekindled the pornography question in concentrated form and again plunged Andrea into the tangle of debate. The Canadian Criminal Code of 1985 had been structured on the principle that one right can be overridden by another right. Citing that principle, the Court in *Butler* voted unanimously to prohibit the production and distribution of obscene materials and defined as obscene any visual or written materials that degraded or dehumanized women, precluding their equality, denying them access to all the rights of citizenship. The Court openly acknowledged in its decision that such restrictions would sometimes abridge freedom of expression, yet defended the curtailment as regrettable but necessary. As precedent, the Court cited the 1983 *Rankine* decision, the first to address pornography "from the point of view of the victims of the sexual abuse, rather than of the sensibilities of the observers," as well as the 1985 *Ramsingh* ruling that women "have a right to demand that some limitation be imposed by government on freedom of pornographic expression." In other words—as Andrea put it in a letter to Erica Jong—the Canadian Supreme Court had weighed "pornography's harms to women against the speech rights of pornographers. They held that women's equality had the higher value."[24]

The Court's underlying assumptions—not previously articulated openly by a prestigious legal body—produced a predictable uproar. On May 7–8, nearly two hundred "anti-censorship" feminists gathered to discuss the issues at a conference in New York entitled "The Sex Panic: Women, Censorship and 'Pornography.'" Leonore Tiefer, president of the International Academy of Sex Research and one of the conference's lead speakers, put the matter bluntly:

legal restrictions on explicit sexual expression, she predicted, "will force erotic experimentation in art, video, books and performances underground, which will deprive most women of access to unconventional inputs to their erotic imagination. . . . Now is the time for more sexual experimentation, not shame-soaked restraint." The witty Texas journalist Molly Ivins had a somewhat different take: "We've all read the studies of pornography and sexual aggression saying yes it does, no it doesn't, yes it does, no it doesn't. You could just shit or go blind trying to figure that one out . . . common goddam sense tells me there probably is some truth to the theory that all those ugly pictures do encourage violence against women." Few of the conference attendees were willing to give even that much credence to their "anti-porn" opponents.[25]

The reasons go deep and range from differing perspectives on sexuality to the legitimacy of social institutions. Without pretending to play philosopher or to be expert in the dozen or so specialties at issue, at least some outline can be made of the underlying assumptions that once again fiercely divided the feminist movement. To focus on Andrea and Kitty, it might be easier to describe the areas in which they did *not* subscribe to the values their opponents commonly attributed to them. Though they did sometimes find themselves—to their own maximum discomfort—on the same side of the pornography debate as right-wingers, they were profoundly at odds with their basic worldview.[26]

Both Andrea and Kitty were—and had long been—committed lefties. Kitty had worked with the Black Panthers and had staunchly opposed the Vietnam War; in 1986 she'd also been co-counsel and the guiding spirit behind a pathbreaking Supreme Court case that established sexual harassment as a legal claim for sex discrimination. Andrea, even as an undergraduate, had been active in left-wing causes, and—unlike those on the Right—had viewed religion, monogamous pair-bonding, and the traditional family as enemies, not exemplars, of the good life. She believed in *lots* of sexual experimentation and, like Kitty, objected to violent pornography because she concluded that it subordinated and harmed women, not because it encouraged lust—which to them was the path not to the devil but to pleasure and human connection.

Nor did Andrea believe, as many of those on the right did, that humankind was intrinsically sinful. As a young woman she held firm to the belief, which some call "utopian"—in the essential goodness and malleability of people, and wholly blamed institutionalized injustice and bigotry for the deformations of human life; faced as an adult with the obstinacy of "imprinting," she gradually (and sadly) modified her faith in utopian notions of progress, yet an intractable and to herself sometimes irritating faith in the possibilities of change remained at the core of her temperament.

She and Kitty *shared* many attitudes and assumptions with pro-pornography feminists—including, primarily, their contempt for patriarchal privilege and sexist assumptions of male superiority. Andrea vehemently agreed with those of her feminist opponents (the majority, probably) who insisted that gender was *not* a biological given; she believed that masculinity and femininity were social constructs, not immutable products of biology. In Andrea's ideal world, the traditional gender binary would be supplanted by androgyny— the view that all human beings are capable of developing all those traits currently parceled out to *either* men *or* to women. But agreement about what men might potentially become elided into disagreement over what men currently *were*.

The pro-pornography camp tended to hold the more positive view of heterosexual men; it saw them, generally speaking, as more negotiable, more emotionally available, more appreciative and considerate of their female companions, and less prone to violence, sexist rigidity, and ruling the roost. As part and parcel of that view, these feminists were less likely to see women as victims, as unwilling or unable to assume active agency (like initiating—or rejecting—sex) on their own behalf. They were more likely to regard sexuality as the *mutual* pursuit of pleasure and an expressive outlet for tenderness rather than as a battleground for asserting control. Neither camp viewed sex, as many on the religious Right did, as the source of sinful temptation or as primarily designed for procreation.[27]

It was, and still is, often claimed by their antagonists that Andrea and Kitty believed all heterosexual sex was rape, though neither did; as Kitty put it in a rather sharp rebuke to a correspondent, "I did not say 'all sex is rape' or anything that amounts to that. Ever. Not here.

Not anywhere. You know it. I know it." Andrea agreed, yet could become heated when a straight woman persisted in describing her male partner as a paragon of gentle tenderness, and she breathed fire when one well-known female writer kept insisting that "when I hear an unqualified narrative of male sexual destructiveness, and do not interrupt it, I feel that I betray my body's deepest friendships."

In that last instance, Andrea let loose with the kind of harangue she currently rarely indulged: "You tell us that there are these millions and millions of men who do not rape or use force or hit or use prostitutes, and that they are the norm. And guess what . . . you made it up. Because the 50 percent of married women who *Time* says are beaten by their husbands are ordinary women beaten by ordinary men. . . . And ordinary men of all kinds from all places in society use prostitutes and revel in their abjectness. And ordinary men of all kinds force sex. Not all men do, no. . . . Study those who don't, commend them, no argument . . . your formulation . . . *demands* a silencing of women: because yr happiness cannot co-exist with so very much that so many women have to say . . . you put yr sexual happiness above her voice, her life, which is yr political choice to make. Nevertheless, we have fought very hard to be able to begin to say these terrible, but very ordinary, things, to articulate these terrible, but very ordinary, experiences. . . . Yr 'agency' shit is pretty pathetic next to this fight. And don't you just wish that I accepted being a victim over agency?"

Andrea in fact had her own doubts about the *Butler v. Queen* decision, though overall she regarded it as "a tremendous victory for women in Western legal systems." Although Kitty had written the legal brief for the Canadian women's group Legal Education and Action Fund (LEAF), Andrea had opposed their attempts at intervention, arguing that no criminal obscenity law—even when reinterpreted to provide greater protection for women—should be actively supported; obscenity laws meant governmental and police intervention, and both agencies were in bed with the pornographers.[28]

Yet overall the *Butler* decision represented a long-sought legal vindication of their insistence that pornography could be harmful. Despite her doubts about the decision, Andrea never voiced them publicly, even after the ruling was later claimed to have had some negative consequences that she and Kitty hadn't foreseen or had dismissed as improbable. They were blamed especially for what their opponents claimed was—as a direct result of the *Butler* decision—a clamp-down by Canadian Customs on material emanating from gay, lesbian, and feminist sources, including the seizure of *Bad Attitude*, a sexually explicit lesbian-feminist magazine.

Andrea and Kitty took the claim with the utmost seriousness and set about trying to pin down the actual extent of the purported censorship. After considerable digging, in which they enlisted the help of various on-the-ground sources, including the progressive Canadian Women's Legal Education and Action Fund, they issued a formal statement summarizing their findings. In it, they pointed out that under *Butler*, it was illegal for Customs to seize materials because they are gay or lesbian, though previously it *had* been legal to do so—and those earlier confiscations had led to "vociferous" complaints from gay and lesbian groups. As Kitty tellingly put it in a letter: "If materials are being seized because they are gay or lesbian, i.e., for moralistic reasons, it is only possible *because* Canada Customs has *not* re-evaluated its standards to conform with *Butler*." She thought "the real problem with *Butler* is lack of enforcement, not excessive enforcement."

Two of Andrea's own books, *Woman Hating* and *Pornography*, were briefly impounded at the U.S.–Canada border on the grounds of their "obscene" content. Her detractors delighted in the "irony," and the *New York Times* printed an op-ed piece, "Censors' Helpers," which gloried in the news. Yet Canadian border seizures had been commonplace long before *Butler*, and no causal relationship has been established between the court decision and the post-*Butler* seizures: Canadian Customs did not, at least not through 1994, officially revise its guidelines to reflect or incorporate the ruling. In fact, as Andrea and Kitty learned, the charge of a crackdown on importing gay and lesbian material had been largely fabricated; according to LEAF, Customs officials "are not using the Butler decision *at all*." Andrea and Kitty believed that the probable source of the false rumor lay with the ongoing and increasingly contentious debate *in the United States* between speech rights guaranteed by the First Amendment and equality rights at the heart of the

Fourteenth Amendment. To date, the U.S. Supreme Court had come down heavily on the side of those declaring that speech rights took precedence. The Canadian Supreme Court's *Butler* decision had taken the opposite position, explicitly adopting the view that "society's interest in sex equality outweighs pornographers' speech rights." As Robin Morgan put it, "having legal recourse to defend one's civil rights is a far cry from censorship."[29]

The week after the *Times* published its mocking op-ed, the latest edition of *Screw* magazine carried the headline "Dworkin/MacKinnon Lesbo Orgy," an editorial entitled "Catherine MacKinnon: Whore for Censorship," and for good measure a doctored photograph with Kitty and Andrea's heads pasted onto other bodies, showing Andrea "fucking" Kitty. The text read, "Sapphic sow Andrea Dworkin has a new battle to fight. Thanks to the efforts of her pussy partner-in-crime, Catherine MacKinnon, some of Dworkin's own books have been banned in Canada because of their violent and sexual content. When will these two book-burning bull dykes learn that the sword of censorship cuts both ways?" Soon after, PBS ran its own version of the story—in the King's English, of course.[30]

11

Prelude to Israel

Back in 1988, at age forty-two, Andrea had decided to go to Israel. In doing so, she was embarking, somewhat to her own surprise, on a double journey: reawakening her childhood as a young Jewish girl and starting on a path of inquiry into the state of Israel and her own relationship to it. For more than a decade the subject of Israel would preoccupy her, leading initially to a 1990 article in *Ms.*, "Israel: Whose Country Is It Anyway?" and eventually her 2000 book *Scapegoat*, arguably her finest—or certainly among them.[1]

The ostensible reason for Andrea's 1988 visit had been the first International Jewish Feminist Conference. Middle-class, male-dominated American Jewish groups (including the powerful American Jewish Congress) had put the conference together, but for Andrea the main goal was to meet with grassroots Israeli feminists who objected to the exclusion of the poor and of Palestinian women from the mainstream conference—women she did manage to meet in Haifa, Tel Aviv, and Jerusalem. In retrospect, she described herself at the time as an innocent, a typical secular American Jew who supported the state of Israel and knew very little about it.[2]

The trip was an eye-opener. She became horrified, above all, by the tales she heard of Israeli soldiers shooting rubber-coated bullets at boys who threw stones at them, and the multiple stories of the troops brutalizing Palestinian women. As for the Orthodox rabbinate, Andrea was appalled at their insistence on the strict observance of ancient Talmudic misogyny that codified male dominance and treated women as an inferior, even unclean, species. She knew that the low status of women in Israel wasn't unique, yet felt "we"— American Jewry—were "uniquely responsible for it."

Andrea's mounting interest in Israel was inescapably linked to a heightened awareness of her own Jewishness, a conscious identity that went back to childhood. She remembered her Hebrew School principal when she was growing up in Camden, New Jersey, who'd told the students that they had the obligation to be first a Jew, second an American, third a human being, a citizen of the world. Andrea, age eleven, had dared to argue with him, had boldly announced that she was primarily a citizen of the world. Enraged, the principal told her that Jews had been killed throughout history precisely because many had felt the way she did. Andrea persisted: if everyone was a human being first, then Jews would be safe. He told her she had the blood of other Jews on her hands and stormed from the room.

Andrea hadn't picked up her views from her own family. Both sets of her grandparents had been immigrants and had refused to talk about the past. To Andrea their attitude represented "an incomprehensible and disquieting amnesia," but that didn't deter her from developing her own set of views early on. She never forgot the time when she was only ten years old that she'd unexpectedly come upon her hysterical, tear-stained aunt, caught up in the midst of a traumatic flashback to the series of concentration camps in which she'd been imprisoned during World War II, and the death march she'd somehow survived. The aunt broke down in front of Andrea only once, but a window had been opened; she'd been profoundly shocked. Many years later, she told an interviewer that the incident had led her in college to sit down in the library with the record of the Nuremberg trials and read it, volume after volume. "I might go through six months," she later wrote, "when I won't read it and a few months when I will and I have been doing that since I was a kid."[3]

In high school she argued that the idea of a Jewish *state* was intrinsically wrong, because "anyone who wasn't Jewish would be second-class by definition," and "we didn't have the right to do to other people what had been done to us." To be a *fair* state, Israel could not be a *Jewish* state. Besides, she insisted, Palestine had not been an *empty* land prior to the establishment of Israel, as the Zionists claimed; "the Palestinians were right," she announced, "when they say the Jews regarded them as nothing." The Jewish state, she declared, was "an imperialist act."

All of this had been moderated in childhood by an awareness that Israel at its inception had declared itself a socialist democracy based on the premise that men and women were equal in all ways, and that "servility was inappropriate for the new Jew, male or female." Israel had even established egalitarian collectives (the *kibbutzim*), where the entire community raised the children and the traditional nuclear family was declared obsolete; children no longer "belonged" to their biological parents. Andrea's disapproval of Zionism had further softened when other issues, relating to race, gender, and the war in Vietnam, had gradually absorbed her attention, and her Jewishness had receded; its conscious influence became dormant.

Andrea in time went off to Bennington College to lead the life of a lusty, literary, non-religious voluptuary. In the decades that followed, she never joined a Jewish group or political organization, nor in her writings ever engaged, except for a passing mention, the many controversies that arose regarding Israel. (The one exception is her 1983 book, *Right-Wing Women*, in which the references are largely scholarly and abstract.) Which isn't to say that as an adult she dismissed her Jewishness or soft-pedaled its importance in forming her character. To the contrary. She told an interviewer in 1980 that "everything I know about human rights goes back in one way or another to what I learned about being a Jew . . . when I began to think about what it means to be a woman, it was that experience that I called on . . . my Jewishness is the background that's most influenced my values."[4]

Her 1988 trip to Israel for the international feminist conference, and writing about her experiences subsequently for *Ms.*, aroused much in her that had been lying dormant. Had her grade school principal after all been right, she now wondered, in telling her that if Jews had no homeland to call their own, then those who disapproved of the creation of the state of Israel—including herself—would "have the blood of Jews on her hands"? The question resonated far more deeply within her when in Israel than it had when sitting as an eleven-year-old in a Camden, New Jersey, classroom.

On one side of the ledger remained her conviction that Israel from its inception had been based on a fundamental betrayal of egalitarianism: it had excluded and stigmatized those who were not Jews. In her view, the starting premise of the state had been implicitly racist. And yet . . . she had now lived long enough to see and understand how profoundly anti-Semitism was rooted—implacably so among Israel's immediate neighbors. The profundity of anti-Jewish hatred in combination with the fact that Israel had been created on the principle of exclusion inescapably meant, as Andrea put it, that "Israel had to become either a fortress or a tomb." She didn't believe that having their own state made Jews any safer, but it did make them different "from the pathetic creatures on the trains, the skeletons in the camps"—and that was "a great relief." Enough of a relief that she resolved not to do or say anything that might "have the blood of Jews on my hands."

And the Arabs? What could one say about the Palestinians whose land—and on this point Andrea remained obdurate—had been appropriated, stolen? As early as the seventies, Andrea had started to read books by and about the Palestinians. Among much else, she'd begun to realize that despite her parents' good intentions, she'd imbibed from them a certain amount of anti-Arab prejudice. They were uncommonly conscientious for their generation in speaking out against racial and religious bigotry, and "went out of their way to say 'some Arabs' when making a negative comment." Yet in truth, as Andrea put it, "my education in the Jewish community made that caveat fairly meaningless."

The more she read, the more convinced she became that the Palestinians were a people wronged, that Israel had violated their basic human rights, even while denying the fact. The land had *not* been empty. The Israeli seizure of Palestinian territory had been, in her view, an imperialist act, and it contradicted "every idea we have about who we are and what being a Jew means . . . we took a country from the people who lived there; we the dispossessed finally did it to someone else." While in Jerusalem in 1988 Andrea joined with some four hundred other women in a vigil against the occupation.

On that particular point, her opinion held firm, but her considerable ambivalence in other areas remained. She reminded herself that in Israel, unlike in the Arab world, men and women were at least officially equal, though in practice a male-dominant structure remained intact. From her perspective, "women were pretty invisible"—and for that she blamed the power of the Orthodox rabbinate in particular. In 1988 there were separate religious courts for Christians, Muslims, Druze, and Jews, and as far as Andrea could see "women from each group are subject to the authority of the most ancient systems of religious misogyny." The husband remained the master, and a "rebellious" wife could easily lose custody of her children and all financial support. And as well, "of course, Israel has all the other good things boys do to girls: rape, incest, prostitution, sexual harassment in public places."

After returning to the States, Andrea wrote up her piece, "Israel: Whose Country Is It Anyway?," for *Ms.* magazine. The article produced a small avalanche of letters to the editor, almost all protesting Andrea's views. She was denounced as an "Israel-basher" bent on attacking the right of "a dispersed people" to have a homeland. One letter dismissed her as "the stereotype of a self-hating Jew," another rejected her opinions as those of a myopic tourist, a third accused her of defaming the Talmud. A few of the letters did thank her for "spreading the word," for "letting the truth be known." Hurt but never deterred for long by criticism, Andrea decided to explore the issues relating to Israel in more depth—and the subject would come to absorb her for nearly a decade. For the time being, though, she felt "far away from writing: it seems like a geographical distance, as if I would have to swim rivers and climb mountains to get anywhere near it. And, while I would like to be there, I don't know how to get there. So nothing seems right."[5]

Yet Andrea felt irresistibly drawn to preparing a full-length work on the subject. Deeply committed to the project, she wrote up what she thought was a persuasive proposal, and Elaine sent it out widely. Only one publisher, the Free Press (which had published *Intercourse*), expressed any interest. Their terms were borderline insulting—very little money coupled to a demand for world rights. To supplement her income she would have to continue the arduous job of traveling around the country giving speeches, leaving her insufficient time and energy to work on the book. She'd also over the years accumulated a multitude of commitments, mostly centered on the ongoing pornography struggle, and she refused to abandon them, though the tug-of-war on her time was often a daily one. Even at the start of her research, she lamented how far away she was from writing the book: "I feel so frightened," she wrote, "because time goes so fast, each day just moves past me, and I have so much to learn, constantly interrupted by whatever, life."

In order to make a living, Andrea traveled widely from 1991 to 1993 giving lectures for more than half of each year. The constant trek upset her natural body rhythms—she wrote at night and slept days—and also kept her from finding enough concentrated time to make significant progress on her book. The brief bursts of free time that were her own were often spent recovering from too little sleep in too many hotel beds, which was more and more difficult as she approached fifty. Late in that year she decided to make yet one more effort—all her previous ones had failed—to persuade a foundation to buy her some release time.[6]

Someone suggested that the Diana Foundation in California might be receptive, and Andrea worked up a provocative proposal that as a secondary benefit helped her to further define the essence of what she hoped to accomplish. Women and Jews, she wrote the foundation, "seem to be nearly universal scapegoats . . . used to represent traits that then are stigmatized and must be extirpated from individuals or nation-states to establish a pure sexual or racial identity." She wanted to explore what the two groups had in common. Though women and Jews have historically repudiated violence, she wrote, "many forms of violence, overt and subtle," have been used against them. Both Jews and women have often been seen as "the carriers of civilizing values," yet each has been maligned "as low, craven, venal—moneygrubbers and sluts respectively." And both groups have managed to find "an affirmative cultural value and identity in the signets of oppression (for instance, for Jews religious learning and ritual, for women, maternity and childrearing)."[7]

Never one to conceal or prettify her views, not even when desperate for money, Andrea audaciously included in her proposal the assertion that "in the fight for statehood, Jews for the first time became associated with violence, and Israel is now widely recognized not only as a military power but as a militarist nation, a warrior nation." For garnish she added this eye-opener: "Inside Israel, Jewish women still have no country, since there is not civil equality for them. . . . Jewish women continue to be scapegoated by Israeli men. How and why? And is there a relationship between the new masculine identity of Israeli men, anchored in a warrior mentality, and the growth of an indigenous Israeli racism: hatred of the Palestinians?"

Miraculously, the Diana Foundation decided to award Andrea a $5,000 grant. It was a huge relief; she was now able for a time to say no to any overnight invitation to speak or to attend yet another conference, to pick and choose based solely on the urgency of the call, how much time would have to be invested, and the importance of the subject. She still cared too much about the issues that affected women's lives to leave the public arena entirely behind; she simply cut back. She basically had a scholar's disposition: a large capacity (and need) for solitude linked to a driven hunger for "getting to the bottom of things," plus a minimal capacity for mere chit-chat. But she scorned scholarship as practiced in academia, with its disdain for "excessive" entanglement with the merely "transient" affairs of everyday life. In one of the speeches on prostitution that Andrea still occasionally gave, she put the issue this way: "Academic life is premised on the notion that there is a tomorrow and a next day . . . or that there is some kind of discourse of ideas and a year of freedom in which you can have disagreements that will not cost you your life. . . . If you have been in prostitution, you do not have tomorrow on your mind. . . . No woman who is prostituted can afford to be that stupid, such that she would actually believe that tomorrow will come." The far more pressing problem for women "is that being hurt is ordinary. It happens every day, all the time. . . . We count ourselves goddamn lucky when whatever happens falls short of rape."[8]

John, at least, seemed to be in a good place. *Refusing to Be a Man* had drawn both good reviews and considerable sales, and he rather easily secured a contract for a second book, and with an advance larger than Andrea had gotten for all of her books combined, making it possible for him to leave his day job in magazine publishing. That second book, *The End of Manhood*—a practical guide for overcoming our "defective conditioning" in masculinity—came out in 1993, and it, too, did well. Its success launched him into a variety of new projects, including a novel, a children's book, and a collaborative effort to write a "rock/rap" opera.[9]

The next stage in Andrea's work on Israel involved two extended visits to the Holocaust Museum in Washington, DC, in September and November of 1993. Each time she spent four days, five hours each day. The experience proved searing; it was "almost unbearable . . . overwhelming." She ended up writing a forty-page article about her visit, though she allowed *Ms.*, given its space limitations, to condense it down to little more than ten pages. The longer piece, fortunately, exists in manuscript form; it gives us far more of Andrea's distinctive voice, and the anguish the experience had cost her. Throughout the eight days she spent at the museum two voices continued to haunt her: the grade school principal shouting his prediction that "the blood of the Jews" would be on her hands; and the terrified, piercing shrieks of her aunt reliving in flashback the horrors of the Auschwitz-Birkenau concentration camp in which she'd once been imprisoned. Andrea would steady herself, needed to steady herself, with the constant reminder that to know more about the Holocaust "would be a victory over it—over the fear it creates, over the hate it incarnates, over the desperate sadness it always evokes."[10]

She took with her to Washington an article Kitty had recently written for *Ms.* on the current rape/death camps in Bosnia, the ethnic cleansing, the hurricane of violence that the Serbs had unleashed against Bosnia's Muslims and Croatians—in Kitty's words "the forced prostitution, the making of a pornography of genocide." Andrea brought the article with her, as she put it, in order to remind her of "the kind of material I needed to find" at the Holocaust Museum. She brought with her, too, many questions, particularly questions about the treatment of women in the camps. In what numbers were they raped? Were some of the camps brothels? Where and how were women used in medical experiments? "What happened to the women? Concretely, the specifics."

She did get some information about the women whose teeth were pulled out and vaginas searched for gold; the women subjected to x-ray and surgical treatment as part of the Nazis' "infertility experiments"; the Polish women whose bones were broken for transplant to German patients; the women sterilized with chemical injections into their wombs. But she would be disappointed in the answers she got.

Andrea had written in advance to the Museum staff, posing some of her questions; they were extremely kind; they presented her with a great deal of material; they guided her to areas that might further inform her particular inquiries. Yet she felt she'd "met a blank wall when I tried to explain that I wanted to know about rape as a genocidal strategy, the sexual destruction of personhood in the brothels (serial rape), the aggression against women's reproductive capacities." She told the "nice" female staff member with whom she'd earlier corresponded "how wrong I thought it was that the Museum, which pays scrupulous attention to the political sensitivities of ethnic groups targeted by the Nazis for slave labor or forced labor or, in the case of the Romani, even for extinction—did not pay any attention to crimes against women." The "nice staff member" revealed that "the women who work at the Museum . . . sort of felt the same way." She gave Andrea the names of seven people to whom she could explain her disappointment in writing. Andrea decided not to: "Critical questions are not really possible; the burden of knowing is too great to ask to know yet more. And who looks *for* the story of women; and if it is missing sees the absence?" The Museum told the story, "brilliantly told" it, "of annihilation, mass murder . . . one emerges sober, sad, knowing more, in grief. . . .

There is a visual eloquence that does not let the mind drift . . . it is an astonishing achievement." It was enough.

But not quite enough, not for Andrea. What about the issue of outside intervention? As word of the Nazi terror gradually leaked out, what was the international reaction? Who tried to intervene? Did anyone try? Andrea turned to the documentary films at the Museum. They told her much: "that Germany was 'morally isolated from the whole world'; that various politicians threatened to sever diplomatic relations; that there was *only* condemnation, no action of any kind; that the U.S. did not want any of the endangered Jews to come here; that labor opposed increases in immigration; that some Jewish groups were afraid more immigrants would mean more anti-Semitism here . . . that the State Department did all it could to keep Jews excluded . . . that F.D.R. never made a move to help; that in 1939 there was an effort to get the U.S. to let in twenty thousand children (the logic being that they would not steal jobs) but the children were not let in; that from 1933–1941 refugees could get out of Germany but could not get in elsewhere. . . . In other words: we knew. We did not like Jews and we kept Jews out."

And then there were the films about the survivors, "straightforward and simple, even though they are narrating horror. They are more like us than not like us, or so it appears. What they have to tell us is substantive and necessary . . . but their other gift to us is in their demeanor, they are generous not to hurt us with their inner world of turmoil, often depression, often terror, often despair. They are calm and reassuring and we can leave believing that they are fine now." Andrea, though, knew better; Andrea had grown up with these people: "I know they are not [fine]. What they are is American now—and Americans like happy endings. Don't accept this part of their gift. Listen to what they say, not how they have learned to say it."

Andrea returned to New York, came back to her home in Brooklyn, knew that for however long it would take she must give priority from now on to years of researching and writing, to preparing her study of how and why outsiders, women and Jews especially, but also others, the Palestinians prominently, had been scapegoated through time—writing subliminally, inescapably, about her own lifelong alienation from "normalcy." Though she wouldn't have predicted it in 1993, the project would consume her until nearly the end of the decade.

She would do her best during much of that time to keep the rest of the world at bay, though now and then it would creep in over her objections. And she did not always object: unrelieved immersion in the historic plight of the downtrodden and the despised would have risked a kind of unbalance, a form of derangement. Besides, there were people she cared about, commitments she valued; in her hermit-like retreat she'd now and then welcome interruption, live voices, needed companionship.

What she mostly got, though, what she had long gotten, were distorted representations of her views; cartoon-like depictions of her as an over-sized, rampaging ogre; dismissive mockery. There was no hiding from all that, though John, with limited success, tried to intercept some of the more scurrilous articles about her. She'd become something of a celebrity, though in the guise of a pariah. In the anti-porn wars, still enflamed, she remained everybody's favorite target, easy to deplore, easy to parody—the unvarying overalls, the lack of make-up, the frizzled hair: the harridan personified.

What was spoken publicly or put in print was, of course, far more mannerly, except for the no-holds-barred gutter treatment of the *Hustler/Penthouse/Screw* crowd. But the professors and the pundits—the "rational" crowd—prided themselves on civility and knew how to hone their urbane vocabulary to a fine edge. Still, there was no mistaking the underlying animus against her *person*, not simply her politics.

Among Andrea's more skillful antagonists was Nadine Strossen, who was president of the ACLU from 1991 to 2008 and author of *Defending Pornography*, the doyenne of sophisticated leftwing dissent and discourse. One could argue that it was an antagonism all but destined to occur. One could even argue that Andrea herself had inaugurated it when, way back in 1981, she wrote a piece (for which she'd been unable to find a publisher) entitled "The ACLU: Bait and Switch" that excoriated the civil rights group for defending the "free speech" of the Nazis in Skokie and the Klan in Alabama. "I am tired of the sophistry of the ACLU," Andrea had written in the article. "It does not even make a distinction between those who have genocidal ambitions and those who do not. The ACLU prides itself on refusing to make these distinctions."[11]

Strossen's 1995 book, *Defending Pornography*, struck back hard, devoting a sizeable chunk of her text to an irate attack on the "MacDworkinites" (as she called them). Though lengthy, the assault was unoriginal, largely repeating the multiple accusations long leveled at Andrea (and often Kitty, too) and fully addressed by them many times over. The two were, Strossen insisted, anti-sex prudes who'd actively sought alliance with the right-wing Moral Majority in an effort to censor offending (pro-sex) material. Yet the Right had favored not the ordinance (if it had, such legislation would have become law under Reagan), but outright censorship of "smut." Andrea and Kitty, oppositely, had made clear on multiple occasions that censorship in the context of the First Amendment involved *state-based* actions of prohibition, which they strenuously opposed.

Nor had they objected to pornography that didn't subordinate *anyone*—not solely women—or in which the performers hadn't been abused and drugged (Strossen saw no reason "to believe that force or violence are endemic to the sex industry," the implication being that Linda Lovelace had been an anomaly—or had lied). Instead, their ordinance allowed individual women to bring civil suits that itemized instances of harm resulting from pornography and the industry surrounding it—changes *they* were required to prove. Yes, Strossen was correct: the right wing *did* indeed oppose any and all sexually explicit material. But Andrea and Kitty did *not*, and had never sought an alliance with the right wing. Nor, for the umpteenth time, had either of them *ever* said that all heterosexual intercourse was rape.

Strossen claimed that she'd carefully reviewed the scientific literature on the harmful effects of pornography and had found it feeble. In a confrontation first on National Public Radio, and then in print, Diana E.H. Russell, professor of sociology and the pioneering author of *Against Pornography*, pointed out to Strossen the gaping holes in her research. As Russell later put it, the scientific discussion in Strossen's book was "a sham." Most of the key researchers on the relationship between pornography and violence against women, Russell charged—"Neil Malamuth, James Check, Dolf Zillman, Bryant Jennings, myself—do not rate a single mention in her book." In reply, Strossen said that she'd relied on what *she* called "the best source on the subject"—which it assuredly wasn't—a short book, *Sex and Sensibility*, by Marcia Pally, a columnist for *Penthouse*. What the scientific evidence *did* show, according to Russell, was that violent pornography predisposed some men to rape and intensified the predisposition in others; that it undermined "some men's *internal* inhibitions" as well as their "*social* inhibitions against acting out their desire to rape." Russell concluded with a show-stopper: Strossen's view that many men who consume porn have never raped a woman, ergo porn doesn't cause rape, is comparable to saying "that because some cigarette smokers don't die of lung disease, there cannot be a causal relationship between smoking and lung cancer."[12]

Russell also took issue with Strossen's charge that anti-porn feminists distorted the evidence by choosing for their educational slide shows "overtly violent, sexist samples." That was analogous, Russell suggested, to "arguing that the horror and devastation of anti-Semitism in Nazi Germany cannot be judged from photographs of the concentration camps, because a lot of Jews weren't incarcerated in them." She made comparable mincemeat of Strossen's assertion that "the more unconventional the sexual expression is, the more revolutionary its social and political implications become." Russell went in for the kill: "I suppose rape doesn't qualify as unconventional sexual expression any more—but would child porn qualify as revolutionary? Or images of sexual mutilation and woman-killing?"

Robin Morgan also weighed in. In a letter to the *New York Times*, she protested its mostly favorable review of Strossen's *Defending Pornography* for having ignored her "vulgar personal invective against women with whom" she disagrees, as well as for mischaracterizing Morgan herself as having repudiated her support of the MacKinnon/Dworkin position. In making that claim, Morgan pointed out, Strossen had used "a manipulated excerpt" from a twenty-five-year-old article: "I have never repudiated my anti-pornography position, knowing as I do how pornography destroys many women's lives and serves as an instrument of social control over all women . . . [but]

I have never supported censorship (nor have Dworkin or Mac-
Kinnon)." Andrea had earlier put the same sentiment in a letter to
Gloria Steinem: "I think it is unbelievable what these women [like
Strossen] do. And get away with, in the name of a movement for
women's honor."[13]

Yet another instance in which Andrea was called away from work on
the Israel book to join in public protest was the 1994 murder of O.J.
Simpson's ex-wife, Nicole Brown Simpson. Flooded with memories of her own battering when married to Iwan, Andrea wrote not
one but three pieces on Nicole, making her story emblematic of
the plight of women whose lives were linked with men determined
to control or kill them. In 1993, Andrea pointed out, there were
300,000 domestic violence calls to the police in New York City
alone. The common reaction to such brutality was the standard,
indignant, question: *"Dammit, why didn't she simply leave?!"* In fact,
Nicole *did* leave: she was killed in *her own* home; besides, more battered women are killed *after* they leave their spouses. And before
Nicole left O.J. she'd tried damned near everything else, including
calling the police multiple times—nine, to be exact. The police had
been incredulous. They were fans; they'd stopped off at Simpson's
house many times for a pat on the back and a beer.[14]

    Five days before Nicole's death, after months of being tracked and
suddenly accosted by O.J., she'd called a battered women's shelter.
She told her mother that she'd reached the end of her rope: "I'm
scared. I go to the gas station, he's there. I go to the Payless Shoe
Store, and he's there. I'm driving, and he's behind me." She wrote
all that in her diary, where she also recorded detailed descriptions
of O.J.'s physical attacks on her. All of which, at O.J.'s trial, was kept
from the jury. The judge dismissed such evidence as "hearsay" or
"inadmissible." He did allow testimony from those who'd witnessed
O.J. hitting Nicole in public—though most battery, of course, takes
place behind closed doors and has no witnesses. "The voice of the
victim," as Andrea put it, "still has no social standing or legal significance. She has no credibility."

    O.J. was acquitted. As Andrea pointed out, the jury was made up
predominantly of women, and polls conducted during the trial con-

firmed that "women were indifferent to the beatings Nicole Simpson endured." Andrea wasn't surprised; *people*, not just men, ignore signs of battering, don't hear the screams, don't see the bruises, assume the woman is exaggerating, or had wanted it. Andrea herself, more than twenty years since she'd laid eyes on Iwan, was still haunted by fears and flashbacks. Andrea's last line in her series of articles on Nicole Brown Simpson says it all: "Everybody's against wife abuse, but who's prepared to stop it?"

It enraged Andrea—and not solely Andrea—that the murder of Nicole Brown Simpson should be so quickly followed by the 1996 Milos Forman film *The People vs. Larry Flynt*. For Andrea, the juxtaposition was classic: in her mind, O.J. Simpson and Larry Flynt were both products of a culture that valorized male brutality while disavowing the value of women. Unlike Hugh Hefner, who'd become elevated in the popular mind to the role of a glamorous sexual liberationist, Larry Flynt had been widely seen as a coarse and gross vulgarian. Then along came Hollywood, waving its magical wand.

Not only did the prestigious Milos Forman direct *The People vs. Larry Flynt*, but the likeable Woody Harrelson played the porn king. *New York Times* critic Frank Rich wrote of the film that what made the movie "so effective is that it doesn't sentimentalize or airbrush Larry Flynt." In an interview, Forman agreed: "I didn't try to cover the ugly side." The two screenwriters made the same point more forcefully: "I don't think anyone will accuse us of whitewashing here . . . we try to be honest." If true, that would mean the real-life Flynt was the authentic voice of plain-talking working-class America, a crusading, passionate defender of the First Amendment, and the faithful, monogamous partner of his beloved wife, Althea. What the movie entirely omits or *merely* downplays is Flynt's unbridled racism, his *five* marriages, his daughter's published accusation of molestation when she was a child, and the repetitive images in *Hustler* magazine of women being tortured and raped.[15]

Thanks to the arrival of Paula Duffy as the new publisher of The Free Press—Andrea described her as "a genuine feminist and extremely down to earth and nice"—she got a contract to compile a third collection of her writings and speeches (after *Our Blood* in

1976 and *Letters from a War Zone* in 1988). Andrea was of two minds about the opportunity: she hated putting *Scapegoat*, her work-in-progress on Israel, aside for a time, but she delighted in the unexpected chance to put her shorter pieces into print. She completed the job in May 1996, and closed her preface to the book with a bold challenge: "I am asking men who come to these pages to walk through the looking glass. And I am asking women to break the mirror. Once we all clean up the broken glass—no easy task—we will have a radical equality of rights and liberty."[16]

The injunction was challenging, and way too optimistic. The book got two wonderful pre-publication blurbs from Simone de Beauvoir's biographer Deirdre Bair ("We should all treat Andrea Dworkin like a national treasure") and the wide-ranging English writer (and Booker Prize winner) John Berger ("She is perhaps the most misrepresented writer in the Western world"). But the good omens went unfulfilled. The book did get published in England, and Andrea went over for a modest publicity tour, but in the United States (as she wrote to Gloria Steinem) *Life and Death* was "a failure"—it got little attention and negligible sales.

That was pretty typical not only for Andrea but also for collections of pre-published short pieces—in her case by someone far better known for her politics than for her writing. Still, "My Life as a Writer," the one new and lengthy piece at the start of the volume, had it been read, might well have brought Andrea some much-wished-for attention *as a writer.* It has none of the oracular, melodramatic provocations that had sometimes marred her earlier work, yet "My Life as a Writer" does have her familiar steely clarity, her eloquent bluntness—as well as a good deal of basic information about her early life that she'd previously avoided or masked in generalities. We were "bad children in adulthood; smart adults in childhood," she tells us at one point about herself and her friends, "precocious; willful; stubborn; not one age or one sex or with one goal easily advanced by a conforming marriage and inevitable motherhood."

And in her brief portraits in the essay of some of the women who'd been of central importance to her survival, Andrea lets her always-present-but-usually-guarded tenderness and generosity emerge. She singles out three women for special gratitude: Grace

Paley, Barbara Deming (yes, despite the furious misadventure of Sugarloaf Key, which Andrea never mentions), and Muriel Rukeyser. "Each of these women," Andrea tells us, "had faith in me—and I never quite knew why; and each of these women loved me—and I never knew why. It was a lucky orphan who found each of these women and it was a lucky striving writer who found each of these writers. They are all taken more seriously now than they were then; but I had the good sense to know that each was an Amerikan [sic] original, wise with common sense and plain talk, gritty with life; they were great craftswomen, each a citizen and a visionary. I know what I took; I hope I gave enough back."

At the moment she doubted it. "I really do have to find some way or place I can live," she wrote Kitty, "to do whatever still is left to me to do, which I fear is not much. You have a right to know this, I think. I'm simply used up. I feel virtually nothing except sometimes pain."[17]

12

Scapegoat

Despite her lapses into melancholy, which now and then dipped deeper into depression, Andrea was determined to finish *Scapegoat*. Having invested the better part of half a dozen years on the book, and with the end in sight, she managed to hunker down for the final lap. Transitioning from typewriter to computer, she gratefully substituted emails for long-form letters (alas, what she gained in time, history has lost in textured detail). She cut back her commitments on all fronts. With rare exceptions, she turned down invitations to lecture that involved extensive travel or preparation, wrote only a few short pieces, and almost never gave interviews; the one notable exception was an uncommonly long session with Susan Brownmiller, who was preparing her memoir *In Our Time* and needed to talk over the early years of the pornography wars.

Andrea also found irresistible an invitation early in 1998 to speak at the Yale Law School on the twentieth anniversary of Kitty MacKinnon's pathbreaking book, *Sexual Harassment of Working Women*. She took the occasion to outline the additional contributions that she felt feminist jurisprudence might make to social justice issues beyond (or accompanying) those relating to women: the need to intervene in "other social hierarchies . . . I mean white supremacy . . . [and] class inequities, which in this country are becoming worse and worse such that whole parts of our population are being thrown away."[1]

Of the few short pieces she wrote during the late nineties, the one standout, published in England's *The Guardian*, was her reflection on the Monica Lewinsky scandal—it was brief, but fierce. She slammed into Bill Clinton: "We are talking about a man who, in a predatory way, is using women, particularly young women. . . . [His] fixation on oral sex—*non-reciprocal* oral sex—consistently puts women in states of submission to him." And she had no sympathy for Hillary: "She is covering up for a man who has a history of exploiting women. If there is one thing being a feminist has to mean it's that you don't do that." In a stab at humor, Andrea offered "a modest proposal. It will probably bring the FBI to my door, but I think that Hillary should shoot Bill and then President Gore should pardon her." The "deafening" silence from other feminists on the Lewinsky case distressed her.[2]

Andrea was concerned in general at the current state of the feminist movement. She and Kitty had in 1997 published *In Harm's Way: The Pornography Civil Rights Hearings*, a compilation of testimony, mostly from women, that had been given over time at various public hearings on the pornography ordinances—women who then had often become targets for harassment and abuse. Much of the testimony was searing, and Andrea and Kitty hoped that *In Harm's Way* would serve as a future source book for resurrecting the idea of giving those who felt injured by porn the chance to sue for damages. John and a friend of his, Adam Thorburn, made a theater piece out of the material called "Freed Speech"; it had a well-received reading, but hopes of performing it elsewhere, particularly on college campuses, went unrealized.

Waiting in the wings instead was George W. Bush. Within two years of becoming president, he would declare himself "a war president" and would embark on a disastrous conflict in Iraq that condoned the wiretapping of American citizens at home and the torture of prisoners abroad. The Christian Right—the true censors—would seize the reins of power during the Bush administration. *Their* war against pornography (unlike that of Andrea and Kitty) had everything to do with the sanctity of marriage, the importance of maintaining the monogamous, male-dominated family unit, and the "protection" of women in their "natural" roles of wives and mothers.[3]

Andrea, by then, had taken the long view. "What we kept trying to do," she told Susan Brownmiller in 1998, "was to make it clear that we were talking about harm to women" and "civil inequality." Now, with the internet, we'd gone a step further "and things are rapidly getting worse than anyone could have imagined. I'm back to not knowing what to do." She placed some hope in the fact that there did exist "a community of resistance to entrenched male violence that is international, militant, [and] across generations. . . . We are the hard core, the front line, the ones who cannot be bought off or scared off. We will not reconcile with male power. . . . We know we have another three-to-four hundred years of struggle. We are committed for the duration."

Scapegoat, from inception to completion, took nine years. (It was published in 2000.) Hugely ambitious, it's a monumental if sometimes problematic piece of work—monumental in the profundity of its inquiry, the boldness of its argument, the lucidity of its prose, and the sheer scope of its inquiry (though it should be said that its bibliography, containing seventy-eight pages of notes citing some fifteen hundred works of scholarship, has—along with attesting to Andrea's profound engagement with the subject—the uncomfortable secondary effect of suggesting the autodidact's self-conscious fear of not being taken seriously. This is further confirmed by the lengthy multiple quotations in the body of the text).

Scapegoat is something of an anomaly in Andrea's body of work. Her long-standing theme of misogyny shares the stage this time around, and is often crowded off it, by her impassioned discussions of anti-Semitism and the militaristic turn taken by the state of Israel. *Scapegoat* is also the most traditionally academic of Andrea's books (though her insights go deeper and the pulsating intensity of her prose is more riveting than can be said for most academic works); it seems a surprising anomaly for a writer who in earlier books experimented with twisting autobiography into fiction, and

then back again, to end up in *Scapegoat* with all the scholarly appa-
ratus of the professoriate and a prose style all but free of onrushing
proclamation. Singular, too, is the near absence in *Scapegoat* of those
occasional apocalyptic outbursts that previously studded her work.
Aside from the innate drama of the subject matter itself, *Scapegoat*
is notably free of showy theatricality or grandiloquence. The tone
throughout is highly sophisticated, the analysis measured, deliberate, exquisitely cerebral.

The central theme of *Scapegoat* is the analogous dehumanization of Jews and women in Nazi Germany, and Palestinians and
women in the state of Israel. Andrea nowhere suggests any equa-
tion between the unmitigated vileness of the German Nazis and the
current behavior of Israeli men. In her view, the link between the
two, though only marginal, is the cultivation in both instances of a
hyper-masculinity reliant for believability and force on the scape-
goating of others. The matter of scale is all-important, as is the
differing cultural context in which the warrior model emerged in
the two countries, and the ways in which it was publicly deployed.

Andrea harshly condemns the Israeli treatment of the Palestinians, and sees its origin—but not its justification—in the Jewish
determination to safeguard the homeland from the enmity of its
Arab neighbors. She stresses the pained consciousness of many
Israelis over their ugly treatment of the Palestinians as far different
from the almost gleeful arrogance of the Nazis as they proceeded
to hunt, torture, rape, and kill millions of Jews, whom they defined
as mere scum, as not human. Andrea avoids any implication that
the Holocaust, murderous and merciless, a lunatic pursuit of racial
purity, is comparable on any level with the Israeli determination to
defend the Jewish state from destruction.

Yet she is exceedingly tough on the Israelis, inviting denunciation
of the new breed of warrior Jews and providing the ammunition for
it. At the very beginning of *Scapegoat*, she outlines her ambivalence:
"The line between self-defense and aggression has been breached
by my particular ethnic group represented by the Israeli government; the line itself is often not self-evident, in that violent acts
sometimes serve to head off enemy attack and are arguably a form
of self-defense. I believe that threatened peoples and individuals

have a right to self-defense. This goes against the pacifism that has been instrumental in my political life."

On her 1988 trip to Israel, Andrea had been able to meet women, both Jewish and Arab, and had been deeply distressed at their stories of widespread prostitution, pornography, rape, and battering. Why, she wondered, should she have expected otherwise? Her answer in *Scapegoat* is simple: "because the Israelis are my guys, a miracle of self-determination and courage." There was no question in her mind that Jewish survival depended on confiscating Palestinian land, and even ten years after her trip to Israel she remained convinced that "they had to." Yet in the course of the armed conflicts that followed, she laments that "brutality has become institutionalized in Israel as expressions of male dominance and state sovereignty—over Jewish/Israeli women as well as over Palestinian men and women." In her view, a radical shift had occurred: the ideal of Jewish manhood that for thousands of years had emphasized the virtues of gentleness, nurturance, and studiousness had given way to the belligerent, macho Israeli male. What had inescapably followed this surge of aggression, Andrea believed, was the increased subservience of Israeli women *and* "the subordination of a racial or ethnic other"; male dominance "needs internal and external scapegoats."[4]

In Andrea's universe, the primary, if not the sole, grounds for hope was that Israeli and Palestinian women, "often motivated by feminist ambitions and feminist ideas," have found each other; "cooperation," she writes, "is the female equivalent of male conflict"—but she stresses that "this is a social, not a biological, point" (though in much of her writing Andrea powerfully argues against any valid biological explanation for gender differences, she herself occasionally slides into what can *sound like* an essentialist vocabulary; for example: "Is it masculinity itself that both causes and motivates violence?").

In several elliptical and passing remarks in *Scapegoat*, Andrea—briefly recapturing her oracular voice—suggests that "women have to be literate in both strategic violence and the violence of self-defense. It is one thing to choose not to kill; it is quite another to be defenseless by virtue of ignorance and socialization. . . . I have become certain of one thing: that women cannot be free of male dominance without challenging the men of one's own ethnic group and destroying their authority. This is a willed betrayal, as any assault on male dominance must be." Andrea can even be read in this passage as suggesting—her old sibylline voice to the fore—that we take the notion of "assault" literally. Meaning an armed gender war? Surely not; the hint is broad enough to allow us to dismiss it as a mere vestige of flamboyance, of Andrea briefly indulging her penchant (and knack) for florid theatrics. The solemn new Andrea of *Scapegoat* would confidently settle for something less apocalyptic, as she does when she proceeds simply to advise women to be on guard.

There are manifold riches to be found in *Scapegoat*: lush yet lucid descriptions ("Muslim women do not have a government that protects them. . . . So women—even though forced—try to prove their loyalty through self-abnegation, covered, often enclosed . . . and the gangs that attack and harass women on the street are the state's voluntary and eager enforcers, self-righteous and swollen with male pride"); epigrammatic insights ("States do not exist in nature; states do have a view of what is natural"); complex summaries of contested material (Israel "could have been an ethical nationalism, a step toward a global family, an obligation of honor to a global community; a first step to making the unit of the state archaic, a non-imperial state with a particular human rights agenda, a state with metaphysical borders rather than military borders, a state beyond the constraints of geography"); highly original and persuasive interpretations that border on the metaphysical ("Even the emancipation of Jews in Europe from the official margins of the ghetto—ciphers in shadows made more monstrous by being nearer—reified hate and created the silencing imperatives of assimilation").

Along with its many distinctions, *Scapegoat* has some less laudable features. Two of its eleven chapters could have used a demanding editor. "Hate Literature/Pornography" takes almost forty pages to make what is essentially a single point. "Religion/Maternity," about human origins ("who are we and how did we get here?") is surprisingly pedestrian, relying almost completely on familiar scholarship, only occasionally relieved by the intervention of Andrea's own unique voice.

An additional disappointment in *Scapegoat* is her glib dismissal of postmodernism: "Deconstructionists . . . learned the mesmerizing tactic of nothing meaning nothing, everything meaning nothing, nothing being both itself and its opposite as well as the absolute unknowable." They are "completely uncompromised by meaning; and non-elite readers and writers, trapped in a false existence (not a false consciousness, Hegel having been taken out by Heidegger), longed for a literate Rabelaisian fart, which would, indeed, signify." That's essentially a cheap shot (if elaborately garbed), not worthy of Andrea's characteristic respect for knowledge she did not have, nor of her usual appetite for learning it.

Andrea had a talent for generalization, only occasionally over-indulged ("The only sheep led to the slaughter in World War II were the Germans"). She raises, succinctly and cogently, questions of profound importance, if perhaps unanswerable ("Can the Jewish state sustain itself without the use of torture on a subject population? Can a secular Jewish morality—which tends to be leftwing and rights-based—withstand the imperatives of militarism?"). Aiming for the sociological summary, she sometimes falls back on the banal, like when her attempted synthesis of "Jew-hate and woman-hate" eventuates in the disappointingly obvious: "both women and Jews were defined as parasites who live off the vitality of the so-called Aryan male."

Though Andrea's passionate eloquence is muted for much of *Scapegoat*, it occasionally resurfaces, and to great effect: "This targeting of Arab civilians . . . has never been part of the Jewish history of Israel. . . . [It] has been ignored in order to maintain, among Jews, a self-conception that repudiates brutality. Arabs commit murder. Jews do not. Arabs terrorize civilians. Jews do not . . . no Jew would have easily believed Arab charges that seem to stain the character of the Jewish people: a morally superior people is a consequence of a history of suffering."

Toward the end of *Scapegoat*, the central theme of all Andrea's books—of her life—re-emerges: the plight of women. "One must ask: if the Holocaust can be denied, how can a woman, raped or tortured or beaten, be believed?" She concludes that "degraded men need to degrade women . . . the struggle to subordinate women becomes a basic struggle for male identity as such; in liberation movements, women get a temporary pass from complete servility, because they can be used and useful in any subversion or underground fighting. Once the liberation struggle is won, the women are re-colonialized." The reversion at the end of *Scapegoat* to her lifelong theme is accompanied by the reappearance of her persistent attempt over a lifetime to come up with a solution for ongoing female degradation. Since none is readily available, she turns back again to a portentous vision: "Women need land and guns or other armament or defense; or women need to organize nonviolently in great masses that grow out of small demonstrations using civil disobedience. The latter is harder than the former but gets fairer results. One needs to target individual men who commit crimes against women and institutions that objectify, demean, and hurt women: using either violence or nonviolence. Indiscriminate violence is never justified; there are always innocents. . . . The harm of objectification and dehumanization must be recognized as prelude to normalized violence."

As if dissatisfied with her own inability to produce "the" answer, Andrea settles for a command: "The past thirty years—1970 to 2000, the time of the so-called second wave of feminism—have been prologue: the question is, To what? Answer the question."

The enormous labor of *Scapegoat* finally behind her—the manuscript completed and the rituals of proofreading and reviews still many months off—Andrea drew a deep breath and, running counter to her nature, tried to relax. Everything seemed to conspire against it. Along with being emotionally drained, she'd developed osteoarthritis in her knees, which caused constant and increasing pain. Her spirits dipped a bit lower still when her editor at The Free Press, after a quick read, gave the *Scapegoat* manuscript what Andrea called a "cold reception."

Her unsettled state ill-prepared her for an incident she might otherwise have taken in stride. Attempting an idle walk one day, she was accosted and threatened by a group of young men who tried to force her into a van. A friend who worked at a local rape crisis center later told her that several women had recently reported being raped inside vans, the rapes videotaped (they never found out who the perpetrators were). Her nerves already taut, her energy depleted, the encounter shook her deeply. She decided it was the ideal time, at age fifty-two, to take a *real* vacation, to treat herself to a wholly uncharacteristic splurge—a first-class flight to Paris, a city she'd always loved, and a week's stay in a five-star hotel. It was a luxury beyond her means, but it felt like a necessity.[5]

Initially all went well. She and John spoke by phone every day, she took long walks, went to several museums and, staying pretty much to herself, rested and read in the hotel's garden. John thought she sounded happy and he felt reassured that her mood had lightened. Then suddenly all that changed. He picked up the phone one day to hear a tearful and jumbled Andrea blurt out the appalling news that she'd blacked out from a drugged drink and been raped. Thinking fast and trying to calm her, John suggested that she locate a gynecologist, call the police, and then take the first flight home. Not speaking French and too rattled to think straight, Andrea simply packed up and left for New York.

Months later, her misery having lessened, she decided to write about what had happened in Paris (writing had always been the most reliable way of understanding her own experience). What came out, though, underscored how incomplete that understanding still was—and would likely remain. John, as always, read Andrea's completed manuscript, "The Day I Was Drugged and Raped," and felt uneasy about it. But he decided that for once he would *not* make any editorial suggestions or give an opinion about whether or not she should go ahead and publish the piece. Ultimately, more than a year after the episode, Andrea did finally decide to submit the article to *The New Statesman*. They published it in early June of 2000 (as *The Guardian* did as well).

According to her article, at the start of the misadventure she'd been sitting in the Paris hotel garden reading a book on French fascism, drinking kir royale. Though she rarely drank, she decided to order a second one, but it tasted peculiar and she didn't finish it.

Then (to quote directly from her own account), "I became sort of sickish or weakish or something, and all I could think about was getting to my bed and not making a fool of myself in public view." She managed to get to her room, where she "conked out." Then suddenly "a boy was in the room" with the dinner she'd earlier ordered, the same boy who'd served her the second drink in the garden. Andrea tried to get up, but couldn't stand; she regained balance only long enough to sign the check. Then she fell back on the bed and again passed out.

Awakening in the dark four or five hours later, she didn't at first know where she was. She became aware of vaginal pain, found blood on her hand and "huge, deep" scratches on her leg, which she cleaned in the bathroom. Hours later—she may have fallen back to sleep—she managed to shower. It was then that she discovered "a big, strange bruise on my left breast, next to the aureole, not a regular bruise, huge, black and blue with solid white skin in the centre, as if someone had sucked it up and chewed it. . . . I thought I had been drugged and raped, but I felt confused. I couldn't stand the thought of making a wrong allegation."

She thought that maybe the bartender had done it since he'd "flirted grandly with me in the hotel garden. . . . I didn't know if the boy had been there or not, but I thought yes." She remembered, before passing out, that when the boy brought her dinner to the room, she'd asked him to report her plight. She remembered, too, that he'd appeared suddenly in her room, though the door had been dead-bolted. "I had literally no memory of what the man and the boy had done. It's like being operated on. You don't feel anything until you feel the pain that comes with a return to consciousness." She'd heard about so-called amnesiac drugs—Rohypnol and GHB—and wondered if one of them had been put in the second drink. Her mind went over and over that day and evening, but could come up with little more. "I had decided long ago," she wrote, "that no-one would ever rape me again; he or they or I would die . . . I was scared. I thought that being forced and being conscious was better, because then you knew; even if no one ever believed you, you knew . . . how can you face what you can't remember?"

In the period immediately after returning to New York from

Paris, Andrea felt weighed down with fear and bewilderment. Then, ten days later, her spirits further wilted: her beloved eighty-four-year-old father, after months of failing health, had broken his knee and been hospitalized; he died in hospital in early December 1999. ("I miss him every day," Andrea wrote. "He's the best person I've ever known.") Three weeks later, she was found wandering the streets in delirium from a high fever and was hospitalized with bronchitis, pneumonia, cellulitis, and blood clots. She remained in the hospital for a month. After being released, still depressed and unable to sleep, she started—for the first time in her life—to see a psychiatrist (she somehow found one "whose specialty is in dealing with people who have been tortured"), and also consulted with a psycho-pharmacologist. She began, on a nightly basis, to take on average twelve pills to sleep—and they only worked now and then. Both specialists told her that she was experiencing "perpetual terror," chronic PTSD that dated back at least to Iwan's battering. At times she blamed herself, as rape victims often do (and as Andrea had been doing for a lifetime). She "couldn't be consoled . . . couldn't talk to anyone," not even John.

Initially, as Andrea would subsequently write in *The New Statesman* article, "John looked for any other explanation than rape. He abandoned me emotionally"—which John later acknowledged had in a sense been true, though Andrea had been unable to accept his explanation: "I desperately did not want her to have been raped again." What also contributed to the misunderstanding was that the more they talked about what had happened in Paris, as they "went around and around about the details of it," she experienced John as remaining skeptical. As she later wrote, "this calamitous experience . . . nearly tore us apart [Andrea actually began making plans to leave him] . . . it was really a tough, rough patch in the relationship." John wasn't alone in his doubts about Paris; several of Andrea's close friends—feminists all—seriously doubted her account, and they worried she might be headed for a breakdown.[6]

It was probably to try and clear the air that Andrea had ultimately decided to write *The New Statesman* piece. Yet the response to it hardly clarified matters or soothed her distress. The ensuing uproar—a mix mostly of scorn and disbelief—caught Andrea by surprise, setting back her still fragile recovery. A torrent of ridicule—yet again—came down on her head, and seems to have triggered a retraumatizing from which many of those close to her, including John, felt she never fully recovered. Longtime friends like Nicki Craft (who managed Andrea's website) immediately rallied to her defense, but the voices of mockery drowned them out. Andrea's article, atypically muddled, in spots contradictory and evasive (what might be called clinical symptoms of trauma), all but invited disbelief—that is, for those already hostile to her and unwilling to accept what now seems obvious: that the Paris experience had reopened multiple wounds from her past—the rape in childhood, her mother's disapproval, the battering by Iwan, the death of her father—leaving her disoriented, her memory dull and scrambled, even her prose uncharacteristically limp.[7]

A number of articles appeared in rebuttal to her own piece, and they were uncommonly mean-spirited. No well-known feminist was part of the posse: indeed, her detractors' lack of reputation in comparison with Andrea's and their possible envy of her may have fueled some of the venom that poured forth. Not that any prominent feminist leapt to her defense either (Nicki Craft was one exception), probably due to the controversy's being pretty much confined to the English press. Had it spread to the United States it seems certain that at the least Gloria Steinem and Robin Morgan—always staunch defenders of Andrea, despite occasional misgivings—would have joined the small chorus of her defenders.

A few of her English critics were civil, even respectful. Catherine Bennett, writing for *The Guardian* on the official day (June 7, 2000) of *Scapegoat*'s publication, used the occasion to point out that although Andrea was "often maddening on paper . . . in real life [is] endearing and seemingly vulnerable." Given "her seniority in both feminism and misery," it seemed to Bennett that "to argue with her would be not just impertinent, but akin to saying: 'I don't give a toss about your tragic life.'" Even the sympathetic Bennett, though, couldn't understand why Andrea hadn't called a doctor "to staunch the bleeding," along with notifying hotel security and the police. She was puzzled that Andrea hadn't behaved *rationally*, apparently unaware that following a rape the victim is often befuddled and terrified; or, sometimes, too busy blaming herself—as Andrea had been trained—for having done something to provoke the rape. Andrea had provided the key explanation long since: "There is always a problem for a woman: being believed."[8]

At the opposite end of the empathy scale, Leah McLaren weighed in with an article that was equal parts malign and ignorant. Using the opportunity of the Paris episode as a starting point, she then moved on to a more general attack, studded with inaccuracies, on Andrea's entire career. Like the far more judicious Bennett, McLaren characterized Andrea's 1999 "nightmare scenario" as "full of inconsistencies and logical gaps." Why hadn't Andrea gone directly to a hospital? Why did she never report the rape to the police? How, if the door to her room had been dead-bolted, did the waiter manage to gain entry? Andrea herself would have loved to be able to answer precisely those questions, and had been unsuccessfully trying to do so over the past year. The only truly pertinent question escaped McLaren's notice: why do some women go out of their way to try and discredit the testimony of a rape victim, while raising no questions at all about the aggressor? Deeply wounded, Andrea told Kitty that "if after all my years of work, I could still be raped and not believed, my life has been worthless."

The reception of *Scapegoat* helped to somewhat dilute Andrea's depression. Though the reviews were far from glowing, they were more benign than she usually got ("While she frequently overstates her case . . . Dworkin makes potent points"). By this point in her life, Andrea was generally regarded as a feminist icon, if of a vaguely disreputable sort; she was assuredly not, like Gloria Steinem, a widely respected household name. She fell more into the semi-lunatic-if-brilliant Shulamith Firestone category, which was a few cuts above Valerie Solanas, the attempted assassin of Andy Warhol and author of the "SCUM Manifesto."

The *New York Times*, weighing in a month after the publication of *Scapegoat*, managed to put a damper—as only the *Times* can—on whatever momentum might have been building for the book. The *Times* usually ignored Andrea; she was not an acceptable *in-house* maverick, not male. *Scapegoat* was a different matter: it had a lot to say about Israel, much of it negative, and had to be addressed. The assignment was given to Richard Bernstein, a *Times* book critic since 1995 and the author of *Dictatorship of Virtue*, an attack on the "excesses" of multiculturalism. He did the needed job expertly, mixing just enough praise ("learned and thought-provoking") into his essential pan to offset any suggestion that he might be an admirer. And most of the criticism he leveled had the patina of considered judgment. He granted that Andrea had "read widely," wrote with "stylistic eloquence," and had distilled "many of her ideas into pithy aphorisms." Yet overall he found *Scapegoat* "more an angry rant than a cogent careful argument . . . troubling in its extremism . . . a kind of agitprop."[9]

By the beginning of 2001, Andrea gradually began to regain her strength. To test her readiness, she took two trial runs—a book review for the London *Times* and an essay for Robin Morgan's planned new anthology, *Sisterhood Is Global*. She completed both pieces, but wasn't at all certain that they were up to par: "I hope I haven't let you down with this," she wrote Robin. "I'm very shaky nonetheless." Still, the successful completion proved a boost, and she felt ready to undertake a larger project. Tired of having other people write about—and often misinterpret—her, Andrea decided to try her hand at writing directly about herself.[10]

In a real sense, as she herself put it, "autobiography is the unseen foundation of my non-fiction work" (one is tempted to add "her fiction as well"), but she now aimed for a succinct, first-person account limited to some of the significant events in her life. Entitled *Heartbreak* and barely over two hundred large-type pages, it appeared in 2002. Andrea's choice of topics for the book seems strangely arbitrary: four pages on Petra Kelly, co-founder of the German Green Party, but the barest mention of Grace Paley, with whom she'd once been so close; a chapter on the conservative group, Young Americans for Freedom, with which she'd never been remotely connected, but not a word about Students for a Democratic Society, which she'd enthusiastically joined. It's almost as if she still needed to distance herself from any topic that carried emotional weight, that might threaten her still unsteady balance.

Spare and episodic, *Heartbreak* has a haphazard, almost random feel to it—more like the skeleton outline for some larger work to come. The prose, too, lacks Andrea's characteristic authority and intensity; it consists mostly of simple declarative sentences, the density and complexity of her earlier work notably absent. It might perhaps be said that *this* is what Andrea currently felt capable of writing, this and no more. And this, with its limited distinction, is nonetheless well worth having for its occasional sagacity.

Heartbreak starts off powerfully: "I have been asked, politely and not so politely, why I am myself. This is an accounting any woman will be called on to give if she asserts her will. In the home the question will be couched in a million cruelties, some subtle, some so egregious they rival the injuries of organized war. . . . So here's the deal as I see it: I am ambitious—God knows, not for money; in most respects but not all I am honorable; and I wear overalls; kill the bitch. But the bitch is not yet ready to die. Brava, she says, alone in a small room."

The impact is startling, the words strong, leading one to expect something of a *tour de force*. Yet it never arrives, or rather does so according to the prescription Andrea shares with us only on the very last page of *Heartbreak*: "A memoir, which this is, says: this is what my memory insists on; this is what my memory will not let go." And like everyone's memory, Andrea's proceeds to retain or repress, highlight or minimize, experiences that when strung together appear puzzlingly random, even specious, especially to those of us who cling to expository notions of logic and ordered causality, ignoring (suppressing) their subordination to the muddled, disordered chaos that actually characterizes our paths through life.

And what, in the end, does Andrea's memory insist upon? What does she find comprehensible in explaining herself to herself? That she was "an exile early on." That she had a cousin who "stuck his penis down the throats of at least two of his children when they were very young." That what she loved about Bessie Smith was that "her detachment equaled her commitment." That her mother's real failure was in telling her "not to lie." That her father had told her that it was "a moral wrong [to] read books of only one view." That what she learned "eventually evolved into my own pedagogy: listen to what adults refuse to say; find the answers they won't give; note the manipulative ways they have of using authority to cut the child or student or teenager off at the knees."

From her father, she remembers learning never to shut down inside, "to defer my own reactions and to consider listening an honor and a holy act." She remembers, too, when starting out as a writer, working four part-time jobs all at once, and every other day—after tithing herself for the Black Panther Party—taking out $7 from her tiny savings account. She remembers—this she could never forget—that Grace Paley, who'd helped her when she got out of the Women's House of Detention, had helped her again— this time to get an apartment in a Lower East Side tenement, for which she bought a desk, a chair, a $12 foam-rubber mattress, one fork, one spoon, one knife, one plate, one bowl; after the disaster of her marriage to Iwan, she "was determined to learn to live without men."

She remembered her anger at pacifists who would not take a stand against violence against women, of feeling "that nonviolence was not possible if the ordinary, violent deaths of women went unremarked, unnoticed." She remembered the years of speaking "in small rooms filled with women," someone passing the hat afterward, sleeping on the floor of whoever had invited her, and eating whatever she was given—"bad tabbouleh stands out in my mind." She remembered that after she became well known, "the more money I was paid, the nicer people were . . . when someone was nasty to me, I just raised my price. It was bad for the karma but good for this life."

It had taken longer for her to learn, after years of "watching rapists and batterers go free almost all the time," that her pacifism "could collapse like a glass tower [and] I began to believe that the bad guy should be executed—not by the state but by the victim, if she desired, one shot to the head." She learned, first from prostituting herself, then from other prostitutes she came to know, that "essential to doing the deed, you had to separate your mind from your body. Your consciousness had to be hovering somewhere near the ceiling behind you or on the far side of the room watching your body." She came to realize that although "most people thought that women prostituted in order to get money for drugs . . . it was the other way around; the prostitution became so vile, so ugly, so hard, that drugs provided the only soft landing, a kind of embrace—and on the literal level they took away the pain, physical and mental."

Though scornful of NOW, finding its "milksop politics" deeply offensive and run on the national level by women "who want to play politics with the big boys in Washington, DC," over the years Andrea spoke at rallies and events organized by local NOW chapters and discovered that on that level the members "were valiant women, often the sole staff for battered women's shelters and rape crisis centers, often the only organized progressive group in a small town or city. I've never met better women or better feminists."

At the end of *Heartbreak*, looking back at age fifty-six on her life, having lived through a cascade of mockery and pain, Andrea saw nothing redemptive in suffering. "Surviving degradation," she wrote, "is an ongoing process that gives you rights, honor, and knowledge because you earn them; but it also takes from you too much tenderness. One needs tenderness to love—not to be loved but to love."

"One is alone," she stoically concluded, "not just at the end but all the time. . . . The orphan is always an orphan." She'd heard "so much heartbreak among us"; she longed "to touch her sisters." Yet she felt, she wrote near the end of *Heartbreak*, that she'd "pretty much done what I can do; I'm empty; there's not much left, not inside me. I think that it's bad to give up, but maybe it's not bad to rest, to sit in silence for a while."

By 2002, Andrea's health had taken a turn for the worse. John blamed the toll on her intense years of work on *Scapegoat*. Andrea blamed the drug-rape in Paris in 1999, though her doctors disagreed. The most significant physical change was the increasing pain in her knees, the loss of mobility. An orthopedic surgeon diagnosed her with severe osteoarthritis, exacerbated by years of obesity, and put her on an anti-inflammatory drug. When it failed to work, he shifted her to Vioxx, which did help—until taken off the market as a dangerous precursor to strokes and heart attacks. The next attempt at relief was a series of painful cortisone shots directly into the knees, which worked only once—a period of blessed relief, though of short duration.[11]

As her mobility decreased, she could no longer travel or give speeches. Six months later, she could walk only a few steps at a time, her knees refusing to bend and the pain excruciating. Back in 1989 she and John had moved to a four-story house in Brooklyn—with a renter in the garden apartment. The kitchen was on the first floor, the toilet on the second and her desk, books, and shower on the third. The only way she could navigate the stairs was to crawl up on her hands and feet and to go down on her butt, one step at a time. As she put it, "my physical world became tiny and pain-racked." By then she'd become almost entirely housebound, leaving only for doctor appointments, and when at home usually confined to bed. The doctors told her that unless she was prepared to live the life of an invalid, she'd have to have surgery. With regard to medical expenses, she and John had decided to marry back in 1998, which meant that Andrea, as his spouse, could receive health insurance benefits.[12]

She soon progressed to painful swelling and burning in her legs, with what was diagnosed as "a life-threatening case of inflammation, with possible blood clot complications"; she very nearly died and had to stay a full four weeks in the hospital. After a period of recovery, she then had bariatric—weight-loss—surgery to reduce the pressure on her heart and her arthritic knees. Following *that* recovery, she then had both knees replaced at the same time. "I was in a nightmare of narcotics and untouchable pain," she later wrote. "The horror is that no-one dies from pain. This means that suffering can be immeasurable, enduring, without respite. So it would be for me for the next two years."[13]

Once able to leave the hospital, she was transferred to an institute for physical rehabilitation. The doctors told her she had only two responsibilities: to take her pain medication and to show up, via a wheelchair, for rehabilitative exercise; the cycle was "hideous." Months later, with the help of a walker, she increased from two steps at a time to three; after several more weeks she graduated to crutches and occupational therapy. She was taught how to stand up, how to water a plant, how to use a "grabber" to pick up something she dropped out of reach, how to shop when disabled.

When finally discharged, she was cautioned against relying on John as her primary care-giver: she needed professional help. The rituals of recovery were divided between a visiting nurse (who turned out to be underpaid and badly trained) and a "social aide" to assist with baths and light housework. Still in considerable agony, Andrea left her bed only to go to a "pain management centre" for basic lessons in movement, and for prescriptions. Fentanyl patches and methadone were added to her armory; they slurred her speech and impaired her memory, but she would need the medications for a full two years. By then the pain finally receded to a more manageable level. She was able to go outside on crutches, and then graduated to a cane. She gave up the pills but had "a nasty withdrawal."

At that point John got a job offer to become managing editor of *AARP The Magazine* in Washington, DC. The salary was good, but a move to DC was a mandatory part of the deal. Andrea had loved their Park Slope home, yet realized that managing the stairs had become too great a hurdle. Fortunately, they found a large, sunny, Art Deco–era condo in Washington on Devonshire Plaza NW, all on one level—meaning no steps—and the move was set in motion for February 2004. It proved, as expected, difficult, yet once settled in, Andrea's pain did dim still further; the mix of medications wrecked her appetite, and she lost a good deal of weight. She now and then began to feel rudimentary optimism.

Then, one day, standing up from the kitchen table, without warning her right knee suddenly gave way. The physical therapist told her that the quadriceps above the knee had simply given out; she was put back on crutches, and a restrictive brace was added to help her avoid the danger of falling. The brace went from beneath her calf to the top of her thigh; Andrea named it Darth Vader—evil incarnate. It took her two months to learn how to position the brace perfectly so that it properly supported the damaged knee; she had to lock the brace when ready to walk and unlock it before sitting. As Andrea described it, her wry humor having somehow revived: "in public, locking it makes me look as if I am masturbating, and unlocking it makes me look as if I am fondling my thigh."

With the help of the brace, she was occasionally able to leave the apartment. At one point she and John went to Christopher Hitchens and Carol Blue's apartment for dinner, joined by the former Bush speechwriter David Frum and his wife, Danielle Crittenden. "Andrea had fun that night," John later recalled; they found common ground talking about how much they all hated Bill Clinton and how they thought he was "a rapist." Once, on a self-dare, Andrea said yes to keynoting a conference in DC on the Holocaust. The organizer, unaware or unthinking, picked Andrea up in a truck; she was unable to climb into it. On another occasion, a party was given in her honor, but she couldn't manage the three flights of stairs; were the hosts even aware, she wondered, that she was disabled? Andrea's political instincts, never dormant for long, kicked in—a sure sign she was getting better. "The low consciousness of the able-bodied," she mused, needed attention: "they don't seem to realize that each disabled person lives always on the threshold of separation, exile, and involuntary otherness," is always seeking a way to "mitigate the loneliness."[14]

She *did* start to write again. She had the idea for a new book, though she didn't want to talk about it yet with John; she thought it might be a mirage and that discussing it would make it vanish. She spent most of her days sitting on a red chair in her bedroom, taking notes on a yellow legal pad. Early in 2005, she finally let John know that she was working on a book of literary criticism combined with—of course—political commentary. She temporarily entitled it *Writing America: How Novelists Invented and Gendered a Nation*, and before long she had accumulated some thirty-five pages. She began to believe that she really did have another book in her; after all, she was only fifty-eight. "I am, I think, healing," she wrote, sounding an optimistic note rarely heard over the past few years. She even had an idea for a second new book: it would be about Lynndie England, the young woman in the photographs from Abu Ghraib; it would have combined (as John put it) "all her themes—pornography, prisons, relationship abuse."[15]

On April 8, 2005, Andrea, retiring for the night, complained of feeling unwell. The next morning, when John went into her bedroom to check on her, she didn't seem to be breathing but was still warm. He tried to rouse her, but she was unresponsive. At some point during the night, as an autopsy would later reveal, Andrea had died of acute myocarditis—heart inflammation. The shock was all the more profound because of late all signs had been pointing upward. John was desolate, unable for months to put his feelings down on paper.

Word of Andrea's unexpected death spread quickly. Encomiums poured in, the obits effusive in praise of her unflinching struggle to challenge the status quo, to protect women from harm, to win them full rights of citizenship. Her efforts when alive had been mostly greeted with cruel derision and mockery. Safely dead, the acclaim consistently denied her during her lifetime was showered on her grave. The irony might have amused her. More likely, the hypocrisy would have made her angry. A few people, those who knew her best, mentioned more than her public accomplishments: they spoke of her essential kindness, her dry, hilarious wit, the sympathetic gentleness that belied her fierce public persona. Robin Morgan had a nickname for her: "Creampuff"—in recognition of her softness, her "fragility."

Months after Andrea's death, when John felt emotionally ready to look through her computer, he found to his astonishment a 24,000-word unpublished manuscript entitled *My Suicide*, dated August 30, 1999. Andrea had apparently designed the piece as an autobiographical summing up, not as a final goodbye; in her six remaining years of life, and despite agonizing debilitation, there's no evidence she actually contemplated suicide. *My Suicide* is more accurately seen as an accounting of the wild, dangerous roller-coaster of a life that she'd led—an account true to the life: no holds barred, scorchingly intense, emotionally raw. And always, the underlay of self-doubt: "I wonder if anything that we've done over these years," she told a reviewer toward the end of her life, "is going to survive in any form. . . . I would hate for another generation of women to have to begin inventing the wheel all over again."[16]

Andrea comes back again and again, in *My Suicide*, to her rape in Paris in 1999: "I take my mind in hand and try to compel it to forget what it can't remember anyway but it won't. In a way it's like a vulture picking at a corpse, tearing the flesh off the bones, it wants to remember what isn't there, to know what happened in the missing hours, it picks and picks at the sopping mess."

And always there is the self-blame—not simply in regard to the rape but for all the bad things that had happened to her and all the good things that *she* had prevented from happening: "I blame me no matter what it takes, no matter how abstract or abstruse I need to be . . . for being someone who insists on everything out of her reach," who "thought moderation was a form of stupidity." In the end she gives Sylvia authoritative control of the narrative: "everything my mother ever said about me pretty much turned out to be true. I feel for myself, not for others. I pretend to care but I don't really. I'm not grateful for what people have done for me. She [her mother] had my number. She'd blame me for the rape. She'd say, I'm sure he knew you were a slut. She'd say, if you dressed like everyone else, it wouldn't have happened to you. She'd say, why were you in such a place, why weren't you home? . . . She'd say, there's no reason for anyone to respect you so what did you expect? . . . She'd say, you deserve it."

In *My Suicide*, Andrea the little girl abjectly replies, "Mother, love me, take care of me, care about me." But mother has her own ill health to contend with, and tells her daughter that "you always want everything for yourself and you don't care about anyone else." But its "the pheromones," little Andrea tearfully says. "I have really bad pheromones . . . huge roaches on New York sidewalks run towards me, I change direction and they do too and keep rushing towards me. The bad men and the bad bugs, or I was a monster in my last life and I'm paying now. I don't want any more lives or any afterlife."

And most of the world for much of Andrea's life had agreed with her brutal self-estimate and had reinforced her self-hate. To this day, her accusers remain multiple; they still denounce her as "sloppy with the truth," a "melodramatic, hysterical crank," an unkempt, fat, hairy, ugly "male-hater," a "feminist Nazi."[17]

Yet remarkably and only recently, the tide seems to be turning, signs of appreciation and admiration have emerged, the naysayers yielding a bit of ground. Detectable at a distant remove is a modicum of acknowledgment of Andrea's insistent bravery, her mesmerizing public voice, her generosity of spirit, even, and often, her flat-out brilliance. The turnabout is welcome and deserved. Though her reputation is still contested, the yeasayers have once more found a voice—if only Andrea had lived long enough to find some solace in the sound.

Acknowledgments

This biography is primarily based on archival materials, most notably the extensive Andrea Dworkin Papers at the Schlesinger Library, Harvard. I'm very grateful to John Stoltenberg for giving me unhampered access to the entire archive, which hasn't previously been available to scholars and which is wonderfully rich and consequential (the correspondence files alone are remarkable, since Andrea was in close touch with many leading figures in second-wave feminism and even kept copies of her own letters to them). I'm grateful to Stoltenberg, as well, for giving me access to the sizeable collection of photographs (most never before published) in his possession.

Additionally, I've utilized the archives of a number of other feminists housed at the Schlesinger Library, especially those of Susan Brownmiller, Charlotte Bunch, Barbara Deming, Catharine A. MacKinnon, and Ellen Willis. The staff at Schlesinger, as I knew from earlier expeditions, is celebrated for the skill and grace with which they assist visiting scholars; their standards, thankfully, are as high as ever, and I'm deeply grateful for their many assists. I'm also thankful to them for putting Jordan Villegas in my path as a research assistant. He proved an ideal one—resourceful, wholly reliable and uncomplaining, and a digital *wunderkind*; I'm much in his debt.

The Rubenstein Library at Duke (cited as RLD in the footnotes) also proved rich in feminist source material. The most relevant collections at RLD for telling Andrea's story have been the papers of Dorothy Allison, Phyllis Chesler, Leah Fritz, Merle Hoffman, Robin Morgan, and Dorothy ("Cookie") Teer. Garrett McKinnon, a graduate student in history at Duke, gave me an invaluable assist in ferreting out relevant materials.

In the hunt for photographs, I had expert help from a number of archivists. At Smith College, I especially want to thank Nicole Calero, Maureen Callahan, and Margaret Jessup; at Schlesinger, Diana Carey and Kathryn Allamong Jacobs. For access to Elsa Dorfman's photographic archive, I owe special thanks to Margot Kempers and Harvey Silverglate. My detailed footnotes on secondary sources fully acknowledge, I hope, my indebtedness to the work of other scholars (and in some cases, my disagreement with their conclusions).

Marcia Gallo, Michael Kimmel, Catharine A. MacKinnon, John Stoltenberg, and my partner Eli Zal, all read the first complete draft of the biography, and I'm profoundly grateful to them for their careful, detailed (and sometimes alarming) commentary. Among the five I deliberately chose two who I knew in advance had polar opposite views of Andrea; they reacted true to form—and I profited greatly from their disagreements. At The New Press, its reigning seer, Ellen Adler, came through with her usual wise supervisory advice; Emily Albarillo handled the production side with an ideal combination of insight and tact. I'm grateful, too, for having had Emily Janakiram as my publicist. The scope of her knowledge about feminism and her insight into the issues involved greatly eased the book's path.

As for my editor Ben Woodward, I can hardly say too much. In today's publishing environment, where accession editors vastly outnumber wordsmiths, Ben restores my faith. His tough-minded scrutiny of every line in the manuscript is not what most writers expect (or get) these days. Ben's sharp eye, keen ear, and acute sensitivity to language are matched by a calm persistence that in *almost* every instance brought me around to seeing things his way.

Notes

1: Beginnings

1. Transcript of Susan Brownmiller interview with Andrea Dworkin (henceforth AD), August 10, 1998, in the Andrea Dworkin Papers at the Schlesinger Library, Harvard (henceforth ADP/SLH).

2. For this and the following paragraph: James Wechsler, "Who Sinned?," *New York Times*, March 8, 11, 1965.

3. AD, "Letter to M.," *WIN*, June 26, 1975.

4. Wechsler, "Who Sinned?"

5. For this and the following two paragraphs: *New York Times*, March 6, 13, 19, 20, 30, April 2, 14, May 4, 1965.

6. AD, *Ruins* (manuscript of unpublished book-length "novel in letters," begun in 1975; turned down by publishers; abandoned in 1979), Part I, chapter 1 ("Once"), ADP/SLH.

7. The chief sources for Dworkin/Spiegel family history are "Draft #7" (ms), date December 7, 1987; AD to Henk Jan Gortzak, March 12, 1984; "Marty" (Spiegel, AD's much-loved aunt) to AD, October 27, December 22, 1981; AD to Suzanne Kappeler, March 2, 1988—all in ADP/SLH; Moorcock/Dworkin, "Fighting Talk," April 21 1995: http://nostatusquo.com/ACLU/dworkin /MoorcockInterview.html; AD, "Feminism, Art, and My Mother Sylvia," first published in *Social Policy*, May/June 1975, and reprinted in AD, *Our Blood: Prophecies and Discourses on Sexual Politics* (New York: Perigee, 1976), chapter 1; AD, "My Life as a Writer," in *Life and Death* (New York: The Free Press, 1997), 3–11; AD, *Heartbreak: The Political Memoir of a Feminist Militant*, especially pages 23–25, 29–30, 53 (New York: Basic Books, 2002); AD to Leah Fritz, Box 20, c.1., Fritz

Papers, Rubenstein Library, Duke (henceforth RLD). Several of Andrea's cousins on her mother's side survived Auschwitz, and their descendants live in Israel (as detailed in "Marty" Spiegel to AD, October 27, 1981, ADP/SLH).

8. AD to "Mother, Dad, Mark," n.d. [1964], ADP/SLH; AD, *Life and Death*, 10.

9. For this and the next four paragraphs: AD's unpublished manuscript *Ruins*, ADP/SLH; a section of it appeared as "First Love" in Karla Jay and Allen Young, eds., *Lavender Culture* (1979), then in Julia Wolf Mazow, ed., *The Woman Who Lost Her Names* (New York: Harper & Row, 1980); AD, "My Life as a Writer."

10. For this and the following paragraph: AD, *Ruins*; AD, "First Love."

11. Sources for this and the following five paragraphs: ten postcards, five undated, five dated: two on September 16, the other three September 21, October 12, and October 14—all 1964; AD to "Mother, Dad, Mark," October 2, 1964 ("deadening"), plus seven other letters with the same salutation but undated [all 1964], ADP/SLH.

12. Leah Fritz interview with AD, n.d., Fritz Papers, Rubenstein Library, Duke (RLD).

13. AD, *Letters from a War Zone* (London: Secker & Warburg, 1988), 49; *Ruins* (Kafka); AD to Michael Moorcock, April 6, 1988, ADP/SLH.

14. http:www.nostatusquo.com/ACLU/dworkin/MoorcockInterview.html

15. AD, "The Rape Atrocity and the Boy Next Door," initially a 1975 lecture, then published in AD's collection of essays, *Our Blood*.

16. For this and the following two paragraphs: AD, *Heartbreak*, 107–12

17. For this and the following two paragraphs: AD to her mother, October 22, 1965, AD/SLH. When still in high school Andrea had written to Judith Malina and Julian Beck of the Living Theater commending them for refusing to participate in the air raid drills then mandatory (Brownmiller 1998 interview with Dworkin, ADP/SLH).

18. AD to parents and Mark, January 21, 1966, ADP/SLH; untitled poem, dated "Iraklion, Crete November 1965," which Andrea published in a 1967 chapbook, *Morning Hair*, in an edition of 120 copies.

19. For this and the next four paragraphs: transcript of Susan Brownmiller interview with AD, August 10, 1998, in ADP/SLH; AD, "The Simple Story of a Lesbian Childhood," *Christopher Street*, November 1977; AD, typescript of unpublished *Ruins*, ADP/SLH.

20. AD to Mark, October 27, 1965, AD/SLH.

21. AD, "Margaret Papandreou: An American Feminist in Greece," originally published in *Ms.*, Vol. XI, No. 8, February 1983, later reprinted in AD, *Letters from a War Zone* (New York: Lawrence Hill Books, 1993), 153–61. A series of far-right military juntas ruled Greece from 1967 to 1974. See Seymour Hersh, *The Price of Power* (Ontario, Canada: Summit Books, 1983) for the links between the Greek fascists and the Nixon administration.

22. For the quotes in this and the political comments in the next few paragraphs: AD to her parents, October 30, November 2, 10, 20, 22, 23, 28, December 5, 17, 1965, AD/SLH; also, AD, "Margaret Papandreou."

23. For this and the following section: the manuscript of her unpublished *Ruins*, ADP/SLH, and a section from it, "First Love" in Mazow, ed., *The Woman Who Lost Her Names.*

24. Two years later, Andrea actually started preparations to return to Crete, but by then civil war had broken out and E wrote her a letter saying that his friends were being tortured and killed, that "I am only bitter," and that Americans were too stupid to understand: "Come if you can bear it, I can't promise you anything." Andrea decided not to return. She blamed herself: "I was so afraid, so afraid of the reality of what had happened/was happening to you. The real guns. The real police. The real torture. The real dying." She was also disheartened that the letter E had sent her had "no image of romantic love . . . to propel me toward you, toward self-sacrifice, toward bravery" (AD, *Ruins*, ADP/SLH).

2: Marriage

1. AD to mother, April 21, 1966, ADP/SLH.

2. AD to family, February 11, March 16, 19, 1966, ADP/SLH.

3. January 31, 1966, plus two letters n.d., ADP/SLH

4. Kathleen Norris, *The Virgin of Bennington* (New York: Riverhead Books, 2001), 14 (Oracle).

5. For this and the next four paragraphs: AD to Mark, April 10, 1967, ADP/SLH.

6. For this and the following six paragraphs: AD to "Mom, Dad, Mark," October 1, 20, 1968, ADP/SLH. The Provo manifesto is printed in Richard Kempton, *PROVO: Amsterdam's Anarchist Revolt* (New York: Autonomedia, 2007), which is the most succinct, reliable account of the movement in English.

7. AD ms., "Whatever Happened to Provo or The Saddest Story Ever Told," ADP/SLH, a short section of which appeared in the *Village Voice*, January 15, 1970. In my account I rely mostly on the manuscript version, which includes excerpted transcriptions of Andrea's interviews with a number of prominent figures in the movement.

8. For this and the following two paragraphs: AD, ms. "The Perfect Social System," ADP/SLH.

9. AD to family, October 1, 1968, ADP/SLH; AD, ms. "Dwarfing the Issues: Kabouters in Amsterdam," ADP/SLH.

10. AD to "Mom, Dad, Mark," October 31, 1968, ADP/SLH.

11. For this and the next three paragraphs: AD, ms. transcript of interview notes for "Whatever Happened to Provo," AD/SLH.

12. AD to "dearest Mom, Dad, Mark," October 31, November 12, 1968, ADP/SLH.

13. AD to "Mom, Dad, Mark," December 2, 10, 21, 1968, ADP/SLH.

14. Ibid.

15. For this and the following paragraph: AD, Ms., "Heroes and Villains: Allen Ginsberg" [1992], ADP/SLH.

16. Their exchange of postcards, n.d., are in ADP/SLH. Andrea became friendly in the early seventies with the photographer Elsa Dorfman, whose longtime companion was the lawyer Harvey Silverglate. When their son Isaac was born, Andrea and Ginsberg became his godparents. Later, when the time came for Isaac's bar mitzvah, both Andrea and Allen traveled to Cambridge, Massachusetts, for the services. In the interim since they'd last seen each other, and on the very day of the bar mitzvah, the Supreme Court announced its unanimous decision that the First Amendment right to free speech did *not* forbid states from passing criminal laws against child pornography. The decision elated Andrea—and infuriated Allen. Out of deference to Elsa and her family, Andrea made the firm decision to avoid Allen and any possible confrontation that might spoil the bar mitzvah. But Allen (as Andrea later described it) "affixed himself to me in a rage over the Supreme Court decision. The Cheshire cat had nothing on me. I ordered Allen into a different car to the synagogue, to no avail. I hip hopped around, the way women do avoiding men, and he tailed me, the way men do refusing to be avoided. It became terrible. Allen shadowed me, even when I directly asked him to leave me alone. . . . He insisted on the rightness of sex with children . . . no child would be hurt [Allen said], because sex is always good. Anyone who would stand in the way of consummation was a tyrant. The right wing, the Supreme Court, wanted to send *him* to jail." At which point, as Andrea tells it, she gave up her vow to hold to "the Trappist discipline" and told him that what he was talking about was rape, and that "rape destroyed people . . . I'd shoot you . . . unless you prefer prison." A stunned Allen said that "of course I prefer prison." Andrea came through with a door-stopper: "Then you should thank the right, though they're a little sentimental for my taste." For a somewhat different version, see AD, *Heartbreak: The Political Memoir of a Feminist Militant* (New York: Basic Books, 2002), 43–47. She later remarked that she still regarded Allen as a "hero . . . a poet standing for freedom," but she now also regarded him as "a sexual predator, a nasty piece of trash. . . . I threatened it but he's the assassin." See: https://drive.google.com/drive/folders /1np_HoNiUzM4uWv5DzKJ2DPpvBaOkLWNV; AD to Sharon Doubiago, December 18, 1990, ADP/SLH; Harvey Silverglate to me, November 6, 2019.

17. From 1968 to 1978, Anne Waldman was the director of the Poetry Project at St. Mark's; during that period she, Ginsberg, and others founded the Jack Kerouac School of Disembodied Poetics at the Naropa Institute. Having first met at Bennington, where both were involved with the undergraduate literary journal *SILO*, Andrea and Waldman stayed in touch for a number of years (e.g., AD to parents, [Sept/Oct] 1965, November 12, 1968). Andrea also met Peter Orlovsky at some unknown point and thought him "so lovely, very kind and gentle" [AD to parents, n.d., 1965?].

18. AD to "Mom, Dad, Mark," January 5, February 3, 1969, ADP/SLH.

19. For this and the following three paragraphs: AD to "Mom, Dad, Mark," January 5, 27, February 3, 11, 19, 1969, ADP/SLH.

20. The wedding and its immediate aftermath: AD to "Mom, Dad, Mark," February 28, March 5, 14, 21, April 7, 16, May 5, 15, 1969, ADP/SLH.

21. AD to "Mom, Dad, Mark," January 5, February 22, March 8, 1969, ADP/SLH. In a letter (September 3, 1970, ADP/SLH) to Mark, Andrea described Grace Paley as "my closest friend."

22. Andrea's advice to her brother is mostly contained in three letters: AD to Mark, November 23, 1965, April 10, 1967, and March 8, 1969, ADP/SLH.

23. AD to Mark, February 13, 1970, ADP/SLH.

24. Andrea to her parents, June 4, 11, 27, July 9, November 7, 14, December 4, 1969, January 14, February 3, 6, 14, March 10, April 8, May 15, June 16, 22, 1970, ADP/SLH.

25. Ricki even trusted Andrea to intervene in an angry dispute she was having with her mother, Gladyce Abrams Axelrod, over her involvement with Thatcher Clark. Andrea wrote Ricki's mother an acrimonious letter denouncing her interference (Gladyce and Sylvia merging into a common enemy). The entire three-way correspondence during the spring of 1970, somewhat hair-raising, is in ADP/SLH.

26. For this and the following paragraph: AD to "Mom, Dad, Mark," June 3, 1970.

27. For this and the following paragraph: AD, "The Third Rape," *Los Angeles Times*, April 28, 1991, and "My Life as a Writer, *Contemporary Authors* (Farmington Hills, MI: Gale, 1995)—both essays reprinted in AD, *Life and Death* (New York: The Free Press, 1991); AD to parents, August 17, 1970, ADP/SLH; AD, ms., "A Survivor's Birthday," in the Leah Fritz Papers, Rubenstein Library, Duke (RLD).

28. For this and the following five paragraphs: AD to Mark, September 3, 1970, ADP/SLH; AD to parents, June 3, October 11, 1970, February 20, 1971, April 1, May 5, 1971, ADP/SLH; AD, "A Battered Wife Survives" (first published as "The Bruise That Doesn't Heal" in *Mother Jones*, Vol. III, No. VI, July 1978), reprinted in AD, *Letters from a War Zone* (New York: Lawrence Hill Books, 1993); AD, ms., "A Survivor's Birthday," Leah Fritz Papers, RLD.

29. For this and the following paragraph: AD to parents, March 13, June 9, 1971, AD to Mark, June 9, 1971, ADP/SLH.

30. For this and the following four paragraphs: AD, *Ice and Fire* (London: Secker & Warburg, 1986), 82–83; conversation with John Stoltenberg, February 18, 2019; AD, unpublished manuscript *Ruins*; AD, "A Survivor's Birthday," Leah Fritz Papers, RLD; AD, "A Battered Wife Survives"; AD, "What Battery Really Is" (about the notorious 1987 Joel Steinberg case, in which he beat to death his adopted daughter Lisa)—a shorter, somewhat more personal version was initially published in the *Los Angeles Times*, March 12, 1989. The two "battery" articles are reprinted in AD, *Letters from a War Zone*. Andrea subsequently wrote as well about the Lorena Bobbitt and Nicole Simpson cases ("Trapped In a Pattern of Pain Where No One Can Help"), *Los Angeles Times*, June 26, 1994.

31. For this and the following paragraph: AD, "A Battered Wife Survives," 101.

32. At the risk of dissolving Andrea's personal experience into a categorical one—and thereby robbing it of its non-repeatable individuality—the trauma specialist Bessel Van Der Kolk (in *The Body Keeps the Score: Brain, Mind, and Body in the Healing of Trauma* (New York: Penguin, 2014) emphasizes certain features of trauma that do seem to apply to Andrea's situation: "The mere opportunity to escape," Van Der Kolk points out, "does not necessarily make traumatized . . .

people, take the road to freedom. . . . Rather than risk experimenting with new options they stay stuck in the fear they know . . . the continued secretion of stress hormones is expressed as agitation and panic and in the long term, wreaks havoc with their health" (p. 30). Van Der Kolk is also suggestive in separating "remembering" from "reenacting"; the former, often as a result of psychotherapy, can be a path to recovery, the latter a panicky lifelong repetition of profound anxiety (p. 184). Andrea *did* write about her history, though whether she remembered it fully or accurately must remain an open question; consciously or not, *writing* about the past can be seen as a self-treating form of psychotherapy (rather than taking the form of consultation with specialists). See also Judith Lewis Herman's classic, *Trauma and Recovery* (New York: Basic Books, 1992). In regard specifically to wife battering, the problem has today reached epidemic proportions: half of all murdered women in the United States are killed by a current or former partner, and domestic violence cuts across all lines of class, race, and religion. Awareness of the issue, moreover, is relatively new: until the 1990s the United States had more animal shelters than women's shelters (for more about the issue, see Rachel Louise Snyder's excellent book, *No Visible Bruises* (London: Bloomsbury, 2019). Finally, it needs to be remembered that at this point in time there were virtually no shelters for battered women. The first one in the United States opened in 1974 in St. Paul, Minnesota; by the early eighties, thanks to the women's movement, there were more than three hundred (see Larissa MacFarquhar's "A House of Their Own," *The New Yorker*, August 19, 2019, 36–49).

33. AD to parents, July 30, September 10, 1971, ADP/SLH.

34. AD, transcript of "A Survivor's Birthday," Leah Fritz Papers, RLD.

3: Joining the Fray

1. AD, "First Love," reprinted in Julia Wolf Mazow, ed., *The Woman Who Lost Her Names* (New York: Harper & Row, 1980). In my view, the most compelling discussion of the early years of the feminist movement remains, despite effective challenges to some of its analysis, Alice Echols, *Daring to Be Bad: Radical Feminism in America 1967–1975* (Minneapolis: University of Minnesota Press, 1989).

2. For this and the following two paragraphs: AD to parents, April 28, July 2, 8, November 20, 30, December 10, 1971; also a two-page untitled, undated [October 1972] "preface" designed, but not used, as an introduction to the second section of *Woman Hating*, ADP/SLH.

3. For this and the following paragraph, AD to parents, December 10, 1971, January 24, February 25, August 26, 1972, ADP/SLH.

4. AD to parents, April 25, June 24, 1972, ADP/SLH.

5. For this and the following paragraph: AD to parents, December 10, 1971, September 15, plus one undated letter, ADP/SLH.

6. Jim Hougan to Andrea, March 8, 1996, four pages; AD, "My Suicide," as excerpted in the script for "Aftermath"—both items courtesy John Stoltenberg. Andrea *had* heard earlier rumors that Iwan had been charged with attempted murder.

7. For this and the following two paragraphs: AD to parents, April 28, June 15, 22, October 10 (five-page untitled "statement"), 19, 29, 1972.

8. For this and the following paragraph: AD to parents, December 13, 1972, ADP/SLH; AD, "Living in Terror, Pain: Being a Battered Wife" (heroin), *Los Angeles Times*, March 12, 1989, reprinted in AD, *Life and Death* (New York: The Free Press, 1997). Her later partner, John Stoltenberg, would subsequently manage to persuade Andrea to pay her back taxes; as he puts it, "I wanted our life together to be as safe from charges of illegality as possible. . . . For the same reason we had no drugs in the house" (Stoltenberg to me, June 16, 2019).

9. For this and the following paragraph: AD, *Heartbreak: The Political Memoir of a Feminist Militant* (New York: Basic Books, 2002), 107, 123–24; AD to parents, December 17, 1972, January 22, February 16, March 12, 1973, ADP/SLH; AD, "On Returning to These States," *Village Voice*, August 2, 1973.

10. AD to parents, January 12, March 12, 1973, plus one undated, ADP/SLH.

11. AD, *Heartbreak*, 123; Stoltenberg to me, June 16, 2019. In a piece published in *Vice* after her death, Andrea described the overwhelming anguish she felt after once having hit Velvet (https://www.vice.com/en_us/article/bnd834/velvet-v13n12). Andrea subsequently acquired a cat, George.

12. For this and the following paragraph: AD to parents, January 12, 22, 1973, plus one undated letter [February 1973]; AD to Mark and Carol (Mark had recently married), March 12, 1973. It was through REDRESS that Andrea and I for a time became good friends, though by 1975 we'd drifted apart. Andrea's recollections of REDRESS in her 2002 memoir, *Heartbreak* (127–28) are a good deal harsher than mine; the group certainly did have its prima donnas, and any number of its members were annoyingly self-important. Yet REDRESS also had a number of committed and even self-effacing members—Noam Chomsky and Benjamin Spock are two that come to mind. Nor do I think Andrea is fair when (on page 128 of *Heartbreak*) she writes, "I would be cut in two for putting an idea forward"; that never happened in any meeting I attended, and I was at most of them. For more on my own take on REDRESS, see Duberman, *Cures: A Gay Man's Odyssey* (Boston: Dutton, 1991), which mentions Andrea a number of times, including her brief involvement with the Gay Academic Union, to which I'd introduced her. According to Stoltenberg, he and Andrea first met Joe Chaikin when Joe invited them both to a GAU meeting in my apartment (Stoltenberg to me, June 16, 2019).

13. I knew Joe better than I knew Andrea in these years, but never spent time with both of them together and so don't feel possessed of any special insight (or bias) about their relationship. For this and the following three paragraphs: AD to "J" [Chaikin], September 15, October 28, November 5, 1974, May 16, 1975; Chaikin to AD, five letters n.d. [October/November 1973], ADP/SLH.

14. Andrea's original title for *Woman Hating* was *Last Days at Hot Slit*; Johanna Fateman and Amy Scholder have used *Last Days . . .* as the title for their anthology of Andrea's writing (Los Angeles: Semiotext(e), 2019). In my 1973 diary I note that Andrea asked both me and Muriel Rukeyser to read the manuscript of *Woman Hating*. She'd already described it to me over dinner with (says my diary) "so much clarity and force" that I felt the book would be "a major event." Yet when

I read the manuscript I felt somewhat disappointed—parts of it seemed (as I wrote at the time) "too summary, un-argued, abstract." Muriel, on the other hand (so Andrea reported to her parents) told her "'it's one of the most important books of our time'—wow!" (AD to parents, April 3, 1973, ADP/SLH).

I still believed in Andrea's gift, and it was then—*subsequent* to reading the manuscript—that I sent her to Hal Scharlatt. He encouraged her, but she complained to me about his "heavy vibes." I told her that I thought she was off the mark about him, that along with being a brilliant editor, he was a gentle, generous man. Hal did end up giving Andrea a contract, though while still in the process of editing the book, he died suddenly of a heart attack at age thirty-eight.

While researching Andrea's biography, I came across a letter to her friend Jackie Lapidus (October 9, 1976, ADP/SLH) in which she writes that, following publication, Jack Macrae, the head of Dutton, "expresses just simple contempt for WOMAN HATING," and that "the person who has most purposefully stood in WH's way [is] Dutton's sales manager, [who] hates the book and just sabotaged it outright—this is intelligence that comes to me from within the company."

As for Hal, Andrea goes on to write Lapidus, he "misunderstood the nature of the book—I think he thought it would be sensationalistic in a way that men would be aroused somehow . . . as if the gynocide would continue to be, in its covers, what is in life for men—exciting." That doesn't sound to me at all like the feminist-conscious Hal. "Many things happened when the book was finished," Andrea continues, "to change his mind—he read it for one thing. For another thing, Martin Duberman who was his close friend and confidant, who had told him to read it in ms. to begin with, didn't like it and called Hal to say so."

Reading that in Andrea's 1976 letter proved a shock. I have no memory of saying such a thing to Hal nor of ever discussing *Woman Hating* with him after making the initial introduction. Nor do I believe I would have tried to sabotage a friend's work, especially after recommending it. But as no one needs reminding, memory is tricky, and I felt the need to reveal here Andrea's take on the situation. If nothing else, it may well help to explain why we grew apart as friends.

15. Huey Newton to AD, May 17, 1974 (with enclosures), ADP/SLH; *The Black Panther*, June 22, 1974 (the review is mostly a summary but the tone positive); AD, *Heartbreak*, 123 (Huey). The second review by the leftwing playwright Karen Malpede was also favorable. As was the writer Leah Fritz's in *Sojourner* (October 1976): she predicted that "Dworkin may prove to be an authentic prophet of feminism." An excerpt of the book appeared in *VIVA* (July 1974), though Andrea had to threaten to withdraw if "crucial political material" wasn't restored; it was. She was equally adamant in denying the charge that in *Woman Hating* she advocated incest; no, she insisted, she was instead pointing out that the frequency of father-daughter rape already broke the taboo (AD to Ellen Bass, August 18, 1981, AD to Dick McLeester, August 20, 1980, ADP/SLH).

16. "w.e.a.n.ed: on women writing," *off our backs*, January 1975; "Towards Androgyny," *Berkeley Barb*, January 17–23, 1975.

17. AD to parents, January 25, 1975; Sandra Parke to AD, August 23, 1975; Reesa Vaughter to AD, n.d.; Sandra Liebenstein[?], September 11, 1975; Kate Millett to Elaine Markson, n.d. [1974]; the programs include "A Feminist Lecture Series"

at the Woodstock Women's Center, the Community Church of Boston, and the Pratt/Phoenix Center, ADP/SLH.

18. "An Open Letter to Rennie Davis," six-page ms., ADP/SLH.

19. Dell Williams to AD, September 16, 1974, ADP/SLH; AD, "Renouncing Sexual 'Equality,'" *WIN*, October 17, 1974.

20. For a fuller discussion of all these points, see AD, *Woman Hating*, "Part Four: Androgyny" (New York: Plume, 1976).

21. AD, *Woman Hating*, 184 (pansexual); the remaining quotations in this and the following three paragraphs derive from an entry I made in my diary.

22. John Stoltenberg shared AD's concern that GAU was disinterested in a serious discussion of sexism within the organization (JS to GAU conference planning committee, October 12, 1974, ADP/SLH. For Andrea's discomfort, see Duberman, *Cures*, 276–77 (New York, Plume, 1997).

23. *OUT*, August 1973; Andrea's article, in typescript, is in ADP/SLH. See also AD, "Lesbian Pride," a speech delivered in Central Park for Lesbian Pride Week (June 28, 1975) and reprinted in AD, *Our Blood* (New York: Perigee, 1976), 73–75.

The second (and last) issue of *OUT* printed a letter from the writer Dotson Rader, a friend of Mailer's, protesting Andrea's piece. Mailer himself, who I knew slightly, sent me—on the assumption that I was the editor of *OUT*—a sharp note denouncing the "attack" on him. I responded in kind, and we went at it for several more rounds. Quotes from the correspondence are in Duberman, *Cures*, 289–90; the letters themselves are in the Berg Collection of the New York Public Library.

24. The chief source for the description of the early period of John and Andrea's relationship derives from John's manuscript, "My Life with Andrea Dworkin," courtesy Stoltenberg (henceforth, "My Life"). Additional information is in John Stoltenberg, "Living with Andrea Dworkin," *Lambda Book Report*, May/June 1994; Stoltenberg's speech, "Refusing to Be a Man," delivered at NOW in NYC, May 19, 1974. I have no memory of it, but John tells me that he and Andrea initially met at a GAU meeting in my apartment.

25. AD interview with Leah Fritz, n.d. (partner), Fritz Papers, RLD. In regard to friends' disapproval of their living together, Barbara Deming wrote Andrea, "It pains me very much to know that you have to brace yourself against challenges from one sister after another—about your living with John. I know that you can understand why so many sisters doubt. They just can't imagine such a relation. But how exhausting for you. Please don't let it make you bitter" (Deming to AD, November 12, 1974, ADP/SLH). John, diplomatically, wrote Andrea's parents that "she is the most important person to me in the world" (Stoltenberg to the Dworkins, July 17, 1974, ADP/SLH).

26. JS, "Toward Gender Justice" (November 29, 1974), typescript in ADP/SLH. See also JS, "Refusing to Be a Man," first delivered at the June 19, 1974, meeting of the NYC chapter of NOW, then published in *WIN*, July 1, 1974 (though John protested their change of "ejaculate" to "ejaculation" and drew a clear distinction between them (JS to "People" [*WIN*], July 6, 1974).

27. Stoltenberg, "My Life," courtesy Stoltenberg.

28. Adrienne to Andrea, December 31, 1975, Barbara Deming Papers, SLH. Barbara was quick to reassure Andrea that Adrienne "is blindly compelled (I do think blindly) to establish with you her *Authority*. . . . That compulsion even prevents her from reading you with complete attention apparently . . . [she's] unable in spite of herself not to have to try and keep one in one's lesser place . . . [though] Adrienne clearly values you" (Deming to AD, July 26, 1976, January 29, 1977, ADP/SLH).

29. AD, "A Letter to M.," *WIN*, June 26, 1975. Andrea had first fallen in love and had sex with another girl when both were fourteen ("though we didn't speak one honest word to each other").

30. For more on Deming's history and political views, see Martin Duberman, *A Saving Remnant: The Radical Lives of Barbara Deming and David McReynolds* (New York: The New Press, 2011), quotation on page 165.

31. For this and the following paragraph: Deming to "friends" [*Liberation*], November 10, 1974, ADP/SLH. To underscore her respect for Andrea's work, Deming gave her a $500 grant from the "mini-foundation" she'd set up with the $20,000 settlement she'd received following a severe automobile accident (Deming to Andrea, November 12, 1974, ADP/SLH).

32. Gwenda [Blair] to Andrea, December 12, 1974, ADP/SLH. For this and the following paragraph: Maris Cakars to AD, December 30, 1974; AD to Gwenda, December 27, 1974, January 21, 23, 1975; Pam Black to AD, December 31, 1974, January 4, 1975; AD to Cakars, January 3, 11, 1975, ADP/SLH; Leah Claire Allen, "The Pleasures of Dangerous Criticism" (intersectionality), *SIGNS*, Vol. 42, No. 1 (2016).

33. AD to Susan Cakars, June 30, 1975; AD to *WIN* collective, July 6, 1975; AD to *WIN* editorial board, November 30, 1975. "Redefining Nonviolence," originally a speech (April 5, 1975, Boston College; "We must not accept, even for a moment, male notions of what nonviolence is. . . . The men who hold those notions have never renounced the male behaviors, privileges, values, and conceits which are in and of themselves acts of violence against us"). Andrea reprinted the speech in *Our Blood*, 66–72.

34. AD to Maris Cakars, January 3, 1975, ADP/SLH. It was particularly galling to Barbara Deming (and doubtless Andrea as well) when *Liberation* published an unusually lengthy article by Gina Blumenfell attacking Andrea's work (in words that echoed Adrienne Rich's earlier critique) as failing to understand that "sexual domination must be understood in the larger context of domination per se," and assailing the women's movement in general as "unreflective" and "anti-intellectual" (Deming to the *Liberation* collective, March 12, 1975; the Blumenfell typescript is in ADP/SLH).

35. As Andrea summed it up: "Believe me, the problems were not resolvable— no effort was spared to try to resolve them" (AD to Paul Rayman, April 29, 1976, ADP/SLH). For the serious problems that subsequently erupted between Barbara and Andrea, see Duberman, *A Saving Remnant*, 189–93. In *Remnant*, I let most of the blame for their disagreements fall on Andrea, but I was then focused on Barbara's story and entirely smitten by her generosity of spirit. Now that I'm

deeply engaged with Andrea and sympathetic to *her* history, I'm less certain of the emphasis I then placed.

36. Mary Daly to AD, May 21, 1975; AD to Daly, May 26, 1975. In her letter, the notoriously testy Daly described *Woman Hating* as showing "great potential" despite its "sloppy" and "weak" fourth section (the one on androgyny).

37. Dean Smith to Lawrence Pitkethly (for the search committee), June 2, 1975, ADP/SLH.

38. For this and the following two paragraphs: AD to Phyllis Chesler, n.d. [1975] ("de-escalate" crisis), ADP/SLH. A copy of the Redstockings press release, dated May 9, 1975, is in ADP/SLH. An earlier piece in the *New York Times*, "C.I.A. Subsidized Festival Trips," February 21, 1967, had originated the controversy.

39. For this and the following three paragraphs: AD to Gloria Steinem, June 18, 1975, ADP/SLH.

40. AD to *off our backs*, May 2, 1980 (twice); AD to Steinem, May 3, 1980, ADP/SLH; Echols, *Daring to Be Bad*, 265–69 (Sarachild). Though the controversy died down, it was no thanks to Betty Friedan, who in her 1976 book, *It Changed My Life*, reiterated, if obliquely, the charges against Steinem, apparently annoyed at her rise to prominence.

4: The Mid-Seventies

1. Anonymous, *off our backs*, September–October 1975.

2. For this and the following two paragraphs: AD, preface to *Our Blood: Prophecies and Discourses on Sexual Politics* (New York: Perigee, 1976).

3. *New York Post*, October 1, 1975. My discussion of *Snuff* has been especially informed by Linda Williams, *Hard Core: Power, Pleasure, and the "Frenzy of the Visible"* (Berkeley: University of California Press, 1989), 189–95; Susan Brownmiller, *In Our Time* (New York: Dial Press, 1999), 297–302; Whitney Strub, *Perversion for Profit: The Politics of Pornography and the Rise of the New Right* (New York: Columbia University Press, 2010), 230–36.

4. AD to Susan Yankowitz, February 11, 1976; Yankowitz to AD, February 19, 1976; AD, two-page typed release dated February 24, 1976, ADP/SLH.

5. For this section on *Snuff*, see the following: Nat Hentoff, "Look Who's Snuffing the First Amendment," *Village Voice*, March 15, 1976; AD to *New York Times*, November 12, 1982, ADP/SLH; Leah Fritz, "Why We Had to Picket 'Snuff,'" *Village Voice*, April 12, 1976; John Leonard, "'Snuff,' Built on Rumor, Lacking in Credit," *New York Times*, February 27, 1976 (genocide); Don Morrison, "'Snuff's' Moral Is Don't See It," *Minneapolis Star*, February 26, 1976; press release re: Dworkin and Karla Jay meeting with the Manhattan District Attorney's Office, March 8, 1976; *Gay Community News*, March 25, 1978. I was also among the signers of Andrea's petition.

6. See, for example, AD, "Feminism: An Agenda" and "For Men, Freedom of Speech; For Women, Silence Please," both reprinted in AD, *Letters from a War Zone* (New York: Lawrence Hill Books, 1993).

7. For this and the following three paragraphs: AD, *Our Blood, passim*. For samples of Andrea's resort to press agentry: AD to Kate Millett, June 15, 1976; AD to Gloria Steinem, June 15, 1976. In discussing the book's contents, I draw especially from two of the nine essays: "The Root Cause" and "Renouncing Sexual 'Equality.'"

8. For this and the following paragraph: AD to Marleen Le Febvre, June 13; AD to Barbara and Jane, July 5; AD to Kitty Benedict, January 6; AD to Mander and Rush, October 17—all 1976; Markson to AD, January 6, 1977, ADP/SLH.

9. AD to Yankowitz, July 23, 1976; AD to Kathy Norris, July 27, 1976, ADP/SLH.

10. AD to Marleen Le Febvre, October 2, 1976, ADP/SLH.

11. For this and the following two paragraphs: AD to Eleanor Johnson, October 4; Karla Jay, October 6 (killing), 16; AD to Yankowitz, October 17; AD to Eleanor Johnson, October 17; AD to Markson, October 18; AD to Leah Fritz, October 24; AD to London and Romero, November 12—all 1976, ADP/SLH.

12. For this and the following four paragraphs: Karla Jay to "Strange Her" (AD), October 2, 16; AD to Wendy Stevens, October 4; AD to Robyn Newhouse, October 10; AD to Leah Fritz, October 10; AD to Yankowitz, October 17 (muscled); AD to Eleanor Johnson, October 17 (prisoner); AD to Markson, October 18; AD to Karla Jay, November 3; AD to London and Romero, November 12—all 1976; AD to Deming, March 14, 1977 (taxes), ADP/SLH.

13. AD to Karla Jay, November 3 (Sylvia), 1976; AD to Jackie Lapidus, December 19; AD to Yankowitz, February 16, 1977; AD to June Duffy Dongel, March 14, 1977, ADP/SLH.

14. For this and the following five paragraphs: AD to Yankowitz, November 11; AD to Karla Jay, November 17 (*Ms.*; crazy), 25; AD to Kathy Norris, to Jackie Lapidus, December 19 (whoring), December 20, 1976 (Barbara); AD to Leah Fritz, November 22; AD to Eleanor Johnson, November 22, ADP/SLH. Barbara's extensive notes, written between October 8 and December 25, 1976, are in the Barbara Deming Papers, SLH. Barbara later persisted in trying to restore the friendship: "I still don't understand it—how you and I could have hurt each other (and yes, angered each other) as we somehow did. This is just to say how deeply sorry I am that I hurt *you*. I love you very much; and I respect you very deeply" (Barbara to AD, January 29, 1977, ADP/SLH). By 1979, not having had a response from Andrea, Barbara temporarily gave up trying to save the friendship (though ultimately considerable cordiality was restored). I've described Barbara and Jane's reaction in more detail in Martin Duberman, *A Saving Remnant: The Radical Lives of Barbara Deming and David McReynolds* (New York: The New Press, 2011), 190–92. Some limited contact by letter resumed in 1979, but on Andrea's side was not immediately friendly, though she did recommend a publisher to Deming (AD to Michalowski, January 13; Deming to AD, March 31, 15, July 2; AD to Deming, April 10—all 1979), ADP/SLH.

15. For this and the following paragraph: AD to Eleanor Johnson, November 22 (Chaikin); AD to Jackie Lapidus, December 19; AD to Kathy Norris, December 20—all 1976 (Chaikin), ADP/SLH.

16. For the section on June Arnold: AD to Karla Jay, November 25, 1976; AD to

Johnson and Kataloni, February 27; June Arnold to AD, April 13; AD to Arnold, April 26, May 20; Steinem to Andrea, May 16; AD to Lapidus, May 18—all 1977, ADP/SLH.

17. The individual involved has asked me to use a pseudonym for her real name. For this and the following two paragraphs: AD to Allen Young, August 22, 1977; AD to "Joanne Kastor," August 22, 1977, May 20, 1978; Kastor to AD, August 24, 1977, ADP/SLH; AD to Anne McCallister, September 27, 1980, Leah Fritz Papers, RLD; Kastor to me, March 27, April 30, 2019. In Andrea's unpublished *My Suicide* (1999 MS, courtesy Stoltenberg), written during a despondent period and found after her death, she wrote these lines: ". . . I want women. I have a flat-out appetite now. But I'm not touching anyone . . . touching is even harder than talking and I'm buried alive."

18. AD to Leah Fritz, February 10, 1977, ADP/SLH. Abbie Hoffman, Alice Hoffman, Grace Paley, and Tillie Olsen were among Elaine Markson's other clients, and Hoffman described her as "a fierce and loving protector." It was probably Grace Paley who introduced Andrea to her. Markson died in May 2018.

19. For this and the following two paragraphs: AD to Leah Fritz, February 10, March 13, 1977; AD to Lapidus, April 25, 1977; AD to Martha Shelley, May 2, 1977, ADP/SLH.

20. Andrea and John only later learned that their actions while at Cummington had more impact than they knew at the time. The women on the community's Board of Trustees organized a Women's Caucus "to act against sexism at Cummington," and passed a resolution thanking Andrea and John for their work on the library (AD to Leah Fritz, September 17, 1977, ADP/SLH).

5: The Gathering Storm

1. For this and the following two paragraphs, AD to Jackie Lapidus, April 25, May 18; AD to Eleanor Johnson, April 25; AD to Elsa Dorfman, May 6; AD to Gloria Steinem, May 16; AD to Ellen Frankfort, May 18; AD to Leah Fritz, May 18—all 1977, ADP/SLH.

2. AD to Steinem, June 12, 1977; AD to Karla Jay, June 28, 1977, ADP/SLH.

3. For this and the following paragraph: "WOMEN FOR THE ABOLITION OF PORNOGRAPHY," three-page statement of purpose, n.d.; "Dear Sisters of the Women's Anti-Defamation League," June 11, 1977; AD to Neil Miller, June 12, 1977 (*GCN* editor); *Gay Community News*, June 25, 1977, ADP/SLH.

4. For this and the following two paragraphs: AD to Martha Shelley, June 17; AD to Susan Brownmiller, June 14, 1977; AD to Karla Jay, June 28; Adrienne Rich to "Sisters," June 28; AD to Rich, June 29; Shere Hite to "Dear Women," n.d. (challenging use of the word "abolish" in regard to pornography—she was for consciousness-raising, not legal action); AD to Lois Gould, July 1; Karla Jay to *Times*, July 1; Leah Fritz to AD, July 1, 7 (a further critique of Brownmiller); AD to Fritz, July 6; AD to Robin Morgan, July 7; AD to Janet Sternberg, July 30; Steinem to AD, September 7—all 1977, all ADP/SLH.

5. For this and the following two paragraphs: Gould, *Times*, June 30; Fritz

to "Dear Sisters," July 1; Fritz to AD, July 1; AD to *Times*, June 30; AD to Jane Alpert, November 6; "Another Memo," September 23—all 1977, all ADP/SLH; AD to Brownmiller, June 14; transcript of Brownmiller interview with AD, August 10, 1998, Brownmiller Papers, SLH.

6. AD to Susan Yankowitz, July 9, 1977, ADP/SLH. It was at just this time that the *Soho Weekly News* unexpectedly reprinted in its August 4, 1977, issue Andrea's "Why So-Called Radical Men Love and Need Pornography" (under the title "Fathers, Sons and the Lust for Porn"). *Soho* paid her a munificent $10.

7. Andrea's most detailed and cogent argument against biological determinism is found in her earlier piece, "An Open Letter to Leah Fritz," *WIN*, November 21, 1974.

8. AD to Shelley, June 17; AD to Fritz, August 8 (hissed), 17 (ghetto); AD to Allen Young, August 22 (GAU); AD to Yankowitz, August 26; AD to Steinem, September 21 (hurt)—all 1977; AD to Laura Lederer, July 19; AD to Robin Morgan, July 19; AD to "Robin, Susan, Lois, and Gloria," August 7—all 1979, ADP/SLH. Andrea laid out her complaints against gay male attitudes in *Gay Community News*, June 12, 1977 (ERA), and in "The Lesbian/Gay Movement," *Gay Community News*, June 25, 1977. Wayne Dynes, the conservative gay art historian answered her in his "The New Victorianism," *GCN*, August 20, 1977, in which he managed to demonstrate precisely the disdain about which Andrea had complained.

9. "The Power of Words" was first published in the *Massachusetts Daily Occupied Collegian*, May 8, 1978. It's included in AD's collection, *Letters from a War Zone* (New York: Lawrence Hill Books, 1993), 27–30.

10. AD to Mark, March 3, 1978; AD to Fritz, May 17, 1978 (NYC), ADP/SLH. Shortly before leaving Northampton, Andrea did participate somewhat more in local activism (*Collegian*, April 10, 15, 1978). She also spoke at the Women's Week Conference at Smith: "Look, Dick, Look. See Jane Blow It," reprinted in AD, *Letters from a War Zone*, 126–32. Because the documentation of AD's lecture dates is voluminous and repetitive, I've decided against detailed citations regarding contracts and so forth

11. For this and the following two paragraphs: AD to Steinem, September 21, 1977, March 30, 1978; Steinem to AD, May 9, 1978, ADP/SLH; AD to Corona Machemer, August 19, 1978, Leah Fritz Papers, RLD.

12. For this and the following two paragraphs: Steinem to AD, January 31, 1981, plus three undated notes, ADP/SLH; AD to Robin Morgan, February 14, 18, 1981; AD to Steinem, February 14, 1981, Robin Morgan Papers, RLD.

13. AD to Paula Rayman, April 29, 1976, ADP/SLH.

14. For this and the following paragraph: AD to Fritz, May 17, 1978; AD to Hite, June 27, 1978, ADP/SLH. AD's defense of Hite is in *off our backs*, May 1978. Hite did an interview with Andrea (June 21, n.y., ADP/SLH); the six-page typed transcript is in ADP/SLH. Andrea subsequently had trouble with her *Mother Jones* article: after "the third revised abridged version of my essay . . . they are being nasty as hell" (AD to Lederer, July 19, 1979; AD to Robin Morgan, July 19, 1979, ADP/SLH). The only part of Hite's book that disappointed Catharine MacKinnon was "the same old humanism" of the chapter on pornography (MacKinnon to AD, January 3, 1982, ADP/SLH).

15. For this and the following two paragraphs: Shere Hite interview with AD, June 21, n.y. [1978?]; AD to Leah Fritz, May 6, 17 (*Mother Jones*); AD to Phyllis Chesler, May 18, 24, June 11; Chesler to AD, June 7; AD to parents, June 15—all 1978, ADP/SLH; Leah Fritz to *Mother Jones*, June 7, 1978, Fritz Papers, RLD.

16. AD to Mark, May 22, 1979, December 26, 1980, ADP/SLH.

17. For this and the following three paragraphs: AD to Phyllis Chesler, January 20, 1977, May 18, 24, June 11, 1978; Chesler to AD, June 7, 14; AD to Leah Fritz, February 10, 1977, May 6, 1978; Chesler to Vincent Virga, May 12, 1978—all in ADP/SLH. Andrea may have had the dispute with Chesler in mind when, in her unpublished article "Sororicide" (ms. is in the Leah Fritz Papers, RLD), she lamented that women "are socialized to despise and distrust each other."

18. In 2018, more than a dozen years after Andrea's death, Phyllis published *A Politically Incorrect Feminist* (New York: St. Martin's Press, 2018). In it (pp. 131, 192), she calls Andrea "a genius" but more than compensates for the compliment with an assortment of negative comments about her—"a fanatic, a terribly wounded one . . . who accused practically everyone of high crimes, never mere misdemeanors"—that perhaps tells us as much about Chesler's capacity for hyperbole as Andrea's for outsized accusation.

In an earlier work, *The Death of Feminism* (London: Palgrave MacMillan, 2005, 68), Chesler had been far more generous toward Andrea, calling her "visionary, both in literary and intellectual terms," and deploring Katha Pollitt's article in *The Nation* (April 9, 2005), in which she'd mocked Andrea as "she of the denim overalls and the wild hair and wilder pronouncements," summarizing her as "an oversimplifier and a demagogue."

19. AD to Robyn Newhouse, July 21, 1978; AD to Yankowitz, July 19, 1978, ADP/SLH.

6: Pornography

1. The literature on the pornography issue is vast. Some good starting points on the debate are Andrea Dworkin and Catharine A. MacKinnon, *In Harm's Way* (Cambridge, MA: Harvard University Press, 1997); Lisa Duggan and Nan D. Hunter, *Sex Wars* (New York: Routledge, 2006); and Whitney Strub, *Perversion for Profit: The Politics of Pornography and the Rise of the New Right* (New York: Columbia University Press, 2010), chapter seven; Caroline Bronstein, *Battling Pornography* (Cambridge, UK: Cambridge University Press, 2011).

2. Transcript of Elisabeth Warren interview with AD, n.d. [October 1981], ADP/SLH. See also, Wilson to AD, November 4, March 6; AD to Wilson, April 10—all 1981, all ADP/SLH. See pages 12–14 for more on Andrea's literary education.

3. For this and the following three paragraphs: Both AD's 1977 speech, "Pornography: The New Terrorism," and her 1978 speech in San Francisco, "Pornography and Grief," are reprinted in AD, *Letters from a War Zone. New York Times*, December 4, 1978. It's worth noting that in her San Francisco speech Andrea included gay men in what she called the male need to "despise" women: "This same motif also operates among male homosexuals, where force and/or convention designate some males as female or feminized. The plethora of leather

and chains among male homosexuals . . . are testimony to the fixedness of the male compulsion to dominate and destroy that is the source of sexual pleasure for men" (*Letters*, 22). Andrea's words make it sound as if S/M was (and is) endemic in the gay male world; I believe it's a good deal less than that. Some would argue that a milder form of dominance/submission is inherent in all sexual coupling.

4. See Paul Chevigny, "Pornography and Cognition," *Duke Law Journal*, Vol. 1989, No. 2 (April 1989).

5. Barbara Mehrhof and Lucille Iverrson, "When Does Free Speech Go Too Far?: https://google.com/drive/folders/1qimgo1YBgjRjsFv8gz46ZSYEWhzlJ239; Women Against Pornography pamphlet: https://drive.google.com/drive/foldrs /1mo34KMB88MG3SelTO5adJ51HizZiH4-0.

6. Susan Brownmiller, "Let's Put Pornography Back in the Closet," July 17, 1979, *Newsday*.

7. For this and the following paragraph: AD, "Pornography and the New Terrorism?," *The Body Politic*, August 1978; AD, "For Men, Freedom of Speech; For Women, Silence Please," *Letters from a War Zone*, 222–25. On the inception of WAP: Bronstein, *Battling Pornography*, chapter 6.

8. Brownmiller interview with AD, August 10, 1998, transcript in Brownmiller Papers, SLH; Brownmiller, *In Our Time*, 308–10. Andrea's difficulties with WAP included (according to one of her fans) "silencing" her at a press conference because she didn't fit with their "carefully cultivated public image. . . . I guess you don't project a 'nice girl' image enough to publicly represent WAP," she wrote Andrea. "WAP is too afraid of freaking people out by using lesbianism as both an alternative kind of sexual relating and a model for eroticism in general." (Julie Melrose to AD, September 24, 1979, ADP/SLH). Yet in regard to lesbianism WAP, as part of its formal literature ("Lesbian Feminist Concerns in the Feminist Anti-Pornography Movement") specifically states that "Women Against Pornography upholds the right of every woman to the self-determination of her sexual and affectional preferences" (copy in ADP/SLH).

9. A copy of Wendy Kaminer's position paper, "Where We Stand on the First Amendment," is in ADP/SLH.

10. For this and the following three paragraphs, the most detailed coverage of the September conference is in *off our backs*, November 1979; see also, Leslie Bennetts, "Conference Examines Pornography as a Feminist Issue," *New York Times*, September 17, 1979 (Abzug).

11. Most of Ed Donnerstein and Neil Malamuth's work lay in the future, and will be evaluated, along with research done by others, at a later point in this book. Of the early work, Malamuth's "Rape Proclivity Among Males," *Journal of Social Issues*, 1981, No. 4, is probably the most significant.

12. For this and the following four paragraphs: Ellen Willis, "Feminism, Moralism, and Pornography," *Village Voice*, October and November 1979, reprinted in Nona Willis Aronowitz, *The Essential Ellen Willis* (University of Minnesota Press, 2014), 94–100. In the Ellen Willis Papers at the Schlesinger Library, Harvard, there are a few dozen pages of undated, handwritten notes apparently representing EW's preliminary thoughts, some of which contain additional reflections on the anti-porn movement. For example, in one set of notes (based on internal evidence, they probably date from the mid–late eighties) Willis writes: "Anti-porn

movement: preocc. w. violence—porn causes violence & is violent. porn=rape. rape loses its status as an act & comes to mean something like 'the assault of this male-oriented sexual culture on female sensibilities' + this assault is to be fought by crusading against porn. What can be the aim/effect of such a movement? 1) eliminate porn. Mostly, anti-porn movement denies they want to do this. Just 'raise consciousness.' In fact their denial doesn't hold up. . . . They are reinforcing right's attempts to censor & right just co-opts their arguments."

13. For this and the following paragraph: AD, "For Men, Freedom of Speech; For Women, Silence Please," as reprinted in AD, *Letters from a War Zone*, 222–25.

14. The transcript of AD's "Rally Address," October 20, 1979, is in ADP/SLH.

15. For this and the following paragraph: AD to Susan Hester, May 22, 1979; AD to Elsa Dorfman, May 22, 1979; AD to Laura Lederer, June 8, 1979; AD to MacKinnon, March 31, August 5, 1978; MacKinnon to AD, August 11, 1979, ADP/SLH; Fred Strebeigh, "Defining Law on the Feminist Frontier," *New York Times*, October 6, 1991; AD to Charlotte Bunch, December 12, 1980 (Doubleday), Bunch Papers, SLH.

16. AD to MacKinnon, March 31, 1978, ADP/SLH.

17. MacKinnon to AD, October 16, 1980; AD to MacKinnon, December 2, 1981, ADP/SLH.

18. AD to Amy Hoffman, December 24, 1979, ADP/SLH.

19. For this and the following two paragraphs: AD to Kathy Norris, July 27, December 20, 1976, AD to Robin Morgan, January 5, 1977, June 26, 1979. It may be—though this is purely speculative—that the antagonism between the two was largely ideological: Andrea strongly resisted the notion of biological determinism in regard to gender, whereas Adrienne found "cultural" feminism—the view that men and women are *innately* different—mostly congenial.

20. AD to MacKinnon, January 3, 1980; AD to Marge Piercy, January 10, 1980, ADP/SLH.

21. Leah Fritz to AD, January 3, 1980, Leah Fritz Papers, RLD (nearly a year later, Fritz itemized her discomfort: "I felt several of the stories . . . corroborated the myth of female masochism & the Marxist notion that the enemy is the 'bourgeois' woman" (Fritz to AD, October 1, 1980, ADP/SLH). See also AD to Gloria Steinem, March 17, 1980, ADP/SLH; AD to Alix Kates Shulman, January 31, March 21, 1980, Shulman Papers, RLD; AD to Letty Cottin Pogrebin, January 18, 1980; AD to Vivian Gornick, February 25, 1980, ADP/SLH. Frog in the Well, not Andrea, sent the manuscript to Rita Mae Brown, who did respond with a favorable blurb: "A remarkable collection of short stories that challenge existing definitions of feminist literature. Andrea Dworkin's passion confounds and frightens the patriarchs. It's pure joy for the rest of us" (Rita Mae Brown to Frog in the Well, April 14, 1980, ADP/SLH); Andrea, in turn, wrote favorably about Brown's *Six of One* ("the book is original and beautiful")—the ms. is in ADP/SLH. Andrea's friend, the poet Jacqueline ("Jackie") Lapidus, also loved the book and reported that Kate Millett had agreed with her that "it was an original, outrageous, beautiful, terrifying and gut-wrenching piece of work" (Lapidus to AD, May 9, 1980, ADP/SLH). The *New Women's Times* (July/August 1980) also carried a favorable review.

22. AD to Robin Morgan, March 17, 1980, Robin Morgan Papers, RLD; AD to Deirdre English, March 10, 1980; English to AD, June 18, 1980, ADP/SLH.

23. AD to "Letter to the Editor," *Mother Jones*, March 10, 1980, ADP/SLH.

24. AD to Vicki Smith, April 2, May 30, ADP/SLH; Grace Hardgrove to AD, June 12, 1980.

25. For this and the following two paragraphs: AD to Loretta Barrett, August 4; AD to Steinem, May 3, August 3, 5; AD to Adrienne Rich, August 5; AD to Jan Raymond and Pat Hynes, August 18—all 1980, ADP/SLH; AD to Charlotte Bunch, December 12, 1980, Bunch Papers, SLH.

26. AD to Wendy Goldwyn, September 1, 1980, ADP/SLH.

27. For this and the following paragraph: AD to Adrienne Rich, September 27, 1980; Karla Jay to Eleanor Rawson, September 3, 1980, ADP/SLH.

28. AD, *Ice and Fire* (London: Secker & Warburg, 1986), 100–2.

29. AD to Steinem, September 28, 1980; AD to Lapidus, December 9, 1980, ADP/SLH.

30. AD to Robin Morgan, February 3, 1981, Morgan Papers, RLD.

31. AD to Letty Pogrebin, November 30, 1980, ADP/SLH.

32. For this and the following paragraph: AD, *Pornography* (New York: Perigee, 1981), 167–78; see also, AD, ms. "The Pornographic View: Women in Private—Harlots and Sadists"; AD to Michael Moorcock, April 22, 1988 (Sontag), ADP/SLH. The Sontag essay, "The Pornographic Imagination," is in her *Styles of Radical Will* (London: Secker & Warburg, 1969).

33. AD, *Pornography*, 81–100.

34. MacKinnon to AD, October 16, 1980, ADP/SLH.

35. *Sojourner*, July 1981; AD to Dorothy Allison, August 4, 1981, Allison Papers, Duke; AD to Ellen Frankfort, July 27, 1981, ADP/SLH. In the all-important *New York Times* (July 12, 1981), Ellen Willis denounced *Pornography* as "a booklength sermon with a rhetorical flourish and a singleminded intensity that meet somewhere between poetry and rant. . . . *Pornography*'s relentless outrage . . . is less a call to arms than a counsel of despair."

36. Leah Fritz, "Dworkin Review," n.d., 8 pp., Leah Fritz Papers, RLD.

37. Willis, "Nature's Revenge," *New York Times*, July 12, 1981.

7: Lovelace; Trans; and Right-Wing Women

1. AD to Leonard Lopate, February 15, 1981, ADP/SLH.

2. Ellen Willis, *New York Times*, July 12, 1981; Barbara Deming to AD, July 22?, 1981, Deming Papers, SLH; AD, *Pornography* (New York: Perigee, 1981), 51.

3. AD's unpublished letter to the *New York Times*, November 18, 1979, ADP/SLH.

4. Julie Bindel, What Andrea Dworkin, the Feminist I Knew, Can Teach Young Women," *The Guardian*, March 30, 2015. See also: Christine Stark, "Andrea Dworkin and Me," *Feminist Studies*, Vol. 34, No. 3 (kind and soft). Asked

by me to characterize what Andrea was like in person, John Stoltenberg replied, "So sweet and funny" (Stoltenberg to me, June 16, 2019).

5. Articles by Pat Harrison and Catherine London in *Sojourner*, July 1981.

6. AD, a *new woman's broken heart* (Frog in the Well, 1980).

7. The chronology of events in this and the following two paragraphs is based on Brownmiller's interview with AD, August 10, 1998, transcript in Brownmiller Papers, SLH; MacKinnon to me, May 29, 2019; phone conversation with Mac-Kinnon, July 25, 2019.

8. There's considerable documentation relating to the case in both the Dworkin and MacKinnon Papers at SLH, but since it did not go forward, I've refrained from further detailing. Some of the key letters are: AD to Steinem, May 18, 1980; AD, "Statement," May 31, 1980; MacKinnon to Marchiano, April 27, July 2, July 14, July 15, 1981, February 21, 1982; MacKinnon to AD, October 26 (cheering), 1981; MacKinnon to Gloria, et al., October 28, 1981, ADP/SLH; Susan Brownmiller interview with AD, August 10, 1998, Brownmiller Papers, RLD. There are many admirable qualities to Whitney Strub's *Perversion for Profit* (New York: Columbia University Press, 2010), but his treatment of Linda "Lovelace" Marciano isn't one of them. Of the *Deep Throat* shoot, he mockingly quotes her as saying "I hated to see it end" (p. 246), and portrays her "victimhood" as Andrea and Kitty's invention—which is wretchedly off the mark. See MacKinnon, *Feminism Unmodified* (Cambridge, MA: Harvard University Press, 1987), 127–33.

9. For this and the following paragraph: MacKinnon to AD, November 22, December 11, 26, 1981; AD to MacKinnon, November 27, December 2, 22, 1981, ADP/SLH; AD to Susanne Kappeler, July 31, 1993, ADP/SLH; see also AD to Moorcock and Steele, June 21, 1993, ADP/SLH; MacKinnon to me, May 29, 2019.

10. For this and the following paragraph: AD to Jane Meyerling, July 12, 1982; AD to Jan Raymond, July 12, 1982; AD to Letty Pogrebin, May 4, 1982, ADP/SLH; John Stoltenberg, "What Is the Meaning of S&M?," *Gay Community News*, February 23, 1980.

11. AD, *Woman Hating* (New York: Plume, 1974), chapter 9.

12. AD to Jan Raymond, January 15, 1978; MacKinnon to AD, December 11, 1981, ADP/SLH. Down to the present day Andrea is sometimes still accused of having been transphobic; John Stoltenberg has written a persuasive reply to the charge: https://web.archive.org/web/20160317032310/http:/www.feministtimes .com/%e2%80%8egenderweek-andrea-was-not-transphobic/.

13. For this and the following two paragraphs: transcript of Kim Fullerton interview with AD, April 16, 1982, ADP/SLH; Michael Kimmel, "Who Are the Real Male Bashers?," in *Misframing Men* (New Brunswick, NJ: Rutgers University Press, 2010).

14. The Barnard Conference has produced a substantial amount of commentary and controversy, though the lack of reflection on it in AD's papers is an index of her detachment from the event—though not from the issues it raised. As a result of her non-participation, I've held my discussion of the conference to a minimum. My own understanding of it, however, has been enriched by the extended commentary in *off our backs* (usually regarded as the feminist newspaper of record), and particularly the several articles in its June 1982 issue—especially Claudette

Charbonneau's unsympathetic and highly controversial one; Gayle Rubin's important letter to *oob*, June 8, 1982; and *New Directions for Women*, July/August 1982. See also: Carole S. Vance, *Pleasure and Danger: Exploring Female Sexuality* (containing the revised proceedings of the conference), especially the Epilogue, pp. 431–39 (Abingdon, UK: Routledge & Kegan Paul, 1984); The Steering Committee of WAP's eleven-page protest letter, December 30, 1983, to *Feminist Studies* (a copy is in ADP/SLH); "Diary of a Conference" (*GLQ* 17:1); Gayle Rubin's important, even essential corrective to WAP's various distortions, "Blood Under the Bridge," in *GLQ: A Journal of Lesbian and Gay Studies*, Vol. 127, No. 1, 2011, Duke University Press; and the June 14, 1982, list of grievances against the conference disrupters signed by ("a partial list") more than 150 women, Dorothy Allison Papers, RLD. A particularly cogent discussion of the conference and its aftermath is in Carolyn Bronstein, *Battling Pornography* (Cambridge, UK: Cambridge University Press, 2011), 297–307.

15. AD to Katherine Thomas, September 21, 1986, ADP/SLH.

16. For more on cultural feminism, see Alice Echols, *Daring to Be Bad*, as well as the central texts of adherents of biological determinism frequently cited, including Mary Daly, *Gyn-Ecology* (Boston: Beacon, 1978); Adrienne Rich, *Of Woman Born* (New York: Norton, 1976); and Susan Griffin, *Pornography and Silence* (New York: Harper & Row, 1981).

17. Laura Cottingham, "Strangers Bed Partners," *Village Voice*, September 27, 1985. Alice Echols quotes one (unidentified) "brilliant but conflicted writer" admitting to sympathy with a conference attendee "who berated academics for 'debating the niceties of leather and shit' while ignoring the 'real, material struggles of women'" (Echols, "Retrospective: Tangled Up in Pleasure and Danger," *Signs*, Vol. 42, No. 1 [2016]).

18. For this and the following paragraph: Alice Walker to AD, February 4, 1983; AD to Steinem, March 21, 1983; AD to Ann Jones, April 25, 1983, ADP/SLH.

19. *In These Times*, April 27–May 3, 1983; *FUSE*, September/October 1983; *The New Women's Times Feminist Review*, November/December 1983.

20. *Womannews*, May 1983; several responses to the review are in the issue of June 1983.

8: The Ordinance

1. For this and the following paragraph: Kitty MacKinnon to AD, February 8, April 19, 1983, ADP/SLH; phone conversation with MacKinnon, July 25, 2019.

2. MacKinnon to AD, n.d. [October? 1983]; AD to "The Editor," October 31, 1983, ADP/SLH. See also, Dworkin and MacKinnon, *In Harm's Way: The Pornography Civil Rights Hearings* (Harvard, 1997), which in an appendix prints the Ordinances drawn up for several cities.

3. Catharine A. MacKinnon, "Testimony on Pornography, Minneapolis," *Butterfly Politics: Changing the World for Women* (Cambridge, MA: Harvard Univ. Press, 2019), 96.

4. See Dworkin, *Pornography* (New York: Perigee, 1981), *passim*.

5. For this and the following two paragraphs: MacKinnon, "An Open Letter

to Adrienne Rich," July 4, 1985, APD/SLH; AD to Editor, *Wall Street Journal*, February 2, 1984; transcript of Brownmiller interview with AD, August 10, 1998, ADP/SLH. "An Excerpt from Model Antipornography Civil Rights Ordinance" was published in Dworkin and MacKinnon, *Pornography Civil Rights Hearings*, 138–42.

6. For this and the following three paragraphs see: phone conversation with MacKinnon, July 25, 2019; "An Open Letter on Pornography," *off our backs*, August/September 1985. For the issue of "proof of harm," see MacKinnon, "Pornography," in *Civil Rights & Civil Liberties Review*, Vol. 2, No. 1 (1985); Carol Anne Douglas, "A House Divided?," *off our backs*, June 1985; AD ms. of the February 1984 Toronto conference on pornography, Pauline Bart Papers, RLD; AD to Dorothy ("Cookie") Teer, April 24, 1985, Teer Papers, RLD.

7. For this and the following paragraph: James E.P. Check and Neil Malamuth, "An Empirical Assessment of Some Feminist Hypotheses About Rape," *Journal of Women's Studies* (1984, 8); Edward Donnerstein, "December 12, 1983 testimony in Minneapolis Hearings," and January 10, 1984 "Interview," both in *In Harm's Way: The Pornography Civil Rights Hearings* (Cambridge, UK: Harvard University Press, 1997), 44–60; Neil Malamuth and Ed Donnerstein, eds., *Pornography and Sexual Aggression* (Academic Press, 1984).

Later studies: Mike Baxter, "Flesh and Blood," *New Scientists*, May 5, 1990; Mike Allen et al., "A Meta-Analysis Summarizing the Effects of Pornography," *Human Communication Research*, December 1995; Catherine Itzin, ed., *Pornography: Women, Violence and Civil Liberties* (Oxford, UK: Oxford University Press, 1992); Diana E.H. Russell, *Making Violence Sexy: Feminist Views on Pornography* (Hoboken, NJ: Blackwell, 1993); Elizabeth Oddone-Paolucci et al., "A Meta-Analysis of the Published Research on the Effects of Pornography," in *The Changing Family and Child Development*, Claudio Violato et al., eds. (Abingdon, UK: Routledge, 2000). For a fuller citation of the research to date into pornography's harm, see Catharine MacKinnon, *Sex Equality*, Third Ed., Foundation Press, 2015), 1716–49. See also *off our backs*: Catharine MacKinnon, "Pornography Left and Right," in *Harvard Civil Rights-Civil Liberties Law Review*, Winter 1995, 143–45 for a persuasive denial of ever having said (or believed) that "all sex is rape." She sued over the misquotation many times over, and consistently won, forcing even the *New York Times* to print a retraction.

8. Gayle Rubin to Nan Hunter, June 5, 1985, Dorothy Allison Papers, RLD. For a detailed and cogent analysis of the issues at stake, see Lisa Duggan and Nan D. Hunter, *Sex Wars: Sexual Dissent and Political Culture*, 10th anniversary ed. (London: Taylor & Francis Group, 2006).

9. For this and the next two paragraphs, see: "An Open Letter on Pornography," *off our backs*, August/September 1985. For the issue of "proof of harm," see MacKinnon, "Pornography, Civil Rights & Civil Liberties Review," Vol. 2, no. 1, 1985; Carol Anne Douglas, "A House Divided?," *off our backs*, June 1985; AD ms. of the February 1984 Toronto Conference on pornography, Pauline Bart Papers, RLD; AD to Dorothy ("Cookie") Teer, April 24, 1985, Teer Papers, RLD.

10. Malamuth and Donnerstein, eds., *Pornography and Sexual Aggression*, Academic Press, 1984. See also Donnerstein, "Erotica and Human Aggression," in Green and Donnerstein eds., *Aggression: Theoretical and Empirical Reviews*

(Academic Press, 1983); and Malamuth and Donnerstein, "The Effects of Aggressive Pornographic Mass Media Stimuli," in Berkowitz, ed., *Advances in Experimental Social Psychology* (Academic Press, 1982).

11. AD to Henk Jan, September 20, 1984; AD to Gale O'Brien Green, June 12, 1984; AD to Joyce Keener, June 12, 1984; AD to Jalna Hammer, May 8, 1984—all ADP/SLH.

12. For this and the following three paragraphs: AD to Priscilla Moree, August 14, 1985 (trembling); AD to Dorothy ("Cookie") Teer, April 24, 1985, Teer Papers, RLD.

13. AD to Fraser, July 5, 1984, a copy is in the MacKinnon Papers, SLH.

14. For this and the following two paragraphs: AD to Johanna Markson, March 26, 1990; *Village Voice*, August 21, 1978, October 16, 23, 1984; MacKinnon to *Voice*, December 26, 1984, ADP/SLH. For Andrea's earlier run-in with the ACLU, see her 1981 piece, "The ACLU: Bait and Switch," in *Letters from a War Zone* (New York: Lawrence Hill Books, 1993), 210–13, in which she deplores the confusion of bondage photographs and movies with "free speech."

15. Emerson's article, "Pornography and the First Amendment: A Reply to Professor MacKinnon," appeared in the *Yale Law & Policy Review*, Vol. 3, No. 1 (Fall 1984); Nat Hentoff, "Equal-Opportunity Banning," *Village Voice*, October 30, 1984.

16. For this and the following two paragraphs: Lisa Duggan, "Censorship in the Name of Feminism," *Village Voice*, October 16, 1984; Donnerstein, Daniel Linz, and Steve Penrod, *The Question of Pornography*, 1987: PsycINFO_Database Record © 2012 APA; MacKinnon, *Feminism Unmodified* (Cambridge, MA: Harvard University Press, 1987). Both the lower and appeals courts, presided over by conservative judges, agreed that violent pornography harmed women, but struck down the ordinance on First Amendment grounds (transcript of Dworkin interview, December 7, 1987, ADP/SLH).

17. Lisa Duggan, "Censorship in the Name of Feminism," *The Village Voice*, Oct. 16, 1984.

18. Dorchen Leidholdt to Alan Sears (E.D. of Commission), April 30, 1985; AD to "Friends," n. d. (Media Coalition), ADP/SLH. Andrea's testimony was transcribed, and she reprinted it in her book, *Letters from a War Zone*, 276–307. The discussion of Andrea's testimony that follows relies on the account in *Letters*.

19. The literature on the relationship between pornography and the First Amendment is vast. I list here only those articles and books that have most influenced my judgments: Mary Kate McGowan, "On Pornography: MacKinnon, Speech Acts, and 'False' Construction," *Hypatia*, Summer, 2005; Nick Cowen, "Millian Liberalism and Extreme Pornography," *American Journal of Political Science*, April 2016; Rebecca Whisnant, "Pornography and Pop Culture," *off our backs*, Vol. 37, No. 1 (2007); Danny Scoccia, "Can Liberals Support a Ban on Violent Pornography?," *Ethics*, July 1996; Catharine A. MacKinnon, *Only Words* (Harvard, 1993); Laura J. Lederer and Richard Delgado, *The Price We Pay* (Hill and Wang, 1995); Thomas I. Emerson, "Pornography and the First Amendment: A Reply to Professor Mackinnon," *Yale Law & Policy Review*, Fall, 1984; Pauline B. Bart and Margaret Jozsa, "Dirty Books, Dirty Films, and Dirty Data," in Lederer

and Delgado, *The Price We Pay*; Rosemarie Tong, "Pornography and Censorship," *Social Theory and Practice*, Spring 1982; Anti-Pornography Laws and First Amendment Values," *Harvard Law Review*, December 1984.

20. The 1868 "Hicklin test" in England offered a comprehensive definition of "obscenity" that was avoided when the United States in 1933 declared James Joyce's *Ulysses* not "obscene." In 1957 in *Roth v. U.S.*, the Supreme Court, discarding Hicklin, defined "obscenity" according to "whether to the average person, applying contemporary community standards, the dominant theme of the material taken as a whole appeals to prurient interest." The vague terminology of "community standards" and "prurient interest" continue to defy exactitude down to the present day.

21. In a speech, "Not a Moral Issue," at the University of Minnesota Law School in April 1985 (transcript in ADP/SLH), MacKinnon summarized the insufficiency of current standards: "liberalism has never understood that the free speech of men silences the free speech of women. . . . The first amendment says, 'Congress shall not abridge *the freedom of speech*' . . . [the assumption is] that which if unconstrained by government, *is* free. This tends to assume that some people are not systematically silenced *socially*, prior to government action."

22. Transcript of AD's speech to Upper Midwest Men's Conference, October 15, 1983, ADP/SLH.

23. AD to Dorothy ("Cookie") Teer, Teer Papers, RLD.

24. In the same month of April 1985, *Newsweek* (in the issue of March 18), ran its own feature article on "The War Against Pornography." It revealed a recent Gallup poll that showed "nearly two-thirds of those surveyed supported a ban on magazines, movies and video cassettes that feature sexual violence" and that roughly three-quarters of those surveyed agreed with the anti-porn feminists that sexually explicit material denigrates women and leads some people to sexual violence." But the poll also revealed that by a wide margin, non-violent porn had become accepted in American life, and with the advent of VCRs home porn proliferated. *Newsweek* also reported on the recent research findings of psychologists Edward Donnerstein and Neil Malamuth that "young men shown sexually violent films and then asked to judge a simulated rape trial are less likely to vote for conviction than those who haven't seen the films." They also found that male college students "who briefly watch porn report that 30 percent of the women they know would 'enjoy aggressively forced sex'"; as many as 57 percent indicated "some likelihood that they would commit a rape" if they knew they would not be caught. *Newsweek* also recounted a number of reputable recent studies documenting that 10–40 percent of men who watched violent porn subsequently attempted to re-enact it forcibly on their partners. For a slew of more recent studies further confirming the link between porn consumption and violence against women, see Gail Dines, *Pornland* (Boston: Beacon Press, 2010), especially pp. 87–88, 95–98, 117–18, 181–82.

25. AD to Suzanne Levine, March 9, 1985, ADP/SLH.

26. For this and the following three paragraphs: *In Harm's Way*, 13–17; AD to Valerie Harper, June 12, July 6, August 14, 1984; AD to Steinem, June 28, 1984; AD to Mikulski, July 5, 1984—all in ADP/SLH; various issues of *Sex & Justice*

(the newsletter of the Anti-pornography Task Group (which John Stoltenberg co-chaired) of the National Organization for Changing Men, especially Issues #1/June 1984 and #2/October 1984); MacKinnon, *Butterfly Politics*, 96–102, 360–4. Harkening back to the controversial 1982 Barnard Conference, Kitty denounced as false Carole Vance's claim (in "Negotiating Sex and Gender in the Attorney General's Commission on Pornography," in *Sex Exposed*, Lynne Segal and Mary McIntosh eds., [London: Virago Press, 1992]) that the Commission "decisively rejected their [anti-porn] remedies."

27. Both Andrea and Kitty predicted early on (1983) that if the pornography industry wasn't legally contained, it would massively expand, and that's precisely what has happened; it became "more visible and legitimate, hence less visible as pornography" (MacKinnon, *Butterfly Politics*, 206, 415–16; Dworkin, "Why Pornography Matters to Feminists," in *Letters from a War Zone*, 206; Rodney A. Smolla, *The First Amendment* (Carolina Academic Press, 1999); Smolla & Nimmer on Freedom of Speech Vol. 2, No. 10 (2009); Cheryl B. Preston, "The Misunderstood First Amendment and Our Lives Online," *Brigham Young University Studies*, Vol. 49, No. 1 (2010); Danny Scoccia, "Can Liberals Support a Ban on Violent Pornography," *Ethics*, Vol. 106, No. 4 (July 1996); Max Waltman, "Rethinking Democracy," *Political Research Quarterly*, Vol. 63, No. 1 (March 2010); Mary Kate McGowan, "On Pornography: MacKinnon, Speech Acts, and 'False' Construction," *Hypatia*, Vol. 20, No. 3 (Summer 2005); AD to Cathy Itzin, April 19, 1990; AD to Ann-Claire Anderson, August 31, 1990—copies in MacKinnon Papers, SLH; Catharine MacKinnon, *Only Words*, Harvard Univ. Press, 1996. For a book-length account generally unsympathetic to the Dworkin/MacKinnon position, see Donald Alexander Downs, *The New Politics of Pornography* (Chicago: University of Chicago Press, 1989).

28. Until the internet made pornography in all its varying forms widely available to the general public, a number of scholars had continued to contend with issues related to the subject. Part of the difficulty in attempting any coherent summary of the ongoing debate is not only its breadth and complexity but also the fact that the disputants, in stating their own positions, often ignore the counter-arguments already put forward by others involved in the argument. As a non-specialist, I can do little more here than give voice to at least some of issues I've encountered that from my limited perspective have not been satisfactorily addressed, let alone "answered." I think, for example, that the apparently varying effects of violent, nonviolent, and "nonviolent but degrading" pornography on male viewers remains ill-defined and murky (see, for example, Lynne Segal, "Pornography and Violence: What the 'Experts' Really Say," *Feminist Review*, No. 36, Autumn, 1990). Similarly, I'd like to see the feminist "anti-censorship" forces explain (rather than merely state) what they refer to as the "chilling effect," especially for sexual minorities, of a civil rights ordinance (see Frances Ferguson, "Pornography: The Theory," *Critical Inquiry*, Vol. 21, No. 3, Spring, 1995). We would also profit, I believe, from a detailed discussion of how to measure—or whether it is possible to measure with any confident precision—when a sexual exchange can be said to have achieved an acceptably "mutual," "equal," "consensual" level of tenderness, intimacy, trust, and pleasure. When we applaud the presence of certain ingredients (tenderness, mutuality, et al.) in a relationship, are we mistakenly conflating love with sex? (as the mainstream culture insistently has through time). If so, does

it not riskily follow that casual, sexual "hook-ups" become implicitly castigated, with lifetime monogamy, in contrast, being elevated as superior morality?

In regard to the *industry* of pornography, we need to know more than we currently do about what percentage of the industry is devoted, say, to "mutually pleasurable" rather than "degrading" imagery and what gestures or acts are or are not constitutive of female subordination. I understand that pornography (or art, or books) are among of the building blocks in creating social reality, but so are poverty and racism, and how or why do we prioritize our concerns? (see Cynthia A. Stark, "Is Pornography an Action? The Causal vs. the Conceptual View of Pornography's Harm," *Social Theory and Practice*, Vol. 23, No. 2 [Summer, 1997]). Perhaps the overarching question in need of further explication is the causal relationship between the representation of an action and the action itself, with particular reference (if possible) to *which* individuals are more likely than others to move, swiftly or otherwise, from viewing an image to carrying out an action.

I think we also need to introduce more than we have into the debate over pornography the scholarly strategies and findings from the discipline of media studies. As Gail Dines has put it, "Media scholars accept that images have some effect in the real world"—that images do, overtly and subliminally, shape how we view ourselves and others, and how we judge the morality of certain actions. Dines usefully employs the analogy of the imagery connected to the history of racism. She points out that "the Stepin Fetchit images didn't change the views of the average white person so much as they delivered to the white population ideas that were floating around in the culture"—namely, that blacks are lazy, shiftless, sex-crazed, and violence-prone—"in a form that was compelling, easy to understand—and even easier to get away with." We need to deal more than we have with Dines' compelling question: "If racist porn images can have a detrimental effect on people of color in general, then why can't images of women—black, white, Asian, Latina—being choked and ejaculated on while being called cunts have a negative effect on women of all colors?" (Dines, *Pornland*, Beacon, 2010, 81–2, 87–8).

Finally, it seems to me critical that we further clarify the relationship between the First and the Fourteenth Constitutional Amendments. As Shannon Gilreath has succinctly put the issue (in *The End of Straight Supremacy* [Cambridge, UK: Cambridge University Press, 2011]), the two amendments are sometimes complementary and sometimes competing. He points out that for a very long time, public signs adorned the American landscape announcing NO BLACKS SERVED HERE and WHITES ONLY. Those "speech acts," clearly discriminatory, are now outside the legal pale. "The courts," Gilreath writes (pp. 126–28), "have weighed the competing rights of the speaker [the First Amendment] with those of the people affected by such speech and have held that equality rights [the Fourteenth Amendment] "were more important than the right to unfettered speech." Gilreath concludes—persuasively, in my view—that when the constitutional commitments both to speech and equality collide, "equality should prevail as the subsequent and preeminent principle of liberty." Ideas contrary to equality—Kill the Nigger! Kill the Jew!—can still be expressed, but they become within the bounds of Constitutional challenge and regulation.

29. For this and the following two paragraphs: AD to Laurence Tribe, May 1, 1985; AD to Moorcock, April 9, 1987 (Cambridge), ADP/SLH; Rich, "We Don't

Have to Come Apart Over Pornography: A Statement by Adrienne Rich," *off our backs*, July 1985. Andrea's article "Against the Male Flood" is collected in her *Letters from a War Zone*, 253–75.

30. For this and the following three paragraphs: MacKinnon, "An Open Letter to Adrienne Rich," *off our backs*, Vol. 15, No. 9 (October 1985) (a draft dated July 4, 1985 is in ADP/SLH); transcript of AD's untitled, undated letter to Adrienne, ADP/SLH. Also relevant, though I've not excerpted it here, is MacKinnon, "Coming Apart: Feminists and the Conflict Over Pornography," *off our backs*, Vol. 15, No. 6, June 1985. If Adrienne responded to Andrea, we can't now know: their correspondence (part of the Adrienne Rich Papers at SLH) is closed until 2025.

31. MacKinnon and Dworkin, *In Harm's Way: The Pornography Civil Rights Hearings* (Harvard Univ. Press, 1997) (henceforth cited as *Harm's Way*).

32. See, for example, Jessa Crispin, *Why I Am Not a Feminist* (Melville House, 2017); Ariel Levy, *Female Chauvinist Pigs* (New York: Free Press, 2005); Jane Gerhard, *Desiring Revolution* (New York: Columbia University Press, 2001); Andi Zeisler, *We Were Feminists Once* (New York: Public Affairs, 2016); Anne G. Sabo, *After Pornified* (Zero Books, 2012); Robert Jensen, *Pornography and the End of Masculinity* (South End Press, 2007); Robert Jensen, *The End of Patriarchy* (Spinifex, 2017); Gail Dines, *Pornland* (Boston: Beacon Press, 2010); Rebecca Traister, *Good and Mad* (New York: Simon & Shuster, 2018); and Christopher N. Kendall's brilliant *Gay Male Pornography* (UBC Press, 2004). Michael Kimmel has provocatively suggested that "both FACT and WAP each had it half right: feminism was about [both] protecting women who were harmed [i.e., Dworkin and MacKinnon] and freeing women to explore their own lusts [i.e., FACT]. They always talked past one another, as they do today in the conversations about 'sex work' and 'prostitution' and 'trafficking'" (Kimmel to me, May 9, 2019).

33. For this and the following paragraph: Richard Dyer, "Male Gay Porn: Coming To Terms," *Jump Cut: A Review of Contemporary Media*, No. 30, March 1985, 27–9. Another gay male critic, Tom Waugh, also expressed his "solidarity in words and actions with women's rightful denunciation of pornography as an instrument of antifeminist backlash." Waugh insisted that "anti-patriarchal gay men still have an important contribution to make" to the feminist debate on sexuality (Waugh, "Men's Pornography, Gay vs. Straight," *Jump Cut*, No. 30, March 1985). If so, gay male porn may not be the best vehicle—as Christopher N. Kendall has recently, and powerfully, argued in *Gay Male Pornography* (UBC Press, 2004): "Gay male pornography . . . works to maintain gender roles by encouraging gay men to adopt an identity that valorizes male dominance . . . hence [it is] anti-woman and does . . . a great deal to ensure the survival of a system of gender inequality that is degrading and dehumanizing and that reinforces, by sexualizing, the power dynamics that ensure systematic inequality" (p. 129).

34. B. Ruby Rich's remarkable review essay "Feminism and Sexuality in the 1980s" is in *Feminist Studies* Vol. 12, No. 3 (Fall 1986), 525–61; the Samois anthology was published by Alyson, 1982; *Against Sadomasochism*, edited by Robin Ruth Linden, et al., was published by Frog in the Well Press, 1982.

35. Reading Rich and MacDonald, I was reminded of the study I came across long ago (and may not remember with entire accuracy) that during the Blitz over England during World War II, far more men had nervous breakdowns than

did women; Scott MacDonald, "Confessions of a Feminist Porn Watcher," *Film Quarterly* 36 (Spring 1983); see also Philip Weiss, "Forbidden Pleasures: A Taste for Porn in a City of Women," *Harper's Magazine*, March 1986, 68–72.

36. AD to Jalna Hammer, March 5, 1986, ADP/SLH; *Sex & Justice*, March 1986; AD to Moorcock, June 7, 1987; transcript of Brownmiller interview with AD, August 10, 1998, ADP/SLH.

9: Writing

1. For this and following paragraph: Julie Melrose to Judy Klemsrud, September 4, 1985 (still and chill), "Andrea Dworkin Fights Back," *New Directions for Women*, Nov/Dec 1985.

2. AD to Charlee Hoyt, July 17, 1985, ADP/SLH.

3. For this and the following paragraph: AD to Linda Zlotnick, February 28, September 21, 1986; AD to Therese Stanton, August 14, 1985; AD to Valerie Harper, May 28, June 12, 1985, August 14, 19, 1986; AD to Gerry Spence, April 4, 1986, ADP/SLH; *The Philadelphia Inquirer*, July 21, 1985.

4. For Bourbon Street: https://chieforganizer.org/2019/06/13/the-story -behind-the-iconic-andrea-dworkin-bullhorn-picture/?fbclid=IwARODODEX OnoDSdhB6cQrQlkgQxcpzMXLq51JjnV4_clXz21QMpuvPpDUMoc. Andrea told the *New York Times* reporter, Judy Klemsrud, that "The National Organization for Women is incredibly cowardly and timid on the issue [of pornography] because they don't want to alienate their liberal supporters." She added a still more encompassing denunciation of liberals: "When the so-called liberals who claim to care about torture in prison in right-wing countries bring themselves to understand that a woman being tortured for entertainment is also a violation of women's rights, I'll be very grateful" ("Joining Hands in the Fight Against Pornography," *New York Times*, August 26, 1985). Klemsrud told Andrea and John that the *Times* refused to let her say that they were lesbian and gay (Stoltenberg to me, June 21, 2019). Andrea characterized the Wyoming postponement as "bizarre. . . . No new date has been set yet and even the place of the trial is uncertain. . . . Meanwhile *Screw* has taken over where *Hustler* left off; and what they are doing to me is vile beyond any imagining" (AD to Susanne Kappeler, August 16, 1986, ADP/SLH).

5. For this and the following paragraph: AD to Gerry Spence, August 30, 1985; AD to Charlee Hoyt, July 17, 1985; AD to Gale O'Brien, August 14, 1985—all in ADP/SLH; *Sojourner*, December 1985; Stoltenberg editorial, Issue #4/March 1986, *Sex & Justice*.

6. "Sex Busters," *TIME* magazine's cover story, July 21, 1986; *New York Times*, April 15, 1986.

7. For this and the following paragraph: FACT "Briefing," [n.d., 1985], Dorothy Allison Papers, RLD; David M. Edwards, "Politics and Pornography," http: //home.earthlink.net/-durangeodave/html/writing/Censorship.htm. See especially Whitney Strub's persuasive argument in his *Perversion for Profit* (198–206) that the Commission's hearings were stacked "toward anti-porn witnesses"—a charge weakened by his determined mockery (see, for example, p. 203) of female witnesses who felt they'd been personally harmed through pornography. Though

Strub's research is admirably comprehensive and his insight rich, I believe he's mistaken in describing the willingness of "anti-porn feminism . . . to call on the power of the state in the name of suppression" (Strub, *Perversion for Profit*, 214); certainly that mischaracterizes the MacKinnon/Dworkin position. Nor is he accurate in implying (215) that Andrea muted her criticism of capitalism—which she never did—to appease her "conservative allies." Strub's further characterization of Andrea's "publishing profile" as with "mass-market imprints and prestigious academic publishers (p. 247) is strangely at odds with her actual struggle to get published *at all*.

8. For this and the following discussion of the Commission's report: Carol Anne Douglas, "Pornography: The Meese Report," in *off our backs*, Vol. 16, No. 8, August/September 1986; AD to Theresa Funiociello, June 12, 1985, ADP/SLH; Barbara Ehrenreich, "The Story of Ed," *Mother Jones*, October 1986; *Time* magazine, June 21, 1986. Two of the four women on the eleven-member panel—Judith Becker, professor of clinical psychology at Columbia and Ellen Levine, editor of *Woman's Day* magazine—dissented from the report. They disagreed with the conclusion that a clear-cut causal link between violent pornography and violence against women had been found and further argued that "no self-respecting investigator would accept conclusions" from a commission that had done no original research.

9. Walter Kendrick, *The Secret Museum* (Berkeley: University of California Press, 1987).

10. David M. Edwards, *Politics and Pornography*.

11. Edward Donnerstein, the other expert whose testimony both sides in the debate would cite, later made a similar point: he stressed "that his studies showed the effects of violent images on attitudes, not the effects of sexually explicit materials on behavior" (as quoted in Lisa Duggan, "Censorship in the Name of Feminism," *Village Voice*, October 16, 1984).

12. *Ice and Fire* (London: Secker & Warburg, 1986), 47–48.

13. For this and the following three paragraphs: AD, *Intercourse* (New York: Basic Books, 1987), 83, 135, 156–60, 230, 246–7.

14. Susan Brownmiller to AD, n.d. [October 1986], ADP/SLH; AD to Brownmiller, October 16, 1986, Brownmiller Papers. Perhaps contributing was Brownmiller's negative reaction to the ordinance campaign. In regard to the Minneapolis ordinance, as she wrote to me years later, "I thought it was terrible and unconstitutional, and told her [Andrea] that I would not support it." Brownmiller to me, December 9, 2019.

15. AD to Leah Fritz, April 21, 1987; AD to Michael Moorcock, March 19, April 9, 1987, ADP/SLH.

16. AD to Gerry Spence, May 3, 1986, ADP/SLH; Marilyn French, "A Lyrical Novel of Violence and Exploitation," *Ms.*, April 1987; Louise Armstrong, "Publish and Be Damned," *Women's Review of Books*, May 1986; Kitty MacKinnon to AD, August 4, 1983, ADP/SLH.

17. For this and the following paragraph: *New York Times*, May 3, 24, 1987. MacKinnon wrote a letter to the *Times* protesting the Sternhell review

(MacKinnon to Iacovelli, May 6, 1987, MacKinnon Papers, SLH).

18. For this and the following two paragraphs: *The Nation*, May 30, August 1/18, 1987; AD to Erica Jong, June 8, 1987; AD to Jan Raymond, June 12, 1987; AD to Linda Steele, June 16, 1987; Steele to AD, June 22, 1987, ADP/SLH.

19. AD to Raymond, June 12, 1987; AD to Moorcock and Steele, July 28, 1987; AD to Elaine Markson, July 23, 1987, ADP/SLH.

20. AD to Moorcock, April 9, June 12, 1987; AD to Sarah LeFanu, June 12, 1987 (garbage), ADP/SLH. *New Directions for Women*, July/Aug 1987; *Reader* (Chicago), October 9, 1987; Paul Seidman to AD, July 1, 1987; AD to Seidman, July 8, 1987, ADP/SLH; *Sojourner*, July, September, December, 1987.

21. The review by Roy Porter in the *London Review of Books* (June 25, 1987) was even more venomous than that in the *New York Times*; Porter called her "a sick lady" who writes "offensive, abominable crap." Lynn Rosen interview with AD, *New Directions for Women*, July/August 1987; MacKinnon to AD, August 4, 1983, ADP/SLH.

22. AD to Alice Schwarzer, July 28, August 2, August 10, 1987; Anne Soyland to AD, August 7, 1987; AD to Agnete Strom, August 18, 1987, ADP/SLH.

23. For this and the following two paragraphs: AD to Linda Steele, August 3, 24, 1987, ADP/SLH. Steinem wasn't the only political friend from earlier times that Andrea still saw. She and Robin Morgan tended to have dinner together roughly once a month and, Andrea wrote, "it always brings me up" (AD to Moorcock, August 10, 1987, ADP/SLH). She also—"at the instigation of Phyllis Chesler"— saw Kate Millett now and then, which she did not enjoy. She described one such evening in a letter to Linda Steele, August 24, 1987, ADP/SLH): "I venerate Kate for all she has taught me; but she has retreated into an almost mindless leftism, it's like autism isn't it? Kate [had] signed the FACT brief even though she didn't *read* it—say 'anti-censorship' and she signs. Her friends have tried to get her to understand what she's done wrong. Kitty has spent much time with her. I haven't the heart."

Subsequently, Andrea and Erica Jong tangled briefly over a misunderstanding that they patched up rather quickly, but Erica did make it clear that she opposed the ordinance route. She did not believe, she wrote Andrea, that it was "depictions of violence against women that *creates* violence against women, because the deep sexism of our culture needs many broader & more far-reaching remedies. . . . We need equal pay for equal work. We need the end of sexual stereotyping in the media. We need health care for women & children." (Erica Jong to AD, April 4, 1993; AD to Jong, April 13, May 25, 1993, ADP/SLH).

24. AD to Rosemary McIntosh, September 7, 1987; AD to Moorcock and Steele, September 4, 1987; AD to Gerry Spence, September 7, 1987, ADP/SLH; *Dworkin v. Hustler Magazine, Inc.*, 668 F. Supp. 1408 (C.D. Cal. 1987).

25. For this and the following four paragraphs: AD to Moorcock, November 15, December 10, 1987; AD to Cathy Itzin, December 15, 21, 1987; AD to Alice Schwarzer, August 2, 1987; AD to Mark and Eva Dworkin, January 25, 1988; AD to Linda Steele, August 24, 1987; AD to Kathy Norris, February 8, 1988; —all in ADP/SLH; AD to Robin Morgan, March 2, 1988, Robin Morgan Papers, RLD;

AD to Cookie Teer, December 3, 1986 (England), Teer Papers, RLD.

26. For this and the following three paragraphs: AD to Sarah LeFanu, November 16, 1987; AD to Moorcock, March 19, 1987, December 23, 1987, January 21, March 20, 1988, ADP/SLH.

27. AD to Moorcock, June 12, 1987, February 26, March 20, 1988; AD to Suzanne Kappeler, December 29, 1987, ADP/SLH.

28. For this and the following paragraph: AD to Moorcock, February 26, 1988, ADP/SLH; AD to Robin Morgan, March 2, 1988, Morgan to AD, n.d., Morgan Papers, RLD.

29. AD to Morgan, March 2, 1988; AD to Moorcock, April 6, 1988; AD to Linda Steele, May 8, 1988, ADP/SLH.

30. Conversation with John Stoltenberg, February 18, 2019. See Andrea's vivid description of life in the East Village in *Ice and Fire*, 106–9.

31. For this and the following two paragraphs: AD to Valerie Harper, August 20, 1988; AD to Kathy Norris, August 20, 1988; AD to Suzanne Kappeler, August 30, 1988, ADP/SLH.

32. For this and the following paragraph: AD to Valerie Harper, August 20, 1988; AD to Cathy Itzin, September 26, 1988; AD to Moorcock and Steele, September 6, 1988—all in ADP/SLH.

33. AD to Lesley Bryce, November 9, 1988; AD to Alice Shalvi, December 10, 1988; AD to Cathy Itzin, December 29, 1988, ADP/SLH.

34. For this and the following four paragraphs: conversation with John Stoltenberg, February 18, 2019; AD to Sarah LeFanu, November 16, 1987; AD to Jane Wood, May 1, 1989, ADP/SLH; AD, "What Battery Really Is," reprinted as the last piece in the American edition of *Letters from a War Zone* (New York: Dutton, 1989), 329–34.

10: Mercy

1. AD to Sharon Doubiago, July 17, 1989; AD to Moorcock and Steele, July 17, 1989, ADP/SLH.

2. AD to Kathy Norris and David Dwyer, August 21, 1989; AD to Moorcock and Steele, August 28, December 4, 27; AD to Charles Morgan, July 28, 1989, ADP/SLH. Bosworth's affidavit is in ADP/SLH.

3. For this and the following three paragraphs: AD to Charles Morgan, July 28, 1989; AD to Moorcock and Steele, August 28, 1989; AD to Norris and Dwyer, August 21, 1989, ADP/SLH; *Penthouse*, April 1987.

4. For this and the following paragraph: AD to Moorcock and Steele, December 4, 1989, April 17, May 21, 1990; AD to Susanne Kappeler, May 29, 1990, ADP/SLH. A copy of the settlement agreement, dated May 17, 1990, is in ADP/SLH.

5. AD to Kappeler, May 29, 1990, ADP/SLH. Similarly, when John Herman, the Houghton Mifflin editor, wanted to do *Mercy* in the United States, the publisher "on principle" refused (AD to Moorcock and Steele, March 8, 1990, ADP/SLH).

6. AD to Moorcock and Steele, May 21, 1990, ADP/SLH. A sample of the divergent reviews: *Publishers Weekly*, July 25, 1991 (*Mercy* "brilliantly captures the narrator's mental and physical degradation") vs. the *Tribune*, October 5, 1990 (". . . breathless . . . sometimes clumsy"). For two of the more considered, yet ultimately negative reviews, see Wendy Steiner, "Declaring War on Men," *New York Times*, September 15, 1991; and Roz Kaveney, "*Mercy* by Andrea Dworkin," *Feminist Review*, No. 38 (Summer, 1991), who accused Andrea of "messianic fantasies," thinking of herself as "Everywoman," and claiming superior moral insight.

7. The "humanizing" argument derives from Marisa Anne Pagnattaro, "The Importance of Andrea Dworkin's 'Mercy': Mitigating Circumstances and Narrative Jurisprudence," *Frontiers: A Journal of Women Studies*, Vol. 19, No. 1; Michael Moorcock, "Political Gets Too Personal," *New Statesman*, May 27, 1988.

8. For a sampling of the reviews: *Independent*, October 13, 1990; *Literary Review*, October 1990; *Tribune*, October 5, 1990; *Sunday Correspondent*, October 7, 1990; *Sunday Times*, October 14, 1990. See also, AD, five-page typescript, "The Reviews of *Mercy* in the United Kingdom: I Answer," ADP/SLH.

9. Martha C. Nussbaum, *Sex and Social Justice* (especially ch. 9: "Rage and Reason") (Oxford, UK: Oxford University Press, 1999). Nussbaum had separately reviewed *Mercy* in the *Boston Review of Books*, and Andrea had sent her a scorching letter in response: "You don't need to like my work to write about it in a way that is not thoroughly and absolutely insulting" (AD to Nussbaum, March 14, 1994, copy in MacKinnon Papers, SLH).

10. For two additional sympathetic readings of Andrea, see Rosa A. Eberly, *Citizen Critics: Literary Public Spheres* (especially ch. 5: "Andrea Dworkin's *Mercy*: Pain and Silence in the 'War Zone'"); and Cindy Jenefsky with Ann Russo, *Without Apology: Andrea Dworkin's Art and Politics* (Westview Press, 1998).

11. https://drive.google.com/drive/folders/11KL14jhWQjjuWz4Gptlvpj5lnrw7uQ_z

12. Walter Kendrick, *The Secret Museum* (Berkeley: University of California Press, 1987).

13. For this and the following paragraph: Rebecca Traister, *Good and Mad: The Revolutionary Power of Women's Anger* (New York: Simon & Schuster, 2018). See also Soraya Chemaly, *Rage Becomes Her: The Power of Women's Anger* (New York: Atria, 2018).

14. For this and the following paragraph: AD to Linda Steele, August 17, 1990, ADP/SLH; "Andrea Dworkin Interview," *off our backs*, January 1990; AD to Robin Morgan, February 8, 1990, Morgan Papers, RDL. In regard to her own self-identification as "lesbian," as early as 1978 when an interviewer (Andrea herself) remarked, "There are a lot of rumors about your lesbianism. No one quite seems to know what you do with whom," Andrea's response was "Good" ("Nervous Interview," in AD, *Letters from a War Zone*, 59). Many years later, Ariel Levy provocatively quoted one of Andrea's "closest friends" as saying, "In 30-plus years of knowing her, I've never heard of a single romance with a woman—not one." Levy herself comments that in Andrea's writings, "there are too many smoldering descriptions of heterosexual sex to count, but the mentions of lesbianism are either bloodless . . . or funny" (http://nymag.com/nymetro/news/people/features/11907/index4.html#print). *Behaviorally*, we have plenty of evidence of Andrea's sexual experiences up through the late seventies, but thereafter, aside from a very

few hints, there's almost no evidence of a lesbian romance or sexual encounter. It may be that Andrea's steady increase in weight in the later years of her life was related, as is often the case, to the earlier sexual trauma with Iwan; as the old chestnut has it: "the overweight girl is the overlooked girl." But we need to be cautious about equating *behavior* with *feelings*. If Andrea at some point stopped having sexual *feelings* for other women—or indeed sexual feelings in general—she never said so.

15. AD to Moorcock, December 27, 1989; AD to Jane Wood, January 1, 1990; AD to Florence King, February 16, 1990, ADP/SLH.

16. AD, "Terror, Torture, and Resistance," keynote speech in May 1991 to the Canadian Mental Health Conference on "Women and Mental Health"; first published in *Canadian Woman Studies; Les Cahiers de la Femme*, fall 1991, Vol. 12, No. 1.

17. For this and the following paragraph: AD to Mark and Eva Dworkin, January 25, 1988; AD to Moorcock and Steele, December 4, 1989, ADP/SLH.

18. For this and the following paragraph: AD to Harry Dworkin, January 10; AD to Joyce Keener, March 19; AD to Linda Steele, November 18; AD to Mark Dworkin, November 23, December 16, 23—all 1991, all ADP/SLH; AD to Moorcock, February 1, 28, March 4, May 10; AD to Florence King, May 13—all 1992, all ADP/SLH; AD to Leah Fritz, December 28, 1992, Leah Fritz Papers, RLD.

19. For this and the following four paragraphs: AD to Moorcock and Steele, September 1, 1992; AD to Agnete Stromn, September 15, 1992; AD to Scheerer and Reemtsma, December 22, 1992, ADP/SLH.

20. The key documents detailing the dispute are AD to Markson, September 17, 18, 30, 1992; Judith Herman to Simon, September 29, 1992; AD to Moorcock and Steele, October 1, 1992; Melissa Farley to Downer, October 19, 1992; AD to Susan Hunter, October 25, 1992; Chalker/Downer/Hekert to "Dear Friends," November 16, 1992; Wendy Smith to AD, January 25, 1993; Barbara Ehrenreich to AD, March 5, 1993; Chalker and Downer to Gloria Steinem, September 15, 1993; Chalker and Downer to AD, February 27, 1994; AD to Chalker and Downer, November 5, 1993, March 24, 1994—all in ADP/SLH; *New York Observer*, October 26, 1992.

21. AD to Moorcock, February 28, 1992, ADP/SLH.

22. John Irving, "Pornography and the New Puritans," *New York Times*, March 29, 1992.

23. AD, "Pornography and the New Puritans: Letters From Andrea Dworkin and Others," *New York Times*, May 3, 1992; Gail Dines, *Pornland: How Porn Has Hijacked Our Sexuality* (Boston: Beacon Press, 2010), especially chapter five. Dines also points out, importantly, that contrary to critics who characterize the Dworkin/MacKinnon position as "watching pornography leads men to rape women," neither of them ever "saw porn in such simplistic terms. Rather, both argued that porn has a complicated and multilayered effect on male sexuality, and that rape, rather than simply being caused by porn, is a cultural practice that has been woven into the fabric of a male-dominated society" (page 85). For a discussion of the research up to 1993 linking porn consumption and violence against women, see Catherine Itzin in *New Statesman & Society*, January 31, 1993, ADP/SLH. For

the post-1993 period, Dines primarily cites the following studies: Neil Malamuth, Tamara Addison, and Mary Koss, "Pornography and Sexual Aggression: Are There Reliable Effects and Can We Understand them?" *Annual Review of Sex Research* Vol. 11 (2000); Pamela Paul, *Pornified: How Pornography Is Transforming Our Lives, Our Relationships, and Our Families* (New York: Time Books, 2005); and Dolf Zillman, "Effects of Prolonged Consumption of Pornography," in *Pornography: Research Advances and Policy Considerations*, Zillman and Jennings Bryant eds. (Erlbaum, 1989). Additionally, there is Max Waltman's notable summation of the data in "Rethinking Democracy: Legal Challenges to Pornography and Sex Inequality in Canada and the United States, *Political Research Quarterly*, Vol. 63, No. 1 (March 2010)—henceforth "Waltman, 'Rethinking Democracy.'" For an invaluable discussion of the roots of the ideological division between pro- and anti-pornography feminists, see Ronald J. Berger, Patricia Searles, and Charles E. Cottle, "Ideological Contours of the Contemporary Pornography Debate: Divisions and Alliances," *Frontiers: A Journal of Women Studies*, Vol. 11, No. 2/3 (1990).

24. AD to Erica Jong, March 26, 1993, ADP/SLH; Waltman, "Rethinking Democracy," 231. For more detail, see Carolyn Bronstein, *Battling Pornography: The American Feminist Anti-Pornography Movement, 1976–1986* (Cambridge, UK: Cambridge University Press, 2011), and Brenda Cossman et al., *Bad Attitudes on Trial: Pornography, Feminism and the Butler Decision* (Toronto: University of Toronto Press, 1997). For a more negative assessment of the effects of the *Butler* decision, see Cossman, Bell, Gotell, Ross, *Bad Attitude/s on Trial: Pornography, Feminism, and the Butler Decision* (Univ. of Toronto Press, 1997). In her brilliant article, "A Sensible Anti-porn Feminism" (*Ethics*, July 2007, 674–715), A.W. Eaton has dissected the points of similarity and difference between pro- and anti-porn feminists with illuminating skill.

25. A copy of the conference report, *The Sex Panic*, with highlights from the proceedings, is in the Ellen Willis Papers, SLH.

26. For further distinctions along these lines, see Alexandra G. Bennett, "Theory to Practice: Catharine MacKinnon, Pornography, and Canadian Law," *Modern Language Studies*, Vol. 27, No. 3/4 (Autumn/Winter, 1997); Berger, Searles, and Cottle, "Ideological Contours of the Contemporary Pornography Debate: Divisions and Alliances," *Frontiers: A Journal of Women Studies*, Vol. 11, No. 2/3 (1990); and, in particular, Nancy Whittier's incisive article, "Rethinking Coalitions: Anti-Pornography Feminists, Conservatives, and Relationships between Collaborative Adversarial Movements," *Social Problems*, Vol. 61, No. 2 (May 2014).

27. For this and next two paragraphs: MacKinnon to Jennifer Brown, January 7; AD to "Naomi," September 28; AD to Michele Landsberg, December 6; AD to Steinem, December 6; AD to Kathleen Mahoney, December 6 (twice); MacKinnon to AD, December 6, 16; AD to MacKinnon, December 7—all 1993 ADP/SLH; MacKinnon to Michael Levitas, January 1, 1994 (gay/lesbian), ADP/SLH; AD keynote speech at October 28–30, 1992, Austin, Texas conference, ADP/SLH; *New York Times*, December 4, 1993.

28. For this and the following two paragraphs: AD to Erin Shaw (LEAF staff lawyer), April 29, 1991, Susan Brownmiller Papers, RLD. For some of the tensions that developed between Andrea and Kitty over the *Butler* decision, see AD

to Kitty, May 8, 25, August 7, 14, 1994; Kitty to AD, May 23, August 13, 14, 1994, ADP/SLH.

29. STATEMENT BY CATHARINE A. MACKINNON AND ANDREA DWORKIN REGARDING CANADIAN CUSTOMS AND LEGAL APPROACHES TO PRONOGRAPHY, six-page typescript, ADP/SLH. See also Michele Landsberg, "Supreme Court Porn Ruling Is Ignored," *Toronto Star*, December 14, 1993; Robin Morgan to *New York Times*, February 2, 1995, Morgan Papers, RLD. There is also considerable correspondence in ADP/SLH between Andrea and Kitty, especially between May and August 1994, discussing the issues at stake and the wording of the statement.

30. AD to Michael Levitas (*Times*), December 27, 1993, ADP/SLH.

11: Prelude to Israel

1. AD, *Heartbreak: The Political Memoir of a Feminist Militant* (New York: Basic Books, 2002); "Israel: Whose Country Is It Anyway?," originally published in *Ms.*, September/October 1990, and reprinted in *Life and Death: Unapologetic Writings on the Continuing War Against Women* (New York: The Free Press, 1997), 217–39.

2. For this and the following two paragraphs: AD, transcript of nine-page "The Sexual Mythology of Anti-Semitism," ADP/SLH; AD, "Israel: Whose Country Is It Anyway?"; AD to Mark Dworkin, December 23, 1991, ADP/SLH.

3. For this and the following two paragraphs: "Take No Prisoners," *The Guardian*, May 12, 2000.

4. For this and the following five paragraphs: Jil Clark interview with AD, *Gay Community News*, Vol. 8, No.1 (July 19, 1980).

5. AD to Moorcock and Steele, July 19, 1993, ADP/SLH.

6. AD to Moorcock and Steele, June 21, 1993; AD, "Aftermath" (ms.), ADP/SLH.

7. For this and the following paragraph: AD's proposal to the Diana Foundation, and the correspondence surrounding the grant are in the Merle Hoffman papers, RLD.

8. AD, "Prostitution and Male Supremacy" (ms.), and "Pornography Happens to Women" (ms.) 1993/4, ADP/SLH. Both are reprinted in AD, *Life and Death*.

9. John Stoltenberg letter to "Dear Friends," May 1994, ADP/SLH. John had long been part of the Task Force on Pornography of the National Organization for Men Against Sexism (as of 1990 known as NOMAS, the National Organization for Changing Men); he had also been active on behalf of local efforts to pass the ordinance (http://nomas.org/history/).

10. For the next section: AD, "The Real Pornography of a Brutal War Against Women," *Los Angeles Times*, September 5, 1993; "The U.S. Holocaust Memorial Museum: Is Memory Male?, published in *Ms.*, November/December 1994; and the forty-page manuscript version ("Pictures at an Exhibition: The United States Holocaust Museum") in ADP/SLH. All quotes, unless otherwise indicated, are from the manuscript version.

11. Andrea was finally able to print "The ACLU: Bait and Switch" in her 1993 collection, *Letters from a War Zone* (New York: Lawrence Hill Books, 1993).

12. For this and the following paragraph: Diana E.H. Russell, "Nadine Strossen: The Pornography Industry's Wet Dream," *On the Issues*, summer 1995. For another insightful anti-Strossen review, see Mark Hussey writing separately in the same issue (summer, 1995) of *On the Issues*. Hussey particularly emphasized a point Andrea had long stressed about the class dimension—who did or did not have access—of the free speech issue: "the abstract principle of absolute freedom of speech will tend to work to the advantage of those whose speech is already privileged by the gendered social relations that exist."

13. Robin Morgan to the *New York Times*, February 2, 1995, Morgan Papers, RLD; AD to Steinem, December 6, 1993, ADP/SLH. In an interview with Vance Lehakuhl (*Z*, May 1995) and in an article for *USA Today* (January 12, 1995), Strossen reiterates most of the same views, though in a still less nuanced way. For example: "a causal connection has *never* been established" between porn and violence toward women"; the MacDworkinites' view is "that *all* sex is inherently degrading to women"; "it is more important than ever for the public to understand the link between the pro-censorship feminists and the right wing." And yet again, this time in *USA Today*: "Anti-pornography feminists believe sex itself is degrading to women"; the MacDworkinites "are a reincarnation of puritanical, Victorian notions that feminists have long tried to consign to the dust"; "the pro-censorship feminists have tried to distance themselves from traditional conservatives like Jesse Helms . . . but both groups are united by their common hatred of sexual expression and a fondness for censorship."

14. For this and the following two paragraphs: AD, "Trapped in a Pattern of Pain Where No One Can Help," "In Nicole Brown Simpson's Words," and "Domestic Violence: Trying to Flee" appeared consecutively in the June 26, 1994, January 29, 1995, and October 8, 1995, issues of the *Los Angeles Times*. Andrea reprinted them in *Life and Death*, The Free Press, 1997, 41–50.

15. Hanna Rosin, "The Larry Flynt Revival," *The New Republic*, January 5 & 12, 1997; Gloria Steinem, "Hollywood Cleans Up Hustler," op-ed *New York Times*, January 7, 1997; AD to Susan Brownmiller, January 9, 1997, Brownmiller Papers, RLD.

16. AD to Steinem, October 15, 1997 (Duffy), ADP/SLH; Preface to *Life and Death*, xvii.

17. AD to MacKinnon, March 5, 1995, MacKinnon Papers, SLH.

12: Scapegoat

1. AD, "What Feminist Jurisprudence Means to Me" (ms.), February 27, 1998, ADP/SLH.

2. AD, "Dear Bill and Hillary," *Guardian of London*, January 29, 1998.

3. For this and the following paragraph: John Stoltenberg to "Dear Friends," September 1998; AD, "the meaning of feminism to me now" (ms.), ADP/SLH;

transcript of Brownmiller interview with AD, August 10, 1998 (internet), ADP/SLH.

4. Curiously, in her vast bibliography Andrea never mentions the important 1997 book, *Unheroic Conduct*, by Daniel Boyarin, a towering figure in Talmudic Studies, whose basic findings agree with her views on the shifting ideal of Jewish manhood. It's hard to avoid the sense, deeply touching, that Andrea's zealous scholarship is somehow a reflection of and compensation for her father's thwarted ambition to complete his doctorate; her book can be incidentally seen as a way of fulfilling his dream—awarding him full accreditation.

5. AD to Cookie Teer, April 18, 1999 (cold), ADP/SLH; John Stoltenberg, *Aftermath: Andrea Dworkin's Last Rape*, http://archive.feministtimes.com/andrea -dworkins-last-rape/.

6. The account combines Beth Ribet's "First Year: An Interview with John Stoltenberg," March 11, 2006 (http://www.andreadworkin.net/memorial /stoltinterview.html) with Stoltenberg, "My Life with Andrea Dworkin," courtesy Stoltenberg; Stoltenberg, *Aftermath*, http://archive.feministtimes.com/andrea -dworkins-last-rape/. See also, Ariel Levy, "The Prisoner of Sex," *New York*: http: //nymag.com/nymetro/news/people/features/11907/index4.html#print.

7. For this and the following paragraph: *The Guardian*, June 2, 2000; *The New Statesman*, June 5, 2000.

8. Catherine Bennett, "Doubts About Dworkin," *The Guardian*, June 7, 2000.

9. Richard Bernstein, "Confronting the Barbarity of Hatred," *New York Times*, July 13, 2000.

10. *The Times*, March 2, 2001; AD, thirteen-page ms. "Landscape of the Ordinary: Violence Against Women"; Robin Morgan to AD, April 9, 2001; Morgan notation May 7, 2001; Morgan to AD, June 17, 2002; Morgan to Stoltenberg, July 9, 2002—all in Robin Morgan Papers, RLD.

11. Ariel Levy, "The Prisoner of Sex," http://nymag.com/mymetro/news /people/features/11907. For the account that follows, the essential source is: AD, "Through the Pain Barrier," https://www.theguardian.com/books/2005/apr23 /features.weekend

12. In November 1999, John got a position as managing editor of *Golf Digest Woman*, and the benefits took effect just in time to cover Andrea's hospitalization costs (Stoltenberg to me, June 21, 2019).

13. Beth Ribet, "First Year: An Interview with John Stoltenberg," March 11, 2006, http://www.andreadworkin.net/memorial/stoltinterview.html.

14. David Frum had a more mixed reaction to the evening: "I can't say I was charmed. But despite myself, I was impressed. Dworkin was a woman of deep and broad reading . . . her mind ranged free . . . I'll just say that although I would never, ever have expected to think so: She'll be missed" (*New York Times*, "Week in Review," April 17, 2005).

15. Beth Ribet interview with Stoltenberg, March 11, 2006: http:// andreadworkin.net/memorial/stoltinterview.html; Stoltenberg to me, June 28, 2019.

16. The manuscript is not in SLH; my copy, courtesy of John Stoltenberg, is John's excerpted version, which he retitled *Aftermath* and (as I've mentioned earlier) had been edited for the stage by Adam Thorburn. The staged reading was performed seven times in New York City in 2014, and nine times in Montreal in 2015 (https://howlround.com/directing-andrea-dworkins-aftermath). "My Suicide" has also been excerpted in Johanna Fateman and Amy Scholder, *Last Days at Hot Slit* (Semiotext(e), 2019), 375–93.

17. For one of the more egregious recent examples of the ongoing mockery and misinterpretation, see Erica West, "The Pitfalls of Radical Feminism" (https://jacobinmag.com/2017/radical-feminism-second-wave-class), in which she characterizes Dworkin and MacKinnon as "relying on the state for censorship"—a total misreading of the model ordinance—and being "noticeably silent on the question of racism" (a claim easily disproven by even a cursory reading of Andrea's essays). Moreover, a prominent thread of "third-wave feminism"—exemplified in the work of Katie Roiphe, *The Morning After* (New York: Little Brown, 1993) and Rene Denfield, *The New Victorians* (New York: Warner, 1995)—has also continued to single out Dworkin, MacKinnon, and Robin Morgan as representative of "victim feminists" with an anti-sex agenda, in contrast to their own focus on expanding sexual possibilities for women and treating sexual pleasure as a positive good. Their analysis manages simultaneously to seriously misinterpret Dworkin/MacKinnon/Morgan and to ignore such decidedly pro-sex feminists of the second wave as Susie Bright and Gayle Rubin. For an antidote to Roiphe/Denfield, see Astrid Henry's astute analysis in *Not My Mother's Sister: Generational Conflict and Third-Wave Feminism* (Bloomington: Indiana University Press, 2004); as well as Andi Zeisler's tart, insightful *We Were Feminists Once* (New York: Public Affairs, 2016) for its reminder to the third wave "that while feminist movements seek to change systems, marketplace feminism prioritizes individuals." Alice Echols, in turn, has emphasized an additional concern: "Those of us who teach college are witnessing a sea change on our campuses as students mobilize for greater protection from all manner of danger, sometimes including our own dangerous ideas. Feminists are not the only students insisting on a less discomfiting curriculum, one that comes with trigger warnings and safe rooms, but they have sometimes played an outsized role in such efforts" (Echols, "Retrospective: Tangled Up in Pleasure and Danger," *Signs*, Vol. 42, No. 1 (2016).

Recently, some generous (and prominent) assessments of Andrea's role in the feminist movement have been appearing, beginning with Gail Dines, *Pornland* (Boston: Beacon Press, 2010), and then—primarily in response to the appearance of Johanna Fateman and Amy Scholder's anthology of Andrea's writing, *Last Days at Hot Slit* (semiotext(e), 2019)—Lauren Oyler, "Sex Ed: How to Read Andrea Dworkin," *The New Yorker*, April 1, 2019; Michelle Goldberg, "Not the Fun Kind of Feminism," *New York Times*, February 24, 2019; Moira Donegan, "Sex During Wartime: The Return of Andrea Dworkin's Radical Vision," *BOOKFORUM*, February/March 2019; Jennifer Szalai, "A New Light for a Feminist and Her Work," *New York Times*, March 13, 2019; Julie Bindel, "Why Andrea Dworkin Is the Radical, Visionary Feminist We Need in Our Terrible Times," April 16, 2019;

Jeremy Lybarger, "Finally Seeing Andrea," *Boston Review*, February 23, 2019; Maryse Meijer, "How to Fuck Your Neighbor," *Los Angeles Times*, April 23, 2019; Elaine Blair, "Fighting for Her Life," *New York Review of Books*, June 27, 2019; and Charlotte Shane, "What Men Want," *Dissent*, Spring 2019.

Yet even some of these respectful appreciations continue to repeat some dated misrepresentations. For example, Moira Donegan in *BOOKFORUM* claims that Andrea and Kitty "partnered with religious and social conservatives . . . working together to try to get" the ordinance passed. They *never* worked together. Nor did Andrea (as Donegan has it) try "to wield the power of the state against pornography." The precise opposite is true: she and Kitty designed the ordinance to allow for *civil* (not criminal) cases, thereby deliberately circumventing any prospect of involving or augmenting governmental power.

Index

The abbreviation AD refers to Andrea Dworkin.

victim's compensation act, 242
as violation of women's civil rights,
173, 174, 184, 190, 192, 199, 201,
204–5, 206, 260, 267, 328n17
violence against women portrayed
in, 90–91, 111, 129, 131, 133, 135,
207
Ellen Willis on, 150
Women's Anti-Defamation League
statement against, 111–12
Porsche, Ferdinand, 119
Porter, Roy, 319n21
postmodernism, 272
Pottinger, Stan, 157
poverty, of women, 70, 120, 152–54,
175, 184–85, 188, 194–95, 205–6,
208, 325n12
Powell, Betty, 114
Presidential Commission on
Pornography, 202, 203
prostitution
AD on, 168, 173, 246, 255–56,
281–82
of children, 211–12
in Israel, 253, 270
liberals on, 215
in Linda Lovelace case, 157
of transsexuals, 1616
Women against Pornography's
position on, 132
Provo (Dutch anarchist movement)
AD's writings on, 33–35, 36, 39, 43,
293n7
Corenlius Dirk de Bruin as
member of, 36–37, 41
manifesto of, 31, 293n6
performance art of, 32
role of drugs in, 34, 35, 37
Roel Van Duyn as member of, 35
waning influence of, 33, 34–35, 37
White Bicycle Plan, 32
Publishers Weekly, 95

Quest, 103–4

Rabelais, François, 272
race and racism
housing discrimination, 194
imagery connected to, 315n28

in pornographic imagery, 149
in pornography ordinance battles,
190
racist speech, 195, 205
racial equality
AD's commitment to, 14–15, 70, 79
Harry Dworkin's commitment to,
6, 7
Sylvia Dworkin's commitment to, 7
Radcliffe College,
Dworkin/Dershowitz debate
(May 13, 1981), 155–56
Rader, Dotson, 299n23
Radical America, 120
Ramsingh decision (1985), 243
Random House, 84, 85, 103
Rankine decision (1983), 243
rape
AD's experiences of, 26, 48,
274–75, 276, 277–78, 282, 286
AD's view of, 236, 241, 245–46,
260, 278, 322n23
and effect of pornography on
behavior, 173, 175, 177, 178
federal civil remedy for gender-
based violence, 190
gang rape, 156, 175
incestuous rape, 211
Catharine MacKinnon on, 245–46,
260, 311n7, 322n23
marital rape, 49, 153, 157, 167
Martha Nussbaum on, 234
in pornography, 188, 204
rate of, 135
Diana E. H. Russell on, 261
John Stoltenberg as rape prevention
educator, 110
women's lack of free speech in, 155,
185
rape crisis centers, 153, 241, 274, 282
Rat, 57
Raymond, Janice, 161
Reagan, Ronald, 152–53, 184, 191,
203, 260
REDRESS, 66, 297n12
Redstockings, 57, 82–85, 87
religious beliefs, legal protection of,
192

About the Author

Martin Duberman is Distinguished Professor of History Emeritus at City University of New York, where he founded and directed the Center for Lesbian and Gay Studies. He is the author of numerous histories, biographies, memoirs, essays, plays, and novels, which include *Cures: A Gay Man's Odyssey, Paul Robeson, Stonewall, Black Mountain: An Exploration in Community, The Worlds of Lincoln Kirstein, Saving Remnant, Hold Tight Gently*, and more than a dozen others. He is the recipient of the Bancroft Prize, multiple Lambda Literary Awards, and the Lifetime Achievement Award from the American Historical Association, and he has been a finalist for the Pulitzer Prize and the National Book Award. In 2012, Duberman received an honorary Doctor of Humane Letters from Amherst College and in 2017 an honorary Doctor of Letters from Columbia University.

Publishing in the Public Interest

Thank you for reading this book published by The New Press. The New Press is a nonprofit, public interest publisher. New Press books and authors play a crucial role in sparking conversations about the key political and social issues of our day.

We hope you enjoyed this book and that you will stay in touch with The New Press. Here are a few ways to stay up to date with our books, events, and the issues we cover:

- Sign up at www.thenewpress.com/subscribe to receive updates on New Press authors and issues and to be notified about local events
- Like us on Facebook: www.facebook.com/newpressbooks
- Follow us on Twitter: www.twitter.com/thenewpress

Please consider buying New Press books for yourself; for friends and family; or to donate to schools, libraries, community centers, prison libraries, and other organizations involved with the issues our authors write about.

The New Press is a 501(c)(3) nonprofit organization. You can also support our work with a tax-deductible gift by visiting www.thenewpress.com/donate.